C0-ARS-491

REVIEW COPY

MAY 4   1942 $3.75

Columbia University Press

𝕷ibrary of the

𝕮atholic 𝕱oreign 𝕸ission 𝕾ociety

of America

55404

The Catholic
Theological Union
LIBRARY
Chicago, Ill.

WITHDRAWN

MARYKNOLL SEMINARY LIBRARY
MARYKNOLL, NEW YORK

THE CHRISTIAN APPROACH
TO THE MOSLEM

THE CHRISTIAN APPROACH
TO THE MOSLEM

A Historical Study

By JAMES THAYER ADDISON

SOMETIME PROFESSOR OF THE HISTORY
OF RELIGION AND MISSIONS IN THE
EPISCOPAL THEOLOGICAL SCHOOL,
CAMBRIDGE, MASSACHUSETTS

The Catholic
Theological Union
LIBRARY
Chicago, Ill.

COLUMBIA UNIVERSITY PRESS · NEW YORK

1942

MARYKNOLL SEMINARY LIBRARY
MARYKNOLL, NEW YORK

BV
2625
A33
1942

Copyright, 1942

COLUMBIA UNIVERSITY PRESS, NEW YORK

Foreign agents: OXFORD UNIVERSITY PRESS, Humphrey Milford,
Amen House, London, E.C. 4, England, AND B. I. Building,
Nicol Road, Bombay, India

MANUFACTURED IN THE UNITED STATES OF AMERICA

TO
MY SISTER
MEDORA

Preface

THE justification of this historical study is the fact that there exists no book which surveys from the beginning to the present time the missionary efforts of the Christian Church to approach the Moslem. The materials for such a comprehensive review are to be found only in hundreds of books and articles, each covering but a limited portion of the field. In attempting this larger treatment of an enterprise in which I have had almost no direct share, I have relied not only upon the work of historians but upon the recorded experience of scores of missionaries. The wide range of their endeavors, both in space and in time, has obliged me to make the record not comprehensive but selective. I have not tried to produce a complete history of Christian missions to Moslems nor to deal with all countries, all Churches, and all societies. My effort, instead, has been to choose what seemed most significant or typical or most likely to be interesting. Many regions, therefore, have been left out of this survey, and the lack has been partly supplied by brief appendices. Rather because of the limitations of space than through neglect of its importance, I have omitted the work of the Roman Catholic Church since 1800; and for the same reason I have given to the subject of Christian literature for Moslems less attention than its immense importance would require in any more extended study. *In view of the magnitude of world events since September, 1939, it will be well to note that my record does not extend beyond the year 1939.*

I am greatly indebted, not only for his writings but also for his friendly encouragement, to the Rev. Samuel M. Zwemer, who has done more than any other man of our time to promote and invigorate the general cause of missions to Moslems. I am grateful to several friends who have given me invaluable help in individual chapters, especially the Rev. Fred F. Goodsell, of the

American Board; the Rev. Paul Erdman, of Beirut; the Rev. J. Christy Wilson, of Tabriz, Iran; the Rev. Jan van den Blink, of Java; Mr. S. A. Morrison, of Cairo; and Professor Edwin W. Smith, of the Kennedy School of Missions, at Hartford. My warmest thanks are due to the Rev. Edwin E. Calverley, formerly of the Arabian Mission and now Professor of Islamics at the Kennedy School of Missions. Dr. Calverley has been good enough to read the whole of my manuscript, and from his advice I have benefited at more points than I can number. In conclusion I would acknowledge how much I owe to the skillful coöperation of my secretary, Mr. Arthur R. Youtz.

J. T. ADDISON

New York City
January 15, 1942

Contents

PART THREE

PROBLEMS AND POLICIES

APPENDIXES

INTRODUCTION

Introduction

FOR thirteen centuries Christians have been in touch with Moslems. Beginning with their first relations in Arabia and its borders, the contacts between the two groups have extended in range, sometimes with the spread of Islam and sometimes with the advance of Christianity, until today the representatives of these expanding religions meet each other in regions as far apart as Morocco in the West and the Philippine Islands in the East, and as widely separated as the waste lands of Central Asia and the Cape Province in South Africa. During most of these centuries misunderstanding and suspicion and hostility have marked the relations between Christendom and its powerful rival. As great political communities they have been in conflict time and again. Yet from the earliest times to the latest the Christian Church has put forth efforts, if only here and there and now and then, to reach the Moslem with the Christian message and to convert him to the Christian faith. For reasons which the ensuing pages will make abundantly clear this missionary task is difficult beyond all others of its kind. It has therefore been seldom pursued at all, and still more rarely with success. But always it has been an enterprise which called for high courage, deep devotion, and the power "to endure hardness, as a good soldier of Jesus Christ." And so the story of that endeavor is worth recording.

To suggest the problems which are involved in the Christian approach to the Moslem and the opportunities which await it, we shall do well to begin with the briefest review of the World of Islam and the Faith of Islam. For the reader who is no expert in this field such a sketch may offer a preparation for the more detailed account which follows.

The World of Islam consists of about 250,000,000 Moslems distributed over Asia, Africa, and parts of Europe. Representing several scores of races and every grade of civilization from the highest to the lowest, they are bound together by their faith, the religion which we call Mohammedanism and which they call Islam. Islam is the latest, and perhaps the last, of the world's great religions. It began in the seventh century after Christ with the ministry of its founder, Mohammed, who was born at Mecca in Arabia in the year 570. At the time of his birth Arabia was peopled by warring tribes of Bedouins and hemmed in on two sides by great empires—the Persian Empire and the late Roman or Byzantine Empire. The religion of the Arabs was primitive, consisting of the worship of clan gods, nature gods, and nature spirits. Yet in some of its towns and along its borders there were Jews and Christians.

In the unknown years before he entered on his ministry, Mohammed must have learned much from these believers in God, for when he began in Mecca his public preaching as a prophet, his message voiced the belief in one God whom he identified with the God of Jews and Christians and with one of the vaguer Arab deities who was known as Allah. He proclaimed Allah to be the sole God and denounced the idolatrous worship of all other divinities. He summoned all his countrymen to repent and submit to Allah and declared that Allah would one day sit in judgment upon all men, rewarding believers in heaven and consigning all others to hell. Though he gradually won a small band to his cause, he met for many years with opposition and persecution. But in 622 a group of believers from the near-by town of Medina urged him and his followers to flee from Mecca and find a welcome with them. This was the famous year of the flight or Hegira by which the Moslem reckoning of years is dated. Once established in Medina, Mohammed slowly forged his way to power by uniting its tribes in the brotherhood of one faith. Here, indeed, Islam was really born—that firm organization which was at once political and religious. By the time of Mohammed's death in 632, the whole of Arabia had been won to Islam, united in a simple faith and conscious of growing power and ambition.

Since Mohammed had been supreme ruler, both temporal and spiritual, and since he left no son, a successor had to be elected, the first of a long line known as caliphs. With the second caliph, Omar, who came to power in 634, there began the series of victories which launched Islam on its world career. Within ten years the Arab armies had met and defeated in a series of battles the forces of the Persian and Byzantine Empires and had conquered Persia, Mesopotamia, Syria, Palestine, and Egypt. By 644 the Moslem world extended from North Africa to the frontiers of India. In the lands subdued by the Arabs, Jews and Christians were allowed to keep their own faith if they submitted and paid taxes, but vast numbers of them accepted the new religion. Thus began the development of that great Moslem civilization, with its seat first at Damascus and then at Baghdad, which from the eighth to the thirteenth centuries equalled and often surpassed that of Europe, marked for centuries by high achievements in philosophy, science, mathematics, and architecture. The story of expansion from the seventh century onward is too long and complex to be rehearsed here. Partly it was the outcome of political and military force, partly of true missionary activity. As a consequence of this vigorous growth of centuries, Islam today is the religion not only of the lands it first conquered but also of Turkey and Central Asia, of North Africa, and large parts of Negro Africa. In India 78,000,000 are Moslems, in China 8,000,000 or 10,-000,000, and in the Netherlands East Indies over 40,000,000. Even in the Balkan countries there are at least 3,000,000 more.

The religion of Islam is essentially simple. Between the eighth and the twelfth centuries it experienced a rich development in the fields of theology, legislation, and mysticism, so that a lifetime can be spent in the study of its philosophy, its law, and its devotional literature. But the fundamental requirements for the mass of believers have always been plain. They may be summed up in the "Five Pillars of Islam":

1. The confession of faith in Allah and in his apostle Mohammed, the last and greatest prophet;
2. The prescribed prayers, five times daily;
3. The regular giving of alms;
4. The annual fast between dawn and sunset during the month of Ramadan;

5. The pilgrimage to Mecca.

The ideal Moslem, however, not only fulfills these requirements, but lives, wherever it is possible, according to all the laws of Islam, which are as numerous and detailed as those which bound the Pharisees.

From the Christian point of view the most interesting aspects of Mohammedanism are its likenesses to Judaism and Christianity. Its sacred book, the Koran, contains many Old Testament stories of Moses and other heroes, and it pays to Jesus the honor of recording him as one of the three greatest prophets, who was born of a virgin and lived a sinless life. Yet it denies the crucifixion and combats the Christian claim that Jesus is the Son of God and the Saviour of the world. For the Moslem, moreover, God is primarily supreme Power whose will dominates the universe and who is somehow responsible for its evil as well as its good. His character is rather that of an oriental monarch than that of a loving Father. Because the Moslem thus knows of God and of Jesus but is certain that the Christian view of God and Jesus is wrong, he is harder to convince and convert than any other type of non-Christian.

For some seven hundred years the world of Islam has made little progress in thought and culture and its civilization has first become stationary and then stagnant. Formerly on a level with that of Europe, it slipped behind when Europe went through the great changes of the Renaissance and entered on the modern period. The contrast between Islam and Christendom, from the worldly point of view, has become all the more marked in the past two centuries during which the West has experienced its amazing scientific and material development and the Moslem East has halted in the Middle Ages. Differences have been further magnified and hostility further increased during this same period by the imperialistic expansion of the Western powers. As a result of European conquests the greater part of the Moslem world is now under the control, partial or complete, of Christian nations, as in India, the East Indies, Syria, and Africa.

The latest chapter in the history of the world of Islam has only recently begun. It is the story of the awakening of Islam during the past generation and especially since the World War, the story of reviving energies in politics, in thought, in education, and in material progress. There has been a world-wide movement among Moslem peoples, stirred by the negative impulse to throw off the control of Western powers and by the positive impulse, quite as strong, to adopt the political institutions, the economic organization, and the educational system of the West by deliberate choice instead of under pressure. Indeed, "the most remarkable feature of the present Moslem World is not that it is *becoming* westernized, but that it *desires* to be westernized." The spirit of nationalism has been the inspiration of most of these movements and the key to understanding them. It has stirred Moslem peoples to maintain or to achieve their independence, to revise their systems of education, to concentrate their energies upon scientific and material progress, to move toward the liberation of their women, and to throw off whatever religious limitations stood in the way of advance. The outstanding example of such revolution is Turkey, whose rapid changes since 1921 are almost unexampled. But Egypt and Iran are traveling the same road, and the spirit and ambition they manifest are spreading.

It is with this world of Islam, old and new, that we are to be concerned. In the succeeding chapters we shall undertake to trace the relations between Christians and Moslems so far as they have taken the form of Christian missionary expansion. For the most part we shall be dealing with past events. Yet though our study is historical, our interest is not chiefly academic. We are to examine what the past reveals and what the present has to offer that they may help us to approach with more realism, more intelligence, and more enthusiasm one of the great tasks which God has set before His Church for the generations to come—the conversion of the Moslem world.

PART ONE

Twelve Centuries of Background

I

Christianity and the Rise of Islam

UNLIKE any other great religion which an expanding Christianity has encountered, Islam arose and spread in a world where the Christian Church had long been established, for Mohammed died six centuries after Jesus began his ministry. Not only was the new religion from Arabia later in time than the religion of Christ; it was also in large measure indebted to the earlier faith for its original tenets and for its developed theology. These familiar facts set the missionary relations between the two religions in a class by themselves and determine in advance the peculiar problems that have beset for thirteen centuries the fluctuating efforts of the Christian Church to win the Moslem world.

Since Christian belief and practice supplied one source for the teaching of Mohammed and since his invading followers marched into a wide area where the Christian faith was dominant, it is important to review, however briefly, the state of Christianity at the beginning of the seventh century. Where was it then to be found and what appearance did it present? What sort of Christianity met the eye of the prophet and surrounded his growing body of believers as they moved forward to conquest? The answer to these questions is of more than merely historical interest, for what they then heard and saw has unfortunately determined to a surprising degree the conception of Christianity which Moslems have held ever since.

With the minor exceptions of western North Africa, Sicily, and Spain, the relations of Islam were almost wholly with the various branches of the Eastern Church, and it is with them, indeed, that Islam has been chiefly concerned from that day to this. From the very beginning the followers of Mohammed have drawn their knowledge of Christianity from sources all too imperfect and have had to form their judgments of its nature from contact with Churches most of which were at a low ebb in intellectual energy, in religious power, and in missionary spirit. For the Eastern Churches in the year 600 were not examples of Christianity at its best. They were disunited and for the most part decadent. In contrast with the Western Church, then under the vigorous leadership of Pope Gregory I, their great days were already in the past and their most valuable contributions to the growth of Christianity had long since been made. It was not until four centuries after the rise of Islam that there occurred the final break between what was to be the Orthodox Church in the East and the Church of Rome in the West; but the differences between them were already marked and growing. Though the Catholic Church was still formally united, the characteristics which distinguished the Orthodox Church and the Roman Church were plainly in evidence.

In the East the Church was organized into four patriarchates —Jerusalem, Antioch, Alexandria, and Constantinople. Jerusalem covered only a very small region; Antioch included the fifteen provinces of Syria, Cilicia, Arabia, and Mesopotamia; and Alexandria comprised the nine provinces of Egypt. The Patriarchate of Constantinople, with its twenty-eight provinces in Pontus, Thrace, and Asia Minor, enjoyed the strategic advantage of having as its seat the capital of the empire. But Alexandria had been a famous Christian center long before Constantine founded his new city, and on grounds both racial and ecclesiastical there had been deadly rivalry between the two great patriarchal sees.

At the beginning of the seventh century, however, it was only on paper that this far-flung organization existed, for theological strife had torn the Eastern Church apart and heavy losses had been sustained by the Orthodox patriarchates. Doctrinal differences had wrought schisms which remain to this day. The details of these long struggles belong elsewhere. It is enough for our purpose to note that after the Arian controversy of the fourth century had been concluded there arose a new subject of dispute —the nature of Christ, the relation in His Person of the divine and the human elements. The struggle involved in the solution of this problem lasted for three hundred years. If it had been confined to Christian discussions among theologians, more good than harm might have resulted; but it was so soiled and embittered by personal rivalry and ecclesiastical politics that though the cause of orthodoxy may have triumphed, the Church suffered irreparable wounds. The Christ of theology was vindicated by a process which derided every virtue for which the Christ of history stood.

The Western Church held largely aloof from this unedifying civil warfare, but the Eastern Church has never been the same since. Each of the two forms of heresy eventually condemned resulted in a permanent schism. The party which was eager to emphasize the humanity of Christ and which laid stress upon the distinction of natures in His Person found its center in Antioch and looked to Theodore of Mopsuestia as its chief theologian. But since the views of this group were introduced to Constantinople by Nestorius, when he became Patriarch in 428, they were subsequently identified with his name. The opposing theology, which was warmly concerned to assert the deity of Christ at almost any cost, found its fierce champions in Cyril, the Patriarch of Alexandria, and in the monk Eutyches. In contrast with "Nestorianism" their doctrine came to bear the name of "Monophysitism."

In 431 a council at Ephesus condemned Nestorius as a heretic, and the emperor subsequently banished him. By the time he died, about 439, his many followers were being driven by the imperial authorities out of the empire and into Mesopotamia and Persia. The final condemnation of Nestorianism at the Council of Chalcedon in 451 sealed the fate of the great body which bore his name. During the fifth century Edessa and its theological school became the strong center of this heretical group; but when the school was closed in 489 by the Emperor Zeno, most of the Nestorians migrated to Persia, whither many of their brethren had preceded them. For more than two centuries and a half the Christian Church had been maintaining itself in the Persian empire under Sasanid rule. Though it was often subject to persecution, it suffered less for its religion than because it represented the faith of a rival empire. But as outcasts of that empire Nestorians were welcomed, and they poured in in such numbers that their doctrines soon became dominant. The Persian Church, always largely free from outside control, declared in 497 its complete independence of all other Churches. Though the state religion of Persia was Zoroastrianism and the Christians were but tolerated aliens, Church and State could at last unite in hostility to the Byzantine Empire. But the Nestorian Church was able not merely to save itself from disaster. It now entered upon that career of amazing missionary expansion which, even before the Moslem conquest, had carried its expanding forces far across Central Asia and into China. In the eyes of a lethargic mother Church, Nestorians may have been heretics, but in their daring missionary zeal they were more truly orthodox than their persecutors. In the age that saw the rise of Islam their record is one of the few aspects of Christianity which need no apology.

In the meantime the Monophysites were faring no better at the hands of orthodoxy. At the disorderly Council of Ephesus, called by Theodosius II in 449, the followers of Eutyches had triumphed through imperial aid. But their victory was short-lived, for Pope Leo I repudiated their proceedings as those of a "synod of robbers," and Marcian, the successor of Theodosius, soon banished Eutyches. In 451 he summoned the Council of Chalcedon, which condemned the doctrines not only of Nestorianism but also of Monophysitism. The Eastern Church was now hopelessly split. The Nestorians of the provinces of Syria and Asia had been forced into one schism and the Eutychians of Egypt and Palestine into another. The former, however, were the more fortunate. By withdrawing to a distance they enjoyed a genuine independence and a vigorous church life relatively free from further controversy. But with the Monophysites the bitter contest still persisted through the fifth and sixth centuries. The theologians continued to evolve further doctrinal refinements, and their ignorant and passionate adherents in Constantinople and Alexandria were always ready to carry the battle into the market place and to advance their cause by bloody rioting. Before Justinian came to the throne in 527 Alexandria had witnessed the murder of a patriarch by orthodox partisans, a Constantinople mob had carried about the streets on a pole the head of a monophysite monk, and at Antioch orthodox monks had been imprisoned and executed. Under Justinian Church and State became more fully than ever one body. The emperor consistently persecuted all heretics and drove them from civil and military offices. If only doctrinal points had been at issue, opposition might have been overcome; but imperial control had always been resented by Egypt, and local patriotism made a national cause out of what was only apparently a theological dispute. The result was the permanent separation of the Egyptian or Coptic Church. The minority who remained in communion with the Greek Church became known as Melchites, or the king's men, retaining their power only by the support of Constantinople. Before the Arab invasion of Egypt the Copts had still to suffer from a Persian conquest, which ended when the army of Heraclius restored their land to the empire. Yet the change brought them no peace, for the emperor only renewed the violent persecution which was to be their lot until the Moslem came.

To add to the spectacle of disunion and to increase the area of strife there had meantime arisen another schismatic body. During the century after Chalcedon the Monophysite doctrine took root and spread in Syria and Palestine where, as in Egypt, heresy was stimulated by national feeling. Antioch was the troubled scene of persecutions, now of one party and now of the other, until Justinian almost succeeded in suppressing the heretics. But the Empress Theodora secretly arranged for the consecration of two heretical bishops, one of whom was Jacob Baradai. By the efforts of this tireless leader throughout all the Near East there took shape what has ever since borne his name as the Jacobite Church. By the time of his death in 578 the majority of Syrian Christians were schismatic Monophysites.

One more split marked by the same heresy has yet to be named. The Armenian Church, established through the work of Gregory the Illuminator at the beginning of the fourth century, had long suffered under Persian rule. It remained for nearly two centuries in loyal communion with the Patriarchate of Antioch; but in 491 the Church rejected the decisions of the Council of Chalcedon. Some sixty years later it finally adopted Monophysitism, proclaimed its complete independence and, as the Gregorian Church, joined in schism the Jacobite and the Coptic.

The North African Church included a population heterogeneous then as now—the people of Berber stock predominating in the country districts, the Phoenician elements providing the lower and middle strata of the cities, and the Italians the upper classes and owners of estates. During the third century this Latin-speaking Church of Tertullian and Cyprian made rapid advance and continued to grow stronger, especially in the cities. But in contrast with Egypt the bulk of the rural population was only partly converted. Though the controversy which weakened the Eastern Church left North Africa undisturbed, another crop of disputes was almost equally effective in disturbing the peace and sapping the vigor of the Church. During the four centuries before the Moslem conquest the heresies of Montanism, Novatianism, and Donatism wrought bitter divisions. More destructive than these internal struggles was the Vandal invasion beginning in 438. The conquerors, who ruled for a century, were heretic Arians who persecuted Catholic Christianity with relentless severity, driving thousands to martyrdom and exile. When Justinian's general, Belisarius, broke the Vandal power in 533 the life of the Church was at a low ebb. Thereafter it enjoyed for a time a more vigorous career, though Donatists and Arians then became the objects of further persecutions. By the middle of the seventh century, with the Moslem armies almost on the horizon, still another struggle broke out, stirred by the rise of Monotheletism, the latest and last of the heresies concerned with the Person of Christ. By this time the Church of North Africa was neither large nor flourishing. Its bishops, once numbering nearly five hundred, were reduced in number to little more than one hundred; its advance against paganism had come to a halt and its power of resistance was broken.

Even so brief an outline of the state of the Church as the Moslems found it will reveal the two characteristics which chiefly marked that Church—its alliance with state power and politics and its absorption in doctrinal disputes and heresy-hunting. Either of these traits is enough to weaken the cause of Christianity at any time; when they are combined in a period of dangerous crisis the result will be fatal. In the year 600 they were not merely combined, but each aggravated the evil of the other. It was because theological controversy was coarsened and corrupted by its union with political force and nationalist fervor that the consequences were so devastating. A further source of weakness was the too-rapid growth of monasticism, which during the sixth and seventh centuries drew into retirement a far larger number of Christians than was healthful for the life either of the Church or of the State. Less spiritually vigorous and socially helpful than the best monasticism in the West, the institution served by this time in the East to impair rather than to stimulate the vitality of popular Christianity. The religion of the masses, whose ignorance the ill-educated clergy did little to dispel, was so largely concerned with the worship of saints and martyrs and the veneration of relics that Mohammedans could hardly be blamed for counting it polytheism and idolatry. All things considered, the Christianity which the Moslem encountered was not likely either to resist him firmly or to impress him favorably.

The relations between Christianity and Mohammedanism might be said to begin with the knowledge of Christianity which helped to form the teaching of Mohammed himself. That meager knowledge was derived from personal intercourse with Christians in his neighborhood, partly, no doubt, with those from Ethiopia but chiefly with those dwelling in Arabia and on its borders. The Ethiopic Church was a degenerate off-shoot of the Coptic, strongly influenced by Judaism. In Northern Arabia Christianity was to be found in the vassal states of Palmyra and Hira and among many Bedouin tribes in the adjoining deserts. To the south, in Yemen and Hadramaut, the population was mainly Jewish and Christian. Most of the Christians with whom Mohammed dealt were schismatics and heretics and nearly all of them were ignorant. But even with their none-too-vital church life he seems to have had little direct acquaintance. The small amount he learned appears to have been picked up here and there by chance. Most of his fundamental doctrines, however, were derived either from Judaism or from elements common to Judaism and Christianity—such as the one God, the Day of Judgment, the Resurrection, Heaven and Hell, the phenomena of prophecy, and the reverence for sacred scriptures. Little distinctively Christian appears in the Koran except the figure of Jesus Himself, who is there acknowledged not only as one of the great prophets inspired by God and endowed with a special revelation, but even as the Messiah and as in some sense a "Word" of God. Though His virgin birth is related and many miracles are ascribed to Him, no genuine portion of His teaching appears; there is explicit denial of His death on the cross and of His deity; and the Trinity is conceived as consisting of God, Jesus, and Mary. To add to the confusion, Mohammed was only vaguely aware of the deep difference between Christianity and Judaism.

If Mohammed's knowledge of a decadent form of Christianity had been thorough, or if the Church which he knew so imperfectly had been stronger and sounder, the relations between the two religions might have been very different. As it was, however, what passed for Christianity in his confused mind was a distorted copy of fragments of a notably defective original. If that copy had merely lived and died within his mind it would have only biographical interest. But it was soon to become part of the infallible Koran and to figure in the eyes of every follower as the one reliable account of the great rival religion. As every syllable of error was thus sanctified, the Moslem has never been able to draw from his own sources any saving knowledge of the Christianity of Christ.

II

Christian and Moslem from the Early Conquests to the Crusades

THE STATE of the existing Christian Church and the conception of Christianity already fixed in Islam were important elements in determining the future relations of the two faiths. A factor far more powerful and obvious was the train of overwhelming events that ended with the Arab conquest of Christian lands and the conversion to Islam of most of their inhabitants. Within the score of years between 634 and 653 Syria, Palestine, Persia, Armenia, Egypt, Tripoli, and Cyrenaica had been conquered and Asia Minor had been widely ravaged. Of the character of that invading wave Professor Arnold has written:

These stupendous conquests which laid the foundations of the Arab empire were certainly not the outcome of a holy war, waged for the propagation of Islam, but they were followed by such a vast defection from the Christian faith that this result has often been supposed to have been their aim.... The spirit which animated the invading hosts of Arabs who poured over the confines of the Byzantine and Persian empires was no proselytizing zeal for the conversion of souls. On the contrary religious interests appear to have entered but little into the consciousness of the protagonists of the Arab armies. This expansion of the Arab race is more rightly envisaged as the migration of a vigorous and energetic people driven by hunger and want, to leave their inhospitable deserts and overrun the richer lands of their more fortunate neighbors. Still the unifying principle of the movement was the theocracy established in Medina, and the organization of the new state proceeded from the devoted companions of Mohammed, the faithful depositaries of his teaching, whose moral weight and enthusiasm kept Islam alive as the official religion, despite the indifference of those Arabs who gave to it a mere nominal adherence. It is not, therefore, in the annals of the conquering armies that we must look for the reasons which led to the so rapid spread of the Muslim faith but rather in the conditions prevailing among the conquered peoples.... This interpretation of the Arab conquests as the last of the great Semitic migrations has been worked out in a masterly manner by Caetani.[1]

And it is Caetani who writes of the sweeping consequences:

When at last there appeared, coming out suddenly from the desert, the news of the new revelation, this bastard oriental Christianity torn asunder by internal discords, wavering in its fundamental dogmas, dismayed by such incertitudes could no longer resist the temptations of a new faith, which swept away at one single stroke all miserable doubts, and offered, along with simple, clear, and undisputed doctrines, great material advantages also.[2]

In all these conquered countries except Armenia the majority of the population joined the ranks of Islam in a series of wholesale conversions, moved partly by genuine conviction, partly by fear, and partly by the desire for material profit. It was to the interests of the new rulers that the Christian minorities should not be exterminated, and the teaching of the Prophet fortunately commanded this restraint. Mohammed had declared that pagans who refused to become Moslems should be annihilated but that "Peoples of the Book"—those whose faith was based on sacred scriptures—might retain their religion if they submitted to Arab rule and paid taxes. By this saving clause Jews and Christians were thenceforth to benefit. After the conquest, therefore, the various groups of Christians found themselves in the position of subject peoples called *dhimmis,* each community a kind of state within the state; and on substantially these terms they were to live, under changing dynasties, until the Turkish reforms of 1923.

The *dhimmis* were granted the protection of the state, which guaranteed them life, property, and security in the practice of their religion. They were not compelled to perform military service or to pay the legal alms demanded of Moslems. In return

[1] Arnold, *The Preaching of Islam,* pp. 46 f.
[2] Caetani, *Annali dell'Islam,* II, 1045 f., quoted in Arnold, *op. cit.,* p. 71.

they were obliged to pay a special tax known as the *jizyah* and to accept a subordinate position in the social and political life of the community. They were set at a disadvantage by certain legal disabilities in regard to testimony, marriage, and protection under the criminal law. They were often required to wear a special dress and were forbidden to ride horseback or to carry weapons. They were allowed to replace and rebuild churches, but not to erect new ones, and were commonly expected to conduct their rites in a manner inconspicuous and inoffensive to Moslems. Such regulations as these, in many countries and throughout a period of many centuries, were subject to every kind of variation. At one time they might be few in number and at another exacting and detailed. Under one ruler they might be laxly regarded and half forgotten and under another enforced to the limit with rigorous severity. There were times, too, when the whole system was abandoned for the time, to give way to open and ruthless persecution.

During the first century after the conquest Moslem rule was comparatively just and beneficent; and several countries, recently under Christian government, enjoyed increased prosperity and unaccustomed toleration. The Copts in Egypt actually welcomed their new masters, who brought them freedom from Byzantine oppression and recognized their patriarch as the civil head of the Christian community. It was the Melchites who now became the harassed minority. In Syria and Palestine, too, life under the Arab conquerors seemed to hold more promise of peace and security than had been known under Heraclius, and here again heretical Christians could once more breathe freely. In Damascus, indeed, there were to be cordial relations between Christians and Moslems for a century or more. To the Nestorians in Persia the change from Zoroastrian to Mohammedan rule made little difference. The Christians there were given the usual terms of *dhimmis* and found themselves free to continue their enterprise of missionary expansion, which was already well under way. It was only Armenia that suffered unmitigated hardship, for in that country Arab control was insecure and more than once the

Eastern Empire rewon its lost territory. The prey now of one and now of the other conqueror, the Armenians were persecuted alternately as heretics and as Christians.

The Orthodox Church itself, ruled from Constantinople, was by this time sadly diminished in numbers and in vigor. The rapid growth of monasticism proved harmful both to the authority of the state and to its material welfare. During the seventh century the monothelete controversy absorbed attention, and throughout most of the eighth century the famous iconoclastic controversy offered a new cause for violent internal quarrels and a new field for the persecution of Christians by Christians. This struggle for and against the use of sacred pictures and images was essentially a contest between people and monks on the one side and on the other side the great reforming emperors Leo III and Constantine V. At the cost of several generations of disturbance the final result was the failure of reform.

Islam had found the Christian Church weak and divided. After a century of Moslem advance the Church was far weaker and its divisions had been confirmed and established. The Christian communities under Arab control, none too virile to begin with, had been further denatured by their masters and tethered where they could do no harm. And those parts of the Eastern Church still free from alien bondage were wasting the substance of a great heritage in riotous controversy.

Yet that great heritage was by no means altogether wasted, for one of the notable features of this period is the extent to which Greek and Christian thought came to permeate the mind of Islam. The conquering Arabs were the superiors of their new subjects in military power and religious enthusiasm, but in education and culture they had little to contribute and very much to learn. The communities over which they now held sway may have been decadent, but they were still the possessors of all the available culture there was—the Greco-Roman culture of the Mediterranean world. Whatever flag might be flying over them, Alexandria, Damascus, Baghdad, and Edessa still remained the centers of intellectual life, and the influence of that life was inescapable. So it came about that from the earliest stages of contact almost until the time of the Crusades, Moslems were engaged, both consciously and unconsciously, in absorbing the learning and the civilization of the world into which they had emerged. And since the Christian Church was then the nursery of learning and the guardian of civilization, it was a culture permeated by Christian ideas which molded the mental development of Islam.

Damascus and Edessa, for example, were centers of scholarship where classical authors, pagan and Christian, were studied both in the original languages and in Syriac translations. After the conquest scholars there and elsewhere were active in translating works of science and philosophy into Arabic. From such sources as these the Moslems could learn what the Greeks had bequeathed of metaphysics, astronomy, and medicine. "This Christian-Hellenistic culture was transmitted to them by Christian scholars, writers, and teachers, and their dependence upon such Christian instructors for the knowledge and culture which they saw to be so desirable, must have made for friendly intercourse, and must have meant that Christians who stood in such a relation to Moslems were held in honor and esteem, and there is no lack of evidence that this was the case in all the countries where such contact took place."[3]

Not only was secular culture transmitted to the Mohammedan through a Christian medium, but the older religion had a direct effect upon the newer. The thought of Christian theologians and the life of Christian monks made a notable impression on the plastic religious substance of Islam. Greek theology supplied the philosophic groundwork and language for Moslem thought. The devotional life and practices of monasticism, everywhere in evidence, provided a stimulus to the rise of popular mysticism. And the mystical strand in Islam has proved ever since to be the element most congenial with Christianity, still offering to the missionary of today a fruitful mode of approach.

The first century of Moslem rule includes the years of conquest and the age of the Omayyad Caliphate, the seat of which was at

[3] Margaret Smith, *Studies in Early Mysticism in the Near and Middle East,* pp. 118 f.

Damascus. The Omayyads were secular-minded Arab emperors whose tolerant attitude toward Christians was partly determined by the fact that they took little interest in religion. In 750 there succeeded to power the first representative of the Abbasid Dynasty, a line of rulers whose capital was Baghdad and who governed greater or lesser portions of Islam for the next five centuries. For some time, under the earlier and stronger caliphs, the Christian communities continued to enjoy a toleration that granted them almost complete autonomy; Christian officials were constantly employed in important service; and the free process of sharing culture was maintained. But with growing frequency, between the ninth and eleventh centuries, there were periods when fanatical caliphs exerted themselves to make life hard for the Christians. Rigid regulations to prevent the Christians from attacking the religion of Islam or influencing the Moslem, decrees driving Christians from civil office, outbursts of persecution that led to the destruction of churches, the imposition of taxes more and more burdensome—these were forms of oppression, appearing at intervals, which increased the insecurity of the Church and added to the number of those who embraced Islam.

The fortunes of the Egyptian Church were typically varied, depending on the degree of rapacity manifested by the local emirs; but except for the fierce persecutions of the mad Hakim, the times of the Fatimid caliphs (909-1171) saw better treatment of Christians than they had hitherto known. The Jacobites, too, suffered intermittent ill usage, but in Palestine and Syria during the early Middle Ages they maintained flourishing schools of theology and science, and even as late as the twelfth century their Church was prosperous enough to maintain twenty metropolitans and one hundred bishops in Syria and Asia Minor. Under the Abbasids the members of the Nestorian Church were more favored than other *dhimmis* and often enjoyed careers as advisers and officials at the Baghdad court. As teachers, philosophers, and scientists, they played a part out of all proportion to their numbers in developing "Islamic" culture. But with the growth in size of the educated Moslem community their services were less in demand and their influence gradually waned. During the tenth century the Nestorian missionary movement reached its widest extent, especially in Central Asia. Yet the converts were all among heathen and never among Moslem populations.

The attitude of the Byzantine Empire toward the Moslem during the epoch between 750 and 1100 varied all the way from cringing submission to victorious counter attack. At the end of the eighth century the emperor was paying tribute to the caliph. While a renewed outburst of the iconoclastic controversy was agitating Constantinople, between 826 and 831, the forces of Islam were conquering Crete and Sicily. During the next century, however, under the great rulers of the Macedonian dynasty, Constantinople became the most brilliant center of European civilization. The Moslem armies were crushed in Cilicia and Syria and the frontiers of Islam driven back for a time to the Tigris and the Euphrates. The reconquest of Sicily before the middle of the eleventh century was the last expansive effort of Byzantium. Thenceforth the story is one of scarcely interrupted decline. By 1054 had come the final break with the Church of Rome and the complete severance of Constantinople from the West. Soon afterwards began the advance of the Seljuk Turks against the Eastern Empire. In 1071 the emperor was defeated and captured at Manzikert, and within eight years more Nicaea had been taken and the Turks were almost at the gates of the capital.

Whether we review the relations between Christians and Moslems in conquered territory or survey the general situation in which the Eastern Empire found itself, it is equally clear why there were no Christian missions to Mohammedans. In lands under the control of Islam the death penalty for apostasy was enforced and the Christian minorities were forbidden to proselytize, even if they had been in the frame of mind to attempt it. Being oppressed subjects, however, lucky enough to be alive at all, they naturally remained passive toward their masters. In the parts of Eastern Christendom that were still unsubdued, the Moslem could only be regarded as a feared and hated enemy who might some day be victor but who could hardly be the present object of missionary solicitude.

The nearest approach to interest in the conversion of Mohammedans and the one exception to these broad statements are to be found in the controversies between Christian and Moslem scholars which were conducted at intervals during this period. Some were carried on entirely within Moslem areas, while others involved combatants on both sides of the dividing line.

Though there are signs here and there of earlier controversies, oral and written, the first outstanding scholar to enter the field of polemic against the Moslem was John of Damascus. Known to history as the most honored of the later theologians of the Greek Church, John was born at Damascus about the year 700. After serving for a time at the caliph's court in the same high office which his father had held before him, he withdrew to a monastery to pursue the theological studies to which he owes his fame. His great dogmatic work on the *Sources of Knowledge* includes an important section "Concerning Heresies," and it is one chapter under this heading that deals with Moslems.[4] The topics the author selected and the arguments he used have been so constantly repeated by similar champions from the eighth century to the twentieth that a brief summary of their content will be useful.

Like many of his medieval successors, John regarded Mohammed as essentially a heretic rather than the founder of a new religion. He was a false prophet who probably derived his knowledge of the Scriptures from an Arian monk. The first point to be made, therefore, is that Mohammed has no credentials as a prophet sent by God. He is never foretold in the Old or New Testaments and he can offer no compelling witness to the authority of his revelation. Denying the Moslem accusation that the Jewish scriptures have been corrupted, John turns to them for proof of the divinity of Christ. Even the Koran calls Christ "the Word of God," and since God's Word can hardly be outside of God, we must believe that Christ was in God and of God. In conclusion, the author rebuts the charge that Christians practice idolatry and counters with an attack upon Mohammed for permitting polygamy, concubinage, and lax divorce. Typical of much later controversy is this combination of assault upon the Prophet's personal authority,

---

[4] Migne, *Patrologia graeca*, Vol. 94, cols. 763-74. For translation, see *Moslem World*, Oct., 1934.

confidence in metaphysical argument, and emphasis upon the low character of Moslem morality.

More extensive and more interesting is John's other polemic work, the "Dialogue between a Christian and a Saracen." [5] This form of argument was a favorite type in Byzantine literature, representing at times an actual event but more often manufactured to suit the purposes of the writer. John's dialogue is first concerned with the theological question as to whether the Word of God is created or uncreated. Since one reply will mean that God had previously no Word or Holy Spirit and the other will force the confession that Christ was divine, "when the Moslem hears this [question] he will flee from you, for he has no answer." After a rebuttal of Moslem objections to the Incarnation, the author then attacks the enemy's assertion that whatever happens is in accordance with the divine will and that God is therefore the author of evil. In opposition John maintains that evil comes through the devil, that our sin is due to human freedom, and that God is the originator only of good.

Throughout all his controversial work John of Damascus displays a thorough knowledge of Islam. Fully at home in the Arabic tongue, he often cites the Koran word for word and shows his familiarity with the Hadith, or traditions. He not only enjoys a complete mastery of Christian theology, but has a keen eye for the weak points of his adversary. It is characteristic, in fact, of all the earlier polemic, during the age when Islam and Christendom were in close touch, that the Christian advocate is in full control of his material and knows at first hand what he is talking against.[6]

A century later appeared a controversial writing perhaps the most effective of its era and certainly better known today than any other—the *Apology* of al-Kindi.[7] Al-Kindi was a learned Nestorian Christian who held a high position at the tolerant court of

[5] Migne, *Patrologia graeca*, Vol. 94, cols. 1585-98. Cf. *ibid.*, Vol. 96, cols. 1335-48. For translation, see *Moslem World*, July, 1935.

[6] A younger contemporary of John was Theodore Abucara (or Abu Qurra), bishop of a diocese in northeastern Mesopotamia, who edited a collection of dialogues which includes thirteen disputations with Saracens. So closely do some of these resemble the work of John that certain scholars have concluded that Theodore's work is the original and John's dialogues unauthentic.

[7] Ed. and trans. by Sir William Muir.

the great caliph al-Mamun. Taking advantage of the freedom then accorded to Christians at Baghdad, he wrote a powerful defense of Christianity in the form of a long letter to the caliph's cousin Abdallah, who had urged him to embrace Islam. He begins with a defense of the doctrine of the Trinity—always misrepresented by the Moslem—combining metaphysical arguments with scriptural proofs often very far-fetched. He then proceeds to deny Mohammed's prophetic claims and to show how the necessary evidence, both from prophecy and from miracles, is wanting in his case but convincing in the case of Jesus. The Koran is derided as disorderly and inconsistent. The ordinances of Islam, when examined, prove to be senseless at their worst and at best inferior to those of Christianity. Islam is too easy a religion, and its appeal to worldly inducements accounts for much of its success. In conclusion, al-Kindi sets forth the life and teaching of Christ and the subsequent spread of the Church, closing with an appeal to Abdallah to embrace Christianity.[8]

When a Christian wrote at the Moslem capital he was moved not only by caution but also by a closer and more sympathetic knowledge of his adversary to speak in terms relatively moderate and fair. But when he wrote at the Christian capital his tone was always more bitter. If al-Kindi's book may be taken as a type of apology composed in a Moslem environment, the work of Nicetas of Byzantium, written some fifty years later, may serve as an example of the harsher sort of polemic produced in a Christian center.[9] At the bidding of the Emperor Basil I, who had hopes of winning his Moslem enemies to Christianity, the philosopher Nicetas undertook a refutation of "the foolish and infamous book of the Arab Mohammed and of the errors of the Agarene contained in it." [10] The first part of his work is chiefly concerned with the fundamental truths of Christianity, such as

8 About thirty years later, after the middle of the ninth century, there appeared a defense of Islam written by Ali Tabari at the command of the Caliph Mutawakkil and entitled *The Book of Religion and Empire* (ed. and trans. by A. Mingana). It seems to have been an attempt to refute such attacks as al-Kindi's *Apology.*

9 Migne, *Patrologia graeca*, Vol. 105, cols. 669-842.

10 Since the Arabs were supposed to be descendants of Ishmael by Hagar they are commonly referred to as "Agareni."

the attributes of God and the deity of Christ, all set forth in dryly syllogistic form. The author then turns to attack Mohammed and the Koran. Not content to call Mohammed a false prophet, he brands him as utterly ignorant, a shameless liar, and the son of Satan. His sacred book (probably known to Nicetas in translation) is declared to be an unintelligible tissue of lies and fables, with no true claim to divine origin. Such errors as denying Christ's death on the cross and putting in Christ's mouth the prophecy that Mohammed was to come can be attributed only to the devilish wickedness of Mohammed himself. In a final section Nicetas assails the teaching that God originates both evil and good and that "He neither begets nor is begotten." So far astray in heresy does he find the Moslems that he will not even concede that they worship the true God.

The influence of this polemic literature during the eighth and ninth centuries was mainly indirect. Its clearest result was to stimulate thought within Islam by posing questions with which Moslem thinkers were bound to wrestle—questions, for instance, about human freedom and about the nature of Christ and the nature of the Koran. Partly from this stimulus, indeed, arose several of the liberal and heretical movements of Islamic theology. But whatever may have been the effects of controversy, the conversion of Mohammedans to Christianity was not one of them. Not often intended as a missionary method, controversy was even less often a missionary success. One trouble was that the Christian writings were chiefly defensive reactions. Too frequently they allowed the Moslem to choose the weapons and fix the setting. Moreover, they were usually heavily loaded with technical arguments and, having little moral or spiritual content, awakened no moral or spiritual response. As a matter of fact, such polemic was really a kind of serious sport engaged in by well-equipped contestants who were mainly concerned to score points with varying degrees of good or ill humor. Sometimes the buttons were on the foils and sometimes not; but always the game was a pretty barren substitute for evangelism.

III

The Period of the Crusades

AT THE END of the eleventh century the relations between Christendom and Islam entered on a new phase with the beginning of the Crusades. Hitherto the Moslem had been the aggressor and, with the one great exception of Spain, had met military opposition chiefly from the armies of the Eastern Empire. Thenceforth for two hundred years there was to be a fluctuating contest between the power of Islam and the martial forces of Western Europe. The area of antagonism grew wider and the spirit of conflict more bitter. Although the struggle was not primarily a warfare of religions, one ultimate result was to sunder more deeply than ever the two great faiths and to exacerbate the mutual hatred of their adherents.

Palestine had been a goal of pilgrimage since the time of Constantine. Even after the capture of Jerusalem by the Arabs, the stream of pilgrims continued with few interruptions and they had never been more numerous than in the early years of the eleventh century. But the invasion of the Seljuk Turks changed the entire situation. Not only was Jerusalem captured and its shrines desecrated but the whole of Syria and Anatolia was overrun. By the year 1081 the new emperor, Alexius Comnenus, was practically confined to Constantinople. In despair at the prospect of further defeat, the emperor finally appealed to Pope Urban II for aid against the infidels. In ready response the Pope proclaimed a crusade first at the Council of Piacenza in March, 1095, and again at the Council of Clermont in November of the same year. Alexius was mainly concerned to save his empire and to retrieve its losses, but the Pope and the Christians of Europe were primarily eager to rescue the Holy Places. This, then, was the theme of the call to action voiced by Urban and by such eloquent pleaders as Peter of Amiens. They summoned the nobility and the people to share in a glorious enterprise that was to recover Palestine and plant there the standard of the Cross.

The First Crusade, under the leadership of nobles from France and Norman Italy, set forth in August, 1096. Within three years the Christian armies had captured Nicaea, Antioch, Edessa, and Jerusalem, and had defeated the Egyptian army near Ascalon. As a result of these sweeping victories the crusaders established the Kingdom of Jerusalem and organized the conquered territories in accordance with the feudal system. At the same time the Latin Church was established, with two patriarchates and eight arch-bishoprics, and numerous monasteries were founded. During this early period, too, arose the military orders of the Knights Templars, pledged to defend the Holy Land and to protect pilgrims, and the Hospitallers, or Knights of St. John. Chiefly upon these orders the new states relied for their trained soldiers and for the strongest elements of permanent occupation.

The Kingdom of Jerusalem lasted for nearly a century, flourishing with fair success during the earlier half of its history but during the latter half slowly decaying in character and power. Under its protection pilgrims of every variety poured in once more in a steady flow. But a growing number were immigrants, rather than pilgrims, for the eastern lands under Latin control gradually became genuine colonies. Not only were the armies constantly recruited but the settled European population increased.

After the First Crusade, as has been truly noted, it is rather misleading to attach numerals to a few of the various waves that followed. Yet the conventional names have a certain advantage in any brief summary. What tradition describes as the Second Crusade followed upon the capture of Edessa by the Turks in 1144. This first defeat of many to follow led Bernard of Clairvaux and others to rouse Europe by a new appeal in 1146. The princes who answered were Louis VII of France and the Emperor Conrad III. The Crusade they led, or failed to lead, was a long series of disasters. Most of their forces perished in Asia Minor, and the remnants were defeated at Damascus in 1148. Conrad and Louis returned to their people with nothing to report but humiliation.

The last half of the twelfth century saw the career of Saladin, who first appears as a Kurdish general serving the Seljuk Turks in Egypt. Within a surprisingly brief time he rose to power by conquering nearly the whole of Syria save a strip along the coast. By 1171 he had become ruler of Egypt, and three years later his forces captured Damascus. Before long Saladin's territories hemmed in the Latin Kingdom on all its land frontiers, and under him the Moslems were at last united. In 1187 he defeated the Christian army at Hattin and captured Jerusalem.

These victories, undoing the work of the First Crusade, were more than enough to arouse Europe to the renewed effort which led to the Third Crusade. Replying to the appeal of Gregory VIII, three great armies set forth under the leadership of the Emperor Frederick Barbarossa, Philip Augustus of France, and Richard of England. The emperor met his death by drowning on the way through Cilicia, and the two remaining captains weakened their cause by constant quarreling. In view of the time and energy consumed the results were meager. After a siege of two years Acre was taken in 1191, and a truce with Saladin provided for the free passage to Jerusalem of Christian pilgrims. But when Saladin died in 1193 the Holy City was still in the hands of the Saracens.

The so-called Fourth Crusade is hardly entitled to figure as a contest between Christendom and Islam, for it was really a sordid civil war among Christians. Armies from France and Flanders, in alliance with the Venetians for commercial ends, assailed the feeble Byzantine forces and in 1204 captured and plundered Constantinople. At the eastern capital was established a Latin Empire under Baldwin of Flanders and at the same time a Latin Patriarchate, to signify the subjection of the Greek Church to the Pope. Not until 1261 were the intruders expelled by the Emperor Michael II. A period of nearly sixty years had seen the increase of hatred between Greek and Roman Christians and had marked the weakening of Christendom in the face of Islam.

Meanwhile, between 1217 and 1230, the Emperor Frederick II

had been conducting the long series of expeditions and negotiations which have been known as the Fifth Crusade. An attack upon Egypt led to the capture of Damietta but soon afterward resulted in the evacuation of the country. In 1229, however, Frederick secured an agreement with the Sultan al-Kamil for the surrender of Jerusalem, Bethlehem, and Nazareth, and a path to the coast. Yet Jerusalem remained under Christian control no longer than fifteen years, for in 1244 it fell again to the Moslem, to remain in his hands until the days of Allenby in 1918.

The twenty years and more between 1248 and 1270 witnessed the expeditions of Louis IX, the so-called Sixth Crusade. With a reckless waste of treasure and of life St. Louis assailed the Saracen forces first in Egypt and later in Tunis, campaigns that met with ultimate failure and closed with the death of the king. In the course of another twenty years came the fall of Acre, in 1291. The last of the Latin possessions had now disappeared two centuries after the victories of the First Crusade. Palestine was to remain under Moslem domination for more than six centuries.

A bare outline of the military events gives only a faint suggestion of the complexity of influences that determined the relations between Christians and Moslems during the period of the Crusades. The effect of the whole movement upon the commerce and secular culture of Europe is the subject of an extensive modern literature but is of relatively small consequence for our purpose. More important from the missionary point of view are some of the social and religious products and by-products of these centuries of varied contact in the Near East.

The outstanding factor, of course, is that the age was one of warfare. For two centuries, off and on, Christendom met Islam as an enemy in the field and built up a tradition of antagonism which other factors did little to modify and the traces of which have never been wholly wiped out. At all stages, it is true, the contest was far from being a purely religious war. There was no great desire on either side to make converts. The Seljuk Turks, the first adversaries, were barbarian invaders who had long been fighting with Moslems; and the Franks, who frequently acted like barbarians, were almost as hostile to Christians of the Orthodox

Church as to the followers of the Prophet. Yet the dire fact remains that the two main camps belonged to different faiths and that countless acts of cruelty stained the records of both sides. The Turk was too often a mere savage marauder from Asia. To match him, the Frank, under the sign of the Cross, decapitated thousands of men, women, and children in the Temple at the capture of Jerusalem and massacred tens of thousands more in the streets of the Holy City.

Warfare in the field, however, was only an occasional episode in an epoch that lasted for seven generations. Most of the time nobody was fighting, and at no time was everybody fighting. As the years passed, there was a growing distinction between the armed crusaders, eager for victory and booty, and the increasing number of Europeans who stayed on in Syria and made the East their home. Even among the former, knighthood was sufficiently international to mediate between religions, so that free intercourse with foes was not unusual. Presents and letters were exchanged and hunting grounds used in common. Indeed, despite the opposition of the Church, there even came to be alliances between Christian and Moslem states. The contest willed by God against His enemies had grown to be a mere fiction by the time of Frederick II, and political and military factors outweighed religion.

But it was naturally among the settled population of Frankish origin that peaceful intercourse with the Moslem natives became almost continuous. In spite of the hostile attitude of the clergy and of newcomers with martial ambition, the rank and file of those who had taken root were ready to engage in trade and to enter into social relations. Since their interests were bound up with the land and its inhabitants, they could afford to be friendly and accommodating. They were able to appreciate what was good in Islam and to distinguish between the worst of the Turks and the best of the Arabs. They often adopted eastern dress and eastern customs. Christian slaves and concubines were to be found in Moslem harems, and among the lower classes intermarriage was common, producing a hybrid group known as the "Pullani." Moreover, as time went on, an ever-larger number of Christians embraced Islam. Some of these were captives in battle and others fugitives from justice; still others took the step to win greater safety and comfort. Especially during the thirteenth century, after the fearful sufferings of the Third Crusade, these "renegades" became so numerous that they were often referred to in the chronicles and statute books. For much the same reasons, on the other hand, a far smaller number of Moslems forsook their faith and accepted baptism.

Despite the growth of antagonism, Moslem rulers seldom made their Christian subjects suffer for the Crusades. When the Saracens finally resumed the full control of Palestine the Christians were given their former status as *dhimmis*. The Coptic Church, too, had little cause for complaint under Saladin's strong government, and during the time of the earlier Mameluke sultans who succeeded him the Copts experienced more enlightened justice than they had hitherto known. The only effect of the Crusades upon Egyptian Christians was to keep them for a while from pilgrimage to Jerusalem, for as long as the Franks were in charge, heretics were forbidden access to the shrines. Not until the Moslem victories could they enjoy their rights as Christians.

The period from the end of the eleventh to the end of the twelfth century, during which the first three Crusades were fought out, was an epoch almost destitute of any activity that could properly be called missionary. One of the few episodes worth recording was the work initiated by Peter the Venerable, Abbot of Cluny, the first name in the polemic of the Western Church against Islam. While visiting the abbeys of his order in Spain in the year 1141, Peter discovered a great need for controversial literature and began to plan for its production. Within the next few years, at his instigation, there was prepared by the Englishman, Robert of Retines, aided by a Saracen named Mohammed, the first translation of the Koran into Latin. With the help of the same Saracen, Herman of Dalmatia composed three small treatises on the life and doctrines of Mohammed, and Peter himself wrote a refutation of the teaching of the Prophet, of which two out of four books are extant.[1] The work is entitled

[1] Migne, *Patrologia latina*, Vol. 189, cols. 659-720.

Against the Loathsome Heresy of the Sect of the Saracens. Despite its many errors and distortions, it remains important as the first attempt of its kind in Latin and as an accepted model for much future western polemic.

Compared with modern arguments against Islam, the treatises of Peter and his associates are inaccurate and unfair; but in view of medieval Christian ideas about Mohammed and his religion, they were relatively enlightened and dependable. At least they were written by scholars who knew the Koran and two of whom lived in close contact with educated Moslems. Throughout Europe, however, during all the Middle Ages, there prevailed the grossest ignorance of Islam not only among the masses but even among cultivated men who might have known better. This mental confusion is the more surprising considering the opportunities for knowledge afforded by constant pilgrimage, by intercourse during the Crusades, and by the close relations between the two faiths for many centuries in Spain. Yet we must remember that no calmly correct estimate of an alien religion could be expected in that age, least of all in the case of Islam. For Islam was the common enemy, and it requires a high degree of impartiality to be scrupulously just to a hated foe. It was much easier to arouse in Christians a crusading ardor if the religion of "the False Prophet" was painted in hideous colors. Like other wars, the Crusades had to be sustained by hate propaganda. Moreover, the life of literature and of the intellect was then dependent almost wholly on the clergy, and the clergy were particularly virulent in their hostility. The little they knew came from prejudiced Byzantine sources, or at second and third-hand from popular legends. Islam, in consequence, was depicted as corrupt and degenerate. Mohammed appears as a veritable devil, engaged in a career of vile falsehood, seeking to lead souls to damnation by appealing to their lusts. It was even widely believed that Moslems worshiped the Prophet as their God and bowed down to his images.[2]

[2] The degree of accuracy attempted by most medieval writers may be symbolized by the different forms in which the name of Mohammed appears in the literature of the period: Mahomet, Machumeth, Mahummeth, Malphumeth, Malphus, Mathomus, Baphometh, Maphomet, Bafum, and so forth.

With the founding of the Franciscan and Dominican Orders in the early thirteenth century begins a new chapter in the story of the Christian approach to Moslems. For the first time we can record the deliberate organization of missions to win converts by peaceful means. Until the rise of these Mendicant Orders the missionary activity of the Western Church had been confined almost wholly to the conversion of pagans in Europe. With that task largely achieved and with new horizons opening, the range of the Church's purpose now included Islam. It is true, of course, that in all Moslem territory the death penalty for apostasy was in full force. It is evident, too, that most of the work of the friars was with Christians, Latin and Oriental, and that only occasionally (and for the most part in secrecy) did they deal directly with Moslems. The results were therefore meager. But all these limitations and failures are equally characteristic of most of our modern attempts at the same hard task.

The new era begins in 1219 with the visit of Francis of Assisi himself to the crusading army at Damietta. With characteristic intrepidity the saint crossed the lines to meet the Sultan of Egypt, with whom he had two fruitless interviews. In the same year he dispatched a group of brothers to Morocco. The fact that five of them were martyred there soon afterwards probably shows that they had not been afraid of a direct approach to the infidel. Another mission, sent to Tunis, was unable to carry on its work because of the opposition of Christian merchants, who feared the consequences of rousing hostility. During the ensuing forty years there were many further examples of efforts on the part of popes and of the heads of the two orders to press forward in Moslem areas. In 1225 Honorius III commissioned Franciscans and Dominicans to enter Morocco, where he appointed a Dominican bishop and where for a century there appears an almost unbroken series of bishops from both orders. The friars worked chiefly among Christian slaves, captives, and merchants; yet there is recorded the conversion of a prince of Tunis, who fled to Rome for baptism. In 1228 the Dominicans established a Province of the Holy Land, with monasteries at Acre, Nicosia, Cyprus, and Tripolis. Five years later both Franciscans and Dominicans were dispatched to the courts of the Sultans of Iconium, Aleppo, Damascus, and Egypt, and to the Caliph at Baghdad. Gregory IX supplied them with letters commending their work, and in 1245 Innocent IV wrote to several sultans pleading for a favorable reception for other emissaries. Both popes were active in urging the conversion not only of Oriental Christians but even of Moslems. There is no evidence, however, of missionary success.

During the second half of the thirteenth century the activity of the Mendicant Orders covered a still wider range. Not only was the mission in Tunis renewed and gradually strengthened, but great numbers of the brethren went out to the Near East, settling in various stations all around the borders of the Mongol Empire. If we may trust the report of Pope Innocent IV, they were chiefly concerned with schismatic Christians yet in part with Saracens as well. The fall of Acre in 1291 dealt a fatal blow to this eastward expansion and forced the missions to contract severely the area of their work. Martyrdoms became more numerous, and the friars soon found themselves restricted to such tasks as the care of the Holy Places and ministry to pilgrims and merchants.

It was during this century, when some measure of missionary effort was directed toward the Saracens, that a few leaders appear whose writings go far to redeem the medieval record of polemic. The opportunities afforded by close relations with intelligent Moslems were not wholly neglected by certain equally intelligent Christians, whose attitude toward Islam was relatively clear-headed and considerate. Oliver the Scholastic, of Cologne, for example, wrote a letter in 1221 to "the King of Babylon" (the ruler at Cairo), pleading with him to accept the Christian faith and stressing the many points of belief common to the two rival religions. In his book *Historia Damiatina* he gives a correct account of what the Koran has to say of Jesus Christ and concludes that the followers of the Prophet should be called heretics rather than Saracens. Jacques de Vitry, too, who took part in the Fifth Crusade and was for a time the Bishop of Acre, made similar attempts to convert the infidels. In one of his letters he writes, "As I was not able to preach in the land of the Saracens I showed

the errors of their religion and the truth of ours by letters which
I sent to them, written in the Saracen tongue." His account of
Mohammed and Islam, though naturally biased, includes much
that is accurate.

More impressive in quantity and quality are the writings of the
Dominican missionaries William of Tripolis and Ricoldus de
Monte Crucis, produced toward the end of the thirteenth century.
They wrote after prolonged acquaintance with the Islamic scriptures and traditions and after many years' experience of how the
religion works in the actual life and conduct of its adherents.
William of Tripolis composed a treatise *On the Condition of the
Saracens,* in which he discusses, with uncommon penetration,
those points on which Islam and Christianity are more or less
in agreement. Never presenting Mohammed as a criminal im-
poster, he dwells upon the praise accorded by the Koran to God's
power and mercy and justice and notes the high honor given to
the Old Testament prophets and above all to Jesus. His conclusion is that Islam has its share of right and truth and that the
Moslem is not far from Christian belief.

Ricoldus de Monte Crucis was already a noted scholar and
professor before he set out on pilgrimage to the Holy Land in
1288. After many wanderings in the Near East, he eventually
settled at Baghdad in 1290. In that populous city, still a center
of religious learning, Ricoldus was warmly welcomed both by
Dominican friars and by Moslem scholars. Acquainted by this
time with Arabic, he was able not only to study the sources of
Islam but to engage in disputations with learned Mohammedans
and to observe at first hand the life of the people. Though he
left Baghdad for a while after the fall of Acre, he later returned
for another stay, to be followed by further journeys throughout
the Orient until his return to Florence at the end of the century.
A record of these varied travels appears in his *Liber peregrinacionis,* but his chief work is the *Contra legem Sarracenorum,* commonly called *Confutatio Alcorani.* Based on a thorough mastery
of the Koran and an extended knowledge of Islamic culture and
theology, this treatise is easily the finest piece of anti-Moslem
polemic in the Middle Ages and exerted a strong influence for

several centuries. It was translated into Greek in the latter half of the fourteenth century and in 1506 retranslated from the Greek into Latin, with a dedication to King Ferdinand of Aragon. It made so deep an impression and was so often reprinted that Martin Luther, who owned a copy, thought it worth while to produce a German version.

The *Confutatio Alcorani* conforms, of course, to the usual type of controversial work in expressing vigorous opposition to the teaching of Islam. The author repudiates the Koran as revelation and enlarges upon its errors. He denies the assertion that the Christian Scriptures have been corrupted and renews the familiar attacks upon the sexual immorality of the infidel. Like others, too, he accounts for the agreements between Christianity and Islam by explaining that Mohammed had been instructed in the Bible by Jews and by a Jacobite heretic. Where Ricoldus sounds a new and welcome note is in his generous treatment of the virtues of Mohammedans. He points out to his fellow Christians that in many respects their opponents can offer them examples worthy of imitation. And he praises the good Moslem for his hospitality, his zeal for study, his charity to the poor, his spirit of unity, his respect for Jesus and the prophets, his devotion to prayer, and his reverence for God.[3]

Notable as are these medieval names, another outshines them all—the name of Ramon Lull. Partly because we know so much of his varied career and partly because his life sums up so vividly and so completely the best that the Middle Ages had to contribute to the winning of Islam, we shall devote to his story the ensuing chapter.

[3] For the works of Oliver the Scholastic see H. Hoogeweg (ed.), *Die Schriften des Kölner Domscholasters ... Oliverus,* Tübingen, 1894. The *Tractatus de statu Saracenorum* of William of Tripolis may be found in Prutz, *Kulturgeschichte der Kreuzzüge,* pp. 573 ff. For Jacques de Vitry see P. Funk, *Jakob von Vitry,* Leipzig u. Berlin, 1909. The letters written between 1216 and 1221 appear in the *Zeitschrift für Kirchengeschichte,* XVI (1895), 72 ff. The *Liber peregrinacionis* of Ricoldus may be found in J. C. M. Laurent, *Peregrinatores medii aevi quattuor,* Leipzig, 1864. His *Confutatio Alcorani* is most easily accessible in the Greek version in Migne, *Patrologia graeca,* Vol. 154, cols. 1035-1170.

IV

Ramon Lull

NO MORE STRIKING and extraordinary personality ever played a part in the Christian mission to Moslems than Ramon Lull. Unlike his many successors in the evangelization of Islam, he was not primarily an active missionary in the field, nor does his fame rest mainly upon what he achieved in that role. As a literary artist, a teacher, a philosopher, and a theologian, he was a noted figure in his day. As a mystic, too, he is worthy of study, and though the Church of Rome has never gone further than to beatify him, he was quite as much of a saint as many who have enjoyed canonization. Yet from the hour of his conversion to the hour of his martyrdom, the central strand of his manifold career and the innermost motive of his ardent activity were missionary.

Lull was born about 1232 in Palma, Majorca, of a family well descended and of some influence at court. Three years earlier King James I of Aragon had taken Majorca from the Moors, and its inhabitants found themselves at last under Christian rule. The new king had two sons, Peter and James, and at the age of fourteen Ramon was appointed their page and companion. When, in 1256, James was made heir to the throne of Majorca, Ramon was his tutor, and for seven years served as an accomplished courtier, skilled in all the ways of chivalry and devoted to the art of the troubadour. Though he married at this time and later had a son and a daughter, he lived a dissolute life with no concern for religion. Not until his thirty-first year was he converted. Then, one day in 1263, while he was composing a love song to his latest mistress, he experienced a profoundly moving vision of Christ upon the cross. Stirred but unconvinced, Lull did not yield until a second and a third vision of the Savior brought him to the point of surrender. After a period of agonizing struggle, his life thenceforward was changed, and during the fifty years that remained he knew only one Master.

What concerns us most at this point is the fact, to which he always bore witness, that it was as a missionary that he was converted. The controlling element in his new experience was the eager desire to spend himself in the conversion of infidels. The career of the evangelist and the martyr he set as his ideal from the beginning. Indeed, within a few weeks of his conversion he had formed in his mind an outline of the very plans he was to pursue to the end—the foundation of colleges to train a growing number of missionaries and the writing of Christian books that should win by irrefutable logic the minds and hearts of stubborn unbelievers. Here, surely, was a new mode of approach. The Crusades had spent their force and ended in bloody failure. Lull came forward, in reaction to the methods of his day, to proclaim, as the only means worthy of Christ, the power of loving persuasion. Determined at any cost to train himself for his new career, Ramon made provision for his wife and children, and, after some months spent on a pilgrimage, he returned to Palma to begin the hard process of education. For nine long years he studied Latin, philosophy, and theology, and mastered the Arabic tongue with the aid of a Moorish slave. Though now and then he held formal disputations with Jews and Saracens at Palma, he counted these years as a time of preparation for his future enterprise.

Toward the close of this period Lull composed the first and longest of his great works, for this, too, was to be part of his equipment. The *Book of Contemplation,* a gigantic composition of nearly a million words, covers the whole field of theology and the devotional life and stands as a monument to his amazing energy and mental fertility. But more important from our point of view is its constant emphasis on the theme of the conversion of infidels. In this earliest document he declares that the winning of the Moslem is of prime importance and calls upon the Pope and upon several rulers to send forth missionaries to Islam. Again and again he frames his argument with a view to overcoming the objections of the Saracens. Though incredibly confident in the power of logic, he maintains toward them an attitude of tolerant calmness then almost unexampled. Nor is he afraid to praise their strong points and to admire their virtues. The same candor and sense of justice mark a lesser work written before 1273—*The Book of the Gentile and the Three Wise Men.* Choosing a Saracen for one of his speaking characters, Lull shows throughout the discussion his deep study of the Koran and other Islamic literature. But the book he counted his greatest, produced in 1275, was the *Ars magna,* or *Ars generalis.* Convinced that its contents had come to him as the direct result of divine illumination, he viewed it as a statement of Christian truth which even infidels could not reject. The scholastic Middle Ages did not despise the mechanical devices of this extraordinary "thinking machine," a complex contrivance using letters and figures in various combinations to answer all possible questions in philosophy, theology, and science. The method, in fact, was taught in France during Lull's lifetime and in Spain for nearly two centuries. Yet there is no evidence that it ever changed the mind of a Moslem.

During the twelve years which had passed since his conversion, Lull had gone far to accomplish the first of his purposes—the production of Christian literature that might serve the cause of missions. The time had now come when he could forward his second preparatory aim—the founding of schools for missionaries. In 1276 James I of Aragon died and his son James became ruler of Majorca. One of his first acts, under the influence of his close friend and former tutor, was to found at Miramar a missionary college. There, under the king's patronage, thirteen friars began their studies in theology and Arabic. It was Lull's first open success in the long course he had set himself to run, and the future for a time looked bright. But within less than twenty-five years the college was abandoned; it was never refounded; and there is no evidence that any of its students sought a missionary career.

At this time, too (in 1277), Ramon undertook the first of his many attempts to obtain papal aid for his scheme of colleges. Journeying to Rome to win the support of Pope John XXI, he found upon his arrival that the Pope had just died and that nothing could be accomplished. The next nine years—an unknown period in Lull's life—were probably devoted to travel; and two succeeding years spent at Montpellier abounded in literary production—the theological *Ars demonstrativa,* the famous novel *Blanquerna,* and the mystical *Book of the Lover and the Beloved.* In 1285, however, persistent and still undiscouraged, Ramon was once more in Rome pleading with Honorius IV, whom he persuaded to require the study of Arabic at the University of Paris. In pursuit of this new opportunity, he had an audience in Paris, during the following year, with Philip the Fair, but the king gave him little but good wishes. More fruitful was his interview in 1288 with Pope Nicholas IV, for in the following year the Pope founded the University of Montpellier, which, though not a missionary college, served Lull as a center for study and teaching for many years to come.

By this time Lull, who had been associating closely with the Dominican Order and receiving from them little sympathy, began to be drawn toward the Franciscans, whose Chapter-General he attended in 1289. Supported by letters from their General, he returned to Rome in 1290 and presented to the Pope a tract on the conquest of the Holy Land. But the following year witnessed the loss of Acre, marking the end of Christian rule in the East, an hour highly unpropitious for aggressive advance.

Contented no longer to write books and to beg for papal support, despairing of any missionary enterprise on the grand scale for which he had planned, Lull determined to take the one step he had not yet taken during nearly thirty years of Christian activity—to sail alone for Africa and by his own powers to convert the infidel. It was a daring decision, almost too daring; for when the time came to embark at Genoa, Ramon's courage gave way and he let the boat sail without him. Though racked by physical illness and mental agony, he soon regained control of his will. He insisted that his friends put him on board another ship and, early in 1292, at the age of sixty, he landed at Tunis.

Fortunately for him, friendly relations then existed between Aragon and Tunis, and in each country mutual toleration was commonly practiced. For a time, therefore, he was able to address large groups of learned Moslems and to present in the enemy's country all the telling arguments which for so many years he had been marshaling. Though his line of approach was metaphysical, and though he dwelt on such thorny topics as the Trinity and the deity of Christ, he aroused so much favorable interest among the masses that the local ruler and his council at a solemn meeting decided to condemn him to death. Only through the earnest pleading of one member was the decree changed to banishment. Yet Lull was not easily persuaded to leave. Escaping a violent mob, he was set on board his ship, but he slipped away before it sailed and worked secretly in the town for some weeks. At length, convinced that conditions made further effort impossible, he reluctantly took passage for Naples, and made no attempt to return to Africa for another fourteen years. As a gesture, the adventure had been magnificent, but, save as a record of heroism, it bore no fruit.

After a short stay in Naples, where he preached the Gospel to Moors living in that city, Lull visited Rome once again and had an interview with the aged Celestine V, whose troubled reign was to last only five months. He presented the Pope with two books containing a statement of his missionary program. Quite familiar was the plea for the founding of colleges and the dispatch of trained missionaries; but for the first time there appeared an added proposal which Lull was henceforward to press—the organization of a new armed crusade against the infidel. Fullest credit is due him for having urged for thirty years no mode of approach to the Moslem but that of friendly persuasion; yet there can be no doubt that in his old age, after many failures, his confidence in the power of earnest argument began to waver. He fell back upon the need for compulsion, if other efforts should prove vain. Celestine, however, was in no position to help in any cause, and when Lull made a further attempt before Boniface VIII in the following year, he met only with denial or delay.[1]

For three or four years there was now small opportunity for any activity but further study and writing at Montpellier and

---

[1] It was in this same year that Ramon joined the Tertiary Order of St. Francis as a friar minor.

Paris. During 1299 and 1300, however, Lull was able to take advantage of the permission of James of Aragon to preach in the mosques of Barcelona and Majorca, where he could appeal to unbelievers under Christian protection. In 1300 he was deeply stirred by the news that the Moslems of Syria had been conquered by the Khan of Tartary, who was then accounted a friend of Christianity. Prepared to exploit what seemed a providential opening, Lull sailed in 1301 for the Holy Land. But at Cyprus he discovered that the Khan had returned to Persia and that Syria had fallen again under the control of Islam. He could do no more than devote a few months to the relatively mild enterprise of disputing with Oriental Christian heretics in Cyprus. After a journey through Armenia, he returned before the end of the year to Majorca.

For the next six years, except for a futile interview with Pope Clement V, Lull devoted himself to study, lecturing, and writing, at Majorca, Montpellier, and Paris, as a teacher everywhere revered and as an author incredibly prolific. He had now reached the age of seventy-five years, when nearly anyone else would have felt glad to retire and more than willing to leave to others both the hazards of adventure and the arduous efforts to promote missionary education and forceful crusading. Yet his most notable achievements in all these fields were still to come.

In 1307 Lull set out again for Africa, landing at Bugia, a town about one hundred miles east of Algiers. In the best of times the setting would have been unfavorable to evangelism. At the moment, however, it was worse than usual, for not only had there been recent warfare between Bugia and Tunis, but a Moslem reformer had been so agitating the conservative elements that the whole population was in a state of excitement. Beginning thus at the wrong time, Ramon contrived also to begin in the wrong way. Standing in the market place, he openly proclaimed the falsity of the Moslem creed until he aroused the passions of the mob and escaped death at their hands only through the intervention of the Kadi (or chief judge), who placed him under what would now be called "protective arrest." After the first few weeks, thanks to pleas on his behalf from Spanish and Italian merchants, he was kindly treated in prison and for six months enjoyed freedom to debate with such learned Moslems as were interested to visit him in his confinement. He even began the composition of an Arabic work to prove the Christian claims. But by the end of this time the king of Bugia had returned to his capital and ordered Lull to be deported. Yet his hardships were not quite over, for, just before the end of his homeward voyage, the ship was wrecked off the coast of Italy and Ramon landed destitute at Pisa. He refused, however, to let a mere accident divert him from concentration on the task at hand and, entering a monastery near-by, he turned at once to study and writing and soon completed in Latin the book he had begun at Bugia. It was *The Disputation of Ramon, the Christian, and Hamar, the Saracen.* Copies were sent to Pope and cardinals with repeated pleas for monastic colleges and language schools, and for the preparation of a new crusade to assail successively the Moslem kingdom of Granada, the Barbary Coast, and the Holy Land.

Though he failed to win support from Clement V at Avignon, his enthusiasm met with marked success at Pisa and Genoa, where large sums of money were raised. By the year 1310 an expedition had been assembled under the leadership of the Grand Master of the Knights Hospitalers. Sailing from Brindisi to Rhodes, the crusaders succeeded in capturing Cyprus, but there the campaign ended.

Meanwhile Lull had begun a sojourn of two years in Paris, where he devoted himself with great ardor to assailing the teaching of Averroes—the greatest of Moslem Aristotelians, whose doctrines were sharply at odds with his own. At the end of this period, in the year 1311, Clement V summoned a General Council to meet at Vienne; and Ramon seized the opportunity to present to its members a petition demanding missionary colleges at Rome, Paris, and Toledo, and the organization of a unified military order to engage in armed propaganda. For once he met with an apparent success beyond his hopes. The Council decided to establish five institutions, where Hebrew and Arabic should be taught—at Rome, Bologna, Paris, Oxford, and Salamanca.[2] Furthermore, the Knights of St. John were urged to plan for active crusading, and the possessions of the Templars, who had so long neglected their function, were assigned to them for this purpose. Yet despite all these favorable resolutions, no crusade was ever undertaken.

Though Lull was now eighty years old, his amazing productivity as a writer showed no signs of weakening, for during the next two years, spent chiefly in Majorca, he wrote some forty books and pamphlets. Nor did his zeal for evangelism and his inner longing for martyrdom grow fainter with the years. In 1314, at the age of eighty-two, he sailed once more for Bugia. After a few months there, working with greater tact and secrecy than before, he journey to Tunis to present to the king letters of commendation from James of Aragon. Thanks in part to royal favor, he was even permitted to engage in preaching tours through the villages, as well as to dispute with learned doctors in the city. With many of these scholars his relations must have been cordial, for his ministry continued for months, and in the course of it he published a book dedicated to the Mufti of Tunis. At length, however, for reasons we cannot now fathom, there came a sharp change in his attitude and method. At some time between December, 1315, and March, 1316, he left Tunis for Bugia, and there, in the open market place, defiantly proclaimed his message. At once an angry mob gathered and began to stone him. Somehow his friends contrived to rescue him, but not before he had met with mortal wounds. It was probably on board the ship which bore him toward Italy that he died. With such a martyrdom in mind, he had once written, "Although I am unworthy, O God, of dying for Thee, nevertheless I do not give up the hope of obtaining this holy and precious death."

Lull was a man at once characteristic of his time and ahead of

---

[2] The practical results of these decrees have been much debated. Some have overestimated and others have underestimated their significance. The truth appears to be that at the papal school the plan was really carried out; that there was probably some meager success at Paris; and that there is no evidence that anything was accomplished at the other seats of learning. See Altaner, "Sprachstudien... im Dienste der Mission des 13 and 14 Jahrhunderts," *Zeitschrift für Missionswissenschaft,* XXI (1931), 113-36.

his time. As a scholastic philosopher profoundly confident of the power of logic to work miracles in the production and impartation of truth, he was typical of his era. But as an enthusiast for missions, whose central purpose was to win Moslems by persuasion and to train with care a growing number of evangelists equipped to that end, he was far in advance of his age. It is not surprising, therefore, that it was as a thinker and teacher that he achieved success and won applause and that it was in the fields of missionary organization and direct evangelism that he almost always encountered misunderstanding, disappointment, and failure. Yet it may well prove in the end that his name will live through the inspiring power of these courageous failures. To have attempted what for the time being was impossible is to have earned the gratitude of all those who have since labored to realize his dreams.[3]

[3] This account of Lull's life is chiefly indebted to the one thorough and scholarly biography available in English—Peers, *Ramon Lull*. A brief and interesting popular story of his life, from the missionary point of view, is Zwemer's *Raymund Lull*.

V

Christian and Moslem in Spain

FOR MORE than eight hundred years there were Moslems in Spain. The story of their relations with Christians is an important chapter in our survey for several reasons. In the first place, it records the only example on an extended scale of Moslem dominance in any part of Western Europe.[1] Moreover, Spain offers the one instance of prolonged Mohammedan contact with the Roman Church. Still more significant is the fact that this epoch, covering so many centuries, includes the widest variety of mutual relations. That variety ranges all the way from the time of almost complete control by Islam, with the Christians a defeated minority, through an age when the two faiths were rivals, equal in culture and in power, to a final period when the Moors were only a hunted remnant. We are thus given the chance to observe how each side bore itself toward the other in every diversity of circumstance.

At the beginning of the eighth century, when the expanding force of Islam was still active, the Visigothic empire in Spain was in course of rapid dissolution. The country was a tempting prey for any vigorous invader. After two hundred years of rule by the Goths the aristocracy was corrupt, the middle classes overtaxed and bankrupt, and both serfs and slaves were in a state of misery. It is not surprising, therefore, that a Berber invasion from Morocco should meet with complete success. In the year 711, 12,000 troops under the leadership of Tarik, lieutenant of Musa, governor of Mauretania, defeated the Visigothic king Roderick and captured Cordova and Toledo. In the course of a few months nearly the whole peninsula was overrun. As one historian puts it,

[1] The period of Moslem rule in Sicily reproduces many of the same features on a smaller scale.

"by an unexpected stroke of good fortune a mere raid had resulted in a conquest." The victory was made even more extensive by the arrival in 712 of a larger army under Musa. Everywhere there was little resistance; at several points the people gladly opened their gates to the invaders; and the Jews especially welcomed the Moors and aided them. The few remnants of Christian power were soon confined to a small area in the northwest corner of Spain. There, however, in 718, the tide began to turn. A Visigothic victory at Covadonga marked the beginning of the struggle for reconquest. Starting with guerrilla warfare, various Christian forces gradually grew together to form the Kingdom of the Asturias, with a wide no man's land between them and the Moors. By the end of the eighth century, the Guadarrama mountains constituted a rough boundary between the Christian and Moslem regions—a bleak northern one-third and a fertile southern two-thirds. Thenceforward the medieval history of Spain is primarily the story of the long crusade to expel the Moors. In the course of that fluctuating movement, the different Spanish kingdoms were slowly evolved; and the final victory at Granada in 1492 celebrated the union of the crowns of Aragon and Castile.

The age of widest Moorish dominion comprises the three centuries of the Caliphate of Cordova. After the first rush of conquest ensued a time of dissension and strife among the invaders, during which there occurred, in 750, the fall of the Omayyad Caliphate in the East. Abd ar-Rahman, a member of the deposed dynasty, escaped from Damascus, and after many adventures crossed the Straits with a force of Berbers from Morocco, won his way to power in Spain, and in 756 established himself as Emir, with his capital at Cordova. The greatest of his successors, Abd ar-Rahman III (912-61), who first took the title of Caliph, reigned for nearly fifty years, and under his sway the Caliphate of Cordova reached the height of its glory. In the best days of the dynasty, as every student of history knows, Moslem Spain was one of the wealthiest and most populous countries in Europe, and the brilliance of its civilization shone in contrast with the relative darkness beyond its borders. There was not only a wonderful growth of industry, commerce, and general prosperity, but culture flourished in all its forms. A standard of literacy prevailed far higher than elsewhere on the Continent; and among scholars the development of theology, philosophy, medicine, chemistry, astronomy, history, and geography was phenomenal. Art and poetry, too, were carried to high levels of excellence. Cordova, indeed, was known so widely as "the brightest splendor of the world" that students flocked thither from all countries.

During these three hundred years the Christians were, on the whole, well treated. From the beginning the Moslems left to the vanquished their own laws and judges, with counts of their own race appointed as governors. Though the nobles lost their property, the peasants gained greater prosperity through the division of lands. The lot of the serfs and the slaves was notably bettered, for members of both groups could become free by conversion. The rank and file of Christians, by paying the poll tax, were allowed to practice their religion; and this tolerant attitude of the new rulers greatly aided the process of conquest. In the course of time Christians came to hold high office at court and even served in the Moslem armies. Social intercourse was sufficiently free to produce frequent intermarriage. Indeed, as H. C. Lea reminds us, during the ninth and tenth centuries "facility of conversion from one faith to another was a marked feature of the period, and shows how little firmness of religious conviction existed." Yet the change of faith was a process distinctly one-sided, for all the pressure of prestige and superior civilization was in favor of the Moslem. By the ninth century the majority of the population had accepted Islam.[2]

While it is true that Christianity was tolerated, it is equally true, however, that the Church continued to decay. Though religion, in a sense, remained free, the Church itself was subject to servitude. The Moslem rulers assumed the right to summon ecclesiastical councils and to appoint and depose bishops. As a

---

[2] The one important exception to the general statement that Moorish rule was singularly free from persecution appears in a series of incidents at Cordova in the middle of the ninth century. At that time a fervent zeal for voluntary martyrdom broke out among certain priests, monks, and nuns. Despite the disapproval of the leaders of the Church, who tried to repress them, these enthusiasts publicly attacked Mohammed and Islam, and not a few of them met the death they sought.

result, bishoprics could be bought by notorious evil-livers, and even Jews and Moslems sat on Christian councils. Christian learning and education declined, and the corrupt clergy, of small value to their own people, were treated as outcasts by the Moors. At the very time, in short, when Islam might everywhere be seen at its best, Christianity, for the most part, appeared at its worst. Whether the appeal was religious, social, or political, the advantages were all on the side of Islam.

With the downfall of the Caliphate of Cordova in 1031, began the period of Christian reconquest. Moslem supremacy and martial power never fully recovered from the loss, and during the next two centuries the leadership of Spain gradually passed to the Christian states. Internal disintegration among the Moors and the increasing economic and military strength of the Christians made possible a general advance toward the south. Despite occasional reverses, more and more territory was reclaimed. Under Ferdinand I, who united the crowns of Leon and Castile, and later under Alphonso VI, the reconquest went forward until the fall of Toledo in 1085. From that time on, however, there intervened for more than a century an age of reaction, during which the Christian forces met a series of defeats and suffered from civil strife within their own ranks. First came the invasion of the Almoravides, rulers of a Berber Empire in North Africa. Summoned to help the despairing Moors, they defeated Alphonso VI in 1086 and soon ruled all Moslem Spain. After some two generations, during which the Moors were united once again and the Christians often persecuted, the dynasty had decayed to the point of impotence. It was overthrown in Africa by a powerful new puritanical sect, the Almohades, under the leadership of Abd al-Mumin, who crossed to Spain with an army in 1149 and within less than ten years held nearly one-half the peninsula under his rule. Thanks to some three decades of warfare among Christians, the Almohades reconquered much territory and badly defeated Alphonso VIII in 1196. As fanatics far more intense than the Spanish Moors, they persecuted Christians on many occasions and at times deliberately attempted conversion by force.

By the opening of the thirteenth century, the tide had turned

again and there began the third great forward movement of
the Christians. In July, 1212, Alphonso VIII won a complete victory at Las Navas de Tolosa. James I of Aragon took Majorca,
Minorca, and Valencia. But Ferdinand III, uniting once more
the kingdoms of Leon and Castile, was the foremost leader of the
period. Before his death in 1252 he had become master of all
southern Spain except the province of Granada. At that point
the campaigns ended, and to that area the power of the Moors
was to be confined for another two hundred years.

In the warfare of the twelfth and thirteenth centuries there was
little evidence of racial or religious hatred, since enthusiasm for
one faith or the other was not the main motive in the constant
struggles of the times. It was primarily a contest for political
control, during which there were many examples of Spanish kings
in alliance with Moors against Christian rivals or rebellious subjects. Religious zeal was so seldom apparent that Christian and
Moor often coöperated and intermingled. With the advance of
Christian power, the rights of Moslems were respected in the
treaties of surrender. Regarded as a valuable part of the population, they were gladly tolerated and granted a large degree of
autonomy. Though they were commonly segregated in the cities
and though eating and drinking and sexual intercourse with
Christians was strictly forbidden, the Moors were not subject to
oppression or to forcible proselytizing. In other words, they met
much the same treatment as they had accorded to Christians.

It was during the second half of the thirteenth century that the
Church began to show a marked concern for the Moslem population. At first this new interest took forms quite desirable and
defensible from the Christian point of view. Though Rome was
sternly opposed to the easy tolerance so long manifest in Spain,
the official position of the Church at the time was that no infidel
could be compelled to embrace Christianity. For the Church to
have power over any Moor, he must first have been baptized.
Such, for example, was the orthodox view of St. Thomas Aquinas.
Peaceful persuasion was the order of the day, and for a brief
period it intervened between the indifference of the past and the
cruel bigotry of a later age. For a season, then, the record of

Christianity was one in which the Church may take pride. And, as in North Africa and the Near East, it was the Mendicant Orders, especially the Dominican, that carried into action these missionary principles. The friars were eager in their attempts to convert the Moors, and their preaching activity was continuous. The force of secular authority was exerted no further than to compel the Moslems on many occasions to attend the preaching services and listen to sermons. But though they were free to decide as they would, there is evidence that considerable numbers accepted the Christian faith. Parallel with these evangelistic efforts went the work of polemic writers. Among these the foremost figure was the Dominican Raymond of Penaforte, who not only wrote controversial treatises himself but is responsible also for persuading Thomas Aquinas to compose his *Summa contra gentiles,* with the Moors of Spain especially in mind. Supported by the kings of Castile and Aragon, Raymond founded schools for the study of Arabic in Murcia and in Tunis, that monks might be prepared for evangelizing the Moslems. Raymond Martini, too, who had studied Arabic for polemic use, produced a defense of the faith against Jews and Mohammedans and labored as a missionary both in Spain and in North Africa.

During the fourteenth century and the larger part of the fifteenth, little was accomplished in the work of reconquest. Though no longer formidable, the Moors were strong enough to resist further advance. Among the Christians there were prolonged dynastic struggles in Castile that led to frequent periods of anarchy among the turbulent nobles; and in the occasional warfare Christians and Moors were often found fighting on the same side. A new era, however, began in 1469 with the marriage of Ferdinand of Aragon and Isabella of Castile. The two kingdoms were now united, and after the queen's death in 1504 a single monarch ruled all Spain. For more than a century before this union of the crowns, the temper of the Church had been hardening and the Christian attitude toward the Moslem had been growing steadily more intolerant. Always opposed to the policy of conciliation, the ecclesiastical authorities had been increasing their efforts to keep the Christians separate from the Moors and to humiliate the latter by prescribing for them special garments or badges and by forbidding various Mohammedan practices. Yet none of these attempts was successful for long, nor were the harsh decrees of councils ever widely obeyed. Not until the days of Ferdinand and Isabella were policies of Church and State at one.

By 1482, however, the Christians were united in devotion to their new sovereigns, while in the Moorish kingdom there were sedition and strife. War against the Moslem was deliberately resumed, and for the first time every effort was exerted to make the last stage of conquest a genuine religious crusade. By 1489 only the city of Granada was left in infidel hands, and at the end of a year of siege the town surrendered, in January, 1492. Even after this final victory in the age-old struggle of reconquest, the usual generous terms were granted to the Moors. They were guaranteed the preservation of their religion and laws; those who wished to remain were promised security in person and property; and all who desired to leave might take with them their possessions. Isabella appointed the saintly Hernando de Talavera Archbishop of Granada; and for seven years, under his gentle rule, persuasive preaching and education brought thousands of converts into the Church.

At the turn of the century, however, a complete change of policy took place, and for the next hundred years the record of Church and State was one of ruthless repression and persecution. In 1499 Ximenes, Archbishop of Toledo, was sent to be associate with Hernando, whose authority was soon ignored and whose methods were at once reversed. There ensued a period of conversions by compulsion and terrorism. Symbolic of the new regime was the practice of mass baptism by sprinklers, often of thousands at one time. Welcoming the revolts which inevitably broke out, Ximenes urged upon the court that the Moors, by their resistance, had forfeited all right to life and property and must now submit to baptism or exile. The court agreed to break all the royal pledges and to support the archbishop in the sternest measures. In short order some 60,000 unbelievers in or near Granada were baptized; and, under the influence of Ximenes, Isabella applied the same treatment to the loyal Moslems in

Castile. In a further effort at coercion, there was issued on February 12, 1502, an edict commanding that all adult Moors in the kingdoms of Leon and Castile who remained unconverted should leave the country. Since the government would not allow them to migrate to North Africa and imposed other conditions that made departure almost impossible, this decree really meant baptism or death. In consequence, the Moors were everywhere baptized in great masses. Thenceforward these new converts formed a special class known as Moriscos.

In 1507 Ximenes became Inquisitor General and found a new armory of weapons ready to his hand. Thirty years earlier the Pope had granted to Castile the Inquisition, an engine of persecution which differed greatly, in its fearful efficiency, from its earlier medieval counterpart. For in Spain it represented not merely the Pope but the king, and could wield without hindrance the sword of the state. Its machine was soon turned against the Moriscos; since now that they were officially converted, force might be applied to them as Christians from which, as infidels, they had been exempt. From then on for several generations the majority of "heretics" dealt with were Moriscos, who were constantly arrested and prosecuted for clinging to the customs of Islam. Most of their sufferings they endured without resistance; but in 1568 a great uprising took place at Granada. After a bitter campaign of several years, it was suppressed. Many of the women and children were sold into slavery, and a large proportion of the Moriscos at Granada were exiled to the mountains of northern Spain.

The Moriscos in Aragon fared better as long as Ferdinand lived; but after his death in 1516, when Charles became king, the pitiless hunt began. Released by the Pope from an oath not to make forced conversions, Charles called upon his nobles in 1525 to expel or enslave all unconverted Moors. Tens of thousands submitted in Valencia and Aragon, and, after a brief revolt had been quelled, still larger masses surrendered to baptism. Now that they were at the mercy of the Inquisition, there were but few periods of moderation to interrupt the process of confiscating, fining, scourging, and burning. "Subjected to the perpetual exasperation of interference with their habits and customs, to the oppression of their lords and the persecution of the Inquisition, denied all opportunity to rise in the social scale, forbidden to enjoy the faith of their ancestors, while sedulously trained to hate the religion imposed on them, and despairing of relief in the future, it is no wonder that the Moriscos were discontented subjects, eager to throw off the insupportable yoke and to rise against their oppressors." [3] But, vastly outnumbered and wholly unarmed, they could no longer attempt resistance. Yet it seemed impossible to extinguish them. They multiplied faster than the Christians and remained throughout the century a problem baffling even to a completely unscrupulous government.

Finally, in 1609, the most drastic measures were decreed by the Council of State. The Moriscos, one and all, were to be bodily expelled. A series of edicts in different parts of Spain commanded deportation at short notice, upon pain of death. Troops and ships were assembled; a few minor rebellions were repressed; and between September, 1609, and January, 1614, about 600,000 Moriscos were deported, chiefly to the Moorish states of North Africa. The miserable victims not only suffered dreadful hardships on the way, but at the hands of Moslems in Africa were plundered and slain in great numbers. What with the ravages of disease and deaths from violence, probably two-thirds of them perished.

Thus, nine hundred years after the overthrow of the Gothic monarchy, Spain purified her land of the invader by a stroke which Cardinal Richelieu qualified as the boldest and most barbarous in human annals. The yearning for unity of faith was gratified, and the anxiety as to attack from without was allayed. That the price paid was heavy is seen in the premature decrepitude which overtook the monarchy during the rest of the century. The causes of decadence were many, but not least among them must be reckoned the fierce intolerance which led to the expatriation of the most economically valuable classes of the population. [4]

If that fierce intolerance had merely hampered the economic welfare of Spain, it would have little significance for religion. But it did more. It defiled the record of the Christian Church, and in the world of Islam it was not forgotten.

[3] Lea, *History of the Inquisition of Spain*, III, 382.　　　　[4] *Ibid.*, p. 410.

VI

The Period of Ottoman Supremacy

WHEN we turned aside to treat of Ramon Lull and to rehearse the story of the Moors in Spain, we had brought our survey of the relations between Christendom and Islam to the end of the Crusades. The close of that epoch coincides roughly with the rise of the Ottoman Turks and the beginning of the long period of Ottoman domination.

But before the Crusades had ended and the Osmanli had begun to be dangerous, the conversion of the Mongols to Islam brought nearer to completion the eclipse of Christianity in the East and extinguished the last hope of the time that Christianity might win fresh reinforcement. In the first half of the thirteenth century, the Mongols under Jenghiz Khan, and later under his son Ogotai, had invaded and ravaged Persia and Mesopotamia and parts of Armenia and Georgia. In 1258 Jenghiz's grandson Hulagu captured and sacked Baghdad and slew most of its population, including the Abbasid caliph. Yet Hulagu professed to be a Christian. Under his rule in Persia and Baghdad the Church enjoyed more favor than ever before, and its members occupied many stations of importance. During this time, in fact, the Nestorian Church reached its widest missionary extent. But in spite of success in other quarters, the Christians failed to convert the Mongols and at the same time they made the fatal error of treating their Mohammedan neighbors with a contemptuous intolerance that sometimes went as far as persecution. Since the Mongols favored Christianity chiefly as an aid against their Moslem enemies, their attitude gradually changed when they met successive defeats in their contest with Islam. In 1260 and again in 1280 the Mongols were beaten by Egyptian forces; and with each disaster the prestige of the conquering religion rose, until the Mon-

gol ruler Abagu was converted to Islam, together with many of
his people. When the capture of Acre in 1291 stamped out the
last trace of Christian control, the Mongols decided once for all
in favor of the victorious faith. From then on the Nestorian
Church in Persia and Mesopotamia, the victim of internal decay
and of frequent persecution, slowly declined. What little life remained in this forlorn minority was nearly extinguished a century
later when the invading armies of the bloody Timur swept over
this area. By the beginning of the fifteenth century, the Nestorian
Patriarch, with a feeble remnant of Christians, took refuge in the
highlands of Kurdistan. A Church once powerful throughout
wide stretches of Asia had dwindled to a negligible fragment.

More significant for the future of Christendom and Islam than
Mongol success and Nestorian collapse were the decay of the
Byzantine Empire and the advance of the Turk. During the fourteenth century and the first half of the fifteenth, the Empire,
under its last dynasty, the Palaeologi, was rapidly disintegrating.
Still suffering from the effects of the Fourth Crusade and the experience of Latin rule, the Byzantine power was the prey at once
of internal dissolution and of alien aggression. There were social
revolts and civil wars, religious dissension and financial disorder.
Meanwhile the Osmanli Turks were making steady progress in
Asia Minor and the Balkans. Under three great leaders, Osman,
Orkhan, and Murad I, whose reigns covered the century from
1289 to 1389, the Turks took Nicaea, occupied Gallipoli, and
later conquered Thrace, thus completely isolating Byzantium.
Pressing on into Europe, they overcame both the Bulgarians and
the Serbians. After a defeat by the hordes of Timur at Angora in
1402, they were held in check for some twenty years. When they
were ready to renew the struggle, there was nothing left of the
Greek empire but its capital; and its last sovereigns turned in
vain for aid to the powers of Western Europe. The forces of the
Christian West had long since yielded their holdings in the Near
East to the advancing Osmanli, partly because the Oriental Christians hated their Latin masters more than they feared the Turk.
At the final crisis, therefore, the bitterness between East and
West removed all chance of a united Christian resistance. Out-

side the walls of the doomed city not a hand was lifted to save the ancient capital of Constantine. In May, 1453, the Sultan Mohammed II captured Constantinople.

From the point of view of grand strategy, as Dr. Cash has pointed out in his *Christendom and Islam,* the Mediterranean had become by this

time virtually a Moslem sea, and Europe was literally pushed out into the Atlantic ocean, and at the same time cut off from her Eastern markets. The Turks sought to isolate the unconquered parts of Europe, to strangle their trade and thus to open the way to further Islamic expansion westward.[1]

But before the end of the fifteenth century the voyages of Diaz and Columbus and Vasco da Gama opened up not only a new world in the West but new routes to the East. By closing the old trade paths, the Turks had actually rendered an immense service to Europe. The discoveries of explorers and

the general awakening in Europe combined to isolate Islam. Instead of traversing Moslem lands as in former days merchants now avoided and went round them. Thus the Moslem policy of isolating Europe really acted like a boomerang, for it came back with redoubled force upon Islam and left the Moslem world separated and isolated in the Near and Middle East. Islam, thus cut off from the fresh springs of learning and having begun to decline in power, turned back to its old conservatism and orthodoxy and eventually stagnated.[2]

For more than a century after 1453, however, the Ottoman domain was expanding far and wide; and it was not until yet another century had passed that Christian Europe could once again breathe freely. Selim I, who assumed the title of Caliph of Islam (to be borne by his successors until 1924), conquered Syria and Egypt in 1516 and 1517 and pushed the Turkish frontier into Armenia and Mesopotamia. He was succeeded by Suleiman the Magnificent, during whose long reign of forty-six years the Ottoman power reached its height. Except for Morocco, the Moorish states of North Africa acknowledged the suzerainty of Turkey, and Arabia was soon brought under control. Suleiman was by this time so great a figure that he could consummate an

---

[1] Cash, *Christendom and Islam,* p. 116.　　　[2] *Ibid.,* p. 118.

alliance with Francis I of France and move to the conquest of Hungary in 1526; but three years later his advance into Europe was halted by a defeat at Vienna. Yet this first check had little effect upon Ottoman vitality. Later in the century, however, came the crushing disaster of Lepanto, where the Turks were overwhelmed in 1571 by the combined fleets of Venice, Spain, and Austria. From then on the Ottoman Empire won but few new areas; its leaders lost aggressiveness; and its wonderful administrative machine began to disintegrate. When the Christian armies in 1683, under Sobieski of Poland, again defeated the Turks before Vienna, the danger point had been passed, and the next century witnessed the slow Ottoman retreat before the forces of Austria and Russia. Hungary was soon redeemed once for all, and before the end of the eighteenth century southern Russia and the Crimea.

From the fall of Constantinople until the nineteenth century, then, the Moslem world and the Ottoman Empire in the eyes of Christian Europe were roughly synonymous. The relations between Christendom and Islam were primarily the relations between Christian and Turk. Wherever the Turk was in control, the familiar status of *dhimmis* was assigned to Christians. Whether they were Greeks or Armenians, Bulgars or Albanians, they were forbidden to bear arms or to serve in the civil government. They had not only to pay the capitation tax, from which Moslems were exempt, but to submit to many other exactions and disabilities, the enforcement of which was often abused. Yet according to the familiar "millet" system,[3] which prevailed until the first World War, each Christian body was a recognized entity over which its chosen chief had control in all matters ecclesiastical

---

[3] "The Millet System is a provision for the government of subject minorities whose religious faith differs from that of the governing institution of the State, and who are therefore limited in their citizenship by virtue of the fact that the laws of personal statute are based upon religious sanctions. Such subjects are hence classified according to their creed or rite, and certain phases of their civil administration are committed directly to the jurisdiction of the ecclesiastical organization of the sect, under the oversight of the Head of the Millet, who is usually the ranking member of the hierarchy . . . and who is, in turn, directly responsible to the State for the administration of all its subjects belonging to that particular religion," Carleton, "Church and State in the Near East," *Moslem World* (July, 1938), p. 280,

and to some degree even in civil affairs. Among these ancient Christian communities that survived on sufferance, the Jacobites, by the sixteenth century, had been reduced to hardly more than 50,000 families, chiefly in Iraq and western Turkey. The Armenians, far more numerous, were widely dispersed through Asia Minor after the Ottoman victories and between 1600 and 1800 were trampled alternately by Turkish and Persian armies. It was the Greek Church, strongest in numbers and in influence, which was especially favored by the conquerors.

During the process of conquest large numbers of Orthodox Christians became Moslems; yet multitudes, resisting the temptation, submitted to the conditions imposed on the minority. The Sultan recognized the Greek Church and maintained official relations with its head. The Patriarch of Constantinople was permitted to summon synods and to hold courts for his own people, among whom were included the Orthodox elements in the patriarchates of Antioch, Jerusalem, and Alexandria. But the Patriarchs were chosen and appointed by the Sultan, with only the pretense of election by the Synod. They usually obtained the office by bribery and held it by a cringing subservience; for whatever else they might do, they must not offend their Moslem master. Bishops likewise bought their positions and were utilized by the Turks not only as magistrates among the Christians but even as taxgatherers. This gain in civil authority was paid for, of course, by a disastrous loss in religious influence. As with every branch of Christianity under Moslem domination, the lack of free leadership and the surrounding pressure of a hostile faith wrought their fatal effects upon the Orthodox Church. Before long its diminished body showed every sign of intellectual stagnation and spiritual torpor. Hardly a name of distinction stands out in the featureless history of these depressing centuries. The one notable leader was Cyril Lucar (1572-1638), a Patriarch of Constantinople, who made a brave attempt to reform the Eastern Church from within, along Protestant lines. But after he was executed by the Sultan and condemned by several later synods, the Church gradually sank to still lower levels of degeneration.

When we realize the outward status and the inner character of

the Oriental Churches throughout this long period, it is plain
that the last thing to be expected of them was any thought of
missionary activity. The mere facts of the law would have been
enough to deter them, for the Christian who tried to convert a
Moslem and the Moslem who deserted Islam were alike subject
to the death penalty. Yet even had the way been legally open,
there were psychological and spiritual obstacles even more fatal.
A despised minority, barely maintaining a church life from which
all vigor of mind and soul has fled, is in no state to initiate and
sustain an adventure in evangelism which even now demands a
hardy and zealous faith.

It was only in the independent Christianity of Western Europe,
whether Catholic or Protestant, that there lay any hope for a
missionary approach to Islam. And even there the hope was dim
and the hindrances almost insuperable. Europe in the Renaissance
remained almost as ignorant of Islam as in the Middle Ages.
The contradictory mass of distorted ideas about Mohammed and
his religion that prevailed in medieval times persisted for centuries, and little was done to dispel the confusion. Of those who
had any notions at all about Mohammed, some still regarded him
as a god whose idols were worshiped by believers. In Elizabethan
times, for example, little images or dolls were often called
"mammets." Others inherited the tradition that he was a heretic
who founded the most abominable of Christian schisms. Still
others, having discovered that Islam was really a distinct religion, branded Mohammed as an impostor and a fraud. The
published works which dealt with Islam were few, and still fewer
were those which gave any reliable facts. Among these exceptional
productions was an anonymous work published in 1597, *The
Policy of the Turkish Empire,* which gave not a little accurate
information about Islamic religion and ethics. More typical of
the period were such treatises as Wybarne's *The New Age of Old
Names* (1609), which describes Islam as "a mongrel religion com-
piled of shadows and impostures"; and Bedwell's *Mohammedis
imposturae,* which dealt with "the manifold forgeries, falsehoods,
and horrible impieties of the blasphemous seducer Mohammed."
Not until the more enlightened eighteenth century was there

any serious attempt to understand Mohammed and his faith, a change which may be said to have scarcely begun before Sale's famous translation of the Koran, published in 1734.[4]

Many of the obstacles to missionary advance which kept the Oriental Churches subjected and silent were equally fatal to Roman Catholic ambition. The law against apostasy and the prohibition of Christian evangelism were no less effective in restricting the efforts of the Church of Rome. But whatever Moslem law might have to say in Moslem lands, the Catholic Church itself was a body wholly independent and immensely powerful, in which the missionary spirit may have fluctuated but never died. Compared with the Oriental Churches, it was a healthy organism still expanding. Despite all hindrances, therefore, the activities of the monastic orders, begun in the early thirteenth century, were continued in succeeding generations. From the fourteenth century to the eighteenth, Dominicans and Franciscans were laboring in Morocco, Algeria, and Tunis, in Egypt, Syria, and Cilicia. Toward the end of the seventeenth century other orders, too, were to be found in some of these areas—the Lazarists, Capuchins, and Augustinians. Nearly all of their work, it is true, was with Christian captives, slaves, and merchants, or with oriental schismatics. Yet the cases of martyrdom were frequent enough to indicate what other evidence confirms—that from time to time they had the courage directly to approach the Moslem.

Throughout this same period, moreover, the work of polemic was not neglected; and the publications of various Christian scholars indicate that the conversion of Mohammedans never ceased to be numbered among the aims of the Church. In 1525, for example, appeared the treatise of Loazes called *De conversione et baptismo Agarenorum,* only one of a number of manuals of that era. More thorough was the long work of Thomas a Jesu, published in 1613 and entitled *De conversione omnium gentium procuranda,* a study that included a discussion of practical methods of evangelism in which the author emphasized the great value of prayer and of example. Of special interest, too,

---

[4] A brilliant and scholarly account of the views of Islam prevalent during the Renaissance is *The Crescent and the Rose,* by S. C. Chew.

were the controversial writings of the Jesuit Father Jerome
Xavier, whose work in India we shall describe in the next chapter. He wrote in Persian for the Emperor Akbar the *Life of
Christ* and the *Life of St. Peter,* and in 1609 composed *A Mirror
Showing the Truth,* wherein the Christian Gospel is set forth
and the vanity of other religions declared. That this treatise was
not without effect is shown by the fact that an Indian Moslem
wrote an answer some twelve years later, which he called *The
Divine Rays in Refutation of Christian Error.* And this in turn
met with a rejoinder by a learned scholar at Rome, the *Apologia
pro Christiana religione.*

Though Catholic missions in the territory of Islam bore little
fruit in the conversion of Moslems, at least the Church was alive
to her responsibility and paid the price of zealous effort. Among
Protestants, on the contrary, there was for a long time not only
nothing accomplished but nothing attempted. For nearly two
centuries the Churches of the Reformation were almost destitute
of any sense of missionary vocation. The foremost leaders—men
like Luther, Melancthon, Bucer, Zwingli, and Calvin—displayed
neither missionary vision nor missionary spirit. While conceding
in theory the universality of Christianity, they never recognized
it as a call to the Church of their day. Indeed some of them even
interpreted "Go ye into all the world" as a command already
executed in the past and now no longer operative. And the very
few thinkers who rejected this deadening view remained without
influence.

With no sense of obligation to evangelize the non-Christian
world, the Protestants were hardly likely to enter the most difficult arena of all—the lands of Islam. The Turks, as the nearest
Moslems, were primarily an object of hatred and fear. Luther,
it is true, had read the Koran in Latin and had published a
translation of Ricoldus's *Confutatio;* but though he knew much
more of Islam than most of his contemporaries, he studied it
with no missionary purpose. For him the Turks were simply
vicious enemies, and on political grounds he supported the warfare against them. Yet at least he declaimed, during most of his
career, against turning the contest into a religious crusade. For

this restraint, however, we can give him little credit, since his chief reason was that the papacy was a worse enemy of Christianity than the Turk and that the real Antichrist was not Mohammed but the Pope!

Before it could be stirred by the spirit of evangelism, Protestantism needed an evangelical revival; and for that the Church had to wait until the end of the seventeenth century, when Pietism began to flourish in Germany under the leadership of Spener and Francke. Thanks to this new awakening, the University of Halle became a center for the inspiration and training of the first Protestants to be primarily missionaries to the heathen. Though these early pioneers were not sent to Moslems, it is worth noting that Callenberg, the founder of the Halle Missionsinstitut, was deeply interested in missions to Mohammedans, especially in India. He devoted much of his life to works on Islam and was one of the earliest enthusiasts for the literary evangelism of the Moslem. During the first half of the eighteenth century Callenberg translated into Arabic not only parts of the New Testament but also the *Imitation of Christ* and Luther's Shorter Catechism. He was fully acquainted with the history of polemic against the Moslem and made his own contribution in this field with two books on Christianity written in Arabic.

Until the end of the eighteenth century, when the Wesleyan revival had begun to take effect in England, the only Protestants, other than the German Pietists, who displayed any zeal for evangelism were the Moravians. From the time when the community settled at Herrnhut, near Dresden, in 1722, under the patronage and leadership of Count von Zinzendorf, its members have been famous for their missionary enthusiasm, especially for their eagerness to enter areas that were apparently barren and hopeless. It was this devoted group which sent to the field of Islam the first Protestant missionaries.[5]

Between 1752 and 1761, Frederic William Hocker, a Moravian doctor, was at work in Cairo, aided for only three years by a fellow laborer, George Pilder. Though the two men made an un-

[5] For an interesting possible exception to this statement, see Soucek, "V. B. de Budov," *Moslem World*, Oct., 1927.

successful journey to Abyssinia, their efforts were chiefly confined to Egypt. After seven years in Europe, Hocker returned to Cairo, there to remain until his death in 1782. During his last twelve years he was supported at intervals by some eight or ten other missionaries, most of whom stayed for only brief periods. Soon after Hocker's death the Synod at Herrnhut decided to withdraw the mission in Egypt, and it was never resumed. In the course of these thirty years the Moravian pioneers received no salaries and had to earn their living as doctors, tailors, or carpenters. Since the direct evangelism of Mohammedans was absolutely impossible, they found themselves almost wholly restricted to preaching and personal work among the Copts. Though on occasion they could interview a Moslem in private, they won no converts from Islam; and even upon the Copts their effect was so slight that they never formed any organized groups. So far as visible results go, they had to confess failure. Yet, like other faithful failures, they deserve a citation for gallantry in action.

From the fourteenth century to the nineteenth, from the days of Lull to the days of Henry Martyn, the records of individual missionaries to Moslems are so few and scanty that the endeavors they relate can be summed up only in the most general terms. The one notable exception is the story of the Jesuit missions to the Mughal court in India. For this enterprise the sources are so abundant, so full of color and incident, that they must be given a place in our narrative. If we are to complete our survey of the twelve centuries before the modern age with a picture of the mission to Moslems that met with most success and best displays the methods of an earlier age, we must conclude with a chapter on the Jesuit Fathers at the court of Akbar and his successors.

VII

The Jesuits at the Mughal Court

TOWARD the end of the twelfth century began the period of Moslem domination in northern India. Entering from Afghanistan, Mohammed of Ghor fixed his main capital at Delhi and founded the first Indo-Moslem empire. Thenceforward, for some 325 years, a series of dynasties, holding the Sultanate of Delhi, ruled wide areas of Indian territory. Unlike earlier invading forces, the Moslem conquerors were not absorbed into the Hindu social system. They brought with them not only the new languages of Arabic and Persian and the new law of Islam, but also a new and vital missionary faith which soon claimed the adherence of a large body of converts among the subject peoples. In 1398 the bloody invasion of the ferocious Timur shattered the power of the Sultanate and left India a prey for fifty years to anarchy and civil strife. An Afghan dynasty, the Lodi, restored some measure of order during the last half of the fifteenth century; but in 1526 its forces yielded to the invading army of Babur, King of Kabul, the founder of the Mughal dynasty. These conquerors, though partly Mongol in blood, were Turks, and Babur himself was a direct descendant of Timur. Within four years he was master of nearly all of northern India. After the reign of his son Humayun, during which the empire suffered more losses than gains, Akbar succeeded to the throne in 1556. Organizer of the Mughal Empire and its ruler for fifty years, this contemporary of Queen Elizabeth has been called the greatest man who ever governed India. However many are his other claims to fame, he is part of the story of Christian missions because, midway in his long career, he summoned to his court a group of Jesuit Fathers.

That the undisputed master of a Moslem state should take the initiative in calling Christian teachers is an event so nearly unique as to call for explanation. The reasons may be found partly in the political situation of the time, but chiefly in the personal character and purposes of Akbar.[1]

By the year 1510 Portugal had established her empire in the East with its center at the port of Goa, a small island off the southwest coast of India. Her power was based on the control of the seas, and its primary purpose was the extension of commerce. In contrast, however, with the Dutch and the English in later eras, Portugal was ready to use both force and persuasion for the conversion of the Indians. This period of Portuguese hegemony corresponded roughly with the first century of Mughal rule, a fact which made it inevitable that political motives on both sides should be mingled with those of religion.

Yet Akbar might well have sought for the Jesuits, regardless of the advantages of friendly relations with Goa. For one of the characteristics of his amazingly versatile personality was a deep interest in religion. The rulers of his line had never been noted for orthodoxy nor bound by the authority of tradition; and Akbar especially was only loosely attached to Islam. In matters of religion he was a liberal eclectic, sensitive and eagerly curious; and in the field of statecraft his chief object was to promote the unity of a people divided into the two hostile camps of Hinduism and Islam. As an individual he was sincerely seeking for enlightenment and as an emperor he cherished the vain hope of artificially uniting his people in allegiance to some one common faith. On both counts, then, it is not surprising that he should have turned to Christianity as a possible solution of his problems. Before taking this step, however, he had made various moves which revealed

[1] In reviewing the story of this Jesuit Mission, I have depended on four recent books of high quality: (1) Maclagan, *The Jesuits and the Great Mogul,* an exhaustive treatment based on every variety of source; (2) *The Cambridge History of India,* Vol. IV; (3) du Jarric, *Akbar and the Jesuits,* trans. by C. H. Payne; (4) Guerreiro, *Jahangir and the Jesuits,* trans. by C. H. Payne. The book on Akbar consists of selections and translations from du Jarric's *Histoire,* which is based entirely on letters and reports written by the Fathers while on service with the missions. Published in six parts, between 1599 and 1610, it is a strictly contemporary document. The book on Jahangir is of similar character, formed of selections from the *Relations of Guerreiro* (1609), which are likewise derived from contemporary letters of Jerome Xavier and other missionaries.

his ambitious disregard of tradition and alarmed his Moslem followers. Having already tasted of Hinduism and Jainism, he had now not only become a serious student of Zoroastrianism and added the worship of the sun to his religious repertoire, but had begun to exert spiritual as well as temporal authority over his subjects.

Akbar had already met with several Jesuits [2] engaged upon a mission in Bengal and, following their advice, he dispatched in 1579 an embassy to Goa with letters to the Viceroy, the Archbishop, and the Jesuit Fathers, asking for Christian priests. Responding to his appeal, the authorities sent three Fathers, who reached his capital (then at Fathpur-Sikri, near Agra) in February, 1580. The missionaries chosen were Rodolfo Acquaviva, a well-born Italian of exceptional sanctity; Antonio Monserrate, a studious and scholarly Spaniard; and Francisco Enriqués, a Persian convert from Islam, who was to act as interpreter. Although their ultimate aim was of course to win the whole people of Mogor,[3] they saw in Akbar not only the greatest figure in the country, but also the most promising subject for their endeavors, and accordingly they centered their efforts upon him.

On their appearance at court, they were received by the emperor with great cordiality. Money was supplied for their support, and quarters in the palace were placed at their disposal. A minister of the king was appointed to instruct them in the Persian language, and Monserrate was assigned as tutor to the little prince Murad, with the duty of teaching him Portuguese. Moreover, Akbar not only allowed the Jesuits to establish a hospital, but even gave them freedom to preach and to make conversions. The members of this first mission, however, were not concerned to appeal to the masses in public. More acceptable both to them and to Akbar were the religious debates at court which began soon after their arrival. Akbar would summon the Fathers and certain learned Moslems to meet before him for open discussion

[2] Founded in 1539, the Society of Jesus had entered India, with the mission of Francis Xavier, in 1542.

[3] At this period the seaboard tract under Portuguese control was known as "India," and the Mughal Empire (chiefly in northern India) was referred to as "Mogor."

of their religious beliefs. The Christians were well equipped for such encounters; [4] the Mohammedan doctors (like all their kin from that day to this) delighted in disputation; and the emperor, alert of mind and ready of speech, took the keenest pleasure not only in listening to the arguments but in talking as freely as he might desire. Since all the participants thus enjoyed their opportunities, these frequent meetings seem to have afforded every gratification except the satisfaction of accomplishing anything really worth while.

The debates dealt with the same topics which had been familiar in the Middle Ages and which were to provide the stock in trade of the evangelist almost until our own time. Among them were the authority of the Scriptures and the rebuttal of the Moslem claim that Jews and Christians had tampered with the text of the Bible. Other favorite subjects were the personal life of Mohammed, the nature of heaven as depicted in the Koran, and always, over and over again, those controversial themes, the Incarnation and the Trinity. In all these contests the missionaries were encouraged by the fact that Akbar generally sided with the Christians and viewed every sign of Moslem discomfiture with the keenest relish. But they were not really making the progress which they imagined, for the king was usually more entertained than impressed, and his learned subjects, so far from being touched at heart, were continuously exasperated.

After two years of activity at the Mughal court the Jesuits realized that their cause had advanced but little. Akbar remained interested and well disposed. He took one or more of the Fathers with him on his journeys or campaigns, he expressed deep respect for the books and the pictures which they gave him, and his distaste for Islam was obviously increasing. But plainly he had no intention of committing himself to Christianity. Though willing to acknowledge that it was the best religion with which he was acquainted, he protested that the dogmas of the Incarnation and the Trinity were insuperable difficulties. And the missionaries

[4] Besides their thorough knowledge of Christian theology, the Fathers were also acquainted with the Koran through the Latin translation of Robert of Retines, which had been printed at Basle in 1543. See Maclagan, *op. cit.*, p. 201, n. 41.

were inclined to add (what he could hardly have denied) that the requirement of monogamy was a stumblingblock quite as fatal. A third obstacle was no less deterrent. If he became a Christian, Akbar would have to submit to the authority of a mighty Church over which he had no control. More congenial to his imperial ambition was the idea of a new religion of which he should be the head. Such a project had long been evolving in his mind; and, in 1582, just at the time when the Jesuits were hoping that he might become their first convert, he set forth publicly his own synthetic religion, the Din-i-Ilahi or Divine Faith. Summoning a council of his high officials, he secured their consent that he should prescribe the beliefs and rites of this eclectic cult. It was a sort of monotheism with a strong dash of pantheism. Its rites included elements from all the religions he had studied except Islam, and the emperor himself was to be half-deified as the vicegerent of God. As might have been expected, the new religion pleased nobody but its inventor; hardly more than a dozen courtiers were browbeaten into allegiance; and its artificial hothouse existence lasted no longer than Akbar's reign.

Recognizing their failure with the king, the Jesuits could find no compensation in the few catechumens whom they had gathered among the lower classes so largely neglected by the mission. And the Moslem nobles and scholars, of course, were even more hostile than before. Quite naturally, then, at the suggestion of the missionaries, the Father Provincial summoned them to return to Goa. By February, 1583, the mission had ended its career, and we hear nothing further of Akbar's relations with Christianity for the next seven years. Though a second mission was summoned to his court in 1590, for reasons that are no longer clear its members returned to Goa within less than a year.

Yet before the end of another three years Akbar was engaged in negotiating for a third mission; and in May, 1595, a new group of Fathers arrived at Lahore, headed by Jerome Xavier (a grandnephew of the great Francis), who was to remain at the Mughal court for nearly twenty years. The others were Emmanuel Pinheiro and Benedict de Goes, natives of the Azores. For the next three years the story of the mission closely resembles that of the earlier enterprises. Its members were cordially received at the capital, with much pomp and ceremony. They were supplied with a residence and were allowed to open a school attended by the sons of nobles. Akbar often came to their chapel and displayed reverence for their pictures and images; and plans were soon made for the construction of a church. Quite as friendly, too, was the support afforded by the heir apparent, Prince Salim, who became a firm protector of the Jesuits. Disputes at court were held now and then, and it became more evident than ever how completely Akbar had broken with Islam. Encouraged by the king's contempt for the faith of his ancestors and by his oral permission to preach and to baptize, the Fathers grew bolder than before in their attacks on Islam. Yet by the end of 1597 there was little to show for the years of work save a few converts of humble station; and the emperor, as one of the missionaries wrote, persisted in his obstinate procrastination. He was too well satisfied with the religion of his own composition to commit himself to any other.

During the greater part of the ensuing three years, Akbar was engaged in a long campaign in the Deccan, on which he was accompanied by Xavier and Goes. In these circumstances of constant change and frequent warfare, there was not much they could accomplish of missionary value. But Father Pinheiro, left alone at Lahore until Father Corsi joined him in 1600, continued the work of evangelism under the protection of the viceroy. Though the prolonged absence of a friendly sovereign was a handicap, from the missionary point of view it was an advantage in disguise. It kept the Jesuits from a too-exclusive concern with the king and drew out their energies toward the people. Thenceforward, as a result, they were both more active and more successful in promoting a wider appeal. After returning from the Deccan, Akbar spent most of the last four years of his reign at Agra, where Xavier remained in faithful attendance. One of the latter's few achievements worthy of record was his success in obtaining from the king a written order permitting his subjects to embrace Christianity. This formal statement was hardly needed at Agra, but at Lahore it gave helpful support to Pinheiro and

Corsi, who had to depend for protection on the variable temper of a viceroy and who were more than once in real peril of persecution. It was during this final period, too, that there appeared in Agra the Englishman John Mildenhall, who bore a letter from Queen Elizabeth asking for free access for English ships to Mughal ports. In his capacity as Portuguese agent rather than as Christian missionary, Xavier asserted himself to thwart this alien heretic, employing every fair means and, according to Mildenhall, a good many that were not. The newcomer, in consequence, was never granted a favorable decree while Akbar lived. It was the first of several such episodes in the life of the Jesuit Mission.

By this time the long reign of Akbar was nearing its close. In October, 1605, he died. Whether in his last hours he counted himself a Mohammedan or a Hindu or was content perhaps to be the one remaining convert to his own "Divine Faith," no one knows. But all agreed, Moslems and Fathers alike, that he did not die a Christian.

His successor, Prince Salim, who took the name of Jahangir (1605-27), had long treated the Jesuits with unbroken cordiality. His interest in helping them to build a church at Agra and his reverent attitude toward Christian books, pictures, and images had encouraged the Fathers to believe that he might one day be their first royal convert. But, as a matter of fact, Jahangir was a candidate far less promising than his stronger father. He had no such deep and genuine feeling for religion as had Akbar; his admiration for the various forms of Christian art which adorned his palace was mainly esthetic; and though he had no respect for Islam, he was too light-minded to be a real seeker after new truth. Indeed, his main motive in favoring the members of the mission was to keep on friendly terms with the Portuguese authorities.

On the surface, however, prospects were as promising as in the days of the first mission. The king gave generous allowances for the support of the Fathers, kept them near his person when he traveled, and at Agra permitted them to preach in the mosques on Fridays. In course of time, moreover, at their urgent request, he gave them an opportunity to renew their practice of public disputes with Moslem doctors. For over a month in the year 1608, at Agra, these doctrinal debates went on—the Jesuits deeply in earnest and confident of a logical victory, the emperor gaily witnessing a favorite form of sport and prodding the champions of Islam to increase the excitement, and the mullahs themselves seething with ill-suppressed fury at the abuse of their religion and at the taunts of so partial an umpire. When all was over, Christianity was more hated than ever by the Mohammedans and no more loved than before by their king.

But though Jahangir had no intention of submitting to an exacting Church, in 1610 he encouraged two of his nephews to be baptized by Xavier at a great public festival. That the move was chiefly political in its purpose seems clear from the fact that the emperor insisted that the viceroy at Goa and the King of Spain should be informed of the event. Moreover, in less than five years the converts had forsaken the Church or, as a Jesuit reported, "they rejected the light and returned to their vomit." At the time, however, these conversions and several others hardly less significant raised the hopes of the missionaries, who felt that "at no period had the mission seemed so near to realizing its object."

Beginning in 1613, a brief war between the Portuguese and the Mughal power threw a cloud over the mission for a time. All the Christian churches were closed and the Fathers were reduced to poverty. But during the last decades of Jahangir's reign, the missionaries enjoyed the royal favor and the financial assistance to which they had long been accustomed. Yet they advanced no further than before in the hopeless quest of winning the king, whose character was decaying year by year, under the influence of strong drink and opium. When he died in 1627, they may have realized that at no point had he even been seriously near to conversion.

For the story of the Jesuit Mission under Jahangir's successors during the next century and a half the sources are relatively meager. There is much of adventure to record; but since there were no new developments of interest for the student of missionary methods, the briefest of outlines will suffice.

Under Shah Jahan (1627-58) and Aurangzeb (1658-1707) the

Fathers had to deal with sovereigns who were orthodox Moslems and to experience growing hostility and frequent periods of persecution. Yet, with all the mounting difficulties and increased restrictions, their work continued, in one form or another, for a surprising length of time. The period of strife, however, in the first half of the eighteenth century, which ended with the break-up of the Mughal Empire, reduced the Jesuits to a handful who remained at their stations neglected and half-forgotten. In 1759 the King of Portugal banished all Jesuits from his dominions; in 1773 the Pope suppressed the Society of Jesus; and by the end of the century there was neither a Jesuit Order nor a Mughal Empire.

A study of the Jesuit Mission at the Mughal court is of value chiefly for the light it throws upon a certain type of missionary method and upon the results achieved. In reviewing the record it is important, first of all, to bear in mind that the congregations to which the Jesuits ministered included a large number of European Christians and that most of their converts were from Hinduism. Thus, as has so often happened elsewhere and at other times, the distinctly Moslem work was only a fraction of the whole. Except for the court debates, however, the methods employed in approaching Hindus and Moslems were much the same. Though the Jesuits preached now and then in the mosques on Fridays, they seldom resorted to street preaching. Open evangelism was rare. They depended chiefly on the power of forms and ceremonies, on the vivid appeal to the eye and to the imagination of impressive ritual and elaborate festivals. These festivals were made as public as possible with street processions, displaying crucifixes and rich vestments and accompanied by music. Even the regular services were open to all, and Moslems often attended them. In short, by letting the people see the visible side of the Catholic Church, they brought not a few to desire what she had to give.

Those who sought baptism were usually subject to a long period of probation as catechumens, during which they were instructed in the faith. Partly because of the linguisitc deficiencies of the Fathers, however, the teaching of the catechism was long conducted in the Portuguese tongue, and not until 1611 in the vernacular. The Jesuits for some time were chiefly concerned to acquire Persian, the language of the court, and only later set themselves to learn Hindustani. There is no evidence that any of them ever mastered Arabic.

Estimating the number of baptized Moslem converts is for several reasons a process of peculiar difficulty. In counting their new members, the Fathers seldom distinguished between Hindus and Mohammedans. Moreover, many dying infants of non-Christian parents were baptized, and often children were purchased from the very poor that they might be redeemed by baptism. To narrow down the list, therefore, to converts who were both conscious and Moslem is not easy. It is clear, however, that they were few. As one Father wrote, in Akbar's time, "In the conversion of souls there was not much progress in this land of the Saracens, who were as hard as diamonds to work upon." It is equally plain, too, that conversions from the higher classes were extremely rare. The great majority of the baptized were from a low grade of society, including many servants of Armenians and Europeans. As a result, most of the new members of the Church lived in abject poverty and had to be maintained partly by the funds of the Society and partly by grants from the king. Such financial aid, accompanying conversion, might easily be interpreted as a bribe and tends further to weaken the effect of statistics. Yet when all due allowances are made and the need for much winnowing of figures is conceded, it still remains true that year by year an appreciable number of Mohammedans were won to the acceptance of Christianity. There are a few definite instances of high-class converts, whose names were sure to be recorded, and a much larger number of more humble station. In 1604, for example, it was reported that there were forty converts from Islam in the church at Agra. But such specific reports are so rare that we dare not attempt more than the rough estimate that in the course of one or two decades genuine adult Mohammedan converts were probably to be counted by dozens, perhaps by scores.

PART TWO
The Modern Age

VIII

Turkey

IN A PREVIOUS chapter we have outlined the relations between Christianity and Islam in the Ottoman Empire as far as the opening of the nineteenth century. The situation as it then existed remained unchanged for another twenty or thirty years, until the beginning of Protestant missions in the Near East. Since that time, however, especially during the last seventy years, the story of the missionary enterprise has been so full of incident and variety that we cannot attempt a complete record of all its aspects in all the lands which owed allegiance to the Sultan. Our purpose to understand the Christian approach to the Moslem will best be served by confining our survey to the areas of most importance and to the problems and achievements that have proved of most significance. Bearing in mind the need for this limitation, we shall deal only with Turkey, Syria, and Egypt; and we shall center our attention on the features which in these three countries have been equally characteristic—the relations of missions with the Oriental Churches, the relations of missions with the state, and the contribution of missions to the spread of Western education. These three factors have been everywhere so closely interwoven in the process of history that they cannot be clearly separated in any historical record.

As early as the year 1818, the American Board[1] determined to send a mission to the Near East and appointed as its first members the Rev. Pliny Fisk and the Rev. Levi Parsons. Though they were to begin with a period of preparation at Smyrna, where they arrived early in 1820, their first permanent station was supposed to be Jerusalem. How broad was the vision of the Board at this

[1] The American Board of Commissioners for Foreign Missions, a body representing the Congregational Churches.

time and how much detail was left for future decision are plain
from the instructions given to these two leaders:

You will survey with earnest attention the various tribes and classes
who dwell in that land and in the surrounding countries. The two
grand inquiries ever present in your minds will be, "What good can
be done?" and "By what means?" What can be done for Jews? What
for pagans? What for Mohammedans? What for Christians? What for
the people in Palestine? What for those in Egypt, in Syria, in Armenia,
in other countries to which your inquiries may be extended? [2]

In view of the fact that Jews are mentioned first in these instructions, that Jerusalem was expected to be the first station, and that
Parsons delivered in Boston a farewell sermon on "The Derelic-
tion and Restoration of the Jews," it is probable that in this early
stage of development there was a primary interest in the conversion of Hebrews. But this particular bias did not survive many
years of work in the field, and it is evident that from the very
start the Mission was expected to embrace other opportunities
wherever they arose. It is clear, however, that as yet it was not
mainly, still less exclusively, an attempt to approach the Moslem.

During the next twelve years the missionaries were chiefly
active in learning the necessary languages and in carrying out
long tours of investigation in western Turkey, Syria, Palestine,
and Egypt. After the early death of Parsons and Fisk, the task
of exploration was carried on by Eli Smith and H. G. O. Dwight,
who ended in July, 1831, an extensive and arduous journey which
carried them across Asia Minor, Armenia, and Kurdistan to
Georgia and Persia. In consequence of their reports, there was
founded within a few years the mission of the American Board
among the Nestorians in Persia, to which we shall later refer.
Meanwhile a press had been established in Malta,[3] and work had
already been in progress for some years in Palestine and Syria.
But after the first occupation of Smyrna in 1820, it was not until
1831 that another permanent station was established in Turkey
proper. In June of that year the Rev. William Goodell arrived

---

[2] R. Anderson, *History of the Missions of the A.B.C.F.M.* . . . , I, 10.
[3] The press was moved from Malta in 1833. The Arabic equipment went to
Beirut, as the basis for the great press still flourishing there. The Armenian and
Turkish equipment went to Smyrna and later to Constantinople.

in Constantinople, where he was joined twelve months later by Dwight. With these two men began the widespread mission among the Armenians which was to be the chief activity of the American Board in Turkey until the first World War. In Constantinople alone there were then as many as 100,000 Armenians, among whom a group had already given evidence of a desire for reform in the ancient Church. To this hopeful project of reform the American Mission dedicated itself, adopting at the outset a policy which has been thus stated by one who took part in framing it:

The object of the missionaries was not to break down the Armenian Church, but, if possible, by reviving the knowledge and spirit of the Gospel, to reform it. They were content that the ecclesiastical organization remain, provided the spirit of the Gospel could be revived under it.... They felt, therefore, that as foreigners their main business was to set forth the fundamental doctrines and duties of the Gospel, derived directly from the Holy Scriptures.[4]

Though circumstances later demanded a change of policy, it remained true for the next eighty or ninety years that

the Armenians most completely commanded both the interest of the missionaries and the attention of the constituency at home. Most of the stations in the country were established especially for this race. They were found at every center.[5]

Chiefly in response, then, to the opportunities for evangelism among these people, the activities of the Mission were extended within the next few years to Nicomedia, Brusa, and Adabazar (all within a hundred miles or so of Constantinople), and to Trebizond, on the Black Sea. In 1840 a station was established as far east as Erzerum, near the borders of Transcaucasia.

From the beginning the methods employed were the development of Christian literature and the promotion of modern education. For the revival of the Armenian Church both were indispensable and, so far as Moslems could be touched at all, both were best calculated to avoid antagonism and to arouse response. By the time of his arrival in Constantinople, Dr. Goodell had completed a version of the New Testament in Armeno-

---

[4] R. Anderson, *op. cit.*, I, 96 ff.   [5] Barton, *Daybreak in Turkey*, p. 144.

Turkish and nine years later finished a translation of the Old Testament. The modern Armenian version of the Bible was produced after another decade by Elias Riggs, the great linguist of the Mission, who spent fifty years in literary work in Constantinople. In the publication and extensive distribution of these fruits of so many years of labor, the British and American Bible societies gave generous aid. And with the new versions of the Scriptures went an increasing production of many other types of Christian literature in the same tongues, such as commentaries and manuals of devotion. Before long, too, with the rise of schools, appeared a variety of textbooks, and with the slow growth of a reading public periodicals later began to be issued.

In this early period of the Mission it was the policy of Goodell and his associates to encourage the Greeks and Armenians to found schools of their own, to be aided, but not organized or controlled, by the Mission. After a number of schools of this character had been in operation for several years, the Mission itself responded to a growing need by establishing a boarding school for boys at Bebek, six miles from the capital. Under its energetic leader, Cyrus Hamlin, this little institution was destined, after several changes and many vicissitudes, to win fame throughout the Near East as Robert College.

Thanks to the fact that influential groups in the Armenian Church were already ripe for reform, the response to missionary effort in the first ten years of labor was surprisingly active. The rapid dissemination of the newly translated Scriptures and other Christian literature, the radiating influence of the schools, despite their small numbers, and the persistent personal work of the few missionaries combined to produce results beyond expectation. Much of the interest aroused was due at first merely to intellectual curiosity. But it was not long before there was ample evidence of a deeper movement genuinely religious, which expressed itself in groups for Bible study and meetings for prayer. Converts to evangelical Christianity began to be numbered by the score; and, since some of them were priests, the effect was all the more marked. The growth of evangelical preaching and the change of moral attitude on the part of these clerical leaders not only affected their own people, but through the coming and going of travelers touched others at a distance from the capital. In the year 1839 there was founded a small secret organization known as the Armenian Evangelical Union, which aimed to plan and pray for the reform of the Church. And by the opening of the next decade it had become alarmingly clear to the ecclesiastical authorities that a movement of revival was gathering momentum, awakening the minds and stirring the consciences of an increasing number. Yet up to this point nearly all of these "converts" were still loyal members of the ancient Armenian Church.

They were not long to remain unmolested, however, for a crisis soon arose which was destined to change the whole situation. A brief persecution had threatened reformers and missionaries in 1839; but for five years thereafter they had enjoyed a period of calm, which ended with the rise to power of a new Armenian Patriarch of Constantinople. Urged on by all the forces hostile to the new evangelical teachings, the Patriarch Matteos determined to exert his full powers to stamp out the dangerous Protestant revival. To the natural incentives which always impel religious conservatives to oppose religious radicals, there was added as a further motive the strong desire to maintain the unity of the Church, upon which the millions of scattered Armenians depended for their social and political as well as their religious security. Matteos began by secretly directing all patrons and customers of the evangelicals to withdraw their patronage, so that many were soon deprived of their livelihood. Not content with these economic reprisals, which proved to be inadequate, the Patriarch proceeded, in January, 1846, to wield the weapon of excommunication. His first victim was a well-known priest whom he publicly anathematized, commanding all members of the Church to avoid him as an outcast. Other leaders were soon singled out for like treatment; and forms of recantation were sent throughout the province, with orders to all priests to summon the evangelicals and to demand that they abjure their new beliefs and confess to have been enticed by the devil. The penalties for refusal included not only excommunication in its religious sense but social ostracism and economic boycott. Since the power of the Patriarch, under the millet system, was civil as well as ecclesiastical, his enemies were all the more at his mercy. In consequence of the vigor of these measures, over a hundred Armenians in Constantinople alone were ejected from their homes or debarred from their means of living, and another thirty or more were exiled, imprisoned, or bastinadoed. At a distance from the capital there was still more violence. At Adabazar and as far as Trebizond and Erzerum the defenseless evangelicals were subjected to every sort of cruel outrage—beaten and stoned by mobs, thrown into jails, and even held for torture. Many, of course, recanted and returned to the fold; but a surprisingly large number were faithful to their convictions and thereby found themselves drawn closer to their fellow sufferers. That they could hope for no truce in the campaign of persecution was made plain by the Patriarch when he issued in June, 1847, another general anathema, permanently excommunicating all who still remained firm in their evangelical principles.

Cast out from the Church of their fathers by the repeated acts of its ruler, the homeless evangelicals had no real alternative to forming a Church of their own. Convinced of this necessity, forty of the evangelical Armenians of Constantinople met with the missionaries on July 1, adopted a confession of faith, together with a covenant and rules of discipline, and organized the First Evangelical Armenian Church. Within a week they had chosen an Armenian pastor, who was ordained by the missionaries. During the same month similar churches were formed at Nicomedia, at Adabazar, and later at Trebizond, Erzerum, and Aintab.

For their adequate protection, however, the little minority needed more than a new Church. Their economic distress was in some measure relieved by charitable aid from Europe and America. But charity could not solve their fundamental problem. For according to the Turkish system of government by millets, the Armenians constituted not only a Church but a civic corporation, of which the Patriarch was chief. Only as members of this group could their civil rights be maintained in all matters concerned with marriage, inheritance, taxation, and even many business activities. Though the Sultan's government was willing to protect them, its own machinery denied them any civil status. They had formed a new religious group, but that group had still to be recognized as a political community. To meet this urgent need the British Ambassador, Sir Stratford Canning, exerted strong pressure upon the Turkish Minister of Foreign Affairs, who issued in November, 1847, a *firman* recognizing the Protestant community as on a level with the others in the empire and declaring that "no interference whatever shall be permitted in their temporal and spiritual concerns on the part of the patriarch, monks, or priests of other sects." Since this decree was only of limited authority, it was superseded in 1850 by an Imperial Firman signed by the Sultan Abdul Medjid, which ordained that the Protestants, then numbering about 1,000, should thereafter constitute a new ecclesiastical and civic corporation.[6]

The American Board and the new evangelical churches were now free to expand. So long as they confined themselves to activity among Oriental Christians, there remained no legal obstacle to their advance; and thenceforward for the next forty-five years there was steady progress in evangelistic, educational, and medical work.

During the decade after the opening of Aintab in 1849, regular stations were established in other centers of Armenian population—at Marash, Adana, Tarsus, Marsovan, and Sivas, and further east at Kharput, Bitlis, and Mardin. In 1872 the Mission occupied Van, some eighty miles from the Persian border. And beyond these centers of missionary residence, there was a growing number of lesser towns where new churches were founded. Since they were organized after the Congregational pattern, on the principle of democratic local self-government, with native pastors elected by the members, it was all the easier for their numbers to multiply. Except on rare occasions for brief periods the missionaries never served as pastors; but their influence and authority were constantly exercised to develop the ambition and the capacity for native self-support. This ideal was so novel that the struggle to realize it was long and difficult, yet in the end it was

---

[6] This new body of "Protestants" was to include former members of Greek, Syrian, and other communities, as well as former Armenians.

accepted and carried into practice in ever-increasing measure. To strengthen the bonds between these scattered churches and to promote the more effective spread of evangelical Christianity, the local congregations were later grouped into regional unions. By the year 1895 there were 14 main stations of the American Mission and 268 outstations. Including wives, the total of American missionaries was 152, and including teachers the Armenian staff counted 800 men and women. The churches had grown in number to 111, with nearly 12,000 full members and about 20,000 adherents. Protestant influence was still increasing, and the prospects of the Mission were bright.

The first great break in this steady advance came with the Armenian massacres of 1895. Into the details of these months of unspeakable savagery we need not enter here. It will be enough to note that, with full support from the authorities, Turks and Kurds, wherever Armenians were to be found, threw themselves upon these defenseless Christians and slaughtered men, women, and children by the thousand. When the hideous storm had died down, it was calculated that more than 88,000 Armenians had been killed, 500,000 robbed of all their possessions, and over 500 churches pillaged and destroyed. No distinction at that time was made between orthodox and evangelical Armenians, so that 25 Protestant ministers and some 10,000 other Protestants were murdered. In the midst of the fearful distress that ensued, the missionary staff and their Armenian helpers were confronted at once with the task of relief; and for three years much of their time was devoted to caring for the destitute, especially the widows and orphans. More than $1,500,000, raised chiefly in the United States, was expended in this enterprise, most of which was administered through the organization of the American Board.

In spite of the appalling loss of life and the devastation of property, the Armenian community recovered gradually, in the course of a few years, from what had looked like a fatal blow. On a smaller scale, during the same period, the restoration of the Protestant groups went forward. Thanks to the loyalty of the evangelical Christians, fortified by American energy, in the face of persistent opposition from the government, by the end of the century most of the traces of massacre and pillage had been wiped out, and the work was once more well under way. In the year 1908 the Protestant community was far stronger in every respect than it had been in 1895. There were only a few more stations and churches than before, but the communicants had increased by more than 30 percent and the number of adherents had nearly doubled.

For at least a generation after the separation of the evangelicals from the mother Church, more or less hostility between the two groups continued to be manifest. Little by little, however, the bitterness of controversy died down. As one evidence of the change, the Armenian hierarchy eventually came to agree that the new Bible in modern Armenian was truly the Word of God, and the authorities were even willing that it should be placed in the hands of their people. Partly because of the noble record of the Mission in the dark days of the massacre, by the beginning of the century ill-feeling had so nearly passed away that Protestant pastors were being asked to preach in the old churches; children of both groups were mingling in the schools; and even priests were occasionally sent for preparation to the Protestant seminaries. Moreover, the older Church itself had begun to feel the effects of the evangelical revival and of the intellectual advance to which it led. A new concern for the study of the Bible had become apparent, as well as a heightened interest in developing schools of the Protestant type.

By this time the educational system of the American Board and its evangelical churches had attained a wide range in extent and influence. After the schism of 1846 there was apparent at once the need for training able pastors for the many new churches and for opening primary schools wherever groups of Protestants were to be found. Four theological seminaries were established, at Marsovan, Kharput, Marash, and Mardin. It was thus made clear from the outset that an educated ministry was to be one of the main contributions of the Protestant body. Hardly less vital was the importance of a literate and enlightened church membership. Since education was not provided by the government but left to each religious community, the infant churches had a

free field. And with the enthusiasm for popular education characteristic of Americans, the missionaries were urgent in developing both the demand and the supply. Beginning with elementary
schools for boys, and sometimes for girls, in the chief mission
stations, the provision of these primary schools expanded steadily
wherever there were congregations, so that in 1908 there were
more than 300. Much smaller in number, but of growing value,
were the boarding schools and high schools for both boys and
girls, located at the main centers and under the direct control
of the Mission. Several of these had gradually risen to a higher
level and were properly termed colleges. Central Turkey College
at Aintab, Anatolia College at Marsovan, Euphrates College at
Kharput, International College at Smyrna, and Robert College
at Constantinople provided nearly all that Turkey then knew of
higher education, and their graduates were eventually numbered
by the thousand.

Among all these Robert College has proved the outstanding
institution in Turkey. In 1840, as we have noted, Dr. Cyrus
Hamlin founded at Bebek, near the capital, a boarding school
for boys, which six years later became the first Protestant theological seminary. At the close of another decade the American
Board unwisely decided to abandon the use of English in its
educational work and to limit all the schools to instruction in the
vernacular. Many schools were closed, and the Bebek seminary
was moved to Marsovan. In spite of much disagreement among
the missionaries and no little friction, the new system was rigidly
enforced. As a foremost dissenter, opposed to so narrow a policy,
Hamlin resigned from the Mission—a fortunate move as events
were to prove. For his eager ambition to establish a college at
Constantinople soon aroused the interest of Christopher Robert,
of New York, who agreed to finance the institution which Hamlin had planned. The college was incorporated in New York state
with an independent Board of Trustees; after many struggles with
the Turkish government, its first building was completed at
Bebek, on a beautiful site above the Bosphorus; and in 1863 its
doors were opened to students. During the ensuing ten years of
Dr. Hamlin's presidency, his farsighted policy was justified not

only by the prosperity of Robert College but by the subsequent adoption of the same policy in the educational system of the American Board. For the next thirty years, under the administration of Dr. George Washburn, the college enjoyed a remarkable expansion in numbers and influence. Very few Turks were among the pupils, for the Sultan had forbidden Turkish boys to enter any but government schools. It was Armenians, Greeks, and Bulgarians that supplied most of the 2,500 men who had attended the college by the year 1903.

Robert College was not missionary in the sense of attempting to draw students from the older churches into the Protestant group. But it was openly Christian in its teaching and atmosphere, and the moral effect upon its heterogeneous members was widely noted. Dr. Washburn had good ground for asserting, toward the close of his career,

We have been so far successful that our students are recognized everywhere as representing a different type of manhood from that commonly seen in the East, and some of our alumni are striking and illustrious examples of this type. . . . Unconsciously and incidentally the College has exerted an influence in this part of the world and in other lands which is worthy of notice.

And he adds a further point of special interest for our subject. "We have certainly had great success in winning the confidence of our Mohammedan neighbors, removing their prejudices, securing their respect and friendship, and giving them new conceptions of Christianity, as well as of America." [7]

During the same generation which had seen the rise of these institutions, the education of girls was provided, through the primary and secondary grades, in schools which soon became almost as popular as those for boys. Even opportunities for college training were eventually demanded by so many girls that the college at Kharput organized a women's department, and collegiate schools for women grew up at Marash and Smyrna. None of these, however, can compare in importance with the institution which began in 1871 as the Home School for Girls at Scutari, opposite Constantinople. Its expansion from 1883 to 1924,

[7] Washburn, *Fifty Years in Constantinople*, pp. 296, 298.

under the leadership of Mary Mills Patrick, made it a counterpart
to Robert College in influence and prestige. Before the war it had
moved to a new site on the European side of the Bosphorus; and
with a new charter, as the Constantinople College for Girls it
enjoyed complete independence and widening opportunities.

Partly to meet the needs of Oriental Christians and partly to
provide the one sure mode of approach to Moslems, the American Mission began very early to develop medical service. The
work of Dr. Henry S. West at Sivas, from 1859 to 1876, marked
the first attempt; and during the succeeding decades hospitals
were established in nearly all the chief stations. At the outbreak
of the war in 1914 there were ten of these in operation, treating
annually over 180,000 patients, drawn from every racial group and
from more than 1,200 towns and villages.

Medical missions in Turkey were less hampered by officialdom and
hindered by opposition than any other form of missionary work.
Physicians were more generally welcomed and their benefits more
widely appreciated than anything else the missionaries could do.[8]

After so many words about Armenians, there may naturally
arise the questions, "What has all this to do with the Christian
approach to the Moslem? What did the American Board contribute toward that difficult enterprise?" The simplest answer is
"Very little." But though the reply is true as far as it goes, it
will require some explanation to make clear why the contribution was little and why that little was highly valuable.

Entering Turkey more than a century ago, the Mission confronted all the obstacles which baffle the evangelist among Moslems everywhere and at all times—that intolerant intensity of
faith which in others we call "bigotry," that pride in belonging
to a brotherhood which scorns all outsiders, that supreme confidence in an infallible Book which cannot easily be shaken,
those misconceptions of Christianity which are firmly imbedded
in the faith of Islam. But added to these difficulties were others
characteristic of nineteenth-century Turkey. In the first place,
the dominant race, constituting a large majority of the population, was Mohammedan, and only the subject races were Chris-

---

[8] Barton, *op. cit.*, p. 210.

tian. Christianity was the religion of the despised under dog. More than that, these Christian subjects were divided into racial communities, each a subordinate political unit, so that religious differences were also national and the barriers between them all the harder to pass. To make matters worse, the Christianity of these groups was so feeble and degenerate as to confirm the worst opinions which the Moslem held of the rival religion. All these deep-seated factors were further aggravated by the complication of international politics—the fear felt by a weak Turkey for her strong Christian neighbors and the suspicion with which the Sultan regarded every extension of European power and influence. And finally, in a country where Christians were hated for so many reasons, with all of which a reactionary government was in sympathy, there was no genuine official restraint upon the Islamic law which prescribes for apostasy the penalty of death. The Sultan Abdul Medjid, it is true, made various promises under foreign pressure. A decree in 1839 pledged protection to the lives and property of all subjects, regardless of religion. A written statement in 1844 gave assurance that the Sultan would "take effectual measures to prevent henceforward the persecution and putting to death of the Christian who is an apostate." And the famous Hatti Humayoun of 1856 affirmed that "no subject shall be hindered in the exercise of the religion that he professes, nor shall he be in any way annoyed on that account. No one shall be compelled to change his religion." But these widely heralded reforms were never seriously carried out, and for the next fifty years it was perfectly evident that the government never really intended to acknowledge the right of a Moslem to become a Christian. The convert could find safety only in flight.

In view of all these thorny obstacles, religious, social, and political, it is not hard to understand why the Mission attempted little direct activity with Moslems and accomplished even less. Any open work of that kind would have ended all work of any kind. To honest and courageous leaders the situation seemed to call for an indirect approach; and in appraising its results it is more profitable as well as more just to dwell upon what was done than to deplore what was not done.

Though the Mission began, as we have seen, with the broadest aims, subject to revision in the light of experience, it was not long before there was general agreement at home and abroad that work with the Oriental Churches was to be the immediate task and the conversion of Moslems the ultimate goal. As early as 1839 this policy was expressed in "Instruction to Missionaries," in a form which was pretty consistently maintained until the war.

The Oriental Churches ... have fallen out of Christendom; and, though nominally Christian, they properly receive attention from us, because our approach to the Mohammedan world must be chiefly through them. The Mohammedan nations cannot be converted to the Christian faith while the Oriental Churches, existing everywhere among them, as the representatives and exemplifications of Christianity, continue in their present state. In a large view of the subject, and considering the ultimate design and final results of the missions to the Oriental Churches, they may be regarded as so many missions to the followers of the False Prophet.[9]

There was a brief period, however, during ten years or more after the appearance of the Hatti Humayoun in 1856, when the American Mission and the English Church Missionary Society attempted to evangelize Moslems, especially in Constantinople. Through private conversations and the use of Christian literature, American missionaries would occasionally find openings of which they were always ready to take cautious advantage. As a result of such rare opportunities, Dr. Hamlin estimates that between 1857 and 1877 as many as fifty baptisms of Turkish men, women, and children may be attributed to the American Mission. These results, however, were the minor by-products of a mission devoted to other aims. But it was with Islam as the main objective that the Church Missionary Society took advantage of what then looked like a new era of freedom. In 1858 the Society sent to Constantinople the Rev. Dr. Koelle, formerly in West Africa, and the Rev. Gottlieb Pfander, who had just been proving himself a mighty controversialist among the Moslems of India.[10] The new missionaries began to preach in public and to talk in private with interested Turks. Conversions and baptisms followed, and

9 *Missionary Herald*, Sept., 1839.
10 See the later account of his work in chap. xiii.

in the summer of 1864 as many as ten adults were confirmed at one time. Partly because of the stir occasioned by this event and partly because of the publication of a Turkish translation of Pfander's vigorous treatise *The Balance of Truth,* the authorities decided to act. On July 17, 1864, twelve Turkish Christians were seized and thrown into prison, the assembly halls of the Mission were closed, and all the books of the Bible Society confiscated. Even the missionaries were ejected from their homes. It was clear beyond doubt that in spite of all promises open propaganda was really forbidden. Pfander had to retire to London, where he died the next year; though Koelle lived on for ten years at the capital, he baptized only three more converts; and in 1877 the C.M.S. abandoned its station. This sharp reaction was confirmed by the continued hostility of the government, which resented the slightest extension of work beyond the Christian groups. Indeed, the Grand Vizier openly declared that, regardless of all *firmans,* conversions from Islam must be made impossible.

Since the conditions affecting the approach to Moslems remained essentially unchanged for the next thirty years, the American Mission in Turkey, as we have noted, concentrated its forces almost wholly upon work with Armenians, both Orthodox and Protestant. The activities to which this policy led affected Mohammedans in two ways—one direct, the other indirect. Through the distribution of the Bible and other Christian literature, Moslems here and there could occasionally be reached and touched. More obvious were the openings afforded by the many schools. Though in most of these there were no Turkish children, there were some which a few were willing to enter. The proportion throughout the country hardly exceeded one in a hundred; but in the high schools and colleges, by the beginning of the century, it was steadily increasing. In the hospitals, on the other hand, the proportion of Moslems was far greater, sometimes running as high as 50 percent. Through these agencies, then, the Mission maintained direct contact with a fraction of the Mohammedan population. And, as a matter of fact, that is all that can be recorded to the credit of not a few missions professedly to Moslems when they are set in any environment equally hostile. Yet the opportunities, rare at the best, could seldom be effectively exploited when the policy of the Mission and the equipment of its members were primarily adjusted to other aims and duties. Few missionaries could speak Turkish well, and still fewer were learned in Islamics.

It is rather through their indirect results that the achievements of the American Mission may be counted as a valuable contribution to the Christian approach to the Moslem. Their successful promotion of Western education in all its grades had a stimulating effect not only upon thousands of students of both sexes and of various races, but also, in course of time, upon the government educational system and upon the cultural life of modern Turkey. The evidences of that influence were so marked as to win sincere tribute from many foreign observers. But to advance the spread of Western thought and its ideals of justice and freedom, while it may aid the progress of civilization, may be only very indirectly a contribution to religion and to the preparation of the Moslem for accepting the Gospel. Far more important from our point of view was the success of the Mission in fulfilling its deeper purpose to show the Turks what true Christianity means. Hitherto they had never had the opportunity to know. But through the years we have been reviewing, the evidence was slowly spread before their eyes. In schools and hospitals all through the land the meaning of service, of charity, and of compassion was acted out for all who could see and hear. And perhaps still more effective was the witness of an ancient Church perceptibly quickened to new life and the spectacle of new churches in which rising standards of Christian living and thinking had created a changed atmosphere. In any Moslem land where Oriental Christianity is stagnant and despised, it is an indispensable first step to make it active and respectable. In the effort to take that difficult step, the American Mission did all that could be done by small numbers in a short time. The missionaries and their fellow workers, through long years of endeavor, remained loyal to the conviction that in hostile surroundings only a genuine Christianity can command respect. And not until it has won general respect can it count upon a growing power to attract and to convert.

Except for the massacres of 1895 and their aftermath, the Mission and its churches maintained their work amid conditions that were altered but little before the year 1908. Under a government antagonistic to their aims, they were constantly subject to interference and annoyance of every sort, which hampered their acquirement of property, their construction of buildings, their travel, and their publication of books. But neither for better nor for worse was there much change until the Revolution.

So much has happened in Turkey since that date that it is difficult now to appreciate the excitement which attended these events a generation ago. Yet there began at that time the transformation which was to be carried after the war to more remarkable extremes. For many years past the absolute government of the Sultan Abdul Hamid had been becoming more and more corrupt and oppressive. The Sultan was not merely conservative. Fearful of the consequences to himself, he had a pathological dread of any sign of reform; and through an elaborate system of espionage he marked out for exile or execution all Turks who were intelligent enough to want better government and influential enough to work for it. But a group of reformers known as the "Young Turks" had been growing in numbers and in activity. Though many had been banished to various parts of the country, they found it all the easier to spread their principles. The increasing restlessness and sense of desperation among the people were at their worst in Macedonia, where anarchy and intolerable oppression prevailed. It was just in this area that the Young Turks, organized there as the "Committee of Union and Progress," were especially strong. When a large and ill-paid army was sent into Macedonia in July, 1908, nearly all its officers were soon won over to the cause of the Committee and took an oath to support its program. The leaders were now ready to strike. They telegraphed the Sultan demanding that he declare a constitutional government at once and threatened, if he refused, to march with their troops upon Constantinople. After a few days of hesitation, Abdul Hamid yielded and on July 24 issued an *irade* restoring the constitution which he had issued in 1876 and suspended the next year. Dismissing the Grand Vizier and appointing a liberal in his place, he solemnly swore upon the Koran to be faithful to the new order. A decree was promptly issued abolishing the secret service. Political prisoners were released and exiles summoned home. The press was free at last and censorship abolished.

Confronted with these sudden and exciting changes, the Turkish people gave themselves over to outbursts of rejoicing. Vast gatherings met in public squares to hear the proclamations of freedom, and salutes were fired in honor of the new era. Everywhere there were spontaneous celebrations. Emotions, indeed, were so strong that Christian and Moslem leaders embraced in public and called themselves brothers.

When the stir had died down, steps were taken to hold a general election, for the constitution called not only for a senate appointed by the Sultan but also for a house of representatives chosen by the people. On December 17, 1908, the parliament was opened by Abdul Hamid, and the Young Turks at last had control of the government. But needless to say, the Sultan had not been really converted, and within four months he achieved a counter-revolution. After recruiting an opposition party, he lavishly bribed the troops in the capital and used them to seize the parliament building and to drive from the city the Young Turk leaders. At the same time he ordered a massacre of Armenians in Cilicia, where in the course of a few days 30,000 were murdered. It was a short-lived triumph, however, for within a brief space of ten days the fallen leaders had reunited in Salonica, rallied an army of veterans and volunteers, and advanced to the gates of the capital. On April 27, 1909, parliament met to hear a proclamation from the supreme legal authority, the Sheikh-ul-Islam, deposing Abdul Hamid on the ground of misgovernment and treason to the Moslem faith. When the decree had been unanimously ratified, the Sultan was transported under guard to Salonica and there imprisoned. His brother, whom he had held as a prisoner for thirty-three years, was proclaimed Sultan as Mohammed V and formed at once a liberal cabinet.

For the first few years after the Revolution, all the changes which it wrought were beneficial to the missionary cause. The stirring movements of the day tended for a time to unite the Christians and the Moslems, who often met on equal terms in the new "Clubs of Unity and Progress." Missionary educators were appealed to for advice, and Christian leaders addressed audiences of varied beliefs, even on religious topics. There was a large increase in the number of Moslems who entered missionary schools, and Moslems proved readier than before to attend Christian meetings. Especially welcome was the experience of enjoying for the first time freedom of the press and freedom of travel, both of which could release activities so long subject to cramping limitation. And beyond these practical gains there was felt the broader advantage of working in a changed atmosphere of general ferment hospitable to novel ideas. Yet it proved that the transformation was less far-reaching than had at first been hoped. The devotion of the masses to Islam had in no way been weakened. Instead, there was a marked revival of Mohammedan religious enthusiasm. In contrast with the revolution after the World War, the conservative Moslem authorities had supported the reforms. The government therefore remained as unready as ever to concede the right of conversion from Islam; the public preaching of Christianity continued to be impossible; and the native Christians were confined as rigidly as before to work among their own people. In spite of these surviving restrictions, however, the foreign missionary could now count on fuller opportunities than he had hitherto known. It was in recognition of this fact that the reports of the Edinburgh Conference of 1910 dwelt upon the need in Turkey for more missionaries trained in Islamics and urgently recommended that through personal evangelism and the use of Christian literature there should be a renewed emphasis upon the direct approach to Moslems.

But the circumstances favorable to peaceful progress were not to last long, for the next ten years were to bring to Turkey nothing but disorder and disaster. During most of that time it was at war with Christian powers. Between September, 1911, and May, 1912, Turkey was engaged in a war with Italy, which ended with the cession of the province of Tripoli. Six months later there broke out the first Balkan War, in which Turkey was overwhelmingly defeated by Montenegro, Serbia, Bulgaria, and Greece. By the following May the Ottoman Empire had been deprived of nearly all its European territory, only a small part of which was restored after the ensuing war among the Balkan countries. Finally, in the hope of victory as an ally of Germany, Turkey entered the World War at the end of October, 1914, and just four years later called for an armistice on terms that amounted to unconditional surrender.

Four years of warfare completely altered the status and the prospects of the American Mission in Turkey. They were years which strangely combined continued success, irreparable disaster, unexpected opportunities, and almost unbearable strain.

Since the missionary work of secondary and higher education was largely under the control of Americans, and since the United States never declared war on Turkey, four of the high schools and several colleges remained in operation throughout the war. In Constantinople, for instance, Robert College and the College for Women, which were independent of the Board, drew a larger number of pupils than before, with an increased proportion of Moslems. The hospitals, of course, were more needed than ever and most of them, under Red Cross direction, continued their activity for both soldiers and civilians.

Yet disastrous loss in nearly every other direction was the inevitable fate of a mission which had found among the Armenian people its chief field of endeavor. To state a really horrible fact in cold terms, their constituency was almost wiped out. Within the first two years of the war about 800,000 Armenians were either massacred or deported; and before the Armistice still more were slain or exiled, or met their deaths through plague or famine. By the year 1922, when all losses could be counted and the new Turkey had begun to emerge, all the missionaries had been withdrawn from the stations in Eastern Turkey. All but a few of the churches and schools had been closed, and 95 percent of the Armenian Protestants had disappeared. Nearly half the foreign missionary force of some 200 men and women had been lost to the work by death, retirement, or disease; and over $2,000,-000 worth of property had been destroyed.

During these years of trial, the missionaries were not only called upon to maintain what little of their former work was still possible and to endure the devastation of so much that they had helped to build. They were summoned also to answer the urgent appeals for relief. With the slender resources that were then available, they were active in this cause from the beginning of the war. By September, 1915, the acute suffering among the Christian population had become so widespread that there was formed in New York an Armenian and Syrian Relief Committee, which undertook at once to raise $100,000 in aid of the stricken and the homeless. These steps marked the modest beginning of what was later to become the Near East Relief, an organization which eventually sent more than 500 workers to the field, spent $108,000,000, and, at a conservative estimate, saved the lives of over 1,000,000. It was not until the Armistice that workers from outside were enlisted in the enterprise, so that for four years the burden of this immense task lay upon the missionary staff already in the field. Though foreigners of several nations, Protestants and Catholics, were active in service, the American leaders were the chief organizers. Hospitals, refugee camps, and centers for the distribution of food and clothing all played a part in the program of relief. But the Commission soon began to specialize in the care of children; and its most notable results were achieved through an expanding system of orphanages. In these institutions 130,000 boys and girls found not only shelter but education and vocational training to fit them for their future as members of new homes or apprentices in industry. In compensation for the crippling or destruction of so large a part of the older work, the Christian forces in Turkey and their supporters at home could find deep satisfaction in this mission to feed the hungry and clothe the naked and heal the sick and visit the prisoners and to receive in Christ's name the children who were lost. There could have been no finer opportunity to show the Near East the meaning of Christianity in action.

While this great undertaking was still at the height of its activity, Turkey was in the midst of a second revolution, which wrought changes far more drastic than the first. The Nationalist Revolution, under the leadership of Mustapha Kemal, aimed first of all at the restoration of an independent Turkey. During 1919 and 1920 Kemal and his followers organized the Nationalist party and established at Angora (now Ankara) a new government with a new constitution. The Grand National Assembly became the *de facto* government of Turkey, with which the Allies had thenceforth to reckon. And the reckoning was not long in coming. The assembly rejected the treaty of Sèvres, which not only dismembered the old empire but even carved out portions of Anatolia. The army, reinvigorated and ably led, defeated the invading Greeks and threatened the allied forces at Constantinople. Mustapha Kemal could now negotiate on equal terms with the war-weary Powers. On all the main points upon which the Angora government insisted, Britain and France had to yield; and the resulting treaty of Lausanne, signed in July, 1923, recognized Turkey as a nation absolutely independent, sovereign over all Anatolia. The Ottoman Empire was dead and gone; and in its place had emerged a new nation, united, compact, and vigorous, determined to assert the rights of Turkey for the Turks. Corrupt and decadent imperialism had been supplanted by efficient and enthusiastic nationalism.

Before the treaty had firmly established Turkey's position among nations, domestic reforms had already begun. Like others which were soon to follow, their aim was to mold and strengthen a secular state of the western type. With the execution of this twofold purpose to secularize and to westernize, no enemies at home or abroad were allowed to interfere. In 1922 the Sultanate was abolished and the former sultan's cousin installed as Caliph only. But sixteen months later, to the astonishment of the Moslem world, came the abolition of the Ottoman Caliphate. So far as the Angora government was concerned, Islam was no longer to retain a shred of temporal power. In October, 1923, there had been proclaimed the Republic of Turkey, with Mustapha Kemal as its first president. By that time the ratification of the treaty of Lausanne had ended the millet system and had also extinguished those extraterritorial rights known as the "Capitulations." Thenceforward the state would share none of its powers either with religious groups inside the country or with foreigners outside.

The next few years were marked by a series of rapid and revolutionary changes. Moslem law was completely excluded from the courts, and the government adopted civil, criminal, and commercial codes of law based on European models. These codes applied to all citizens, irrespective of race or religion; for all without distinction were now regarded as Turks. One result of this new legal system was the abolition of polygamy. Another was a degree of religious freedom which, on paper at least, was all that could be desired. Though Islam was still the state religion, the government was so determined to be rid of every reactionary influence that it dissolved the religious orders and closed the monasteries. Even more drastic was a further reform which did away with all Moslem schools from top to bottom. Education as well as law had to submit to complete secularization. Finally, in the year 1928, the next logical step was taken by striking from the constitution the clause which declared Islam to be the state religion.

The legislation of the last ten or twelve years has brought about changes sufficiently remarkable. It is only in comparison with the earlier reforms that they can be called minor. They include, for example, the compulsory introduction of a modified Latin alphabet, together with an active campaign for mass education, the translation and public recitation of the Koran in Turkish, the law permitting woman suffrage, and the law abolishing titles and requiring the use of surnames by all citizens.

A further factor in the transformation of the old Turkey was the virtual elimination of the familiar racial and religious minorities. By death and exile this process had been partly achieved through the tragic years before 1922. Its completion was authorized by the treaty of Lausanne and carried out under the auspices of the League of Nations. At the cost of great hardship and suffering, more than a million Greeks were removed from Turkey to Greece, and nearly half that number of Turks were transferred from Greece to Turkey. During the same period most of the surviving Armenians outside of Constantinople had to find other homes, partly in Syria and partly in what is now the only Armenia—the Armenian Soviet Socialist Republic, in Transcaucasia. In consequence of these wholesale readjustments, Turkey became homogeneous to a degree never before known.

Twenty years after its first steps toward recovery, Turkey is now a powerful state of the totalitarian type. The present constitution virtually recognizes only one party, and the president, though elected, is practically a dictator. After twenty years of irresistible leadership, Kemal Atatürk died in 1938 and has been succeeded by his right-hand man, Ismet Inönü.

In the Turkey of today we find a population of about 18,000,-000, at least 98 percent of which is Moslem. Though most of the people are engaged in one form or another of agriculture, two Five-Year Plans of the government have been chiefly aimed at industrializing the country so that it may gradually achieve economic independence. The dominating role which the state plays in agriculture and industry is matched by its equally energetic management of education. The few schools not directly controlled by the government are under strict supervision. Though the law requires the compulsory education of all boys and girls, the facilities for their training are not yet available. In fact, the 765,000 children in primary schools in 1938 include less than half the children of school age. The secondary schools, though still few in number, provide for only 74,000 pupils, since as yet there is but little demand for training beyond the elementary grades. But for those who can take advantage of higher education there is the University of Istanbul and, since 1934, a smaller university at Ankara. Outside of this regular educational system, the state has conducted since 1928 a widespread campaign to reduce illiteracy. Through obligatory attendance at night schools, nearly 2,000,000 (half of whom are women) have learned to read.[11]

[11] Between 1928 and 1934 the percentage of literacy rose from 22 to 45.

Far more than any other Moslem country, far more, indeed, than some western countries, Turkey has been opening opportunities to women. Most of the elementary schools include both boys and girls in the proportion of two to one. Education in the secondary grades is provided separately for girls, and higher education in all its branches is open to them on a basis of complete equality with men. So fully have girls taken advantage of these privileges that during the first decade of the republic their numbers in the schools increased nearly fourfold. Even in Istanbul University more than one-sixth of the students are women. Not only do girls fill most of the minor positions in business and government offices as stenographers and clerks, but more and more of them are entering professions. Over half the teachers in Turkey are women, and a small but growing number have become lawyers and doctors. A still more startling break with the past was the granting of woman suffrage in 1934, together with the right to run for office. Within two years there were thirty women representatives in the Grand National Assembly.

The official status of Islam in the Turkey of today is much like that assigned to Christianity in Nazi Germany. The government is neither pro-Islam nor anti-Islam. Recognizing religion as one of the major forces to be dealt with, the state aims to keep it in its place and to use it for what it is worth to further national purposes and policies. Typical of this practical opportunism is the publication by the government, for use in the mosques, of books of very modern sermons. These prescribed addresses are chiefly concerned with inculcating the virtues of good citizenship, the need for scientific progress, and above all the duty of patriotic loyalty. For patriotism, in the form of passionate devotion to the state, has become, as it has elsewhere, almost a new religion.

The part which Islam now plays in the lives of the people has of course been affected by the attitude of the state. Among the masses its hold has been but little shaken, for in all reforms these conservative millions have remained passive. Yet surely we must allow for some effect upon their religion of the extinction of Moslem law and the suppression of all Moslem schools. When we remember, moreover, that there are no longer any seminaries for training the clergy, the decay of Islam among the common people seems almost foreordained. Among the educated classes, at any rate, that decay is already far advanced. Within this large and growing group, the average Turk has come to think of religion as reactionary bigotry, opposed to that amazing national progress in which he glories. When he is not frankly agnostic he is at least indifferent to Islam. He applauds the complete divorce between a backward religion and a secular state. And it is the state which commands his loyalty and absorbs his energy.

The revolutionary changes which crowded the eventful years from 1914 to 1924 completely altered the whole environment in which the American Board Mission had so long been conducting its work. With its Armenian constituency virtually eliminated,[12] with a vigorous nationalism stimulating every move of a dictatorial government, and with education rapidly becoming secularized, the Board was faced with the question whether or not it should end its career in Turkey. How and why the decision to remain was reached has been clearly stated by a leader of the Mission. Writing in the autumn of 1923, Dr. Ernest W. Riggs declared,

For many months the American Board has been earnestly facing the objections to continuing missionary work in Turkey raised by serious Christian leaders.... This thorough examination of the question led the Board at its annual meeting in October 1923 to decide on the continuance of its work in Turkey and for the Turks.... Several strong reasons have led the Board to take this positive action.... In the first place, as the work of one hundred years is reviewed, it has become increasingly evident that we had made no adequate presentation of the Gospel to the Turkish people. We have been satisfied with the marvelous success among Armenians and Greeks. Few of the Turkish youth were gathered into our schools. Still fewer of the Turkish adults had any real opportunity to hear our presentation of the Christian message. The literature which was printed for the Turks was far from adequate, and aside from the Bible and Pilgrim's Progress, most of it is even now out of date. Few of the missionaries have ever been qualified in language or knowledge of Moslem beliefs and practices to present the claims of the Gospel to the Turkish

12 There are still 16 small churches (chiefly in Istanbul), whose 820 communicants are Armenians and Greeks.

people. Our very failure to do this in the past demands from us a new consecration to the task. Moreover, the American Board cannot lightly withdraw from a field which has been assigned to it by the common consent of other missionary societies. . . . Were we to refuse to present this Gospel because of the hardships and difficulties which we face, we would be denying the efficacy of our message.[13]

As the same writer has pointed out in an earlier article,

We cannot but recognize in the sacrifice of the Christian peoples the opening of a new door to the Moslems. . . . Through the complete overturning of the work of the past and the elimination of the native leaders, the foreign workers themselves are brought back to the primitive and personal presentation of the Gospel to the Turks by life and word.[14]

It was a wise and courageous decision, which the future was to justify. The new nationalism having adopted the slogan of "Turkey for the Turks," the new missionary policy was to take the risk for the sake of the opportunity, and to stay in Turkey in the service of the Turks.

There remain to be reviewed, then, the obstacles which have had to be faced and the achievements which have still proved possible.

The key to understanding the difficulties is the fact that the threatening power which watches with jealous alertness for signs of an expanding Christianity is no longer a reactionary Islam but an ardent secular nationalism. That same nationalism, having dealt the heaviest blows to Islam, is naturally not prepared to be much more lenient with Christianity. The state is all the more reluctant to grant full freedom to the missionary forces because of the Moslem principle of associating religion with nationality. The heritage of the past makes it easy to believe that to cease to be a Moslem means to cease to be a Turk, and that foreign influence, even when religious, must be anti-Turkish. The familiar charge against missions is not that they weaken Islam, but that they appear as a discordant note in an otherwise unanimous and well-regimented nationalism. The restrictions laid upon missionary activity are therefore no longer the expression of religious

13 E. W. Riggs, "The American Board and the Turks," *Moslem World*, Jan., 1924.
14 E. W. Riggs, "The Missionary Outlook in Turkey," *Moslem World*, April, 1923.

rivalry or hostility. They are the result of the same growth of state domination from which Christianity suffers in Germany and Italy. Though it may thus appear that the Church has only exchanged one enemy for another, it is generally agreed that the change has been to her advantage.

So far as evangelistic work is concerned, the freedom granted to Christian missionaries is at least legally satisfactory. The treaty of Lausanne guaranteed the free exercise of any religion not incompatible with public order and good morals. All citizens, without distinction of religion, were to be equal before the law and to possess the right to establish schools and charitable institutions. These provisions, moreover, were promptly incorporated in the constitution. Though for several years existing legislation made it difficult to carry out such pledges, the way was soon made easy by the abolition in 1926 of all Moslem law and by the disestablishment of Islam in 1928. The new civil code declared that adults of eighteen years or over should be free to adhere to any religion they chose. This seemed to mean that a grown Moslem was at liberty to become a Christian. And there is some reason to believe that the government is ready to support this radical conclusion. For cases are on record, during the last seven years, of Moslems who have adopted Christianity; and "though some of them have met with petty persecution from minor officials and have been subjected to social ostracism, they have claimed and been accorded the support of the central authorities in the action they have taken." [15] The chief present obstacle to successful evangelism, then, is the force of public opinion, expressed in social pressure and economic persecution. Yet any institution openly responsible for conversions would undoubtedly, in some form or other, feel the weight of official displeasure.

Though all Moslem schools have been closed, Christian schools are still permitted. But the limitations under which they operate are severely definite. Only children who have passed through the primary grades may enter these "foreign" schools, so that elementary education has been eliminated from the missionary pro-

[15] Morrison, "Religious Liberty in Turkey," *International Review of Missions,* Oct., 1935, p. 455.

gram. Moreover, religious instruction in Christian schools must be strictly confined to Christian pupils. In view of the fact that Moslems seldom receive religious training in government schools and that elsewhere only parents can teach religion to Moslems under eighteen, these rules do not discriminate unfairly against Christianity.

The present work of the American Board is conducted on the principle of complete conformity with official regulations and whole-hearted coöperation with the government. Only on such terms could the Mission hope for present success and for widening opportunities in the future. The staff of foreigners now consists of about sixty missionaries at seven main stations, where their activity is chiefly in education and medical service.

The medical work, ministering almost wholly to Turks, includes a hospital at Gaziantep and dispensary clinics at Adana and Talas. The large American Hospital at Istanbul is independent of the Board. The government is greatly interested in the improvement of public health, not only through training a growing number of doctors at the university but also through promoting health campaigns by means of literature, the movies, and the radio. Yet the fact that even now there is only one doctor for every 4,500 people and only one hospital or dispensary for every 45,000 is enough to make the small missionary forces a welcome addition to the slim resources available. Though the law still forbids the enlistment of new medical missionaries, the skillful service of the present staff is fully appreciated by Turkish leaders.

In the field of education, the Mission is obliged to adjust its work to the national program and to submit to the cramping effect of following the government curriculum, which lays great emphasis upon teaching natural science and stimulating the spread of nationalism. Only a willing conformity can prove that there is no intent to teach an alien culture. Within these limits, however, every effort is made to offer a special contribution by demonstrating the value of new experiments in educational method from which the state system may profit. More important is the success of these schools in developing features of their own that are morally distinctive. By maintaining relations between teacher and pupil far closer than are found in government schools, by combining discipline with freedom, by a deep concern for the training of character, and (despite the absence of formal Christian teaching) by the witness of the Christian way of life in the school community, they justify their place in the system of a secular state. And leaders in that state are readier than they once were to note the value of factors which their own scheme ignores.

The Mission is now responsible for the American Academy for Girls at Scutari (Istanbul) and the American Collegiate institute for girls at Izmir (Smyrna). At Tarsus there is the American College for boys; and at Talas the school for boys has met with such marked approval that scores of students have recently been sent there by the government, to be supported at the expense of the state. In all these schools practical vocational training plays a large part. Still flourishing as independent institutions are the two centers of higher education, Robert College and Istanbul Woman's College. The latter now numbers among its graduates many leaders in the growing activities of women, and its present popularity has made necessary a waiting list for entrance. The remaining independent organizations of real importance are the Y.M.C.A. and the Y.W.C.A., initiated and inspired by foreigners but now largely under Turkish leadership. Since 1939 they have been operated as schools, rather than as religious associations. Their program of work includes vocational education and various forms of social service.

The work of schools and dispensaries does not quite include all of the activities in which the American Board is engaged, for there are a number of missionaries whose function is simply to establish friendly contacts with the people. On a very small scale, too, a beginning has been made in several types of community service, such as the provision of playgrounds and reading rooms. More influential at the present moment is the Publication Department of the Mission. Its aim is not only to keep English and American readers in touch with the cultural life of Turkey, but to provide for Turkish readers pamphlets and books of various kinds which will make clear to them the meaning and power of Christianity—books as different, for example, as Wallace's *Ben-Hur* and Axling's *Life of Kagawa*. The department's chief contribution in recent years has been the publication of Dr. Mac-Callum's translation of the whole Bible into modern Turkish. Fortunately there is now wide freedom for the circulation of many types of Christian literature, and the sale of the Scriptures is active and continuous.

In its new form and with its new purposes, the American Mission in Turkey has been at work for only sixteen years. That is too short a time for a small group to affect the religious life of 18,000,000 people. But it is a time long enough to achieve genuine results and long enough to develop a distinctive method and attitude. Aside from the specific results of boys and girls educated and patients healed, the chief consequence of the present policy has been the growth of real friendship between missionaries and the leaders of thought and action among the Turks. Fidelity to the restrictions prescribed by the state has everywhere diminished suspicion, and sincere coöperation in medical and educational service has produced a marked increase in mutual understanding. During these years the representatives of the Mission have come to live, more than ever before, on intimate terms with the Turkish people and to keep in close touch with the currents of their life. With confidence on both sides growing stronger, the way has been prepared for an expanding influence. As a further preparation for the future, we may count the fact that "there is a large number of loyal Turks who realize the desperate prospects of a nation without spiritual elements in its life." The opening that lies ahead is the opportunity to convince them that the values which they recognize in the contributions of Christian missions can be truly and permanently theirs only through the acceptance of Christ and that loyalty to Him is compatible with loyalty to race and nation.[16]

The attitude now characteristic of the American Board in its

[16] See H. H. Riggs, "The Missionary Situation in Turkey," *International Review of Missions*, April, 1938.

approach to the Moslem is declared in one of its own publications, a leaflet entitled "If Your Project Is in the Near East"
(1937).

We are attempting a non-proselytizing, non-dogmatic, disinterested
service.... Our interest is not fundamentally in pulling men out of
one body and transferring them to another. It is nothing less than the
process of leaven or salt within the whole of life.

This policy is partly the result of conditions imposed upon all
Christians in Turkey and partly a reflection of the theological
position and general temper of the American Congregational
churches in the twentieth century. The interpretation of Christianity and of the function of missions for which these churches
stand has made it easier for them than for some others to adapt
themselves to such limitations as Turkey prescribes. For this
reason their Mission has quite naturally made a virtue of necessity. The most useful conclusion to be drawn is not that their
method is superior to any other, but that in a great enterprise like
the winning of the Moslem there are more ways than one to express the purposes of Christ. And we have a right to assume that
He approves and rewards them all.

IX

Syria

THE Mission of the American Board, which has been the only large Protestant group at work in Turkey, played an equally important part in Syria for nearly fifty years. The story of its founding and of its initial purposes has been already reviewed. Its work in Syria began in October, 1823, with the arrival at Beirut of the Rev. William Goodell and the Rev. Isaac Bird, who were joined by the Rev. Eli Smith in 1827, four years before Dr. Goodell was transferred to Constantinople. Strengthened by further reinforcements in 1838 and 1840, the station was by that time firmly established.

The missionaries encountered in Syria a situation rather more confused than their colleagues met in Turkey. The suspicious attitude of the government and the familiar features of Ottoman rule under the millet system were the same in both countries. But though Syria was far smaller than Turkey and much less populous, it presented—and still presents—complexities of its own. In the field of religion the distribution was different from that in the larger country. In Syria, the Christians probably constituted (as they do today) about one-fifth of the population, the majority concentrated in the Lebanon and the larger cities—Beirut, Damascus, Aleppo, and Tripoli.

Both Moslems and Christians were split into a greater number of groups than in Turkey. Though the bulk of the Mohammedans were orthodox Sunnis, the others were divided among sects of various degrees of heretical belief. Least extravagant were several types of Shiahs, such as certain Ismaili groups and the Metawileh. More numerous, and more extreme in their doctrines, were the Druses, an intractable people living in large colonies, partly in southern Lebanon but chiefly in the district of Hauran. The leading article of their creed is that Allah was incarnated in the sixth Fatimid Caliph, the insane Hakim, who died in Egypt in 1021. With this eccentric feature are combined other doctrines, like those of the Gnostics and Manichaeans, which introduce the ideas of emanations and of a dualistic conflict between Light and Darkness. Like the Gnostics, too, is the division of Druses into the Intelligent, an esoteric inner circle, who are superior to all Moslem law, and the uninitiated Ignorant, who usually conform to the customs of the country. Still more divergent from the parent stock are the Nusairis, now commonly known as the Alawis, who live in northern and central Syria and in parts of Cilicia. "The religious system of the Nusairis forms a bizarre syncretism of Christian, pagan, and Moslem elements, the latter borrowed from the most fanatical Shiah theories and closely resembling Ismailism." [1] In their festivals and in their liturgy, with its use of wine, Christian influence is apparent. Yet they regard Ali as an incarnation of God and with this and with other Moslem ideas they combine a belief in the transmigration of souls. Their community, which now numbers over 228,000, is exclusive, and its creed and practices are retained in strict secrecy. But in their association with the members of other faiths, the Alawis are allowed to conform outwardly to the majority and to be Christians with Christians and Moslems with Moslems.

Among the Christian minority the missionaries found an equal diversity. There were the members of the Greek Orthodox Church under the Patriarch of Antioch, and in smaller numbers there were Jacobites [2] and Armenians. To increase the confusion, were other bodies which in one form or another owed allegiance to the Roman Catholic Church. One of these was that of the Greek Catholics—Arabic-speaking Syrians once in the Orthodox fold but now loyal to Rome. Far more important were the numerous Maronites, who were settled chiefly in the Lebanon mountains between Tripoli and Tyre. The ancestors of the Maronites, who had strayed into heresy in the seventh century, went over to the Church of Rome during the Crusades. Their descendants, though

---

1 H. Lammens, *Islam*, p. 170.
2 The remnants of the ancient monophysite Syrian Church.

retaining their own liturgy, accept the doctrines of the Roman Catholic Church and remain subject to the Pope under their own elected Patriarch. Catholic in the same sense and on the same terms were the Uniate Armenians and the Syrian Catholics.

The adverse conditions which confronted the missions in Turkey were present likewise in Syria—the opposition of the government to the Christian foreigners and the hostile rigidity of the mass of Sunni Moslems. The eccentric half-Moslem groups were slightly easier to approach but not much easier to convert. And the multiplication of Christian bodies only added to the number of ecclesiastical authorities who were soon ready to view the newcomers as enemies. By way of adding to this burden of difficulties, the country was involved, off and on for the next twenty years, in both foreign and civil warfare. During most of the decade before 1829 Greece and Turkey were intermittently at war, a struggle which at times involved Beirut. Much more disturbing was the invasion of Palestine and Syria in 1831 by the Egyptian army of Ibrahim Pasha, son of the great viceroy Mohammed Ali. The forces of the Turkish Sultan were defeated, and Syria was subjected to Egyptian rule for nearly ten years. After the Sultan had met a second reverse in 1839, the European Powers intervened; a British squadron captured Beirut and Acre; and in 1840 the lost provinces were restored to Turkey. But the very next year there broke out a civil war between the Maronites and the Druses in which the latter were successful, and four years later came a still bloodier contest between the same peoples, ending with another Druse victory.

It was in the face of all these obstacles and in the midst of all this discord, now chronic and now acute, that the little group of foreigners had to initiate and expand their mission. Though the direct approach to Moslems was next to impossible, there were tens of thousands of Christians whose spiritual needs were evident. To reach these people, the most obvious methods were the use of literature and the establishment of schools. It was upon literary and educational work, then, that the Mission concentrated from the beginning.

The production of evangelical tracts and books had begun with the founding of the Press at Malta in 1822, and with the removal of its Arabic section to Beirut in 1834 its activities increased. In the next fourteen years there were printed over 7,000,000 pages of some fifty different books and pamphlets, which were sold or distributed every year by colporteurs on long journeys reaching as far as Aleppo. Much more important was the translation of the Bible into Arabic, for the need for a new and accurate version had long been apparent. That heavy task was begun in 1847 by Eli Smith, who died nine years later, after the printing of only Genesis and Exodus. But his preliminary labors on most of the other books lightened the work of his successor, the Rev. C. V. A. Van Dyck. After nine more years of skillful and tireless effort, Dr. Van Dyck completed in 1865 the translation of the entire Bible—a version which has been acclaimed ever since as a masterpiece.

Schools for the children of Christian parents were soon opened, and within four years of their arrival the missionaries and their helpers were conducting thirteen schools in Beirut and near-by towns. Their pupils numbered as many as 600, including 120 girls. But these initial successes were soon ended by the troubles arising from the war with Greece, which obliged the missionaries to withdraw to Malta for two years. After their return, the work of education, though resumed with difficulty, went forward steadily for several decades. It was in 1834 that the first school exclusively for girls was begun at Beirut—a step that marked an epoch in Syrian education. A boarding school for boys, established at Beirut in the following year, was closed in 1842; but its place was filled a few years later by a new seminary for boys at Abeih, which was to continue for the next thirty years. By 1870 the number of small mission schools had so increased that their total enrollment was over 1,200, including 250 girls. Before that time there had been founded two institutions destined to prosper for generations to come. The lesser of the two was the Beirut Seminary for Girls, opened in 1862 by Syrian teachers, which in course of time was to become the present flourishing American School for Girls.

A more distinguished future awaited another institution begun at this time. The opposition of the American Board to education through the medium of the English language, which had resulted in the founding of Robert College as an independent organization, produced in Syria the same results. With the consent of the Board, Dr. Daniel Bliss resigned from the Mission and set himself to organize a college. After raising $100,000 in the United States and smaller sums in England, he arranged for the incorporation by the New York legislature of the Syrian Protestant College. The bill was signed in May, 1864, the constitution of the College was adopted by the new trustees, and Dr. Bliss was elected president. Two years and a half later the College opened at Beirut in a rented house with a preparatory class of sixteen students. In the mind of its wise founder, the future university was almost as real as the existing school. To his foresight is due the gradual purchase of the greater part of that superb tract of land facing the Mediterranean, which even now is adequate to the needs of an expanding center of learning. Under his guidance, a School of Medicine was established as early as 1867 and a School of Pharmacy in 1872. During the thirty-six years of his presidency, Dr. Bliss saw the College develop from a handful of students housed in a few rooms to a body of more than 600 men and boys, taught by 40 professors and tutors (half of whom were American) and divided among five departments—Preparatory, Collegiate, Commercial, Medical, and Pharmaceutical.

In the production of literature and the expansion of schools, there were difficulties and hindrances, and progress was by no means uniform. But advance in these directions was fairly encouraging, compared with the trials and hazards of evangelism. For the effort to present the Gospel to native Christians and to reawaken their Churches proved far more discouraging than in Turkey. Yet from the beginning that purpose was urgent in the minds of missionaries. In the use of tracts and books, in preaching services, and in personal intercourse wherever there was an opening, their activity was continuous. From the very outset, too, the opposition of the ecclesiastical authorities was vigorous and bitter. The foreigners had not been at work for a year when the Maronite Patriarch was sufficiently alarmed to threaten with excommunication whoever consorted with them. Three years later he renewed his solemn warning, in a proclamation which damned the missionaries as "infernal dragons." And he meant what he said, for the first Maronite convert was tortured and imprisoned and ended his life in a filthy jail. Hardly less hostile were the leaders of the Greek Catholics, who thundered in similar tones against the diabolical Americans and all who aided them.

To judge by the results of the first twenty years, however, there was little cause for excitement. For a year or two after 1834, it is true, there was a strong movement toward Protestant Christianity among the Druses of the Lebanon. But the missionaries were convinced that the chief motive was to escape the military service which the Egyptian government was then requiring of all Moslems. Though urgently besieged by many applicants, the leaders of the Mission were reluctant to act before submitting the Druses to a prolonged period of testing; and in the course of time the agitation died away, leaving but a handful of converts. The Mission was not equipped psychologically or physically to deal with mass movements; it could apply only the most rigid individual standards; and for better or worse it missed whatever chance there may have been to win these heretical half-Moslems. Some ten years later another movement confronted the missionaries. At Hasbeiya, a small town fifty miles from Beirut, more than a hundred men and women seceded from the Greek Orthodox Church, declared themselves Protestants, and asked for ministers and teachers. To meet these demands, the few workers available made every possible effort; but the violent persecutions which ensued broke up the little group and put an end to any orderly training. It was not until seven years had passed that the loyal remnant of these seceders was formed into a church with a Syrian pastor.

Meanwhile, as we noted in the last chapter, the Turkish government had recognized the Protestants as a distinct religious community; and in response to this concession there was organized in 1848 at Beirut the first indigenous Protestant church. Considering that the Mission had been at work for twenty-five years, the new body was small indeed, composed of only twenty-seven members. Ten had come from the Greek Orthodox Church, three were Druses, and the remainder represented four other divisions. During the next seven years, similar churches were founded at Hasbeiya, Abeih, Aleppo, and Sidon. By 1857, besides these churches, there were preaching stations at sixteen other points, including Tripoli. The legitimacy of Protestantism had been accepted by the government; the anathemas of patriarchs were now fewer in number and feebler in their effects; and the missionaries were welcomed and honored in many places where they had once been threatened with violence. They were even on speaking terms with some of the oriental clergy. Yet the leaders of the Roman and Greek Churches were as unrelenting as ever in the set purpose to extinguish what was pure Christianity to the missionaries and dangerous heresy to their opponents. In almost every town and village entered by the Mission, there had to be a severe contest before those of the ancient faith would tolerate the Protestants.

Just as the Mission was beginning to hope for better days, there occurred in 1860 the great Druse rebellion and its attendant massacres. Despite their previous defeats, the Maronites once more fell upon their Druse neighbors in several villages of the Lebanon. Retaliation was so prompt and merciless that the Christians soon became the chief sufferers. Encouraged by the Turks, the Druses slaughtered Christians wherever they found them; and as far away as Damascus, Kurds and Arabs joined them in plunder and murder. Before foreign aid could intervene by the dispatch of a fleet to Beirut, as many as 14,000 Maronite, Greek Orthodox, and other Christians had perished. In the midst of the widespread suffering that followed, the missionaries were everywhere active in the work of relief. More than $150,000, raised in the United States and Europe, was placed in their hands for the care of the starving and homeless, the sick and the wounded. But prevention was needed as well as cure. To make certain that the Turks should not again throw the Christians to the wolves, the European Powers insisted that the whole Lebanon district, with its Christian majority, should thereafter be ruled by a native Christian governor, a provision that insured for many years to come comparative order and notable prosperity for the Lebanon.

During the next ten years there was but little progress in the field of the American Mission. At a number of centers there were new movements toward Protestantism, usually in the face of violent opposition; several stations were opened and several abandoned; and the number of missionaries, which had reached in 1856 its maximum of thirty, had dropped by 1870 to only eighteen. For this marked contrast to the continued success of the mission to Armenians in Turkey there were several reasons. In Turkey the Armenian was a strong national Church, not under the control of Rome, not influenced by Jesuits, and less dominated by its priests than the various Uniate bodies in Syria. There was therefore far less organized resistance to the inroads of evangelical Christianity. Official opponents were fewer and weaker and more easily reconciled. Confronted with antagonism more stubborn and bitter than their colleagues found in Turkey, the missionaries in Syria seem also to have been less successful in their methods of approach. Partly, perhaps, because of that very antagonism, they were more polemic in their attitude and spent more time in directly attacking abuses and in emphasizing doctrinal differences. Less hopeful of stimulating reform from within, they were more given to assault from without, especially against those outward aspects of oriental Christianity which always scandalize Protestants. Then, too, they were not only very slow to train Syrian helpers, but they remained inflexible in their demands for a long probation in dealing with would-be converts. In consequence of these external and internal causes, there was never any large and concerted movement toward Protestantism. By the year 1870 there were about 1,300 pupils in the mission schools; but the Syrian workers numbered only 50, and after forty-seven years there were only 245 church members.

If the results were thus meager in the attempt to revive the Eastern Churches, they were almost negligible in the attempt to touch Islam. Reviewing them from this point of view, a historian of the American Board reported that (1) The Scriptures had been widely circulated, and the Bible was open to all who could read. (2) Protestantism had proved influential in gradually changing the minds of Moslems in regard to Christianity and increasing their respect for it. (3) Moslems had been among the attendants at preaching services; and (4) Druses had been taught in schools especially organized for them and some had been baptized.[3] It is only fair to add that a small number of Moslems were already to be found in a few of the schools.

It was at this point, in the year 1870, that the Mission was transferred from the American Board to the Board of Missions of the recently reunited Presbyterian Church in the United States of America.[4] Though most of the missionaries remained at their posts under the new regime, it was the Presbyterian Mission which thenceforward became the chief representative of Protestantism in Syria. By this time, however, other missions had entered the field. To name only the chief organizations which have survived, the British Syrian Mission began in 1860 the first of its schools for girls, which numbered at the end of the century as many as fifty-six. The Irish Presbyterians and the Edinburgh Medical Mission Association opened work at Damascus, and the English Friends at Brummana, close to Beirut. Writing thirty years ago of these and other minor missions, Julius Richter says,

Their united forces were hardly equal to that of the American Board or the Presbyterian Mission of a later date. A characteristic common to these smaller undertakings is that they did not aim at the formation of congregations. When their labors resulted in conversions to Protestantism, their converts, if they did not remain in the service of the mission, joined the congregations established by the Americans. But there were never many such converts, and the influence of these missions has been in general small. . . . The waste of energy that results from the dividing of the missionary undertaking in Syria among so many small, independent missions is to be regretted. Though considerable sums have been spent, but little abiding effect has been produced in this religiously and politically distracted country. Yet . . . an energetic pushing of English and Protestant influences is a necessary and valuable step in the direction of the preaching of the Gospel. . . . In the course of the twenty-five years succeeding 1860, every considerable village in the whole of Syria . . . has been occupied by Protestant missions. Herein is to be found an explanation of the fact that the predominant mission of the American Presbyterians has

[3] R. Anderson, *History of the Missions of the A.B.C.F.M.,* II, 395 ff.
[4] The so-called Presbyterian Church, North, had in 1837 suffered a doctrinal division into the "Old School" and "New School" Presbyterians.

never thought it necessary to vie with other societies in the formation of stations. Its work has been intensive rather than extensive.[5]

During the forty-four years between 1870 and the World War,
the Presbyterian Mission maintained its main stations at Beirut,
Tripoli, and Sidon and at Zahlah in the Lebanon, with missionaries in two other villages. Before the end of the century the
churches in these districts has been organized into three presbyteries. Through the pastoral work and preaching of missionaries and of the Syrian Protestant clergy and through the
increasing use of Christian literature, the enterprise of evangelism went steadily forward. Advance was still slow, not only
because of ecclesiastical opposition but also because of constant
interference by the government. The Turkish authorities prohibited street preaching, forbade the ownership of property by
foreign corporations, required permits for all kinds of buildings
and repairs, carefully censored all publications, and regulated the
curricula of schools. These numerous rules, combined with
chronic procrastination in their administration, served as continuous hindrances to normal progress. Nor was there much improvement in relations with the Oriental Churches. The Maronites, supported by the Jesuits, and the Greek Orthodox, backed
by Russian power, commanded far larger funds and far more
political influence than the Protestants; and they took full advantage of their position to check their unwelcome rivals. Yet
in spite of the hampering effect of these hostile forces, by 1914
the number of organized churches had grown to 39, with over
3,100 communicants.[6]

The outstanding contribution of the Mission, however, was in
the field of education. Though here, too, the same authorities in
Church and State were active in creating obstacles, success was
both more marked and more easily measured. The elementary
day schools in towns and villages multiplied in number, until at
the outbreak of the war there were nearly 100, with more than
4,500 pupils. They not only served the purpose of educating the

[5] Richter, *History of Protestant Missions in the Near East,* pp. 201 f., 211 f.

[6] As a further handicap should be counted the heavy emigration of Syrians,
especially to the United States, in the early years of this century, a movement
which included a large number of Protestant Christians.

Protestant children, who supplied only one-fourth of the total; they were equally valuable as an evangelistic agency in helping the Mission to secure a foothold in many villages otherwise inaccessible. During the same period there had been developed 8 secondary schools, of which the most important were the seminaries for girls at Beirut, Tripoli, Suk al-Gharb in the Lebanon, and Sidon, the boarding school for boys at Tripoli, and Gerard Academy for Boys at Sidon, which introduced in 1895 an industrial department, teaching farming and handicrafts. At the top of the scale, and independent of the Mission, was the Syrian Protestant College. By the opening of the century, nearly all of these American schools were full to overflowing, for by that time the process of westernization in the Near East was well advanced and appetite for foreign education was growing. Stimulated by the same movement and meeting many of the same demands, was the increasing activity of the American Press at Beirut, which had become one of the most powerful missionary agencies in the Levant.[7]

When we turn to assess the results of all this work, we must remind ourselves first of the purposes that lay behind it. Essentially the same as the aims which prompted the Mission in Turkey, they have been clearly stated by one of the foremost leaders of the Syrian Mission, Dr. Henry H. Jessup. After a missionary career lasting from 1856 to 1910, he wrote, "The chief and ultimate object of missionary work in Western Asia is the conversion of the Mohammedans to the Christian faith." But he adds that "the Oriental Churches are among the greatest obstacles to the conversion of their Mohammedan neighbors." Since "there is no hope of reforming the higher ecclesiastics and through them the people," another plan has been

to preach the Gospel and give the Bible to the people, leaving them in their own ecclesiastical relations, in the hope of reforming the Church from within. This plan has been patiently tried . . . in Syria, Asia Minor and Egypt, without success. For no sooner do men read the Bible and become enlightened, than they make haste to "come

---

[7] In 1905, for example, the Press printed 47,000,000 pages of various Bible editions. The publication of the Arabic Scriptures has been financed by the American Bible Society.

out and be separate.". . . The result has been that the people themselves have demanded and compelled the organization of a new
Oriental Evangelical Church. . . . It has vindicated the claims of
Christianity to be a pure non-idolatrous religion. Mohammedans can
see the Bible acted out in life in the teaching and practice of the
Protestant Churches. . . . The Oriental Churches have lost the spirit
which might enable them to evangelize Islam. They care not to do it.
They cannot do it. They will not do it. This "kingdom" of privilege
and service "shall be taken from them and given to another," even
to the Churches of the Reformation.[8]

In its efforts to stir the Churches of the East to new life, the
Mission had met with little visible success. There had been no
general awakening among these ancient bodies. But in the formation of evangelical churches the Mission could report over 3,000
communicants. As representing a different type of Christianity
more worthy of Moslem respect, these Protestants might be said
to aid the approach to Islam; but they felt themselves in no
position to evangelize Moslems and seldom if ever attempted it.
As a new agency for winning Mohammedans they were negligible. The reasons for their failure we have reviewed at some
length in treating of Turkey. The complex of difficulties which
made it so hard to convert Moslems in Turkey was present likewise in Syria, and whatever hindrances held the missionary in
check served with double force to restrain the indigenous Christian. Probably no American leader was better equipped than
Dr. Jessup to take advantage of the few opportunities to reach
the Moslem. Yet his detailed account of his long career makes
mention of hardly more than a score of conversions with which
he was personally concerned. It was rather in the possibilities
of a gradual indirect approach that hope for the future was to
be found. Reviewing these other lines of advance at the Cairo
Conference in 1906, Dr. W. K. Eddy noted that in Syria open
evangelism and public discussion were illegal. There was still,
however, wide room for activity in the distribution and sale of
the Scriptures and in medical service. Even more promising were
the openings afforded by the mission schools, where Moslems
were always welcome and where Bible study was an essential part

[8] Jessup, *Fifty-Three Years in Syria*, I, 85-93.

of the course. In spite of frequent government orders against attendance at Christian schools, an ever-growing number of non-Christians was to be found there; and in the Sidon district there were counted among the pupils as many as 250 Moslems. The Turkish revolution in 1908 and 1909, which, as we have seen, fell far short of bringing to missions the benefits anticipated, had at least the effect of gradually increasing the number of Mohammedans in these Christian schools.

The attitude of the Mission toward its responsibility for Islam was expressed at this time in the findings of a conference held at Beirut in 1910, resolutions which were later transmitted to the Edinburgh Conference. It was declared

1.) that direct evangelistic work among Moslems, which has been going on quietly for several decades in Syria and Palestine, is more than ever possible today, whether by means of visiting, conversation, the production and careful distribution of Christian literature, Bible circulation, medical missions, and boys' and girls' schools. 2.) That the promulgation of the [new Turkish] Constitution has already, in the more enlightened centers, made this direct evangelistic work easier, and will, we trust ... make it increasingly so. And, on the other hand, we are face to face with a Mohammedan educational and religious revival which makes necessary this missionary advance if the prestige gained in the past is to be preserved and increased. 3.) For which reasons it is certain that the time has come for a wisely planned and carefully conducted and intensely earnest forward move in work among Moslems in Syria and Palestine, and the attention of all the Societies already working in the field is to be directed toward immediately making that forward move.[9]

Before these plans could begin to take effect, the Turkish Empire entered upon that series of wars which lasted, with but few intermissions, from 1911 to 1921. From the beginning of the World War, Syria was so close to the zone of hostilities that the activities of the mission were seriously restricted and hundreds of thousands of the people were plunged into suffering. Before the end of 1916, disease was everywhere rife, there was a huge increase in crime, famine was widely prevalent, and more than 70,000 had died of starvation in Syria and Palestine. British missionaries had been obliged to leave Syria, and much of their work

[9] World Missionary Conference (Edinburgh), *Reports*, IX, 255.

was carried on by native Christians. The Syrian Protestant College, however, managed to continue in operation. As in Turkey, the chief task of the foreign missionaries and of the college staff was the administration of relief. For four years they had to serve as secretly as possible, since the government prohibited all such philanthropy. Yet they contrived to render aid on a large scale, partly by arranging for the transmission of gifts from Syrians in America to their relatives and friends in the homeland. Through the careful organization of the whole Mission force, nearly $2,000,000 was thus distributed during the war. On October 8, 1918, Allenby's cavalry rode into Beirut, and for Syria the war was over. With the British forces came an American Red Cross Unit from Palestine, which took over the local volunteer work. Six months later the Near East Relief contingents began to arrive from the United States, bringing ample supplies of men and money. At length the Mission was free to face the task of reconstruction in the midst of changed surroundings and under a new government.

Just what that new government should be was a problem not easy to solve. The British remained in control for some time, but only to maintain order during the period of transition. In the Sykes-Picot Agreement of 1916 they had agreed that France should obtain the coastal strip of Syria and a wide sphere of influence in the interior, which should include the four leading cities of Damascus, Aleppo, Hama, and Homs. Regardless of this pledge, the Arab leaders Husain and his son Feisal had been promised an independent Arab state, embracing all Syria outside a part of the Lebanon. Both these conflicting claims could not be realized, and the conflict between them soon came to a decision. The Inter-Allied Council at San Remo in April, 1920, assigned the mandate for Syria to France. Meanwhile, in March, with the full support of the vast majority of the Syrian people, Feisal had been proclaimed king at Damascus, and four months later the Syrian National Congress adopted a democratic constitution for a united Syria. Roused by this defiance and suspecting that the British had approved it, the French government acted promptly. In the wake of an ultimatum, a small French force under General Gouraud advanced upon Damascus, defeated the Arab troops, and drove Feisal out of the country.

In the course of the next five years what had once been Syria in the broader sense was organized into five different states. Lebanon, much enlarged, became Great Lebanon. The remainder of the coastal region northward was divided between the State of the Alawis[10] and the autonomous Sanjak of Alexandretta, adjoining Turkey.[11] In the southeast appeared the small State of Jebel ad-Druz, the center of population of the Druses. And deprived of all direct access to the sea, the rest of inner Syria, including Aleppo and Damascus, was united in the single State of Syria. Except for a provisional constitution in the Lebanon, which produced little but dissension and disunion, there was no serious attempt for some years to develop representative government. Syrian hopes for freedom and unity had been balked, and the alien government of France was active in suppressing both personal and political liberties. By the opening of the year 1925, therefore, large groups of the people were eager for revolt. Beginning among the Druses but extending to Damascus and as far as Aleppo, there then broke out a violent insurrection which was not wholly suppressed until June, 1927. During the first year Damascus was bombarded and partly burnt, many villages were destroyed with much loss of life, and a genuine reign of terror was maintained by cruel reprisals. After another year of military occupation and in an atmosphere of deep bitterness and suspicion, the French set themselves at length to answer the demands for self-government. The constitution of the Lebanese Republic had already been restored; and in 1930 the Syrian Republic received a similar constitution providing for a president, a legislature, and a responsible ministry. In both republics, however, the High Commissioner retains the power of veto, and the ultimate authority of the Mandate remains unimpaired. Six years later treaties with both these states were negotiated, according to which the Mandate should end in January, 1939, and their sovereignty should then be recognized. But these treaties have never

10 Known after 1930 as the Government of Latakia.
11 Ceded to Turkey by treaty in 1939 and now known as Hatay.

been ratified by the French parliament and no further action upon them will be taken until after the present war.

It was naturally with the evils attending the French occupation that the Syrian people were most impressed—the presence of large bodies of troops (sometimes half of them black Senegalese), the elaborate system of espionage, punitive raids, and the deportation of leaders without trial. The missionaries, however, could join with a minority of Syrians in appreciating the benefits which were no less clearly a result of foreign rule—the construction of public works and motor roads, the modernizing of cities like Beirut, progress in industry and farming, the development of a sanitary and medical service, and, more important if less tangible, a marked improvement in the morale of the Christian population. With increasing facilities for travel, with a welcome sense of physical security, and with widening opportunities for reaching the Moslem, the Mission continued its work.

In reviving its educational activity, the Mission has enjoyed advantages which it had never known before. It can count upon freedom from official restrictions and a friendly attitude on the part of the government. No less encouraging has been a new readiness among Moslem parents to send their sons and daughters to Christian schools. Since the French have fostered the establishment by the government of a system of elementary schools, there is now less opportunity for missionary institutions of this grade, so that the number today is only 44 for the Presbyterians, and for the British Syrian Mission only 11. In secondary education, too, there has been a decline in numbers. Yet the increase in the proportion of Mohammedan pupils in the high schools at Beirut, Tripoli, and Sidon, where they number 40 or 50 percent, marks a hopeful enlargement of influence. Though a shrinkage in quantity has thus occurred, the quality of Christian schools justifies their place in the national scheme. They offer what cannot be found in the government schools—not only regular religious training, but an intimate relation between the Christian teachers and the pupils. Standing as a witness before the nation to Christian aims and ideals in education, they serve not only to build up the Evangelical Church, but to touch and sometimes to mold an ever-larger number of Moslems.

It is in higher education that the missionary forces encounter the least competition and can claim the most easily visible progress. Dominating the field as the foremost institution of Western learning in the Near East is the American University of Beirut.[12] After seventy-five years of expansion, the university today, under the presidency of Dr. Bayard Dodge, is impressive in part by the remarkable variety it represents—variety of personnel and variety of activity. Its 1,700 students[13] are drawn from 43 different countries. Nearly half, it is true, come from the surrounding area of Syria and the Lebanon, but Palestine adds 300 more and Iraq another 145. To catalogue the remaining sources of supply would fill a page. Just as examples of the diversity might be named Arabia, Zanzibar, France, Lithuania, the United States, and Chile. Hardly less varied is the religious composition of the student body, drawn from eighteen different religious groups. Nearly a third are Mohammedans and about one-eighth are Jews, while the Christians are chiefly Eastern Orthodox and Protestants, with a sprinkling of Armenians, Copts, and Maronites. Socially, too, the students cover a wide range, from the sons of families living almost in poverty to the sons of aristocratic Moslems of political note. Quite as striking as the diversity of the personnel is the variety of work. The departments themselves are numerous enough—the Elementary School, the École française (a secondary school), the Preparatory School,[14] the College of Arts and Sciences, the Schools of Medicine, Dentistry, Nursing, and Pharmacy, and the recently founded Institute of Music and Institute of Rural Life. Beyond the regular academic work there are all sorts of enterprises that engage the interests of teachers and undergraduates. Members of the faculty are busy in various types of valuable research and of service to the government, while a dozen different

---

[12] The Syrian Protestant College was thus renamed in 1920.
[13] Statistics of 1938.
[14] In close affiliation with the university and housed on the same campus is the International College, formerly of Smyrna, which has taken over these departments of elementary and secondary grade.

groups of students are active in such social work as night schools, village welfare centers, social surveys, and the like.

In view of its high ideals and of the scope of its influence, it is small wonder that the university is known and trusted over so wide an area and that its graduates fill hundreds of important posts throughout the Near East. Its moral effect in raising the standards of public service has been immense. When it comes to religion, however, the university is extremely cautious. Not only is no religious instruction required, but very little is offered, even to Christian students; and "Assembly" meetings, with singing of hymns and ethical talks, have supplanted services in the chapel. Of general uplift and moral training the authorities approve; yet they are shy not merely of exerting religious pressure but of any such Christian emphasis as might disturb the most sensitive Moslem. The present ideal of the institution, which grows more secular every year, is that each student should remain in whatever religious status he may happen to be. The conversion of a Moslem to Christianity would be as unexpected as it would be inconvenient.

Aleppo College, though very small in comparison and not yet of full college grade, is an interesting and promising example of Christian coöperation. Long before the World War there had been a college at Aintab, supported by the American Board and the Armenian Evangelical Church. After the war what remained of the institution was transferred to Aleppo, where it has recently joined forces with the North Syria School for Boys of the Presbyterian Mission and the Syrian Evangelical Church. Established in new buildings on an excellent site outside the city, the college has doubled its enrollment in the last two years and now includes over 400 students.

The first opportunity for the women of Syria to profit by higher education has been offered by the Presbyterian Mission in the American Junior College for Women at Beirut. From small beginnings in the form of advanced classes at the American School for Girls, there has grown up in the last fifteen years a college of about 90 students, housed in attractive buildings on a site not far from the university. By providing the training of Freshman and Sophomore years, it meets the needs of an increasing number of girls, some of whom complete their studies in the two higher classes at the university. The role it can play in the life of Syria is small as yet, for in notable contrast with Turkey the emancipation of women proceeds at a cautiously conservative pace. Very few Moslem women have completely discarded the veil or venture to seek employment in clerical positions, still less in the professions. Yet about 40 percent of the college girls are Mohammedan, including not a few from Palestine and Iraq.

To confine our survey of educational missions to these various schools and colleges would be to omit two vital factors in the life of the Church in Syria—the Bible Lands Union for Christian Education and the American Press at Beirut. Though their contribution might be counted no less truly an element in evangelism, it is equally indispensable to the cause of Christian education. The Bible Lands Union, organized in 1925, is international not only in its affiliations[15] but in its sphere of work, which includes Iraq, Palestine, and Transjordan as well as Syria. It is likewise interdenominational, for its officers and committees include representatives of the Eastern Orthodox, Anglican, and Protestant Churches. Its center of gravity, however, is Protestant, and Syria its chief field. In addition to supplying the education material for a monthly Christian journal and serving at Beirut as a center for the distribution of Christian literature, the Union is active in the organization of Sunday schools and of conferences and institutes for leaders in Christian education. Perhaps its most remarkable success has been in the development of Daily Vacation Bible Schools, of which there are now in Syria as many as 72, with 2,700 pupils. Though these activities do not touch Moslems directly, they serve as a genuine stimulus to the youth of the evangelical churches, and they have already produced a perceptible effect upon Orthodox leaders and even upon Maronites.

The founding of the American Press and its share in the production of the Arabic Bible we have already noted. Since these earlier achievements, its work has steadily advanced in quantity

[15] Affiliated with the World's Sunday School Association, the World's Christian Endeavor Union, and the World's Association of Daily Vacation Bible Schools.

and quality. When it celebrated its centennial of service in Beirut in 1934, the Press could report that it had printed 2,200,000 volumes of Scriptures—whole Bibles, Testaments, and portions. In that year alone it produced 143,000 volumes of Bibles and religious and educational books and in the same year had sold a number almost equally large. Its present catalogue lists more than 550 titles in Arabic, including such diverse works as a *Phonetic Guide to Colloquial Arabic, Elementary Botany, Lawrence and the Arabs,* commentaries on the New Testament, translations of Fosdick's *Meaning of Prayer,* and Jones's *Christ of the Indian Road,* together with scores of Christian tracts and devotional books. The range of its influence may be measured by the fact that it has regular customers not only in Syria and Palestine, but throughout the whole of North Africa and in Turkey, Egypt, the Sudan, Arabia, Iraq, Iran, India, and South America. Wherever Arabic is read, the Press serves as a powerful auxiliary to the Christian approach to Islam.

The results of evangelism in Syria are to be found chiefly in the body for which the Presbyterian Mission is responsible—the Syrian Evangelical Church. The Mission staff has now only 39 members, including wives; but the national force numbers 268, of whom 22 are ordained. In the 4 stations and 68 out-stations there are 40 organized churches, with 3,700 communicants. The majority of these are second-generation Christians, drawn originally from the Greek Orthodox Church; for today there are relatively few who follow their fathers' footsteps in seceding from the parent bodies. The Evangelical Church is completely controlled by Syrian Christians, in whose hands is the government both of the congregations and of the presbyteries. They administer not only the local funds but such foreign contributions as are intended for their work. For this task of leadership in the ministry it is not easy to find volunteers, though the quality of candidates, both Syrian and Armenian, appears to be better than a generation ago. Their training is now provided in the new Near East School of Theology at Beirut,[16] which sets higher

16 Founded in 1932 by the union of the School for Religious Workers of the Presbyterian Mission and the School of Religion of the American Board at Athens.

standards of education than have hitherto been required. Outside of the Syrian Evangelical Church, the only other Protestant body of importance is that of the Protestant Armenian churches of northern Syria, a strong self-governing group which took shape in 1931 as the Armenian Evangelical Union.

The effect of the evangelical movement upon the Oriental Churches during the past hundred years has been far slighter than the Protestant leaders once hoped. Yet genuine results have been achieved that are worthy of record. Scarcely any perceptible impression, it is true, has been made upon the Maronites or the other Uniate bodies under Roman rule. But the effort to influence the Greek Orthodox Church has met with greater success. Though the evidence is often intangible and hard to estimate, its members have unquestionably benefited from the development of Protestantism. There is little doubt, too, that their clergy have improved in quality. They are readier than before to meet on friendly terms with Protestant leaders and to admit the need for reforms. More significant is their recognition of the value of the Bible in the lives of their people. Quite as hopeful is the fact that the more enlightened and advanced among their members need live no longer in the dread of excommunication. Remaining where they are, they can work from within. Rather more clear, as in Turkey, has been the favorable effect upon the Armenians, for members of their ancient Gregorian Church often attend Protestant services and even some of their clergy come for training to Protestant institutions. It is just because of these varied consequences of several generations of evangelism that there is but little attempt at present to revive the Oriental Churches by direct methods. The chief influence by which they are now reached is exerted through the schools. The claim, therefore, can now be justly made that the Mission is not interested in proselytizing from the older bodies.

The question of prime importance, however, is how far the Christian forces in Syria are enlisted in the effort to win Moslems. The changes following the war were all calculated to encourage a new emphasis upon that enterprise. In the first place, the government of the Sultan was gone, and a Christian nation had assumed the responsibility for the welfare of Syria. The mere change of attitude and atmosphere was an immense advantage. Yet certain restraints upon legal freedom still remain. In contrast with the Turkish movement toward complete secularization, Syria still retains the ancient grouping of its people into religious communities. In one or another every citizen must be registered, in order to preserve his civil rights. The constitutions of both the Lebanese Republic and the Syrian Republic provide for "absolute liberty of conscience." But it is only in the Lebanon that this broad declaration has been implemented since 1925 by definite legislation prescribing the procedure by which men and women may change their religious registration. And in the Lebanon it has been proved on a number of occasions that this law will operate in the case of a Moslem who has become a Christian. In the Syrian Republic, however, there is no established method except for a change *to* Islam, so that there the process works only one way. To become a Christian, therefore, is not only socially perilous; it involves the loss of civil status. Politically and legally, then, there have been improvements, even though unhappy hindrances still persist. Ecclesiastically, too, the postwar era finds the churches and missions in better condition for advance. A growing unity of feeling and action has strengthened the Christian bodies. As early as 1919 there was formed the United Missionary Conference of Syria and Palestine, with the aim to limit the number of competing denominations and to bring order out of too much confusion. As a further step in federation, the Near East Christian Council was established in 1927,[17] with its executive center first at Cairo but since 1934 at Beirut. Like its sister councils in Japan, China, and India, it serves both to coördinate and stimulate the work of otherwise scattered units, to aid them in common efforts, and to represent them in relations with governments. Affiliated with the Council is the invaluable Central Literature Committee for Moslems, under the leadership of its editorial secretary, Miss Constance E. Padwick. Its headquarters is at Cairo, and its influence reaches out to touch every quarter of the world of Islam. Thanks to the spirit which made these

[17] First known as the Council for Western Asia and Northern Africa.

organizations possible and the coöperation to which they have led, the missions in Syria are now working in increased harmony. With a more open road before them and with the bonds between them closer, they have begun seriously to face their main task.

Clear evidence of a new concentration of purpose appeared at the Brummana Regional Conference held in 1924, which recorded with regret that "the number of missionaries definitely devoting the whole of their time and strength to the evangelization of Moslem, Druse, and Nusairiyeh peoples is almost negligible." The members expressed their conviction "that in view of changed conditions in the Near East, and the new openings for preaching Christ to non-Christians, the Home Boards and the Missions in the field should shift the emphasis of their objective from the Christians to the Moslems of these lands, thus setting an example and starting a movement that we hope will lead the native Church to make missionary work the center of all its activities." It was further resolved "that all the missionaries and native workers among Moslems should be trained in Islamics through courses of lectures and conferences and that picked men should be set aside by the Missions to specialize on Islamics." [18]

In carrying out these good resolutions, no group has been more in earnest than the British Syrian Mission, whose twenty-two workers are nearly all women. The conversion of non-Christians has long been its primary aim. Through its schools, through informal dispensary service, but chiefly through personal evangelism among women, the Mission is in active touch with Mohammedans, orthodox or heretical, in all its stations and finds them today increasingly ready of access. Work with Moslems is likewise the main concern of the Edinburgh Medical Mission in its Victoria Hospital at Damascus. In that rigidly conservative Moslem city of 200,000 inhabitants, no open preaching or discussion is possible; but in the hospital, which hundreds of Mohammedans enter each year, there is freedom for Christian services and for daily contact with patients in the wards. Similar opportunities, though with fewer Moslems, are open to the hospital of the English Friends at Brummana.

[18] *Conferences of Christian Workers among Moslems,* pp. 103-23.

It is to the Presbyterian Mission, however, and to the Evan-gelical Churches that we must look for most of the evidence for growing efforts on behalf of Islam. Theirs are the largest and strongest bodies and theirs the chief responsibility. With the de-termined aim to carry out its change of policy, the Mission re-opened in 1922 its station at Aleppo, where two-thirds of the 300,000 people are Moslems. Other stations at Hama and Homs were later established and staffed with foreign workers who could concentrate upon the difficult task of pioneering. Still later Na-batiyeh was added to the list and several smaller outstations that can serve as demonstration centers. Already the Kennedy Memo-rial Hospital at Tripoli was in active operation, with direct evangelism as part of its program.[19] But another hospital was opened in far more unfriendly territory at Deir az-Zor on the Euphrates, 400 miles inland. When doctors can minister to pa-tients in these settled institutions, the problem of making con-tacts is easily solved. Elsewhere, however, the solution is far less simple. Yet by one means or another friendly relations have been established. It may be by the sale of the Scriptures, or by village preaching, or by giving aid in agricultural improvement. In the larger and more hostile centers, the work must begin with reading rooms, or with stereopticon lectures on general subjects, or per-haps with athletics for boys and girls, or with child welfare groups.

Not only is the missionary today far readier to approach the Moslems; the Moslems themselves are easier to reach. Especially during the last six or seven years there has been testimony from many quarters that their attendance at Christian services is much more frequent than before and that wherever the Gospel is preached in the villages they are more willing than of old to listen. The orthodox Sunnis are of course the hardest to touch, for Syrian Mohammedans are intensely conservative, and the presence of foreign rule and a Christian minority has tended to solidify them and to encourage an attitude of self-protection. It

[19] The hospital now treats annually about 1,200 patients, drawn from more than 100 towns and villages.

is therefore among the Nusairis and Ismailis that greater headway is made.

But the foreign missionaries have not been content to accept for themselves alone the responsibility for reaching the great mass of unevangelized Moslems. They have been quite aware that that privilege, however unwelcome, belongs ultimately to the Syrian Christians. At the Brummana Conference, from whose findings we have already quoted, it was resolved "that the great force latent in the native Churches be brought into action by finding means to inspire and direct them to reach the Moslem population with the Gospel, and that in so doing special efforts be made to dispel their manifest feeling of reluctance and lack of faith in the matter of the conversion of Moslems to the Christian faith." [20] And nine years later, in 1933, the Presbyterian Mission voted not only that it should prosecute more vigorously its policy to occupy non-Christian centers but that it should "develop in the thinking of the Syrian leaders and religious workers their joint responsibility for this task." For it has had to be recognized that the clergy in the old Oriental Churches are no more interested in the winning of Mohammedans than they were a hundred years ago. The one hope for a long time to come is that the Protestant Christians may be stirred to prove themselves a missionary body.

Until recently, it must be confessed, such a hope has been difficult to cherish. As an acute observer has remarked, "today the evangelical churches in the Near East are differentiated from other churches by their evangelical creed, their mode of worship, and their knowledge of the Bible, but not by their attitude to the Moslems." [21] This verdict still holds good for the majority in Syria, Palestine, and Egypt. But during the past decade in Syria there has been evident a growing recognition on the part of Protestant Christians of their responsibility to evangelize Moslems. Though more clearly manifest among the Armenian churches, it is notable, too, among the Syrians. Every year the

[20] See n. 18.
[21] Levonian, "Islam and the Evangelical Churches in the Near East," *International Review of Missions* (July, 1935), pp. 392 f.

presbyteries are being gradually educated and stimulated to such activity, and an ever-larger number of pastors and members of the Evangelical Church are now in touch with individuals and families among their Mohammedan neighbors. And the effect of their endeavors is more real than apparent, for outside of the Lebanon there remains the thorny obstacle of the communal organization and the difficulty of transferring converts to Christian registration. Accepting this limitation more readily than most missionaries would approve, the Evangelical Church will not baptize Moslems until they have succeeded in changing their registration. This rule, of course, severely limits the already small number of baptisms and increases the number of secret believers who cannot or will not take the critical step of joining the Church. In other words, under conditions of genuine religious freedom where Christianity could be judged entirely on its merits, the chances for advance would be immensely increased and forces now restrained would be released for action. As things stand, however, the slight degree of liberty already won is so precarious that there is a marked reluctance on the part of missionaries and Syrian Christians to further any policy that would provoke a strong reaction. The Evangelical Church and the missionary institutions have become vested interests, whose welfare must not be jeopardized by the persecution which would arise if Moslems deserted their religion in appreciable numbers. There are moments, then, when the workers wonder if perhaps they are not almost more afraid of success than of failure. But we may assume with confidence that these are only their weaker moments. The coming years will prove them equal to a beckoning opportunity.

X

Egypt

AT THE OPENING of the nineteenth century, Egypt had been a part of the Ottoman Empire for nearly 300 years, ever since the Turkish Sultan Selim I executed the last Mameluke Sultan in 1517. But the hold of Constantinople upon Egypt had always been relatively loose, and for some time past the governing aristocracy of the Mamelukes had confined the Turkish Pasha at Cairo to merely nominal authority. The victories of Napoleon over both Mamelukes and Turks brought only a temporary change of masters; for in 1801, thanks to British aid, Egypt was restored once more to Turkish sovereignty. The further disorders which then ensued gave an opening for the rise of a Macedonian Moslem then in the Turkish service, the amazing Mohammed Ali. In the course of the next ten years, he defeated the British, extinguished the remaining Mamelukes by massacre, and fought his way to power as sole ruler of Egypt. By the year 1833, he was master of an empire that stretched from Khartum to the borders of Anatolia. At the height of his success, however, the British government joined with Turkey to limit his advance; and the contest, which we have noted in the story of Syria, ended with the Treaty of London in 1841. By this agreement Egypt was granted autonomy under Turkish suzerainty, with Mohammed and his heirs as ruling Pashas. After half a century of startling achievements, Mohammed Ali died in 1849. If he had failed to maintain a growing empire, he had at least saved Egypt from foreign domination and had won the right to be accounted today the founder of Egyptian independence. It is his descendants who have reigned in our time as kings of Egypt; and it was under him that there began that long process of Europeanization, guided by the French, which gives to the culture of modern Egypt its special character.

Five years of reaction under his cruel son Abbas retarded progress; but in the reign of the genial and liberal Said Pasha (1854-63) European influence was again predominant. More eventful was the long administration of Ismail, Mohammed's grandson, who established more firmly the autonomy of Egypt and received from the Sultan the title of Khedive. During his years of rule, the Suez Canal was constructed and opened, the material development of the country was greatly advanced, and foreign trade prospered. But no benefits could atone for the chief contribution of Ismail—the colossal borrowing which raised the public debt of Egypt from $16,500,000 to nearly $300,000,000. It was this wild extravagance, accompanied by corruption, which dismayed foreign creditors and led to complications with the European Powers. At the bidding of Britain and France, the Sultan deposed Ismail in 1879 and named his son Tewfik as Khedive. Controllers General appointed by the two Powers and an International Commission of Liquidation strove for several years to to bring order out of Egyptian chaos. Their efforts were thwarted by the menacing rise of nationalist feeling, inflamed and organized by the military party under the Egyptian Colonel Arabi. By the spring of 1882, the civil government had become paralyzed and the need for intervention grew daily more pressing. A massacre of Europeans at Alexandria in June called for prompt action; and when both France and Italy declined to coöperate, Great Britain undertook the task alone. The bombardment of Alexandria and the landing of marines on July 11 were followed by the dispatch of an army to Egypt. On September 13 the forces under Wolseley defeated Arabi's army in a thirty-minute encounter at Tel al-Kebir, and soon the British flag was floating above the Citadel at Cairo. There then began that British occupation which for more than fifty years was described as "temporary" and which even now is not quite ended.

For thirty-two years, until the World War, the government of Egypt was theoretically the same as ever, with the Khedives Tewfik and Abbas II holding office under Turkish suzerainty. But Lord Cromer, though ostensibly only British Agent and Consul

General, was the *de facto* ruler of the country. Aided by a growing staff of British civil servants who acted as advisers to every Egyptian official of importance, he held in his hands the reins of government. "Advice" from him and his assistants was all that was needed to set in motion and to bring to gradual completion the varied and radical reforms which remade Egypt in the course of one memorable generation. This veiled protectorate was a method of rule as curiously left-handed and uniquely illogical as it was astonishingly effective. The unobtrusive mastery of "the great proconsul," who accepted full responsibility without demanding executive authority, wrought wonders for the social and material welfare of the people. These years of change brought to them financial stability, economic prosperity, even-handed justice, and honest and humane administration. The one notable failure was in the field of education, for the primary purpose of the system introduced by the British was the provision of clerks for government service. In consequence, not only was popular education neglected but no effort was exerted to train for future self-government the upper classes who were certain in time to demand it.

The first Protestant body to begin missionary work in Egypt in the nineteenth century was the English Church Missionary Society. As early as 1815, the Society had established a "Mediterranean Mission" with its center at Malta, where a printing press was set up and where versions of the New Testament in Arabic, modern Greek, and other tongues were published for use in the Near East. In 1825 the C. M. S. sent out to Egypt five Germans, who had been trained at the Basel Seminary, including Samuel Gobat (later Bishop in Jerusalem), W. Krusé, and J. R. T. Lieder. Restrained from direct work with Moslems by the same severe limitations which later confronted other evangelists in Turkey and Syria, they confined their labors chiefly to the Coptic Christians. Since for many years they met with no opposition from the Coptic Patriarch or his clergy, they found a free opening for the sale and distribution of the Scriptures and of Christian tracts. They were even allowed to preach in Coptic churches and monasteries; and, taking full advantage of their opportunities as colporteurs and preachers, they made frequent and extensive tours throughout the Delta and up the Nile as far as Nubia. At Cairo they established a girls' day school and a boarding school for boys, which had grown by 1842 into a theological seminary for Coptic clergy. Services, too, were held at several places in the capital, with the same intent—to promote the spread of evangelical Christianity among the Copts.

For a time these efforts to revive the Coptic Church, especially by reforming its clergy, seemed likely to meet with success. But the quality of candidates for the seminary proved to be so poor that the institution was closed in 1848. Moreover, the government began to be suspicious of anything like a Christian revival and encouraged the most conservative elements among the Copts to win full control over their Church's policy. In the face of this strong reaction, the missionary group, already reduced to two men, was further weakened in 1852 by the transfer of Krusé to Palestine, so that Lieder alone remained. Since his work was thenceforth largely with English-speaking residents, the C. M. S. officially ended the Mission in 1862. An estimate of its record for a generation may fairly be given in the words of Bishop Gobat:

Besides the dissemination of the Word of God and other good books in all parts of Egypt, and the scriptural though imperfect education of youth, the results of the Mission were the conversion of a few individuals, some of whom have died in the faith, a few enlightened young men dispersed through Egypt—while many members of the different communities have been led to doubt the truth of their superstitions and traditions. Yet upon the whole it must be confessed that the Egyptian Mission has not had the success which might have been expected.[1]

Just as the C. M. S. enterprise was gradually fading out, new Protestant forces arrived to found a mission which has since become the largest and strongest in Egypt. In 1854 there arrived in Cairo the first three representatives of the "American Mission," sent out by the United Presbyterian Church.[2] As with the Congregationalists in Turkey and Syria, their commission was to

[1] Watson, *In the Valley of the Nile*, pp. 130 f.

[2] A small body, chiefly centered in Pennsylvania, which was formed in 1858 by the union of two sects. Strictly speaking, the Mission was originated by only one of these—the Associate Reformed Church of the West.

preach the gospel wherever it was needed—to Moslems, Jews, or Christians. But again like their compatriots elsewhere, they found that only the native Christians were accessible, and soon their attention was largely concentrated upon the Copts. Their methods, quite naturally, were those of their English predecessors —preaching, personal work, the distribution of religious literature, and the opening of small schools. By the year 1857 the Mission had established a second station at Alexandria, with schools for both boys and girls; and between 1865 and 1869 Assiut, Medinet-al-Fayum, and Mansura were occupied.

The C. M. S. Mission had consistently refused to organize its converts into separate groups, and the American Mission in Turkey and Syria had refrained from this step until persecution drove them to take it. But the United Presbyterians proceeded almost at once to receive converts into their own body. As early as 1860 the first presbytery was formed, and three years later the first native congregation was organized at Cairo. An independent Protestant Church, therefore, instead of being the result of persecution, was at least in part the cause of it. For in the year 1867 violent opposition began to be manifest. Supported by the authority and influence of the government, the Coptic Patriarch and his leading clergy set themselves to stamp out this alarming new movement. A bull of denunciation was read in all the churches, Protestant books were collected and burned, and at a number of places Egyptian Protestants were attacked and beaten in the streets. Yet compared with the sufferings of evangelical Christians in Turkey and Syria, the disturbances in Egypt were mild and of brief duration. In spite of interdicts and threats, the young Church continued to expand, so that by 1870 in the two organized congregations and among smaller groups elsewhere there were 180 communicants and 11 schools.

During the next twenty-five years progress in nearly every direction was almost unbroken. By the close of that period the native Church included 33 organized congregations, with 19 ordained Egyptians and 4,500 communicants. It was in 1899 that these were later organized into four presbyteries constituting the Synod of the Nile. Among the 119 schools with their 8,000 pupils were now to be counted large girls' boarding schools at Cairo, Assiut, and Luxor, a theological seminary at Cairo, and a thriving college for men at Assiut, founded by Dr. John Hogg. Three more important towns in the Delta had just been occupied— Tanta, Zagazig, and Benha. Everywhere, however, the work was almost wholly with Coptic Christians. Yet opportunities for reaching Moslems were not entirely neglected. Partly by the sale of the Scriptures and the use of controversial literature but chiefly through the schools, in which about a third of the pupils were Mohammedan, there was contact with Islam. And in the year 1896 Dr. Andrew Watson estimated that since the Mission began, 75 Moslems, most of them from the lower classes, had been baptized.

The next fifteen years of work were attended with such success that by the year 1910 the figures for native clergy, communicants, and pupils in the schools had more than doubled. By this time, too, the openings for an approach to Moslems had increased, for there were 4,000 Moslem boys and girls in the schools, hundreds of women in harems were in touch with the women evangelists, and there were now two hospitals in operation at Assiut and Tanta. Yet very few of the 90 or more missionaries were equipped for evangelizing Moslems; the center of interest was elsewhere; and it was seldom that more than 6 or 8 conversions from Islam were annually recorded.

Long before this date the Church Missionary Society had reëntered Egypt. The British occupation of the country in 1882 offered a stimulating opportunity to renew the endeavor which had been abandoned twenty years earlier; and the Society determined to found a new Mission which should be inspired by the sole purpose to win Moslems. The first step was to transfer to Egypt a German member of the Palestine Mission, the Rev. F. A. Klein, who was already distinguished as an Arabic scholar. In Cairo he not only continued his literary work but began to hold public services in Arabic, and opened a reading room to which Mohammedans resorted in large numbers. Seven years later, at the urgent suggestion of Klein, Dr. F. J. Harpur, who had been serving at Aden, was sent to Egypt to begin medical work at Old

Cairo. By the end of the century the Mission was still small and feebly manned; but new hospital buildings had been erected, schools in Cairo had been opened, and women missionaries were active both in teaching and in visiting Moslem homes. Yet the nineteenth century had almost ended before any mission in Egypt had produced a leader ready to give himself entirely to direct evangelism among Moslems.

The outstanding pioneer in this hardest of vocations was Douglas M. Thornton, a Cambridge graduate who had been at work for some years in the Student Volunteer Movement in England and who volunteered for service in Egypt under the C. M. S. Arriving in Cairo toward the close of the year 1898, he set himself at once to prepare for a task long neglected and bristling with difficulties—the presentation of the Christian message to educated Moslems. It was an enterprise for which Cairo was an ideal center, for, unlike other cities in the Near East, it is a famous seat of Islamic learning, the home of the great Azhar University, which for centuries has drawn thousands of students from all over the world of Islam. It was likewise the center of whatever European education was then available to Egyptians. As Thornton's biographer puts it,

"Educated Mohammedans" is a term embracing very divergent types. These divergences, however, reduce themselves to two main classes, between which there is a great gulf fixed: those who have had a traditional Islamic education ending with the Azhar University, and those who have had a Western education ending with the Government Secondary School or Higher College. In dress the same divergence is for the most part marked; the former (the "Sheikh" class) wearing orthodox Oriental costume, and the latter (the "Effendi" class) wearing Western dress, with "tarboosh" (or fez).[3]

The plans which Thornton wrote out to guide his future work in Egypt are significant not only because they foretold what were to be the achievements of his short career, but even more because they offer us a remarkable forecast of what have been ever since the chief methods and policies of the C. M. S. in Egypt. Among them were these ambitious agenda: (1) *evangelizing the educated men of Cairo*—by Bible and other classes; by personal interviews,

[3] Gairdner, *D. M. Thornton*, p. 73.

controversial or apologetic or otherwise; by evangelistic services; (2) *evangelizing by literature*—the whole Arabic-reading Moslem world by means of Arabic literature; conference of all workers among Moslems for expediting this end; (3) *training*—training workers by means of Bible classes; training them by advanced classes; a hostel for promoting these ends; training missionaries by residence in Cairo as being the literary and intellectual center of Islam. Nor did he or his successors forget that no missionary to Moslems in Egypt can afford to neglect the Copts. A further item, then, was (4) *helping the Copts*—in Scripture instruction; in encouraging their priests; in literature; through their theological students; in their missionary life.[4]

During the eight years before his premature death in 1907, Thornton labored with an energy so unremitting and so contagious that a large part of his designs was carried into vigorous action. In nearly all these enterprises, his companion and complement was the Rev. W. H. Temple Gairdner, who joined him in 1899. An Oxford graduate of brilliance and charm, who, like his friend, had been a leader in the Student Volunteer Movement, Gairdner carried on for more than twenty years after Thornton's death the endeavors they had begun by sharing. Thornton and Gairdner opened a religious bookshop, with adjoining rooms for reading and for conference. Through the opportunities afforded by the chance to sell the Gospels or to welcome the passers-by, they soon came into touch with a growing number of sheikhs and effendis and found opportunities for friendship and for personal work. To reach larger audiences and to make a wider impression, Thornton advertised and organized public meetings which he addressed on general topics. Some were for effendis who could understand English, others in Arabic for the sheikhs. In course of time many of these gatherings were given freedom for questions and discussion, often with lively results; for when groups of Azhar students were in attendance, controversy would wax warm, and meetings would sometimes break up in disorder. Progress among the effendis, however, met with less friction, and Thornton was even invited to speak at their own societies, so

4 *Ibid.*, p. 125.

that each year his effect upon students grew more marked. In the last years of his life the range of his influence was extended by two tours to several important centers in Upper Egypt, where he delivered evangelistic addresses to thousands of Copts and Moslems.

Before the close of Thornton's ministry, the two colleagues had initiated the literary work which Gairdner was to continue with such distinction and success, for both of them realized the immense value of Christian literature as a pioneer agency for reaching the educated classes. Besides developing and enlarging the meager supply of booklets and tracts which the Mission had been able to offer, they began in 1905 an Arabic monthly periodical, *Orient and Occident*. Twenty-five years later the magazine had more than 3,000 subscribers in fourteen Moslem countries. Thus, by one means or another, every avenue was explored by which those groups in Islam which had hitherto been most inaccessible could be reached and won. Very few indeed, as might be expected, were brought to the point of baptism—perhaps forty or fifty in the first ten years and only a fraction of these from the student class. What was even more important for the future was the skillful and fearless experimentation, which showed what could be done by concentration of purpose and which originated and tested the varied methods which the next generation could follow with brighter promise of success.

The decade which witnessed the joint efforts of Thornton and Gairdner saw the founding in Egypt of two other agencies which shared in their aims. In 1898 there was established the Egypt General Mission, an interdenominational body of British Protestants, whose missionaries were laymen and lay women and whose central purpose was the evangelization of Moslems. Representing no one Church, they have organized no group of their own but have urged their converts to join other bodies, in most cases the Evangelical Church. With the same special concern for the Christian approach to the Moslem, the Nile Mission Press was founded in 1905 to provide literature in Arabic. As an interdenominational society, it aims to serve the needs of all the missions in Egypt. In the course of the last generation it has issued 800 different publications and during the year 1938 distributed 500,000 books and tracts for readers in at least 12 countries.

Another encouraging event in this period was the Conference of Missionaries to Mohammedans, held at Cairo in April, 1906, the first gathering of its kind in the history of the Church. Organized by the Rev. S. M. Zwemer, of the Arabian Mission, it drew together more than sixty delegates from nearly every Moslem land. For six days they conferred, through the reading of papers and discussion, upon the state of the cause in each country and upon the many problems, methods, and policies which were of common interest. As a memorial of their meeting, they later published two volumes of addresses and papers, and issued to the churches of the Protestant world an appeal for renewed effort and increasing support. The conference not only helped to guide and strengthen the work of all its scattered members. It served to remind Christians far and wide that missions to Moslems were no longer a series of isolated and negligible endeavors, but a coöperative enterprise of growing strength, the beginning of a campaign that was to be pressed with unswerving determination.

The opening decade of the twentieth century, during which the evangelization of Moslems showed signs of a new vitality, was a period of ferment in the public life of Egypt. After the retirement of Lord Cromer in 1907, the spread of nationalism, which had not been formidable since 1882, began once more to be manifest. Though the mild administration of his successor, Sir Elden Gorst (1907-11), afforded it room for growth, its activities were firmly repressed by Lord Kitchener, who ruled Egypt until the World War. In 1914 Egypt was declared a Protectorate, the Khedive Abbas II was deposed, and Ismail's son Husain was appointed Sultan. For the next five years British control became open and direct, and, under the stress of war conditions, nationalism was driven below the surface. Throughout these years, however, the fellahin (the peasant population) accumulated many grievances, such as compulsion to volunteer for the army's Labor Corps and the loss of crops and livestock, for which compensation was always slow and inadequate. All classes, moreover, noted the growing deterioration of British personnel and resented the harsh methods employed by the local Egyptian authorities in towns and villages. By the time of the Armistice, then, the fellahin had for the first time grown hostile to British rule, so that the nationalist outbreak which followed was supported by a wave of intense popular feeling. Its vigorous leader Zaghlul headed a delegation (the Wafd) calling for complete independence and demanding representation at Paris. When both claims were denied and Zaghlul deported, the whole of Egypt began to stir with revolt; and violent disorders wracked the country for weeks before they were suppressed by armed forces. During the next three years negotiations and concessions alternated with demonstrations and riots. The upshot was a compromise—a Declaration by Great Britain published in February, 1922, which announced that the Protectorate was ended and that Egypt was to be thenceforth an independent sovereign state. The Sultan Fuad (Husain's successor in 1917) was proclaimed King, and fourteen months later there was promulgated a national constitution. But along with these large concessions went unpopular restrictions. Certain phases of government were "reserved" to Great Britain, pending satisfactory negotiations in the future. The British were to assume responsibility for guarding the Suez Canal; they were to retain a garrison in Egypt to preserve the country from foreign interference; and the protection of minorities and of foreign interests was to be secured by the dominating presence of a British High Commissioner. Since the political events of the next thirteen years are too numerous and complicated to form part of a missionary sketch, it will suffice to note that nationalism, represented chiefly by the Wafdist party under its leaders Zaghlul and Nahas, continued to press, in and out of the parliament, for complete independence, and that a succession of High Commissioners contrived with varying degrees of firmness to maintain the reserved powers of Great Britain. During this restless era, two constitutions were successively in operation, premiers rose and fell, and parliament was occasionally suppressed for long periods. At four different times negotiations between British ministers and Egyptian premiers produced treaties to end the deadlock, but none of them was ratified. Finally, in August, 1936, there was signed in London a treaty which brought the long struggle to a close. The treaty provided that the independence of Egypt should be rendered complete by the ending of military occupation, the admission of Egypt to the League of Nations, and the exchange of ambassadors between the two countries. In return, Egypt agreed to a military alliance with Great Britain and to the quartering of British troops in the zone of the Canal. It was further agreed that with the consent of the Powers the "Capitulations," which had given them extraterritorial rights, should be abolished by the action of a conference, which was held at Montreux in 1937. Fifty-four years after the British occupation began, Egypt thus achieved full sovereignty; and today, under its popular young king, Faruk I, and with its growing population of 16,000,000, the country has taken its place in the community of free nations.

From the point of view of missions, these political developments have been far less important than those cultural changes which were proceeding at the same time and at a steadier pace. For though nationalism involves a struggle against the political domination of the West, it does not exclude a widespread enthusiasm for Western thought, Western customs, and Western standards of education and social life.

During the last twenty years the improvement in the status of women in the cities has been encouraging. Among the educated of the middle and upper classes in Cairo and Alexandria, the veil has been almost wholly discarded; and while polygamy is still legal, legislation (not wholly effective) has fixed the minimum age for the marriage of girls at sixteen. At least the professions of teaching and nursing are open to women, and a few have begun to find their way even into medicine and law. It is in education, however, that the most notable advances have been made, for not only are parents awakening to the need for training their daughters, but the government has been energetic in providing opportunities. Twenty years ago there were no government secondary schools for girls and only a few primary schools. Today there are about 1,500 girls in government secondary schools and nearly 5,000 in the primary schools. But if we include those in the village elementary schools and a smaller number in private schools, we

find more than 400,000 girls in all grades, with a ratio to boys
of four to seven, a truly remarkable showing for a Moslem country. At the other end of the scale is the Egyptian University,
which for ten years has admitted women on equal terms with men
and where some 375 girls are now studying.[5]

But schools for girls are only part of a long series of reforms
which during the last twenty years have remade the educational
system of Egypt. When the British entered the country, there
were thousands of Moslem *kuttabs,* village schools teaching a little
reading and much memorizing of the Koran. Progress before the
war consisted chiefly in improving the quality of these schools
by subsidies conditional upon higher standards and in beginning
slowly the organization of government primary and secondary
schools with a Western curriculum. But little money and less
enthusiasm went into the cause of education, and the whole
system was inadequate and inefficient. Since 1922, however, rapid
advances have been made both in quantity and in quality. By
1933 the number of schools had so increased that it was feasible
to pass legislation making education compulsory for all children
between the ages of seven and twelve, though facilities still remain unequal to their training. Yet the improved *kuttabs,* still
the base of the pyramid, are now teaching about 843,000 children.
The government primary schools, with a European course of
study, include over 30,000 pupils; and even in the secondary
schools, now 41 in number, there are some 18,500 boys and girls.
At the peak of the educational structure is the Egyptian University—refounded and reformed in 1925—which comprises 8 different faculties, the most popular of which are those of Arts,
Medicine, Law, Engineering, Commerce, and Agriculture. In all
departments over 9,000 students are now to be counted.

The quality of education has been improved through the en-
richment of the curricula by a greater variety of modern subjects
and through raising the standards of teacher training by the development of two Institutes of Pedagogy. Nor has the need been
forgotten to provide industrial, technical, and agricultural schools
of both elementary and secondary grade. Most recent among the

[5] Not counting a larger number in the School for Nurses.

reforms has been the movement to encourage such extracurricular activities as athletic sports and musical, dramatic, and gardening clubs. Yet it would be wrong to give the impression that quality has kept pace with quantity. The constant entanglement of education with politics, the passion for bureaucratic centralization, the lack of interest in the individual, and the exaggerated value attaching to examinations—all operate to keep education in Egypt well below the best standards of Europe and indeed below the best that Christian schools and colleges can offer.

Outside this Westernized framework stand the ancient Azhar University and its subsidiary schools, representing the Moslem heritage of the past. Founded in Cairo in the year 988, with the mosque of al-Azhar as its center, the university in modern times has often included as many as 18,000 pupils in its whole system, with perhaps half that number studying in Cairo. The training begins with young boys in the lesser schools and ends with four years of advanced work at the central mosque, where the old curriculum is maintained—Moslem law, tradition, and theology, the exegesis of the Koran, together with logic, grammar, and rhetoric. Though hundreds of students are drawn from every quarter of the Moslem world, more than nine-tenths are Egyptians. Until recent times it was easy to attract large numbers, for instruction was free and open to all classes, and graduates could find positions as sheikhs of village mosques or teachers in village schools, while the gifted could rise still higher.

Nine centuries saw little or no alteration either in the methods or the matter of teaching. Some forty-five years ago, however, a very few meager changes were made to modernize the curriculum, with the result that the students rioted in protest. But by 1925 the students of another generation had become acutely aware that their training was ill designed to fit them for most kinds of employment that a new Egypt was offering and they besieged the government with demands for reform. Roused by their protests and alarmed by the rapid drop in the number of entering pupils, the government proceeded to plan cautiously for the modernizing of the Azhar. Hopeful schemes, already beginning to take effect, were checked some years later by conservative obstruction, and it needed a students' strike to oust a reactionary Rector. Since 1935, however, under the Sheikh al-Maraghi, reconstruction has been firmly carried out. All instruction will soon be given outside the ancient mosque, in new buildings with up-to-date equipment. Already there is a scientific course parallel to the religious studies, and the knowledge of one foreign language is compulsory. The modernistic office from which the new Rector rules is symbolical of the changes that are yet to come.

The same spirit of nationalism manifest in political and educational reforms has recently shown itself in the growing interest in social service, especially in the active promotion of public health. Among the Egyptian masses bilharziasis, hookworm disease, pellagra, and trachoma are so prevalent that probably nine-tenths of the population suffer from one or more of these diseases. And the conditions under which children are born and reared account for a very high rate of infant mortality. In the effort to remedy these notorious evils, the government has begun to follow Western models and to reproduce nearly every type of social service hitherto confined to missionary agencies. The Department of Public Health has established more than sixty hospitals, some of which deal especially with the plagues we have mentioned. It has developed forty itinerant clinics, which care each year for several hundred thousand patients. The Child Welfare Section of the Department is responsible for a large number of baby welfare centers, children's dispensaries, and maternity schools. Increasing attention, moreover, is now paid to public health propaganda and to health education in the schools. And this concern for the welfare of the masses is not confined to government officials, for there is an encouraging growth of voluntary agencies like the Egyptian Association for Social Studies and the new Social Workers' Alliances in Cairo and Alexandria. It is unfortunately true that most of these activities are chiefly centered in the large cities and that the vast village population has still been only slightly touched. The government, however, has recently instituted a Ministry of Social Welfare, including a department for the improvement of the condition of the fellahin.

The powerful movements of the past generation, invading

every sphere of social life, have not left religion untouched. A struggle closely parallel to our own contest between fundamentalists and modernists has been slowly brewing in more than one Moslem land, and signs of it in Cairo have been evident. Of course the illiterate millions in Egypt and even the majority of their religious guides are scarcely affected by Western thought and modern science. Then, too, at the other end of the arc, are thousands with a Western education who have reacted from religion so sharply as to swing over into agnosticism and who remain Moslems only in the social and political sense. Between the two groups there are only a few genuine religious liberals. Yet they have been far more articulate and influential than their numbers would indicate. Today, however, they are less effective than they were a dozen years ago; for orthodoxy, as represented by the Azhar group, is in the ascendancy for the time being and too strong to be tampered with. Egypt, in fact, is wavering between the conservatism which puts Islam first and nationalism second and the progressive nationalism, like Turkey's, which puts Westernism first and Islam second. No clear leadership has yet arisen to make the choice definite and effective.

This hesitation between two general policies for the nation is reflected in the behavior of the government when it is called upon to deal with the problem of religious freedom.

Sometimes the one party and sometimes the other gains the ascendancy and, as a consequence, there arises a frequent fluctuation in policy and in the government's attitude on questions of religious liberty. On the whole, however, it would be true to say that Egypt's newly acquired independence has strengthened the position of the more conservative elements.[6]

Certain clauses in the constitution seem to offer adequate safeguards for complete freedom in religion. The constitution guarantees absolute liberty of conscience and the free exercise of every religion not conflicting with public order and good morals. It even provides that past laws are to remain in force only if they conform to the principles set forth in the constitution. There is no method, however, by which an appeal can be taken to the

6 Morrison, in "The Church and the State," Madras Series, VI, 90 f.

constitution from a decision made in the lower courts. Further-more, there is an article of the constitution which declares that "Islam is the religion of the State," a clause which can easily be cited to give Islam a preferred position in all cases of doubt or conflict. To these legal points must be added the obvious fact, of broader significance and fraught with greater danger, that the population of Egypt is more than 90 percent Moslem and that chronic hostility to Christianity can readily become acute.

The practical situation which results from these factors, and with which the Christian forces must reckon, is that there is still no way of registering officially a conversion from Islam to Chris-tianity. The only form of registration recognized by the govern-ment is that *to* Islam. The convert to Christianity, therefore, suffers not only social persecution but serious legal disabilities. He cannot claim inheritance from his Moslem relatives, and his wife is usually separated from him. Should the convert be a woman, she is in even worse case, for if she is unmarried her person can be claimed by her father or guardian and if she is married, by her husband. She will thus be subjected to every kind of pressure in a wholly Moslem environment. Evangelism is restricted not only by this legal difficulty but also by the prohi-bition of all out-of-door preaching and even more by the resent-ment felt by all classes against Christian propaganda. "Moslems object to missions just because they are evangelistic and also on account of the methods they are supposed to adopt.... Missions are frequently charged with exploiting the helplessness of the sick, the poor and the young, and are said to use 'moral' and 'spiritual' coercion to effect a change of faith." [7] "The government is frequently called upon 'to defend Islam' against the evangelis-tic activities of the Christian Church, and it usually does so not by forbidding evangelism as such, but by charges against evange-lists of attacking Islam and so endangering the public peace." [8] Hostility roused by these deep-seated prejudices led to a violent antimissionary campaign in press and parliament during the years between 1932 and 1934, an agitation which has since died down.

It is an environment characterized by the many modern changes

[7] *Ibid.*, p. 99.   [8] *Ibid.*, p. 93.

we have reviewed as well as by the persistence of ancient traditions that the missionary work of the Churches has been conducted for the past thirty years. As we survey its status and its policies today, the feature which most readily attracts attention is the enterprise of education. Here the restrictions and control imposed by government are less severe than in certain other Moslem lands such as Turkey and Iran. Christian churches or missions are allowed to conduct schools of all grades. But those under government inspection and receiving government aid must relieve Moslem pupils by a "conscience clause" which permits them to avoid Christian teaching if they so desire. Moslem children may even receive their compulsory education in Christian elementary schools if they can certify to their instruction in Islam at home or in some other school. Recently, however, the government has begun to exert pressure upon Christian institutions to provide this Islamic teaching for their Moslem pupils. But for the time being at least, the authority of the state is rather more a restraint upon educational methods than upon religious liberty. For the intense and widespread ambition to obtain certificates from primary and secondary schools, as a step toward employment in government service, tends to press all the mission schools into the government mold and to standardize them at an illiberal level. Nearly all the institutions, even including those for girls, have to contend with this threat to some of the higher values of education.

The greater part of the Christian elementary education, begun by the United Presbyterian Mission, is carried on at present by the Evangelical Church, which is responsible for 174 schools with 17,000 pupils. The Egypt General Mission conducts only 7 such schools and the C. M. S. only 5. Save for one boys' school under the C. M. S., the Christian high schools and boarding schools are those of the U. P. Mission, whose 7 institutions—5 for girls and 2 for boys—now include about 1,500 students. The same mission offers training of a still higher grade at Assiut College for boys and at the Cairo Girls' College which have long furnished most of the Christian leadership for all missionary organizations in the Nile Valley. Most of the 600 or more students at Assiut are

Protestant or Coptic Christians; but in the smaller Girls' College the percentage of Moslems is far higher. The same college enjoys the further advantage of such complete detachment from the government system that it is able to give its own emphasis to moral and cultural training. Small as these totals may seem in summary form, they represent an enterprise of long standing which is responsible for the fact that while only 11 percent of Moslems are literate, the percentage for Copts is nearly twice as high and for Protestant Egyptians more than three times.

The special contributions which justify the Christian schools are partly educational and partly religious. The great majority of the elementary schools, under the care of the native Evangelical Church, are ill equipped, staffed by miserably paid teachers, and, though they are attended by a fair proportion of Moslems, their chief justification is that they enable Christian children to avoid attendance at Moslem schools. But the few primary schools conducted by the missions, together with their high schools and boarding schools, offer advantages seldom found under the government system. Despite the influence of the latter, they still show a greater flexibility and readiness to experiment with new methods and types of training. They lay greater stress upon preparation for the life of the home and the community. They are more active in promoting extracurricular activities and in developing school spirit. Of far higher value is their Christian quality, manifest not only in continuous and definite religious instruction but in worship, in the personal influence of the teacher, and in the reality of their character-training. It is these factors, wherever they are vital, which mark them as indispensable aids in the indirect approach to Islam.

Independent of missionary control and only partly aligned with the government system, the American University at Cairo is the only Christian institution which supplies education of full college grade. Like the American University of Beirut, it is incorporated in the United States with an interdenominational board of trustees. After several years of planning and organization by Dr. Charles R. Watson, Dr. Robert S. McClenahan, and others, the university was opened in 1920, with Dr. Watson as president and

with two departments in operation, the Preparatory School and
the School of Oriental Studies. At the close of twenty years of
steady development, the university now includes four departments. The College of Arts and Sciences embraces three courses—
a Secondary School which strictly follows the government curriculum, a Junior College offering six years of work leading to
the University of London Matriculation Certificate, and a Senior
College with a course of three years leading to the degree of
Bachelor of Arts. In all these groups the students number about
270, including 12 girls. Three-quarters of them are Egyptians
and more than a third are Moslems. The Division of Extension
has been notably successful in promoting the education of the
public through lectures, forums, and educational films, at which
the annual attendance runs as high as 30,000. The Department
of Education is still in a rudimentary state so far as instruction
goes. Its most valuable activity is the publication of the *Journal
of Modern Education* (the first Arabic magazine in this field),
which has proved influential in Egypt and which counts among
its subscribers the government educational authorities in the
Sudan, Palestine, Iraq, India, Tripoli, the Hejaz, and Sumatra.
The School of Oriental Studies had been in operation for eight
years before the university was opened. Begun under the leadership of Gairdner and Zwemer as a center for teaching Arabic and
Islamics to missionaries, it has since sent out hundreds of trained
workers to all parts of the Arabic-speaking field.

So far as numbers go, the college is handicapped by living
under the shadow of the powerful Egyptian University, which is
naturally the first choice of most Moslem parents. But in maintaining the values of a liberal education, in reproducing some
of the virtues of American undergraduate life, and in the enlightenment of the Egyptian public the university renders service
that has been widely recognized. From the missionary point of
view, its contribution has been a steadfast insistence upon its
Christian purpose. While shunning the methods of direct evangelism, its teachers succeed in making religion interesting and
in presenting Christianity in an atmosphere of friendly discussion
and tolerant give-and-take, as appropriate to a university as it is

unfamiliar to the tense bigotry of the Egyptian environment.

The forces of Christian education in Egypt are further strengthened by those other undenominational institutions, the Y.M.C.A. and the Y.W.C.A. Each is represented by active centers, chiefly at Cairo and Alexandria. The facilities they afford for athletics, for educational classes, and for social life are all the more valued in a society where wholesome alternatives are much rarer than in America and where rival opportunities of the same sort are so few.

As in other Mohammedan countries, medical work has proved in Egypt a mode of approach of almost unrivaled value; and for some fifty years both the American Mission and the C. M. S. have maintained medical service of growing extent. The United Presbyterians have hospitals at Tanta and at Assiut. The latter is large enough to care for 2,300 inpatients every year in addition to 22,000 out-patients; and its leper clinic and nurses' training school enable it to make a distinctive contribution. At Shebin is the hospital of the Egypt General Mission. Besides a hospital at Menouf and four dispensaries elsewhere, the C. M. S. supports at Old Cairo the most famous and influential hospital in Egypt. Expanding gradually from a small nucleus, it has long been treating an average of 25,000 new patients annually, the large majority of whom are of course Moslems. On the medical side alone its achievements during a generation have been a blessing to the country. By specializing in the treatment of bilharziasis and in the care of sufferers from the hookworm disease (at least 6,000 of whom attend the clinics each year), the doctors at Old Cairo have rendered distinguished service in the fight against the worst plagues in Egypt. Reaching out from their city headquarters, the members of the staff have always maintained the closest contact with village life and with the rural population through the use of house boats and country outstations and medical mission camps. No hospital, moreover, has ever taken more seriously or exploited more effectively its opportunities as a center of evangelism. Prayer is offered before every operation. In every ward, morning and evening, and in the waiting rooms for the out-patients both physicians and evangelists share in conducting Christian services with short addresses. Many Moslems, too, are ready to buy portions of Scriptures and to receive leaflets on Christian themes. But beyond the effort to reach the patients who are present at any one time, the hospital has extended its influence by frequent tours of itineration in the more accessible of the thousand towns and villages from which former patients have come. Through the use of careful records this follow-up work has led to many openings for personal evangelism.

On a smaller scale than the strictly medical work are new forms of missionary social service which have begun to prove effective in touching the lives of many Moslems hitherto unreached. Among these is an educational center for the blind, where handwork and the use of Arabic Braille are taught. To meet the needs of quite different groups, several of the missions have started child-welfare centers at various points in Cairo. Perhaps the most interesting of the recent experiments in service is the Boulac Social Settlement begun by the C. M. S. and now under the direction of the native Anglican Church. Founded in 1925 as a small club for boys in vicious slum surroundings, its growing activities with girls and mothers and little children have helped to change the atmosphere of a whole neighborhood and to express the meaning of Christianity in welcome terms unknown before to hostile Moslems.

Schools, hospitals, and social-service agencies not only afford innumerable opportunities for evangelism. If they are genuinely Christian, they are themselves forms of evangelism—modes, that is, by which the Christian message can be expressed and the Christian spirit embodied. Yet there still remains that direct work of the Church as such which we commonly call evangelistic. In Egypt, as we have seen, it is concerned with the effort to present Christianity both to Copts and to Moslems.

The American Mission of the United Presbyterians is the only mission of importance which has long concentrated upon the aim to win Copts to evangelical Christianity. In furthering that purpose, as our review has shown, it has relied chiefly on building up a strong native Protestant Church. In 1926 this Evangelical Church in Egypt though retaining organic connection with the parent body in the United States, became entirely self-governing, self-supporting, and independent. Its autonomy was made possible by separating the organized churches, the Theological Seminary, and the missionary work in the Sudan from the unorganized congregations and small bodies of enquirers. It is the former group of institutions which constitutes the Evangelical Church, over which missionaries have no further control save as a very small minority in presbyteries and in the Synod. The Church now includes 155 Egyptian clergy, 150 organized congregations, and 22,000 members. In what it has done for these thousands, past and present, who have left their ancestral Church lies the most obvious achievement of the American Mission. In making better Christians out of poor Christians its enterprise has succeeded, for the Evangelical Church maintains a vastly higher level than the Coptic, not merely in general enlightenment but in Christian morality and religious vitality.

When the Church Missionary Society reëntered Egypt in 1882, its declared purpose, as we have noted, was to be the evangelism of the Moslem population. In contrast with the policy of the American Mission, the C. M. S., therefore, deliberately avoided the organization of an Anglican Church at the expense of the Coptic Church. It chose for a while to neglect the development of a native Church, rather than to neglect the direct approach to Moslems. In course of time, however, the formation of an Anglican Communion became inevitable. At several points there had grown up small congregations for whose care the Mission was responsible. Some of their members were Syrians from Palestine, some were Copts in the service of the Mission, and an increasing number were converts from Islam. To meet the needs of these varied types of Christians and to give them such corporate life as would increase their evangelistic power, there was founded in 1925 "The Episcopal Church in Egypt in communion with the Anglican Church." But only those are admitted who are prepared to endorse the principle, officially formulated, that this Church has "no other objective than to preach the Gospel of Christ among those in Egypt who know Him not, that is, the Mohammedans, and [that it] is still working with this as its sole primary aim." The new Church, with its own Council, has since taken over from the C. M. S. the responsibility for the literary, social, and evangelistic work. Three Egyptians have already been ordained to the ministry, and in the four churches there are 658 baptized members.

In spite of its small size and its characteristic emphasis upon the approach to Islam, the C. M. S. mission has had a perceptible effect on the Coptic Church. Just because it does not appear as a dangerous rival, its leaders have long been able to enjoy cordial relations with the Coptic clergy, to offer counsel and encouragement to those who sought reform, and to enlist the interest of Copts in the movement toward Christian unity, to which we shall later refer. The American Mission, on the other hand, following an opposite policy, has always met with official Coptic opposition, ranging all the way from the earlier persecution to the present state of none-too-friendly truce. Yet the expansion of its vigorous offspring, the Evangelical Church, however unwelcome it may have been, has been a factor in the life of Christian Egypt far too powerful to be ignored.

If in some degree or other it has been one aim of all the missions to work toward the reform of the Coptic Church, what has been the result of their endeavors? That there has always been urgent need for reform is beyond question. Honor is due to the million Copts of Egypt and to their ancestors during many centuries for their fidelity to a persecuted faith. The mere existence of the Church today is a tribute to their tradition of loyalty. But it is no secret that the Coptic Church is one of the poorest specimens of organized Christianity now on exhibition. And it is under the daily observation of some 15,000,000 Moslems, who have long since drawn their own conclusions. The majority of the priests are deplorably uneducated, many unable to read the ancient Coptic of the liturgy and some unable even to read Arabic. Their prevailing ignorance of the essentials of Christian life and doctrine and their impotence as spiritual leaders account for the low moral tone of most of their people and for the widespread superstition which always flourishes in darkness. Among the masses of the village population, in fact, there is all too little difference, either in morality or in popular belief, between Copts and Moslems. The tradition which keeps them separate is more nearly loyalty to a community than loyalty to a life or a faith. And even that tradition is insecure, for there is a steady drift from Coptic Christianity to Islam. Seldom instructed in their own faith at home or at school or in church, the Christians are often a prey to the many inducements to join the confident and urgent majority. The motive is almost never religious. It is rather the desire to obtain a Moslem wife or a Moslem husband, or the need to secure a position in government or commercial service. The missions, in consequence, are faced with the discouraging fact that if ten or twenty Moslems turn each year to Christianity, there are perhaps four or five hundred Copts who permanently embrace Islam.

But the long years of missionary pressure upon the ancient Church have not been without effect. Whatever might be the results of other methods, it must be granted that

the building up of the Evangelical Church and the reaction caused thereby, did more to revive the Coptic Church than all the previous efforts directed to this end. The present movement toward reform is strongest just where the Evangelical Church and its influence are the greatest. Experience has abundantly proved, therefore, that the revival of the Coptic Church from within, and the formation of evangelical congregations without, are not opposed to each other, but rather lend each other mutual support.[9]

More than a generation ago signs of change had begun to appear, chiefly among younger laymen, in the formation of societies and the publication of journals to promote reforms, in the use of lay preachers in certain churches, and in the agitation for providing Christian teaching for Copts in government schools. All such tokens of life, however, were resisted for many years by the hierarchy headed by the Patriarch. But the Patriarch "Cyril V died at a great age in 1927, having governed his Church for fifty-two years and having on the whole successfully opposed all reforms good and bad."[10] After a year of quarreling, a new Patriarch was elected, who had pledged himself to certain reforms.

[9] Stanley, "The Policy of the Christian Church in Egypt," *Church Missionary Review,* June, 1922, p. 152. [10] Attwater, *The Dissident Eastern Churches,* p. 242.

But as he was the leader of the conservative party, the chance for any radical improvements is slight. The groups now working for revival are largely recruited from among those laymen whose education has been of the Western type and who are striving, with little support from the ecclesiastical authorities, to improve the education of the clergy and to purify the corrupt financial administration of the Church. Several societies of lay workers have been formed, such as The Friends of the Bible, The Society of Faith, and The Society for the Revival of the Church. And a few of their more enthusiastic members are active in preaching to unenlightened Copts and in developing Coptic village schools.

The efforts to evangelize Copts and to invigorate the Coptic Church form an indispensable part of the Christian approach to Islam in Egypt, because "the key to the problem of Moslem evangelism lies in the hands of the indigenous Churches." For foreign missions to confine themselves wholly to work either with Copts or with Moslems is to ignore one essential factor in the total process. It is only through coöperation with Copts, orthodox and Protestant, that the enterprise can be pursued with any hope of success. What, then, is the present record of the native Christian bodies as forces in evangelizing the Moslem?

Accustomed to the status of a tolerated minority, commonly despised and sometimes oppressed, the Coptic Church has never attempted the task of converting Moslems. Under a Moslem government it has been able to maintain its existence only by remaining quietly inoffensive. Faced with the choice between static submission and wholesale martyrdom, it has chosen static submission. And only those Christians who are ready to run risks which the Copts have declined are in any position to cast the first stone. But however disqualified we may be for passing harsh judgments, the fact must be noted that today the Coptic Church, as a body, is completely indifferent to the cause of winning Mohammedans and finds it difficult even to imagine such an enterprise to be either possible or advisable. Neither the Church as a whole nor any official organization within the Church has yet committed itself to such a policy. Yet there are some signs of missionary instinct worth observing. A few Copts, for instance, attended the conference held at Cairo in 1929 to consider the relation of the indigenous Churches to Moslem evangelism. Moreover, the number of Coptic clergy who are prepared to teach and baptize enquirers is slowly increasing. More significant is the readiness of a growing number of young Coptic laymen to engage in voluntary evangelism not only among their backward fellow Christians but likewise among Moslems. Thanks to the initiative of the C. M. S. Mission, which has supplied both encouragement and training, these groups meet frequently for conference and conduct preaching centers in and around Cairo, where they speak at meetings for both Copts and Moslems.

The difference in missionary spirit between members of the Coptic Church and members of the Egyptian Evangelical Church is discouragingly slight. It had been the hope of the American Mission that the Protestant Christians would become missionaries to Moslems, but that hope has not yet been realized. In spite of their far better training in the Christian faith and its principles, they still share with the other Copts the reluctance to approach the Moslem and the conviction that genuine conversion from Islam is next to impossible. Like their fellow Christians in the ancient Church, they fear the hostility of the great Moslem majority and view with suspicion the sincerity of the few Moslems who seem drawn toward Christianity. In consequence, they count it unwise and unsafe to alter the existing equilibrium. This inherited attitude has been made all the easier to maintain by the mission policy, which has assigned to the Evangelical Church the organized congregations and which has thus promoted the tendency to regard pastoral work as the function of the native clergy and missionary work as the vocation of the foreigners. Both clergy and lay leaders, therefore, center their interest in the administrative affairs of their own Church and postpone to some happier future the unattractive task of approaching the incorrigible Moslem. Even if their readiness to expand were far greater than it is, they would still be handicapped by the fact that nearly all of them lack the knowledge and training required for effective work with Mohammedans. Indeed, the only members of the Church who are definitely engaged in preaching to Moslems are two or three converts from Islam. Among the few grounds for encouragement, we may note the greater interest and concern manifest in some of the younger clergy and laity and the very limited activity of ecclesiastical committees on work among non-Christians. Nor should we overlook the undeniable fact that the mere existence in Egypt of a Christian Church worthy of respect is a marked advantage to the cause.

Any candid review of the present status and temper of these indigenous Churches, old or young, will warrant the conclusion that they are not yet ready to pursue the evangelization of Moslems on their own initiative. For the time being the advance of the enterprise depends on the activities of the foreign Mission. And their opportunities have never been wider than during the last fifteen or twenty years. For it is agreed by all observers that ever since the first decade of the century there has been a greater ease of access to all classes of the Moslem population. The movements of nationalism and Westernization have modified the attitude of rigidity toward any kind of change. For this reason, among others less obvious, there appears an increasing readiness on the part of Mohammedans to listen to the Christian message and to study it.

A sign of these encouraging new openings and of the missionary resolve to utilize them was the Helwan Regional Conference, held in 1924. The resolutions agreed to by this gathering sum up the status of the enterprise at the point it had then reached and indicate many of the lines of development which it was later to follow. The delegates were unanimous in the conviction that the winning of non-Christian Egypt for Christ must ultimately be accomplished by the Egyptians themselves, and their report offers many suggestions for the stimulation and training of Copts toward that end. But they were equally conscious of how much still depended on their own forces. Their findings point out that the classes to be reached include the sheikhs and students of the Azhar, the effendis, the fellahin, and the hareem ladies of the upper and middle classes, each group demanding distinctive modes of approach. But while recommending a variety of methods, direct and indirect, the members were ready to assure all their fellow workers that "there is unbounded scope for evangelistic work throughout the whole country."

During the fifteen years since the conference, the missions have set themselves to answer its call with varying degrees of enthusiasm and of success. The United Presbyterians have found it difficult to shift their emphasis, for their work for Moslems has so long been accidental rather than definite or deliberate. They have not yet undertaken any organized evangelism of Moslems which can claim to be properly staffed or adequately financed at strategic centers. Very few of their older missionaries are trained to undertake the task. In the last few years, however, there has been a distinct change of attitude, especially on the part of the younger members of the Mission. No longer content with following the line of least resistance, they are ready to reach outward toward neglected opportunities for direct contact with Islam. And this new ambition is now an acknowledged feature of the Mission's program. A committee reporting to the meeting of the Mission Association in January, 1938, affirmed that "Our aim as a Mission should be to evangelize the Moslem directly as well as indirectly" and demanded that men and women should be set apart for such work and equipped with sufficient resources.

True to its original purpose, the Egypt General Mission has continued to center its activities upon evangelizing Moslems. Its sixty or more missionaries, two-thirds of whom are women, are engaged at eleven stations not only in teaching and medical service but in varied forms of evangelism. Their methods include meetings for Moslems, the production of literature, colportage, and a growing amount of work with women. In coöperation with the Nile Mission Press, the Mission has recently begun to publish a periodical journal especially designed to meet the needs of Moslem readers.

Equally loyal to the same professed aim, the C. M. S. Mission has an advantage over the Egypt General Mission in being able to operate through an indigenous Church. Its present policy, in fact, is primarily to educate the leaders and members of the native Episcopal Church to do their own evangelizing through the congregations and the literary and social agencies for which they are now responsible. The church at Gizeh, for example, sends out its members regularly to visit neighboring Moslem villages for personal work and the distribution of literature; and at the Sunday services both at Gizeh and at Menouf a considerable number of Moslems is always in attendance. The Student Evangelistic Center in the busiest part of Cairo has proved an effective means for reaching both sheikhs and effendis. For some ten years, hundreds of Moslems have been taught there through education groups, personal talks, and the active use of a lending library. The method most recently and successfully employed has been the private Bible study of individuals with a Christian teacher.

Within the Church's administration comes also the work of the Egypt Committee of the S. P. C. K.[11] Council for Egypt and Palestine, upon which has fallen the mantle of the former C. M. S. Literature Department. Built upon the foundations so firmly laid by Canon Temple Gairdner, it has ever kept before it his two-fold aim of strengthening the intellectual and devotional life of the Anglican Church, and of expounding to Moslem leaders in a clear and constructive way the riches of the Christian faith. The same motif ... inspires all efforts to promote the circulation of the Scriptures.[12]

As in Syria and Palestine, the effectiveness of the Christian forces in Egypt has been hampered by the competition of too many sects and societies, among which relations have sometimes been less than fraternal. For in addition to those we have described, there are a dozen other groups which we have ignored chiefly because their work for Moslems is negligible. To further more friendly relations and to secure more effective coöperation among the missions, the Egypt Inter-Mission Council was organized in 1920. During the past twenty years, the Council has amply justified its existence, though there are still some eight minor societies which reject even this moderate attempt at joint endeavor. Still fewer are the bodies which have affiliated with the Near East Christian Council. Both Councils are of course loose federations of Protestants and Anglicans, which aim at promoting

---

[11] The Society for Promoting Christian Knowledge.
[12] Morrison, *The Way of Partnership*, p. 73.

fellowship and at increasing efficiency. A wider scope character-
izes the Fellowship of Unity. As a result of the appeal for unity
issued by the Lambeth Conference of 1920, Bishop Gwynne, of
the Anglican Diocese of Egypt and the Sudan, founded the Fellowship in 1921, to draw together the leaders of the different
Churches, clerical and lay, for social, intellectual, and spiritual
comradeship. Since then its annual services and conferences have
been attended by representatives of the Greek Orthodox, Coptic,
Armenian, Evangelical, and Anglican Churches. Sharing the
same fundamental ideals as the Faith and Order movement
among the Churches of the world, the Fellowship in Egypt is
chiefly concerned to develop mutual understanding among separated bodies, and to work slowly toward intercommunion and
the more distant goal of organic unity. It marks the earliest stage
in the realization of that ideal upon which the winning of Islam
depends—a vigorous and united Christian Church of Egypt.

XI

Iran

IRAN, long known to the West as Persia, covers the broad area of 628,000 square miles between Iraq (Mesopotamia) on the west and Afghanistan and India on the east. Equal in size to the United States east of the Mississippi (minus the Gulf States), the country is chiefly a lofty plateau, the greater part of which is either arid or mountainous. A wide variety of temperature marks a climate that ranges from the severest cold to extreme heat. Centuries of migration and invasion have produced an extraordinary mixture of racial stock which is yet predominantly Aryan. Of Aryan origin, too, is the prevailing Iranian language, though five others, including Turkish, Kurdish, and Arabic, are spoken by millions.

Before the middle of the seventh century, the Sasanian rulers of Persia had been overthrown by the Moslem armies, and within a few generations the ancient faith of Zoroastrianism had given way before the creed of the victors. For more than twelve centuries, therefore, Iran has been a Moslem country, and since 1502 the Shiite branch of Islam has been the state religion.

At the beginning of the nineteenth century and throughout its whole course, Iran was governed by a Shah who was an absolute monarch of the oriental type, ruling through a Grand Vizier whose control extended to all departments of the government. The law administered was chiefly Shiite Moslem law; and in all legal matters the power of the mujtahids—the leading Moslem clergy—remained the one check upon the royal authority. The general state of civilization was still medieval. Corruption and bribery, injustice and oppressive taxation, prevailed in increasing measure.

From 1800 until 1922 the history of Persia revolves around

Anglo-Russian rivalry. Throughout this long period Iran was held in a vise between the two great empires, Russia slowly creeping southward and Britain, to protect India, extending its influence northward in Afghanistan and southern Iran. Before the century was half gone, Persia had given up her territory in the Caucasus, had granted extraterritoriality to the Powers, and had recognized the independence of Afghanistan. Thwarted and controlled within and without, she had yielded all real independence. By the first decade of the present century, economic concessions in the north to Russia and in the south to Britain were rapidly drawing the kingdom toward the loss of all national identity.

Before the end of the long reign of Nasr ad-Din (1848-96), Western ideas of progress and reform were already in the air; but it was not until 1906, after his weak successor Muzaffar had ruled for ten years, that there occurred a series of popular uprisings which led to the demand for a parliament and ended in the granting of a constitution by the Shah. Muzaffar, however, died in the following year, and the new Shah set himself to overthrow the constitution. Roused by his reactionary policy and indignant at the Anglo-Russian agreement of 1907, which had marked out the country into spheres of influence, the leaders of the rising nationalism took advantage of a second rebellion in 1909. Their forces succeeded in capturing the capital and replacing the Shah by his twelve-year-old son. But in spite of two revolutions, both of which had been supported by the Moslem clergy, Iran was not really ready for stable constitutional government. Domestic inefficiency and corruption and constant foreign intrigue baffled every effort of the liberal group. Before the first World War, the constitution had been practically nullified and the days of Persian independence seemed numbered.

Through the resulting four years of warfare, despite a declared neutrality, the land was a battle ground for Turkish, Russian, and British troops. Forbidden representation at Versailles, Persia was obliged in the summer of 1919 to sign an agreement with Britain which converted the country into a virtual protectorate. No wonder that a Persian patriot then declared, "Iran is a corpse, but there is no one to bury her." Yet within two years the whole situation had changed, for a leader had arisen through whom Iran has found political salvation. Seeing his native land threatened with invasion by a Bolshevik army, before which the British and Persian forces were slowly retiring, Col. Reza Khan, with the unofficial support of Britain, carried out in February, 1921, a coup d'état which gave him command of the army and virtual control of the state. Before a week had passed he had concluded a treaty with the Soviet government, which renounced all previous concessions to Russia and canceled all debts. Though Britain might thus claim to have given aid in saving Iran from the Soviets, the Soviet threat had really helped to save Iran from Britain. With a strong new independent government, the English position in the country became increasingly untenable. Within three years the last British troops had been withdrawn, and Iran was free at last from all foreign domination. Her rebirth as a nation was signalized at the close of 1925 by a vote of the National Assembly which deposed the Shah, abolished the reigning Kajar Dynasty, and conferred the crown on Reza Khan, who ascended the throne as Reza Shah Pahlavi.

For fifteen years the story of Iran has been the record of the strong rule of the new Shah, who, like his contemporary the late Kemal Atatürk, is a skillful soldier, an organizer of dynamic energy, an enthusiast for Western progress, and a passionate nationalist. Reza Shah Pahlavi, in fact, incarnates that spirit of nationalism which is at once the explanation and the inspiration of all the movements and changes which have been so rapidly transforming Iran. "Nationalism," it has been reported, "is almost a new religion, and to a large extent monopolizes the thought of leaders of the younger generation." Patriotic pride and loyalty to the throne find expression in a new sense of unity. All distinctions of dress and title have been wiped out by law, and diversities of race and religion are largely ignored by the recent reforms. For once every man is primarily an Iranian. The official change of name from Persia to Iran symbolizes a return to the great days of pre-Moslem empire, no less than does the title of the dynasty—Pahlavi.

A large standing army, supported by compulsory military service, and an efficient police force have brought under control the nomadic tribes and wandering brigands, so that internal order makes travel and commerce safe. Travel is now not only secure but increasingly easy and cheap, for more than 13,000 miles of motor roads have been completed and a railroad of 1,000 miles between the Caspian and the Persian Gulf spans the country. With motor cars and trucks superseding animals and with airplanes in growing use, journeys that once took 18 days by mule can now be made in 9 hours by auto or in 2 by plane. And 10,000 miles of telegraph keep all parts of the country in touch with one another and with the outside world.

The basis of all the rapid changes is direct legislation by an active parliament, thoroughly subservient to the Shah. Modern commercial and penal codes have been adopted over the vigorous opposition of the Moslem clergy. Nearly all the reforms, indeed, have been at the expense of the rights of the clergy and in more and more complete disregard of Moslem law and tradition. Their views and vested interests, once all-powerful, are now seldom consulted and commonly ignored. The future welfare of Iran takes precedence over the waning prestige of Islam.

From the point of view of Christian missions, no reforms are of more importance than those which have changed the position of women and completely transformed the educational system. By gradual steps, in the course of the last twelve years, and thanks in large measure to the resolute initiative of the Shah, marriage has become a civil ceremony no longer under control of the mullahs. The minimum age for women has been set at sixteen, in defiance of Moslem custom; the wife is given the right to sue for divorce in certain cases; and the use of the veil has been strictly forbidden. One immediate result has been that many new careers, such as nursing, stenography, and teaching, have been thrown open to women. And still more important has been the increasing demand for the education of girls.

Free primary education for all boys has been set as the goal, and rapid progress to that end has been achieved. In 1906 the government spent only $40,000 on education, whereas now it spends more than $6,000,000 a year. As a consequence there are primary schools in most villages of any size, though there is hardly accommodation yet for more than one-third of the boys and girls. With adult education available in night schools, illiteracy is steadily decreasing. And at the other end of the scale, a new government university and the support by the government of hundreds of students abroad provide for the higher education of teachers and professional leaders. In comparison with the past, the present regime has brought even more benefits to girls than to boys. Though in rural districts little attention has yet been paid to the schooling of girls, the speed with which their opportunities have been enlarged may be measured by the fact that in 1919 there were only 10 public schools for girls, while in 1933 there were 870. Even the government university is open to women; but thus far there are relatively few girls who can pass from the primary to the middle grade, and still fewer who seek a college training.

Shiite Islam is still the official religion of Iran, and according to the constitution the Shah and his cabinet ministers must be Moslems. But though Islam has not been formally disestablished, its influence upon government policy has been reduced to the vanishing point. Since Reza Pahlavi became Shah, the power of the clergy, as we have seen, has been completely broken. While the secularizing of education has not proceeded so far as in Turkey, religious teaching in government primary schools has been gradually reduced and in secondary schools is no longer required. The large income from religious endowments now goes to support public-welfare projects, and even the theological seminaries are under state control. In contrast with Turkey and Egypt, where religious liberty is guaranteed by the constitution but in practice does not always include real freedom for Moslems to become Christians, in Iran such liberty is not proclaimed as law, but in practice is a recognized principle. Under the present scheme for the registration of all citizens, converts from Islam can be registered as Christians and thus win official recognition of their change of status.

In consequence of the spread of Western education and of the rise of a secular-minded nationalism, Islam has been gravely weakened not merely in its control of the government but in its hold upon the educated classes. Patriotic Iranians, trained in modern schools and eager for the advance of their country, attribute to Islam and its officials the decay of the old Persia. In their eyes the mullahs, once a serious obstacle to progress, are now but little more than a laughingstock. To rapidly increasing numbers, the formal observances of the faith seem irksome and needless; many are ready to acknowledge the waning of their belief; and thousands are drifting openly into agnosticism. Whatever may prove to be the evil consequences of such a falling away from all religion, one good result has been the growth of a liberal tolerance in matters religious. Today there is a degree of friendliness between Christian and Moslem unknown before; and while converts to Christianity are still subject to minor persecution, they may now live in comparative security.

Even so brief a summary of modern Persian progress would not be complete without a reminder that the country is still oppressed by social evils, old and new. Education is largely a class affair, with the ignorant masses as yet untouched and unchanged, living at a low level under primitive conditions. Official life is still tainted by corruption. Temporary marriages remain legal and highly popular; divorce is free and easy; prostitution and venereal disease are widely prevalent; opium is still a scourge; and there is an alarming increase in the consumption of alcohol. Yet however baffling may be the evils that have still to be dealt with, the achievements since 1922 are amazing in the range of their success. Even with the support of a vigorous and enlightened minority, one man can hardly be expected in fifteen or twenty years completely to remake an oriental society.

The Iran of today has a population of about 15,000,000, spread over so wide an area that the density is hardly more than 19 to the square mile. Three-fourths of the people live in villages, and there are still almost 3,000,000 nomads, such as Kurds, Kashgais, and Bakhtiaris. The government, however, is gradually forcing these tribes to settle in villages. The remainder of the people dwell in towns of 10,000 or more, of which the largest are Teheran (360,000), Tabriz (219,000), and Meshed

(139,000). Nearly 95 percent of all Iranians are Moslems of the Shiah sect, with only 850,000 registered as Sunnis among the Kurds and Turks. Too heretical to be classed as Mohammedans are the Bahais, whose number no one seems to know. It may be as low as 100,000 or as high as 500,000. Far smaller are the other religious groups—the 50,000 Armenian and the 30,000 Nestorian Christians, the 40,000 Jews, and the 10,000 Zoroastrians, the last remnants in Iran of the ancient faith.

The work of Protestant missions to the Moslems of Persia began with Henry Martyn, who, after five years in India, spent ten months at Shiraz in the years 1811 and 1812. As one of the most winning and heroic figures in the whole company of pioneer witnesses and as a kind of patron saint of all later missionaries to Islam, Martyn must be accorded fuller treatment than we can give to most of his successors. Since his attitude and methods are typical of an earlier period, there is all the more reason to tell his story not too briefly.

The son of a merchant's clerk who had once been a laborer in the mines, Henry Martyn was born in Cornwall in 1781. In spite of the slender means of his family, he was sent to St. John's College, Cambridge, where, before graduation, he became Senior Wrangler and won a first prize in mathematics. By the time he was made a Fellow of the College in 1802, he had experienced a deep and lasting conversion of the evangelical type; and, moved by what he had learned of the work of Brainerd in North America and of Carey in India, he had determined to give his life to the missionary cause. After ordination to the priesthood, he was appointed as chaplain to the East India Company and in August, 1805, sailed for Calcutta. Impulsive and emotional by nature, Martyn was dominated by a piety highly subjective and of an almost morbid intensity. It was in keeping with both the depth and the narrowness of his tradition that after a taste of Roman Catholicism at Bahia (where his ship touched) and after witnessing some Moslem sailors celebrating a religious festival, he should write in his diary of the "shocking examples of the range and power of the devil in the form of Popish and Mohammedan delusion." But unlike many others of his type, Martyn combined a vivid sense of sin and a burning zeal for the Gospel not merely with the most perfect manners but with a disarming humility and an attractive simplicity. Like such other saints as Francis Xavier, he united virtue and charm. Yet even with this rare union, he could never have achieved what he did had he not possessed also intellectual gifts of a high order. As a linguist he was positively a genius, adding to his native capacity an unquenchable enthusiasm. Even before he left England he had been laboring at the grammar not only of Bengali and Hindustani but even of Arabic and Persian. And every ounce of his varied endowments, mental and spiritual, was dedicated to a divine Master. The very day after he arrived at Calcutta he wrote,

I feel pressed in spirit to do something for God. . . . I want nothing but grace, I want to be perfectly holy, and to save myself and others who hear me. I have hitherto lived to little purpose . . . now let me burn out for God.

With Martyn's work as translator and evangelist in India, we shall deal in a later chapter. During those five strenuous years he had literally been "burning himself out," contending in the midst of intense activity with the increasing symptoms of tuberculosis. But nearly a year and a half of life still remained to him when, after an exhausting journey under a scorching sun, he reached Shiraz early in June, 1811. His chief purpose was to revise a defective translation of the New Testament into Persian, which he had already made in India. He carried letters to a leading citizen of the town, who provided him with a room and offered to give him assistance. Thanks to this cordial welcome, Martyn was soon at home and at work. "Imagine a pale person," he wrote, "sitting on a Persian carpet, in a room without table or chair, with a pair of formidable moustachios and habited as a Persian, and you see me."

James Morier, a British diplomat then resident in Persia, later wrote of Martyn:

The Persians, who were struck with his humility, his patience and resignation, called him a man of God. . . . When he was living at Shiraz, employed in his translation, he neither sought nor shunned the society of the natives, many of whom constantly drew him into arguments about religion, with the intention of persuading him of the truth and excellence of theirs.[1]

Though he persisted without relaxation in his linguistic work, he still found time for numberless conferences with learned visitors, as they crowded in to talk with "a holy man" whose reputation soon spread far beyond the borders of the city. In moral character, in mastery of his own kind of theology, and in knowledge of the Koran, Martyn was admirably equipped for such controversy. But he was true to his type and his time in his utter contempt for Islam. Since he loathed it as a form of sin, he was naturally not interested in it as a form of religion. Keen polemic was a contest between the powers of light and the powers of darkness; in his own words, it was "aiming a stab at the vitals of Mohammed." The teaching of "the impostor of Mecca" was for him merely "all this Mohammedan stuff." To his general detestation of Islam, he added a further disqualification for success in Persia: he was ignorant of mysticism in any religion and he scoffed at the Sufi doctrines as arising simply from the "vanity" of believers.

Yet because he was a warm-hearted Christian and a gentleman of rare charm, the Moslem doctors were only too glad to talk with him at any time and at any length. Most of these countless interviews were conducted along the usual lines familiar in past centuries to John of Damascus, Ramon Lull, and Jerome Xavier. The Trinity, the Divinity of Christ, the Atonement, the definition of "miracle," the evidences for the inspiration of the Scriptures and of the Koran—these were the stock themes for argument. The mystical doctrines of Sufiism, too, were often debated—the meaning of emanation, of immanence, and of union with God. The larger the company present and the more doctrinal the issues, the more barren were the results. But even in Martyn's brief experience a century and a quarter ago, there were signs that confidence in the efficacy of debate was wavering. At different points during his months at Shiraz Martyn wrote, "Frigid reasoning with men of perverse minds seldom brings men to Christ. However, as they require it, I reason." Yet "I have now lost

[1] G. Smith, *Henry Martyn*, pp. 391 f.

all hope of ever convincing Mohammedans by argument.... I know not what to do but to pray for them." There was another mode of approach, however, which we might too easily call modern were it not that Martyn had already begun to use it effectively—the method not of controversy but of sharing religious experience. When one Aga Baba asked him whether, independently of external evidence, he had internal proof of the doctrine of Christ, Martyn answered, "Yes, undoubtedly: the change from what I once was is sufficient evidence for me." To the question of another as to how he had obtained his peace of mind, he replied by telling of his own religious history, "the substance of which was that I took my Bible before God in prayer, and prayed for forgiveness through Christ, assurance of it through His Spirit, and grace to obey His commandments." And again when his friend Sayyid Ali was genuinely seeking for help, Martyn reports, "I then went through all the different states of my mind at the time I was called to the knowledge of the Gospel. He listened with great interest, and said, 'You must not regret the loss of so much time as you give me, because it does me good.'" Such moments of intimate witnessing could be found in the lives of all good missionaries to Moslems from that day to this. Yet it took the workers in the field of Islam a long time to discover how much more fruitful are these moments than the hours devoted to doctrinal debate.

Martyn had not come to Persia primarily as an evangelist, and we have no right to measure his success in terms of converts. One Persian, it is true, was long afterwards won to Christianity through his memories of Martyn and through studying a copy of the New Testament which Martyn had given him. But the visible achievement of these months of toil was the complete revision of the Persian translation of the New Testament and the translation into Persian of the Psalms. The New Testament version was subsequently printed both in St. Petersburg and in Calcutta. Meanwhile, before leaving the country Martyn undertook a wearisome journey of nearly two months from Shiraz to Tabriz, where he left with the British ambassador a handsome copy of the New Testament for presentation to the Shah. Thence, after à long illness, he set forth early in September, 1812, to travel 1,500 miles through Azerbaijan and Armenia to Constantinople. In failing health and amid endless hardships, he kept up the struggle day after day until his frail body could stand no more. He died at Tokat on October 16, 1812. During his seven years in the field he had accomplished as a linguist enough to make a lifetime notable. Yet it is not chiefly as a translator that he is famous. In the history of the Church and in the lives of those who have come after him, he is remembered less for what he did than for what he was—a radiant spirit who, in a great adventure for God, gave all that he had, and for whom "the trumpets have sounded on the other side."

After Martyn's death there was an interval of eighteen years before members of the Basel Mission, which had been working for some time in Transcaucasia, began to make pioneering tours in Persia. The famous Karl Pfander, who was later to serve in India, journeyed through Persia in 1830, and in response to his recommendation the Basel Mission opened a station at Tabriz in 1833. In the following year the American Board of Commissioners for Foreign Missions entered upon its work for Nestorian Christians at Urumia and sent the Rev. J. L. Merrick on a long reconnaissance to Teheran, Isfahan, and Shiraz. His report declared that public preaching was not only inexpedient but impracticable. In the face of this testimony, for which there was plenty of evidence, the Mission abandoned the effort to appeal to Moslems; and within a few years the Basel group, on the same grounds, withdrew from Persia. While the Nestorian Mission continued to prosper and was not without effect upon its Moslem neighbors, there were for thirty years and more no missionaries in Persia devoted mainly to touching Islam.

Not until fifty-seven years after the death of Martyn did a missionary of his own Church enter the field of Persia. In 1869 Robert Bruce, of the English Church Missionary Society, who was then in India, obtained a year's leave for study and translation in Persia and settled at Julfa, outside of Isfahan. His persistent desire to stay there finally induced the reluctant officials of the C. M. S. to adopt his growing work as their own, and by

1875 the Mission of the Church of England had thus taken root. Bruce, like Martyn, had confined himself chiefly to literary labor. "I am not yet reaping," he wrote, "I am not yet sowing; I can hardly be said to be plowing, but I am gathering the stones from the field." Meantime, in 1870, all the work of the American Board in Persia had been transferred to the American Presbyterians,[2] who proceeded thereafter to hasten the process of direct approach to the Moslem. Within three years their forces were active at new stations in Teheran and Tabriz. Their schools for the Armenian children in both cities were attended by only a handful of Moslems, and official opposition was strong. Yet Moslems were soon attracted to their weekly services, and a few even reached the point of baptism.

During the remaining decades of the nineteenth century, the Presbyterian Mission not only expanded and prospered among the Nestorians in the Urumia district, but established a station at Hamadan and strengthened its forces and its influence at Teheran and Tabriz by beginning medical work and enlarging its schools. Successful contact with Mohammedans was still rare and difficult, and among the little Christian communities in each city hardly a score were faithful converts from Islam. By 1885, however, the custom of administering baptism in secret had been abandoned in favor of the more hazardous but sounder practice of public baptism. Not until the last few years of the century did the sister Mission of the English Church in southern Persia show any signs of marked expansion. But before 1900 the C. M. S. had six clergy on its staff and had opened stations with either hospitals or dispensaries at Kerman, Yezd, and Shiraz.

The political and social reforms in Persia which made the period between 1905 and 1910 so eventful were almost wholly favorable to the missionary cause. The new zeal for Western education wrought a change in the Moslem attitude toward Christian schools. Within a few years Mohammedan boys and girls began to appear in such numbers as often to constitute 40 or 50 percent of the whole; and a large proportion were from

[2] The Board of Foreign Missions of the Presbyterian Church in the United States of America.

prominent and influential families. By 1912 there were at least 1,000 of them enrolled in the schools of all the missions—a total double that of five years before. The death penalty for apostasy, though not enforced, was still on the books, so that converts to Christianity had no legal protection and were liable to severe persecution. Open evangelizing was out of the question and the sale of Christian literature was often obstructed. Yet the atmosphere in changing Persia had become tolerant enough to make possible a more immediate approach to Moslems and to encourage a growing number of enquirers. At the C. M. S. stations in 1911, for example, there were over 100 baptisms of converts from Islam. It was now through such accessions, rather than through the winning of Oriental Christians, that the small churches were increasing. In southern Persia improving conditions justified the formation in 1912 of an Anglican diocese of Iran and the appointment of a bishop. The same year witnessed the first inter-mission conference, which was held at Hamadan and at which the thirty-one delegates devoted two weeks to the discussion of such common problems as the training of recent converts, the development of self-support, and the production of Christian literature. The gathering reflected in all its sessions a general tone of optimism and emphasized the need for energetic advance.

During the World War, the whole missionary enterprise in Persia was gravely dislocated and most of its normal work broken up. Massacres and pestilence completely wiped out the flourishing Christian center at Urumia. At one time or another famine prevailed in nearly every area, as well as frequent epidemics of disease. Hospitals were filled with refugees, and the depleted staff of missionaries was everywhere active in the exhausting work of administering relief. It was not till after 1920 that the aftermath of war had been largely cleared away and the hopeful progress of prewar years had been resumed with surprising promptitude.

As but one occasion for encouragement we may cite the advance at Meshed, that intensely Moslem city in eastern Persia, a sacred place of pilgrimage for more than 100,000 devotees every year. Dr. Esselstyn, of the Presbyterian Mission, had founded a station there in 1911, the only Christian center in a huge province covering a quarter of the area of Persia. Serving alone for four years, until he was joined by the Rev. D. M. Donaldson and others, Esselstyn traveled over wide areas, preaching openly and distributing the Scriptures, yet at the same time winning everywhere the confidence of the leaders and gentry. By 1915 a hospital had been equipped, where starving thousands were fed and cared for during the war and where Esselstyn himself died of typhus in 1918. By that time the doctor in charge was treating about 15,000 patients a year. In 1920, at this most unpromising spot, was organized the first church in Iran to be formed entirely of converts from Islam. Today it numbers more than 90 communicants and has spread its branches to three neighboring towns. At other stations in the less difficult areas there was not only similar growth in church membership but steady progress in educational work, especially at Teheran where the Iran Bethel School for girls and the college for boys were profiting by recent gifts for buildings and endowment.

The new regime of Reza Khan, like its feebler counterpart of twenty years earlier, soon began to work changes which for the most part aided the advance of the Church. Peace and order, improved communications, the eclipse of the Moslem clergy, and general enthusiasm for Westernization were all favorable factors. A larger degree of tolerance and a relaxation of tension between Christianity and Islam were added advantages. But as in other countries striving toward a secularized nationalism, points of conflict arose in the field of education. In 1927 the government issued regulations requiring that all Moslem pupils must be taught Moslem law and must not be instructed in any non-Moslem religion. Unwilling to accept this stiff rule as final, the mission boards began negotiations with the government which lasted for a year and a half, with useful results. It was finally agreed that though Moslem pupils must take government examinations in the Koran and the Law, they might prepare in these subjects outside of the schools; and that while the Bible itself must not be used in the courses on religion, selections from the Bible might supply material for ethical teaching. With these opportunities still open and with freedom to carry on worship and religious instruction outside of the curriculum, it has been possible to maintain the Christian character of mission schools and colleges. A harder blow, however, was a later decree, in 1932, forbidding foreign missions to conduct any elementary schools—a prohibition that eliminated nearly three-quarters of the pupils in missionary institutions. Yet even here the situation was partly redeemed, for in several stations the primary schools were taken over by the local Protestant churches and conducted independently of the missions.

Indicative of the growing cohesion and power of the Church in Iran were the three interchurch conferences held between 1925 and 1931. All of them produced valuable discussions and findings in regard to evangelistic methods, the training of workers, the care of converts, and other familiar problems. But the developments most significant for the future were the increasing influence of the Iranian members and the determined purpose to work for organic Church unity. Even at the first conference the delegates included eight converts from Islam, and three of the meetings were led by some of these members. In 1931 all the important officers and more than two-thirds of the delegates were Iranian.

The need for closer Church unity was a major consideration in each of the conferences. The prospects for success appeared brighter than in most fields of the same size and importance, for there were only two missions of any consequence in the entire country and these had long maintained such harmonious relations that they were already practicing intercommunion. The conference of 1925 appointed a committee of fourteen, with ten Persian members, to investigate the matter and report. The next conference, held in 1927, agreed on certain fundamental principles of union, including the acceptance of the Scriptures, the two sacraments, and the two creeds, and the recognition of both presbyters and bishops. It was further decided that the future United Church must be independent of any other existing body. But as the enthusiasm for unity is nearly always greater in the mission field than in the home Church, the conference held four years later was able to report only that "since the differences in the churches in the north and in the south [of Iran] depend upon differences of organization in the churches in America and in England, the matter should be referred to the American and British missionaries themselves, so that they may confer together and make the necessary decisions." Yet if union is still not close at hand, important steps have been taken toward independence. The diocese of Iran is already accounted an "independent see" and held its first synod in 1933. Of its 1,200 members, a majority were formerly Moslems. And the "Evangelical Church" in Iran, with its own General Assembly, ended by agreement in 1935 all control by the Presbyterian Church in America.

Of all the Moslem countries in the Near East, Iran has been for a generation the most religiously approachable. How vigorously the Christian forces have taken advantage of this opportunity is attested by the state of the Church in Iran today. What has been achieved is not simply the conversion of many hundreds of Moslems but their incorporation into churches that are becoming more and more truly Iranian and more and more capable of self-expansion. There is now Persian leadership both in the councils of the Church and in the work of preaching, for in almost every station converts from Islam are active in public and private evangelism—not in anti-Moslem argument but in the positive presentation of the Christian message. What has been said of the Anglican branch might be said also of the Presbyterian—"The Church is small at present; but it is a witnessing Church, it is a praying Church, and it is a Persian Church."

The growing power of the Church has been heavily reinforced by its widespread institutional work, educational and medical. Above the primary and middle schools there stand out especially those pioneers of higher learning in Iran—the Alborz College of Teheran and the Stewart Memorial college at Isfahan. Each has clearly maintained its Christian character, and from both institutions hundreds of graduates now fill positions of trust in all parts of the country. Smaller but hardly less notable in their influence have been the Stileman Memorial College for Women at Isfahan and its counterpart at Teheran, the Nurbakhsh School for girls,[3] where the course has been extended in a new junior college now known as the Sage College for Women. Until August, 1939, these colleges had been looking forward to a prosperous future; but in that month the government announced its intention to assume control of *all* educational work in Iran—the logical outcome of the process of nationalization. Not only the colleges but the six schools of secondary grade connected with the Presbyterian Mission are thus to become government property, with due compensation to the owners.

While none can dispute the right of a government to assume responsibility for education, many will regret it if the Iranian Government takes over a phase of mission work which has been so useful in the upbuilding of Iran, and so effective in bringing to many a knowledge of Christ. It will, however, release for other types of service that part of the appropriations of the Mission which has been devoted to the educational work, and the missionaries who have been engaged in it. The net result may be no less valuable to the nation as a manifestation of the Christian spirit of love and helpfulness and no less effective from an evangelistic point of view.[4]

Reaching an even larger number than the schools are the twelve hospitals in all the chief cities of Iran. Their staffs today are active not only in the familiar work of healing, through which they find access to the lives of hundreds of thousands every year, but also in newer types of service in coöperation with the government, such as the training of nurses, the promotion of public education in hygiene and preventive medicine, and welfare work for mothers and infants.

A brief record of such achievements is worth making for the encouragement it rightly brings. Yet perhaps more important for the future is a summary of those special problems with which the Church in Iran is faced.

The most obvious characteristic of Iran as a Moslem mission field is that nearly all the Moslems are Shiites. Members of that sect are found in other countries, especially in India and Iraq, but nowhere else do they constitute even a clear majority. The

---

[3] Formerly the Iran Bethel School.   [4] *Moslem World*, Jan., 1940, p. 98.

Christian forces, therefore, are usually confronted with one or another variety of this type of Islam, and its peculiar features have in some measure affected both the presentation and the reception of the Christian message. The extended treatment of Shiism for which a work on Islam would call we must here reduce to those few main points that touch the enterprise of Christian evangelism.

Shiah means sect or party, and in this case stands originally for the partisans of Ali. Ali, the cousin and son-in-law of Mohammed, was the fourth successor, or caliph, to rule after the death of Mohammed. Yet from the beginning a small group had asserted the claim that he and his descendants should be the only successors of the Prophet; and after his death in 661 these partisans refused to acknowledge the new line of caliphs, the Omayyad Dynasty. Instead they gave allegiance to his son Hasan and, after Hasan's retirement, to his brother Husain. When Husain, leading a hopeless revolt, was slain at the battle of Kerbela (680), he became thenceforth the chief martyr in their holy cause. To this day he is commemorated at an annual ten-day celebration of mourning in the month Muharram (a sort of Shiah Holy Week), when manifestations of grief are mingled with curses on his slayers and their descendants. Though the schism was thus political, it soon involved also a different view not only as to who should be Mohammed's successor but as to what he should be. He must be no merely temporal chieftain like the false caliphs, but an Imam, the spiritual heir of the Prophet's ministry, entrusted by him with esoteric wisdom and gifted by God with a nature sinless and infallible. Of these Imams in the line of Ali the great majority of Shiites count twelve, the last of whom disappeared, to become the "Hidden Imam," who will one day return to reign in righteousness. Zealous and intolerant in these heretical beliefs, the Shiites were for several centuries in frequent revolt against the governing powers; but for a long time past open conflict has died out and the geographical grouping of the minority has been stabilized. There remain within Islam, then, the vast majority of Sunnites, following the Sunna or tradition of the community, acknowledging the caliph (as long as the office lasted); and the opposing Shiites, who number perhaps 22,000,000 out of more than 250,000,000.

This split in the body of Islam has naturally led to differences of doctrine. With its half-mystical theory of the Imamate, the Shiah not only stood opposed to the caliphate and its pan-Islamic ambitions, but differed further in beliefs less political than religious. The Imams came to be regarded as intercessors with Allah, and Husain has been exalted, in practice if not in theory, even above Mohammed. Since the shedding of his blood is thought to have sacrificial value, the element of atonement appears, with Husain as a mediator. Even an approach to the idea of incarnation may be found in the doctrine that a particle of divine light is transmitted from one infallible Imam to another, a dogma carried by the more extreme sects to the point of belief in Ali and Husain as actual incarnations of the Godhead. Though the Shiah as a whole have been openly hostile to mysticism (known in its Islamic form as Sufiism), so many of the mystics have been Persians that their teaching and ideals have long constituted one strand in the religious thought of Iran. Still another factor has been the influence of that liberal theological movement of the school called Mutazilite (first active more than a thousand years ago), which prevailed especially in Shiite areas and which kept Shiite thought less strict than Sunnite. Yet speculation has been held within bounds by those learned doctors, the mujtahids, who are revered as the final interpreters of orthodoxy.

In addition to the sharper contrasts on major issues, there are minor points of difference in law and custom. The Shiites, for example, approve a form of temporary marriage [5] and refuse to permit the marriage of a Moslem to a Jew or a Christian. Until very recent times, too, they have always regarded contact with an unbeliever as involving ritualistic uncleanness. Another characteristic peculiar to the Shiah is the principle of religious dissimulation,[5] in obedience to which a Shiite may hide his true faith when it would be inconvenient to reveal it. In the presence

[5] Authorized in the Koran and practiced in early Islam, but later rejected by the Sunnis.

of opponents, he is permitted to speak and act as if he were one of them. This taint of unreliability in all religious discussion has naturally been a baffling obstacle in the personal work of the Christian evangelist.

The chief difficulties which the missionary encounters in Iran are raised by those deep convictions in which Shiites and Sunnites are at one. Insofar as their religious thought differs from the orthodox, Shiites offer the more favorable openings.

In the first place they understand more readily, or at least resent less promptly, the Christian dogma of the Incarnation, for their own tendency is to approach the idea of God made manifest in the flesh. The theory of the Imamate, moreover, partly prepares them for the conception of Christ as an ever-living guide and mediator, so that the will of God is revealed not merely in laws but through a Person. More clearly advantageous is their acceptance of the fact that most of the Imams met violent deaths and that their sufferings have eternal meaning. So the Cross seems to be no fatal rock of offense. And since the suffering of Husain and others has given them the right of intercession with Allah and may be thought to have value as an expiation, there appears a setting congenial to the doctrine of the Atonement.

Another peculiar feature of the Persian field is the presence of an undetermined but very large number of Bahais—the product of a religious movement now nearly a century old. Beginning as an intolerant and dogmatic little sect whose leader declared himself to be the Bab or Door of communication with the hidden Imam,[6] this group was first known as the Babis and, as harmful heretics, they were bitterly persecuted by the authorities. Like all zealous dissenters, however, they later split more than once into rival subsects. The only one of these to prosper and expand was that founded by Baha Allah and led in later years by his son Abd al-Baha. Baha Allah wrote a book, the *Kitab Akdas,* or *Most Holy Book,* which was to supersede the Koran; and after his death in 1892 Abd al-Baha declared himself to be its sole interpreter. This later Bahaism, though it had abandoned the politically dangerous dogmas of Babism, has always been

[6] He later claimed to be the Imam Mahdi himself.

opposed as a heresy by the Persian government, and its exiled leaders have carried on their work in such alien centers as Acre in Palestine. But thanks in part to their peaceful program and in part to their practice of dissimulation, most of its members are still to be found in Iran. Their beliefs cover a wide range. The more conservative would accept the extreme claims of the Founder and revere his book. For more than a generation, however, the movement has been denaturing its doctrines to suit the taste of the Occident and to add to its followers in Europe and America. By ancestry it is a minor subsect of the Shiah, yet to the world it claims to aim at "the establishment of true religion and universal peace among mankind" and to stand for "love and harmony" and "the unfettered search for truth" and even for "compulsory education" and "work for all." Many Iranians, too, are Bahais only in this diluted sense.

As a field for missionary endeavor, Bahaism has always been most unpromising, and converts to Christianity from that faith are far fewer than those from Islam. A small number, it is true, have found in Bahaism a halfway house to Christianity; but more numerous are those whose discontent with Islam has led them to become Bahais rather than Christians. For Bahaism aims to be vaguely all-inclusive and requires of the Moslem no such sharp decision as baptism demands. In view of its plea that a man can be a true Bahai without ceasing to be a Moslem or a Christian, it is less an aid than an obstacle to the missionary cause.

If Shiite and Bahai doctrines have long been characteristic of religion in Persia and are distinct marks of that field, there are yet other features which stand out in the newer Iran—all the symptoms of a secularized nationalism. These symptoms, of course, are familiar, in sharper or in milder forms, throughout a score of other countries, from Germany to Java. They present problems common to the Christian Church everywhere. So far as the new nationalism is secularized, it is both the product and the cause of an agnostic attitude toward all religion. In a series of meetings, for example, held at Kermanshah some years ago, the largest single group of questions, handed in for discussion by those who attended in great numbers, demanded reasons for be-

lieving in any God at all. In Iran it is clear, as in Japan or
Turkey, that Christian evangelism has to deal, to an ever greater
degree, with skeptics and atheists. Yet this new patriotism does
not simply ignore religion. It offers itself as a substitute and
tends to view other religions as rivals. So far as this ambition
sterilizes the old Moslem fanaticism and wipes out the influence
of the clergy, it works to the advantage of Christianity. But the
expanding Church itself becomes another rival, viewed all the
more as calling for control because it is partly foreign. Hence
arise the vexatious limits placed upon educational and medical
work and the widespread conviction, far more dangerous, that
to adopt an alien religion is not consistent with an ardent devotion to the state. Confronted with these forces, the Church today
seeks to become more and more plainly and genuinely Iranian
and so to present the Gospel that it may be seen not as a subtle
hindrance to a greater Iran but as the power of God unto
salvation not alone for individual souls but for nations.

XII

Arabia

ARABIA is a huge peninsula. With Transjordan, Syria, and Iraq on its northern borders, it is elsewhere surrounded by water—the Red Sea, the Indian Ocean, and the Persian Gulf. Though the land covers about 1,000,000 square miles, nearly two-thirds the size of India, so large a proportion is desert and mountainous wilderness that the population probably numbers not more than 10,000,000. These Arabs today may be found in various stages of civilization, from the nomadic Beduins of the interior to the more highly developed town dwellers in such larger centers as Mecca and Medina. Here is a land where Islam is completely dominant, where the civic, social, and economic life of the people is bound up with the religion which began in Arabia thirteen centuries ago.

From the rise of the Ottoman Empire until the World War, the more settled coastal regions of the Hejaz and Yemen in the west and of Hasa in the east were directly governed by the Turks; and Turkey at times laid claim to the whole peninsula. Yet even in the districts which they controlled, the Turks were only a small minority, and in the greater part of Arabia the inhabitants remained free to lead their ancient tribal life. As in most other parts of the empire, modern Turkish government was as bad as it could be. The officials of the alien ruling caste from top to bottom were entirely corrupt and incredibly inefficient. Failing utterly as a civilizing force, they succeeded only in stimulating dissension and discord among their Arab subjects.

When the war came it was not difficult to sever the slim thread of connection between Turkey and Arabia. The Arabs went further than that, for, with British support and under the guidance of Lawrence, Husain, the Sherif of Mecca, and his followers bore a valuable part in the later defeat of the Turks in Palestine. At the close of the war Husain was King of the Hejaz; but he had soon to reckon with an opponent more formidable than the Turk —Ibn Saoud. Since the opening of the century, Ibn Saoud, a powerful chieftain in the central area of the Nejd, had revived the Wahhabi movement of former times and had welded together the unsettled Beduin tribes into such a vigorous body that as early as 1913 he had captured the Hasa province from the Turks. With Ottoman rule ended by the war, Ibn Saoud turned his growing forces against his rival Husain. After several years of intermittent civil warfare, his success was so complete that he was proclaimed King of the Hejaz. In the following year, 1927, Great Britain accepted the situation by recognizing his title and the independence of his dominions. Ibn Saoud, then known as King of the Hejaz and of Nejd and its Dependencies, is now King of Saoudi Arabia. His domain includes the vast interior of the Nejd and the coastal regions of the Hejaz and Asir, affording its ruler a paramount position throughout the greater part of the peninsula. The masterful personality of Ibn Saoud, whom some have called the greatest Arab since Mohammed, gives him immense prestige, and everywhere his authority is supreme. Though he maintains the religious law of Islam as the common law of the land, he exerts all the power of an absolute patriarchal monarch. Thanks to his rule, Saoudi Arabia is knit together as it has not been for centuries. The habitual tribal raiding is now scarcely known, crime has been reduced to a minimum, and there are few countries where life and property are safer.[1] Sharing, furthermore, in the wide movement of Arab nationalism, Ibn Saoud has recently negotiated treaties of friendship with Iraq and Transjordan and has made his influence felt in the nationalist agitation of Syria and Palestine.

Though the area of Saoudi Arabia covers the greater part of the peninsula, there are a number of other political units in the remaining coastal regions. Most of these units are important for

---

[1] In this increase of order and unity, the growing use of the motor car has played a notable part. When journeys that once took thirty days can be accomplished in five, tribal independence is inevitably lessened, and ruler and people brought closer together.

our purpose because they include the centers of missionary work. At the southwestern tip of Arabia is the independent kingdom of Yemen, with a population of about 3,000,000. Next to Yemen is the Aden Protectorate, under British control, which covers not only the little Colony of Aden and its hinterland but also the great tract called Hadramaut, which stretches along the southeast coast for 500 or 600 miles. Further on, at the easterly corner of Arabia, is the independent Sultanate of Oman, with a seaboard nearly 900 miles long and a population of 500,000. The largest towns are the ports of Muscat and Matrah, where the inhabitants are chiefly Baluchis and Negroes. A much smaller geographical unit is Bahrain and the adjacent islands lying in the Persian Gulf off the coast of Hasa. Here a population of 120,000, mostly Shiah Moslems, is governed by a Ruling Sheikh under the guidance of a political agent of the British government. Finally,[2] up in the northwestern corner of the Persian Gulf is the little state of Kuwait, where the Sheikh's foreign relationships are under the eye of an agent of Britain. In both Kuwait and Bahrain the oil industry, with its accompanying influx of Europeans and Americans, is now thriving, and modern civilization has begun to work rapid changes in the life of the people.

Most of the characteristics of the Arabs are to be found among all classes of the people, but they appear in their purest and least modified form among those typical Arabs, the Beduin. The Arab is physically hardy, with an extraordinary capacity for endurance. Though illiterate, he is mentally active and direct. Always an extreme individualist, he is passionately insistent upon complete personal liberty. His courage and cheerfulness are almost uniform and his hospitality unrivaled. Though his form of government is autocratic, he is socially a democrat, and when approached on terms of fearless equality he is ready to respond with the most loyal friendship. But alongside his virtues, many of which are both noble and rare, there are defects manifest even to his admirers. For the Arab is emphatically lazy, with a special distaste for manual labor. His individualism makes any-

[2] Omitting a number of other minor divisons, such as the "Trucial Sheikhdoms" and Qatar.

thing like partnership or public spirit excessively difficult. He carries pride and sensuality to a high degree. Except where his faith is solemnly pledged, he is always ready to lie and cheat. And especially if he is a Beduin, he has for centuries made robbery, raiding, and intertribal warfare an almost normal mode of life.

Until the collapse of the Ottoman Empire, missionaries were excluded from all parts of Arabia over which the Turks maintained control. There were other districts, however, where their prohibition was of no effect. Among these was Aden, of which the British took possession in 1839. The possibilities of this small outpost had never been brought home to the Christians of Great Britain until 1882, when Major General F. T. Haig, a devoted member of the English Church Missionary Society, wrote an article for its periodical, *The Intelligencer,* in which he pointed to Aden as the "Gate of Arabia" and sketched plans for a mission in southern Arabia. In 1886, at the request of the Society, he undertook a long tour of exploration which included Yemen, Aden, and Muscat. During the same year Dr. Harpur, of the C. M. S. Egyptian Mission, was stationed for a time at Aden and spent some months at Hodeida in Yemen, where he served as the first medical missionary in Arabia.

A more notable result of General Haig's personal influence was the impression he made on a young Scot, Ion Keith-Falconer. The third son of the Earl of Kintore, Keith-Falconer had already graduated from Harrow and Trinity College, Cambridge, where he had won renown not only as an athlete but as a brilliant scholar. For seven years he had been studying Arabic at Cambridge, at Leipzig, and in Egypt, and had begun an academic career as lecturer in Semitic languages. By 1884 he had become deeply interested in the missionary cause, and in the following year a conference with General Haig determined him to seek Arabia as a field. Throughout the autumn and winter of 1885-86, Keith-Falconer and his wife made a visit of reconnaissance to Aden, during which they decided to fix their station at the village of Sheikh Othman, ten miles from the port. In the course of the subsequent summer in England, he obtained formal recognition from the

Free Church of Scotland as its representative in Arabia, where he
was to found a mission and to pay all its expenses. Accompanied
by his wife and Dr. Stewart Cowen, of Glasgow, as his medical
colleague, he reached Aden before the close of the year. The little
group settled at Sheikh Othman in temporary quarters. There
were only shacks and sheds to use for hospital and dispensary,
but the medical work began at once, and Dr. Cowen was soon
treating scores of patients from the surrounding country. Though
Keith-Falconer found some time for preaching and for personal
evangelism, he was chiefly occupied with building construction
and language study, the wearisome preliminaries of a career that
in reality was nearly at its end. For within a few weeks he was
attacked by malaria; during the greater part of March and April
he lay prostrated with fever; and on May 11, 1887, he died at the
age of thirty.

But with the death of the leader the work did not lapse. His
mother and his widow supplied means for its continuance, and
the Free Church of Scotland adopted Aden as a main station.
From that time onward there has been a succession of missionaries, most of whom have been doctors, for Sheikh Othman became primarily a medical mission. There the Keith-Falconer
Memorial Hospital was completed in 1909. Though for six years
during and after the war the work was in abeyance, the hospital
was reopened in 1920, and now treats every year nearly a thousand
in-patients drawn from a wide area.

Though not the first Protestant enterprise in Arabia, by far
the greatest in its size and range has been the Arabian Mission of
the Reformed Church in America, founded fifty years ago. In
1889 at the Theological Seminary in New Brunswick, New Jersey,
James Cantine, Samuel M. Zwemer, and Philip T. Phelps were
fellow students. Under the leadership of Professor John G. Lan-
sing, they began to form plans for missionary work in Arabia and
applied to the Board of Foreign Missions of their Church to be
sent out as evangelists to some Arabic-speaking country. When the
Board replied that it could not afford to support an additional
enterprise, the four men set themselves to organize and finance

an independent Arabian Mission. While that heavy task was in progress, Cantine sailed for Syria in October, 1889, to begin study at Beirut, and nine months later Zwemer set out to join him. By the beginning of the year 1891 the Arabian Mission had been incorporated with a Board of Trustees, and later in the same year Cantine and Zwemer opened the first station at Basrah, in southern Iraq, then a part of Turkey, near the head of the Persian Gulf. Before the close of 1893, the pioneers had been joined by Peter Zwemer and had established two more stations, at Bahrain and Muscat. So clearly by this time had the missionaries proved their case that in June, 1894, the Reformed Church adopted the new mission, though the latter retained its identity as a distinct body.[3] Within five years the courageous venture of a very small group had not only won official recognition at home, but in spite of Turkish opposition and popular hostility had laid in a difficult field foundations that still endure. Though forbidden to preach in public, the missionaries were active in the sale of Scriptures through extensive touring and in exploiting every opportunity for personal contacts among the people. Before the end of the century, the work had been further strengthened by the arrival of two physicians and the beginning of medical service at Basrah and Bahrain.

The next fourteen years preceding the war were years of rapid expansion, during which the number of missionaries increased from nine to thirty. Great care was exercised in training these new workers, for they were given at least two years of preparatory study in Arabic and Islamics. New stations were established at Kuwait and Matrah. Hospitals were completed first at Bahrain and then at Basrah and Kuwait. Educational work began at Muscat and Bahrain, but it was chiefly at Basrah that the schools for boys and girls flourished. And with this institutional advance there went continued activity in wide itineration through the country by missionaries and colporteurs and the maintenance of regular preaching services at all the stations. These had come to

[3] In 1925 the Arabian Mission was completely amalgamated with the Board of Foreign Missions of the Reformed Church in America.

attract a small but growing number of Moslems, so that enquirers appeared each year, and there were already a few baptized converts.

The World War added many new difficulties to an already trying task. The hospital at Basrah was transferred to Amarah on the Tigris River, and the native helpers, most of whom had been Christians from Turkey and Iraq, were greatly diminished in numbers. Yet at most of the centers work continued, and six years after the Armistice there were more missionaries than in 1914. A new hospital for women had been built at Kuwait and another at Bahrain, the latter aided by gifts from the ruling Sheikh. More significant for the future were the increasing opportunities for pioneering in the interior. As early as July, 1917, Dr. Paul W. Harrison accepted an invitation from Ibn Saoud to visit Riadh, his capital in the Nejd, a successful venture which he repeated in the spring of 1919. In the winter of 1921-22 Dr. L. P. Dame, of Bahrain, engaged in a similar tour, during which he worked at Riadh and other towns in central Arabia. Both the missionaries moved in an atmosphere of bitter hostility and were cursed by the people wherever they went; but the authority of Ibn Saoud protected them, and they succeeded in treating thousands of patients.

Another period of advance, completing the first half century, found the Arabian Mission with a staff of thirty-seven missionaries (including wives) and fourteen native helpers. The institutions include three elementary schools and one high school and the three hospitals and ten dispensaries, in which the patients number about 25,000 a year. The evangelistic services at the main centers are primarily for Moslems, who are now attending, sometimes by scores. But though perhaps a half dozen baptisms occur every year, there is as yet no organized church of former Moslems, for the forty communicants now listed are too scattered to constitute a single group. The certainty of social and commercial ostracism and the danger of persecution still operate as preventive warnings. Yet the fanaticism of twenty-five years ago, then heightened by the Wahhabi movement, is fast disappearing, and in the coast cities toleration has markedly increased.

The lines of approach to the Arab, as in other countries wholly Islamic, are chiefly through the schools and the hospitals in settled communities and through tours into the interior, which combine evangelism, the sale of the Scriptures, and medical service.

Of these activities the least prosperous at present is the educational work. But the achievements at one center, Basrah, have long been of notable value. Though Basrah is in Iraq, it is a station of the Arabian Mission and presents problems and opportunities much like those in Arabia. In this city, ever since 1913, there have been a school for boys and a school for girls, established by the Rev. and Mrs. John Van Ess. After twenty years of service as head of the Boys' School, Dr. Van Ess wrote rather too modestly of its influence:

Roughly two thousand boys and men have met Christ face to face for from two to eight years each, every school day of the year. Many of these now hold posts of responsibility and trust in state and society. I know definitely of only half a dozen who have gone wrong. The sons of many of them are now in school profiting by their fathers' newer outlook and by the home environment of at least a friendly attitude toward the Gospel, and with the promise of an early arrival of the time when the convert's enemies shall not be those of his own household.[4]

The secret of the school's missionary success may be traced to the principles which have inspired its leadership, principles which might well serve as a model for those many schools and colleges elsewhere that are yielding to the temptation to grow more and more secularized. In the words of Dr. Van Ess,

The missionary should capitalize that in which government and secular schools, by their own confession, cannot compete with them, namely, the personal influence which he can exert, the lofty motives which inspire him, and the development of high character. . . . Christ must be at the very heart of the curriculum. I personally would not care to spend five minutes of my life in the East teaching in a school where Christ is not made such. I should leave that task to any philanthropic agency which cares to treat the symptom rather than the disease. . . . A Christian missionary is contributing nothing whatsoever

---

[4] Quoted in Dodd and Dodd, *Mecca and Beyond*, p. 60.

to the alleviation of the world's woe unless he brings to bear that which he possesses in unique measure.[5]

The study of Christ is therefore given "an inviolable place in the program." With all the 300 or 400 pupils, the daily required Bible study is one of the most popular courses. Taught in the vernacular, it is as scientifically planned as any other branch of the curriculum. More than that, the aim of the course is discipleship.

Now, of discipleship the crux is not knowledge but obedience, surrender. To be a disciple implies a conflict of wills, and when I have led the Arab to surrender his will to that of Christ, I have made him a disciple. Does this method work? In my experience it is the only method that does work. It eliminates from the Arab's mind the idea that I am in conflict with him. It represents a constructive purpose rather than a destructive process.[5]

However great may be the possibilities of the right kind of school, it remains true that in Arabia today the range of opportunities open to the medical missionary is the widest. What can be accomplished by a man who is at once a skilled surgeon and an undaunted Christian is evident from the career of Dr. Paul W. Harrison. Soon after he joined the Arabian Mission in 1909, Dr. Harrison was one of the pioneers who opened the station at Kuwait and later he served for a long term as head of the Mason Memorial Hospital at Bahrain. Today he is one of the only two doctors at Muscat, on the Gulf of Oman. There in his stone and concrete hospital in a suburb of the town he treats, on an average, 125 patients a day and performs 15 to 20 operations a week. One day a week, with his wife and a native assistant, he drives 60 or 70 miles into the desert or up and down the coast to reach patients who cannot come to Muscat.

Mostly Dr. Harrison's work is with the ragged hungry poor who live with their goats in date-stick huts . . . with sore-eyed Beduins who never bathe; with over-burdened laborers who carry heavy bags of dried fish all day long for ten cents; with wounded bandits; with men whose hands have been cut off because they were caught stealing; with girls whose throats have been cut by their brothers because they committed adultery; with pearl-divers with running ears and burst eardrums; with water-carriers, date cultivators, camel drivers,

[5] Van Ess, "Educating the Arab," *Moslem World*, Oct., 1931, pp. 386, 380 f.

fishermen: with children, hundreds and hundreds of children, who in Arabia die like flies.[6]

Of the policy of the Arabian Mission and of his own experience in carrying it out, Dr. Harrison has written vividly in his book *The Arab at Home.*

The approach [to the Arab, he writes], on the basis of simple, unaffected, democratic equality is ninety per cent. of missionary method. Associating with the Arabs in this way you may easily meet them and have them meet you as warm friends, and many details take care of themselves. . . . The missionary has no weapons to force an entrance except prayer and friendly service. He is not able, nor does he wish, to enter a place until he is invited. So the method of procedure has been to work out from a base hospital and school and evangelistic station on the coast and gradually so to commend ourselves to the people that our presence inland is desired. This has been a slow method, but time has demonstrated its wisdom. Moreover, it is the only possible method. . . . So the Mission's policy has been to gain the good will of the people by steady, thorough medical work, by educational institutions and by a quiet uncompromising evangelistic campaign. . . . Even the evangelistic missionary is eventually made welcome because of his obvious good intentions and practical benevolence. . . . This is a task of years. In accomplishing it our most powerful instrument is the example of Christian family life lived in full view of the people. . . . Next to the influence of the missionary's family life, the most effective means of getting acquainted is the work of the mission hospitals. . . . If the doctor can add to his professional skill an unfailing human sympathy and personal interest . . . he becomes almost irresistible. . . . He can present and explain Christ's teachings to every one of his hospital patients. He can associate on terms of friendly equality even with the fanatical *Akhwan* [the Wahhabis]. In twelve years' experience I have never met a patient with whom it was impossible to do this sort of personal Christian work.[7]

As Dr. Harrison has pointed out, however, "the fond imagination that the Beduin can be adequately reached by dispensary talks in mission hospitals, located in the coast cities, is an idle dream." Aware of this limited range of institutional work, both Dr. Harrison and other physicians and evangelists have been taking advantage, during the last ten years, of the new opportuni-

[6] Jerome Beatty, "Desert Doctor," *American Magazine,* Oct., 1938.
[7] Harrison, *The Arab at Home,* pp. 290-94.

ties to penetrate into the interior. A remarkable example of such an expedition was the four months', journey of Dr. L. P. Dame in the Nejd, beginning in November, 1923. Answering a summons of Ibn Saoud, who was then very ill, the doctor set out for Riadh with four helpers and an ample store of surgical supplies. On an earlier visit to the capital, as we have previously noted, he had encountered much hostility and many insults. This time, however, his welcome was far more cordial. He not only cured the king and stayed long enough to give over 3,000 medical treatments, but went on to include in his tour three other inland towns which had never before been visited by a doctor. Everywhere his clinics were crowded, and each day his patients were ready to listen to preaching or to stories from the Bible. Nine years later he conducted an even-more-successful expedition; and in the following year Mrs. G. D. Van Peursem won the distinction of being the first Christian woman to enter the Nejd, where she was not merely tolerated but welcomed by Ibn Saoud. A still later instance of pioneering was the tour through Hadramaut made in 1935 by Dr. Harold Storm, of Bahrain, the first Christian to penetrate this untouched part of Arabia.

When we consider how few are the mission stations and how little has yet been accomplished by occasional expeditions elsewhere, it is clear that the million square miles of Arabia are a field still mainly unoccupied. Even excluding the great desert areas without habitation, there are immense stretches of country quite unreached. In the territory that extends for over a thousand miles along the eastern coast of the Red Sea, from the Gulf of Akaba to Aden, there is not a single permanent missionary.[8] In other words, the Hejaz, Asir, and Yemen are as yet unclaimed. Hadramaut, along the southeastern coast, has been no more than visited, and on the east coast, both between Muscat and Bahrain and between Bahrain and Kuwait, a long extent of territory awaits the expansion of the missionary forces.

[8] It may be noted, however, that in 1937, at the invitation of the ruler of the Yemen, the Church of Scotland Mission at Aden set free Dr. and Mrs. Petrie of Sheikh Othman to work for two years in Yemen at the expense of the government.

XIII

Northern India and Its Borders

ISLAM began its career in India with Arab raiding expeditions into Sind as early as the year 712; and thenceforth this western province was so strongly influenced by the religion of Moslem marauders and traders that three-fourths of its people are Mohammedans today. It was not through this entering wedge, however, but from Afghanistan that the great Moslem conquerors entered the country. At first they were only destructive plunderers like Mahmud of Ghazni in 1001; but by the end of the twelfth century Mohammed of Ghor had established at Delhi the capital of an Indo-Moslem empire which, under one dynasty or another, was to endure for more than five centuries. By the year 1202 the invaders had occupied Hindustan, Rajputana, Gujarat, and Bundelkhand and controlled the regions as far east as Bihar and Bengal. Two hundred years later Moslem rulers were pressing southward into the Deccan, and during the reigns of the famous Mughal emperors from Akbar to Aurangzeb (1556-1707) the empire reached its greatest extent in power and in territory.

Since for so long a time and over so wide an area the spread of Islam went hand in hand with the expansion of political control and military domination, it is fair to count the use of force as the chief instrument of conversion. It is plain, moreover, that until the days of Akbar the religious motive for conquest was strong in the minds of ambitious leaders. They were fighting to extend not merely their sway over Hindus but their faith among infidels. Yet even in the earlier centuries of Moslem rule, and still more in the later, there were peaceful influences steadily at work toward the same end. As in Africa and the East Indies today, traders were a powerful factor in interesting and winning the natives. Traveling preachers, too, proved effective in many areas, as they have in larger numbers in modern times. Among other causes of conversion may be counted the suffering from oppression endured by members of the lowest castes (such as oil-makers and leather workers) many of whom have long since entered the brotherhood of Islam. In fact the welcome to outsiders of every grade, which that brotherhood extends, has exerted in India, as elsewhere, a magnetic attraction. It is right to note, however, that these milder methods and inducements would hardly have proved as successful as they did, if they had not been reinforced by the immense prestige of the reigning Islamic power and by the political and military force always at its disposal.

In view of these favorable factors, the spread of Islam in India is not at all surprising. What is remarkable, on the contrary, is its failure to win more than a minority in the vast areas under imperial control.

Political extension and religious extension have always coincided in the history of Islam ... political supremacy in Islam is synonymous with religious supremacy, because Islam is at once a religious, social, and political system. ... Yet ... India is the only country in the world in which Islam has had for centuries such a strong and predominant political position without conquering it religiously. ... Islam came to meet in India a religious and social polity, entirely different and antagonistic in spirit and outlook, a luxuriant and deep-rooted civilization, one of the subtlest and highest growths in human history. Probably the caste-system and the Brahmanical supremacy are the main factors that have proved successful against the conversion of Hinduism to Islam. To borrow a phrase from the well known Hindu historian of Islam, Sir Jadunath Sarkar, in the domain of religion provincial Hinduism has withstood imperialistic Islam.[1]

There could be found no clearer testimony to this invincible fidelity of the Hindus than the fact that their Moslem overlords, well knowing that Hindus were idolatrous polytheists, still granted them the status of *dhimmis,* accorded elsewhere only to such "People of the Book" as Jews and Christians.

With the rise of the British power in the eighteenth century and its attainment of complete control during the nineteenth,

[1] Kraemer, "Islam in India," *Moslem World,* April, 1931, pp. 152 f.

Islamic political domination ended, and Moslems became no longer the rulers but the ruled. As has elsewhere happened, however, the loss of temporal power has not hindered expansion. All the other factors making for growth in numbers have continued to operate. Since the middle of the last century, indeed, Islam has experienced a widespread revival all over India, with conversions amounting to tens and even hundreds of thousands in the course of a year. The losses to Islam have been negligible and the gains considerable. Even during the decade between 1921 and 1931, the Mohammedan numbers increased 13 percent, or 3 percent above the general gain in population.

After more than twelve centuries of experience with Islam, the people of India now include 78,000,000 Moslems out of a total of 336,000,000,[2] or about 23 percent of the whole. In other words, we find in India far more Moslems than in any other country and about 30 percent of all the Moslems in the world. As might be expected from the history of Islam in India, the vast majority live in the north and east, chiefly in the Punjab, the United Provinces, and Bengal. Of the minority in South India, the largest groups are those in the Hyderabad State and the Mappillas along the Malabar coast.

The wide variety and heterogeneity which are characteristic of all things Indian are marks also of Indian Islam. Not only do the usual mixtures of Aryan and Dravidian appear in the racial stock of Moslems, but also elements of Arab, Turkish, and Afghan origin. In language, too, there is like diversity. Urdu is a kind of lingua franca for all Moslem India, but Bengali is the native tongue of an even larger number, and at least seven other languages are spoken by 1,000,000 or more. In social status and education there are similar sharp differences, ranging all the way from Western-educated leaders of aristocratic lineage to the backward peasantry of eastern Bengal. Sectarian differences, moreover, are fully represented. About 92 percent of believers are Sunnites, but the remaining Shiites are split into sects and subsects. Everywhere, too, are to be found active members of the

2 Exclusive of Burma.

Dervish fraternities, of which fourteen major and five minor orders may be counted.

If it is natural that Islam should reflect the variety of the Indian scene, it is likewise not surprising that it should bear many traces of the Hindu tendency to blend religions; for even Islam, among the masses, has yielded to syncretism. The Hindu inheritance of polytheism and the ancient custom of yielding an almost adoring reverence to the religious teacher have made easy a rich development of saint-worship. For millions of Indian Moslems the shrines of these *pirs* are the true centers of religious devotion. Not only are the same "saints" often revered by Hindus and Moslems alike, but local Hindu gods and godlings are worshiped by Mohammedans. Animistic and magical practices, persisting from the remote past, are sometimes as characteristic of one group as of the other.

The diversity of Indian Islam, of course, long antedates the modern period and would constitute a problem for the Christian missionary if there had been no British regime. But the far-reaching changes of the last eighty years are equally important from the missionary point of view, and most of these are directly due to the rule of Britain. As early as the year 1835, the British had decided to promote the Western system of education as the path to employment in the service of the state. In 1857, with the aid of loyal Indian troops, their forces suppressed the great upheaval of the Mutiny, in which Moslems had played a leading part. The next year the government of the Indian Empire was transferred from the East India Company to the crown. Before 1860, then, it had become quite clear that British rule was to be permanent and that progress along Western lines was inevitable. But though the better classes among the Hindus had long since adapted themselves to both ideas, the Moslems remained embittered and reactionary. Partly through resentment at the complete loss of their power and prestige, but chiefly through religious conservatism, they would have none of the new education. Their mullahs, trained only in narrow Islamic studies, declared a boycott against modern learning and aroused the fears of their followers that the true faith was in danger. The Mohammedans, in short, refused to play the game according to the new rules. In consequence, the many offices in government and business open to educated natives fell more and more into the hands of Hindus.

Just when the prospects of the Moslem community seemed at their darkest, the rise of a great leader brought new hope and ambition. Sir Sayyid Ahmad Khan, who had already enjoyed a distinguished career in the British civil service, held the firm conviction that Western science and education were compatible with loyalty to Islam and that only through embracing and exploiting their new opportunities could the Moslems of India find their salvation. His attitude toward the learning of the West was the easier to maintain because he was a staunch supporter of British rule and because he was too rationalistic to be strictly orthodox. With his zeal for changes in the field of education went an almost equal enthusiasm for social and economic reform. In all these directions he was far ahead of his time and his people and had to suffer slander and persecution at the hands of conservatives. Yet he carried on for nearly forty years a vigorous campaign on behalf of the causes he had made his own; and to his farsighted vision and masterful energy the Indian Islam of today is indebted for the progress it has made in every field.

It is chiefly in the sphere of education that the Sayyid's work has borne fruit. In 1875, in the face of stubborn opposition, he founded Aligarh College, with the aim of combining thorough instruction in Islam with Western scientific training and in the hope, as he said, "that this college may expand into a university [3] whose sons shall go forth throughout the length and breadth of the land to preach the gospel of free inquiry, of large-hearted tolerance, and of pure morality." To further the same end, he initiated in 1886 the All-India Mohammedan Educational Conference. From living sources of inspiration such as these has flowed a stream of influence reviving the hopes and increasing the strength of Islam. In spite of orthodox resistance and reactionary movements, the main trend of the last generation has been an increasing readiness to profit by Western education and to take advantage of the many opportunities for service which it afforded. Since the beginning of the century, Moslem illiteracy has been slowly diminishing,

[3] It became a university in 1920.

though even now there are only 64 Moslems out of every 1,000 who can read, as compared with 84 Hindus and 279 Christians. The change of attitude is reflected also in the number of Mohammedan boys and girls who attend modern schools. Fifty years ago the proportion of such pupils was hardly more than half the total proper to their share in the population. Today, however, the Moslem record in primary education is slightly better than the standard for all India. Such a transformation has been made possible both by the modernizing of Moslem schools and by the increased enrollment of Moslems in missionary and government institutions. Further testimony to the intellectual advance of recent times is the rapid expansion of Moslem publications not only in Urdu but also in English. The present output of newspapers, magazines, and books justifies the statement that "the literate Mohammedans of India are more active and aggressive through the press than their co-religionists in any other part of the world." [4]

Affecting a relatively small number is another sign of Moslem vitality—the progress of liberal religious thought. This modernist movement began in India with the rationalism of Sir Sayyid Ahmad Khan. It was carried further, toward the end of the century, by the work of the Sayyid Amir Ali, whose *Spirit of Islam* and other writings are frankly defensive in their attitude and distinctly anti-Christian. Both more radical and more tolerant has been the little group led by the late Khuda Bakhsh, who went still further in the effort to rehabilitate Islam by concession and adaptation. All of these writers have in common the aim of simplifying their religion by getting "back to the Koran." Since their interests have been chiefly social and ethical, they have contributed little of great philosophical value. The latest apologist has been Sir Mohammed Iqbal, a famous poet in the Urdu and Persian tongues, who, like his predecessors, sought to combine the essential teachings of the Koran with the tenets of Western philosophy. Under his treatment, however, little is left of the purely religious values of Islam.

Of a quite different type and with far more influence today is

[4] Zwemer, "Islam in India," *Moslem World*, April, 1925.

the Ahmadiyya movement. As the only Moslem group seriously trying to convert Western Christians and as the most energetic Moslem sect in India, its position calls for a word of description. It began with the activity of Mirza Ghulam Ahmad in the village of Qadian, in the Punjab. In 1891 this Sunni Mohammedan declared himself to be both the promised Messiah and the coming Mahdi. Though condemned by the mullahs as a heretic, he maintained for the next seventeen years a vigorous propaganda in support of his claims. Three years after his death in 1908, his followers were estimated at nearly 50,000. In 1914 the sect split into two divisions, since known as the Qadian group and the Lahore group. The Qadian party holds loyally to the claims of Ahmad and emphasizes its distinction in this respect from both orthodox and liberal Islam. The Lahore party, more free in its tendencies, is despised by the Qadiani and repudiates all connection with them. Like the Bahais, its leaders aim to denature their original gospel to make it attractive to Westerners or to Westernized Moslems. They are eager to adapt their message to what they take to be the fashions of the present hour and to present Islam as "the cosmopolitan religion of Humanity, Toleration, and Progress," a religion practical and rational and opposed to all dogmas. In keeping with their wider ambitions, they refer to their founder not as the Messiah but only as a reformer. Both parties are distinguished for their missionary zeal. Missions of one or of both sects are to be found not only in every province of India, but also in such areas as the Malay States, West Africa, and Palestine, where Moslems live under European control. Moslem governments, responsive to orthodox fears, are usually careful (as in Egypt) to exclude their agents and their literature. It is in India, then, that their efforts are most widespread and fruitful. There the Qadian group was for long the larger; but in recent years the Lahore group has made greater strides, for its looser views of the Founder are less sharply antagonistic to the standards of Islam. Both wings of the Ahmadiyya are busy in the production of literature and the promotion of reforms and they offer to the young Moslem today his best chance for fellowship with a community, which, though heterodox, is thoroughly alive and in many directions progressive. The whole movement, it should be added, is markedly and often bitterly anti-Christian.

It would be misleading, however, to underestimate the strength of traditional orthodoxy. The illiterate masses remain under the control of mullahs still trained in medieval fashion. The chief center for educating the clergy, the college at Deoband founded in 1895, is hostile to all forms of change and yet retains a powerful influence. The leading Moslem association, moreover, "The Society for the Aid of Islam," is so defensive in its attitude as to be distinctly more conservative than progressive, for it aims "to perpetuate the hold of Islam on the minds of the people."

Defense, too, has been the watchword of increasing Moslem political activity throughout the last generation. The formation in 1906 of the All-India Moslem League expressed the determination of Moslems not to be overwhelmed by the Hindu majority in the coming advance toward self-government. The same resolution to maintain their rights as a religious community has marked their vigorous share in the constitutional agitation of the past ten years. Only the divisive system of separate electorates for Hindus and Moslems could satisfy Indian Islam. Yet no mere political scheme can allay the bitter feeling between the two religious groups—a hostility all the more deep-seated because it is grounded in causes not only religious but also social and economic.

The few Protestant missionaries who worked in southern India during the eighteenth century had no relations with Islam; and Carey and his associates at Serampore early in the next century were primarily concerned with the conversion of Hindus. The first Protestant who gave himself mainly to the cause of evangelizing the Indian Moslem was Henry Martyn, whose early career we have described in our study of Iran. Appointed as chaplain to the East India Company, he landed at Calcutta in May, 1806, and within a few months had been assigned to serve at Dinapore, near Patna. In India, as in Persia, he was to be an inspiring pioneer, the model for successors through many years to come. Several of the methods typical of the next few generations were characteristic of Martyn's six short years of labor—the production of literature, the practice of personal evangelism, and the conduct of controversies.

Before he reached India Martyn had begun the study of Hindustani (Urdu), Persian, and Arabic; and his mastery of Hindustani was nearly complete within a year of his arrival. In June, 1807, the clergy of Calcutta urgently invited him to translate the New Testament into that language and promised to send him two natives as helpers. He had already commenced the task and, with the aid of the proffered fellow workers and other experts, completed and revised his version before 1810. Meantime, he had translated into the same tongue a large part of the Book of Common Prayer and a commentary on the parables. After his removal to Cawnpore in 1809, he was busy with the translation of the New Testament into Persian, which he was to revise at Shiraz before his death.

Though Martyn's contribution as a linguist was to prove of more lasting value than anything else he attempted, his work with the Scriptures filled only a part of his time. Since he was a chaplain of the Company, his duties included preaching and pastoral care among the British soldiers and civil servants. As an ardent evangelist, too, he was moved with compassion at the sight of the swarming heathen masses around him and often gathered large groups of low-caste people and beggars, who would listen to his sermons calling them to repentance and proclaiming a Saviour. But it is in his personal contact with educated Mohammedans that we are chiefly interested. In that congenial activity his powers were at their height. As his biographer, Miss Padwick, has observed in a striking passage, these intimate conversations have significance for us "as the first meeting after centuries . . . of two gigantic spiritual forces all unguarded and unaware, coming together with a first rude clash, unsoftened by intercourse and interaction of thought." [5] Though, as we have noted before, Martyn despised Islam as the work of Satan and regarded the "paltry precepts" of its sacred Book as "despicable," he soon came to respect the skill of the Moslem in argument. During his first year in India he wrote, "A new impression was left on my mind;

[5] Padwick, *Henry Martyn*, p. 204.

namely, that these men are not fools, and that all ingenuity and clearness of reasoning are not confined to England and Europe." [6] But, despite his readiness for controversy, he was ready to admit, "I lay not much stress upon clear arguments; the work of God is seldom wrought in this way." [7] "I find that seriousness in the declaration of the truths of the Gospel is likely to have more power than the clearest argument conveyed in a trifling spirit." [8] "A tender concern manifested for their souls is certainly new to them, and seemingly produces corresponding seriousness in their minds." [9] Yet in close association with his scholarly aides and with other learned doctors who would sometimes join them, he naturally found it impossible to avoid the thorny subjects which for eleven centuries had provided the stock in trade for such debates. Month after month there would be many hours spent in argument about the authority of the Scriptures and of the Koran, the miracles of Mohammed, God's power and man's free will, and the doctrines of the Trinity and the Incarnation. But though the eager intensity of the frail evangelist impressed them deeply and they could not but be awed by his claim that "if our word is true you are lost," they remained unconvinced. And Martyn himself was often conscious of the hopelessness of his efforts.

I am preparing [he wrote in a letter to England], for the assault of this great Mohammedan Imam. I have read the Koran and notes twice for this purpose, and even filled whole sheets with objections, remarks, questions, etc.; but, alas! what little hopes have I of doing him or any of them good in this way! [10]

The one convert he is known to have made before he left for Persia in 1810 was not persuaded in the course of controversy. Sheikh Salih, a learned teacher at Lucknow, heard him preach in public to a mixed crowd and was so deeply touched that he could not rest until he had found access to the Persian New Testament which Martyn was then completing. After long study of it, he made his decision for Christianity and in the following year was

6 Sargent, *Memoir of the Rev. Henry Martyn*, p. 158.
7 G. Smith, *Henry Martyn*, p. 233.
8 Sargent, *op. cit.*, p. 192.
9 G. Smith, *op. cit.*, p. 217.
10 *Ibid.*, p. 233.

baptized at Calcutta as Abd al-Masih. His later work as an evangelist among Moslems, chiefly at Agra, was so vigorous and successful that he was ordained by Bishop Heber in 1825 as the first native priest of the Anglican Church in India.

After Abd al-Masih's death in 1827, the mission at Agra suffered a lapse of ten years before the arrival of the famous Karl Pfander. Pfander, as we have earlier noted, had been a leader in the Basel Mission in Transcaucasia and Persia, devoting himself almost wholly to work with Moslems. When the mission in Persia was given up, he went to India, where at Agra and Peshawar he labored until 1858 in the service of the English Church Missionary Society. Pfander is a stalwart example of the older type of controversialist, a dynamic campaigner against the embattled forces of the False Prophet. In public debate and in written polemic he was the foremost combatant of his age. As a noble specimen of his kind (a kind now almost extinct) and as a writer whose books still live, he fills an honorable place in the history of missions to Moslems. The work by which he is chiefly known is the *Mizanu'l Haqq: The Balance of Truth,* written before his arrival in India, translated since then into many tongues, and reissued with revision as lately as 1911.[11] To review it as a type which long served as a model will reveal one well-known Christian method of approaching the Moslem.

Pfander begins with the axiom that we can win a satisfying knowledge of God only through divine revelation. The two great monotheistic faiths which claim to transmit this revelation are Christianity and Islam. Since on so many vital points they differ, only one of them can possibly be the right way. The True Revelation can be distinguished from all other religions by these six marks: (1) It must satisfy the yearnings of the human spirit to obtain the knowledge of the truth, pardon, and purification. (2) It must be in accordance with the moral law of Conscience. (3) Its God must be just and holy, rewarding the good and punishing the evil. (4) Its God must be one, eternal, almighty, and unchanging in purpose. (5) It must make clear the way of salvation, through gradual progress in the knowledge of God. (6) No book

11 Pfander, *The Mizanu'l Haqq: The Balance of Truth.*

or prophet can fully reveal God to men; there must be a visible personal manifestation of God. After this general introduction, the author proceeds to prove in Part One that the Old and New Testaments have never been abrogated and in all essentials are incapable of being changed or annulled. Moreover, the Scriptures we now possess are those which existed in Mohammed's time and they have never undergone corruption. In Part Two are set forth the main doctrines of the Christian faith, beginning with the attributes of God, the Fall of Man, and the need for a Saviour who is more than merely a man. In succeeding chapters we find an exposition of how Christ has wrought salvation for all men and the proof from Scripture of the doctrine of the Trinity. The section closes with a treatment of the "Life and Conduct of a True Christian" and a study of the manner in which the Christian faith was propagated in the first few centuries. From the evidence assembled, it becomes clear that Christianity fulfills all the requirements of the True Revelation.

It is in Part Three that Pfander attacks the claims of Islam to be God's final revelation. After first demolishing the pretense that the Bible contains prophecies concerning Mohammed, he refutes the assertion that the perfection of the language of the Koran is a sign of its divine origin and points out that so far from being miraculously free from self-contradiction, the book contains many conflicting statements. Turning to the contents of the Koran, we find that the great doctrines which largely coincide with those of the Christian Scriptures are themselves derived from the latter and can certainly not be cited as proving the divine commission of the Prophet. As to the alleged miracles of Mohammed, the Koran supplies no evidence whatever, while those recorded in the traditions are too absurd and too ill-attested to entitle him to the prophetic office. Neither prophecy nor miracle, then, afford any witness to the claims of Mohammed. The record of his character and conduct, moreover, is equally fatal to his cause, a point which the author elaborates by citing Mohammed's relations with women and his treatment of his enemies. Quite as discreditable to Islam, he then proceeds to show, were the methods by which the religion was first spread in Arabia and in the neighboring lands. In a final chapter, Pfander sums up the claims of Islam to be the final revelation. Of all the six criteria laid down in the Introduction, Islam can satisfy only one—the belief in one, eternal, almighty God. Christianity, on the contrary, satisfies them all. And the conclusion is obvious.

Two less-famous works of Pfander appeared in India before 1844—*The Way of Salvation,* dealing with sin and redemption, and *The Key of Mysteries,* treating of the doctrine of the Trinity. What far-fetched arguments are employed in the latter may be judged from its assertion that the triune character of God is to be found throughout all Nature and that the necessity for the use of trigonometry is an obvious consequence! These published books, however, were only one product of Pfander's polemic energy. Another was the long controversy with various leading *maulvis* of northern India, in which he engaged for several years after 1842—protracted debates carried on by letters of increasing length, some of which were printed. The heaviest artillery employed was a work of 806 long pages by the Sayyid Ali Hasan of Agra and a rejoinder by Pfander called *The Solution of Difficulties.* A modern verdict upon these vigorous publications is not unfair.

Despite the vogue Pfander's writings once had [writes Bevan Jones], it has to be admitted that they chiefly serve today as a guide to something better. It was one of his failings that he either could not, or would not, issue a treatise on the Christian faith without turning aside to pass adverse criticisms on the teaching of Islam or the character of Mohammed. In places, too, his own arguments are weak, a fact of which Moslem controversialists took full advantage.[12]

In these earlier stages of the approach to Moslems in India, the story may be outlined more easily in terms of successive leaders than in terms of societies or institutions. For when pioneering is called for, it is the pioneers who count. And none counted for more during the next forty years than Thomas Valpy French. A graduate of Oxford with high honors and a priest in the Church of England, French was sent to India in 1850 by the Church Missionary Society. The task assigned to him was the

12 Jones, *The People of the Mosque,* pp. 238 f.

founding of a college at Agra, then the seat of the British government in the Northwest Provinces. Within six months of French's arrival the school had already been established as St. John's College; two years later it was installed in a new building; and by the year 1857 there were over 300 pupils. But the new institution was heavily handicapped by competition with the Government College and by the hostility of the Mohammedans. Though most of the pupils were non-Moslems, French declared that "in actual conversions the visible results were very small"; and of the general attitude of the people he wrote, "Their utter unsusceptibility is almost heartbreaking." During his eight years at the college only one Moslem boy was baptized.

French, like Martyn and Pfander, engaged also in preaching in the streets and bazaars. "You know," he wrote, "how greatly I feel the importance of energetic, widely diffused preaching of the word, incessant aggressive efforts on the great bulwarks of Satan." [13] But he was ready to confess that "the lack of interest displayed by the majority is *appalling,* and I have been filled at times with something not far short of *consternation* at the gulf which has seemed to separate my hearers and myself." [13] In the face of this open hostility, he reached a conclusion which has been confirmed by many evangelists in recent times.

I begin to find in the bazaar . . . that little is gained by the exposition of these mysteries of our faith. . . . The love of God, the character, work, and words of Christ, the effects produced by the Holy Spirit, seem to be the really effectual topics: others, in which more mystery is involved, lead to such blasphemous remarks.[14]

Yet the logical tournament in full armor was still difficult to avoid. In 1854 French was persuaded to join with Pfander in accepting the challenge of two maulvis to meet them in public debate. Even Pfander agreed with reluctance, "well aware," he said, "that generally very little good is done." But as their opponents had been studying the Bible for several years, as well as many controversial works, the chance for effective discussion was fairly promising. For two days, before large and growing audi-

13 Birks, *Life and Correspondence of Thomas Valpy French,* I, 78.
14 *Ibid.,* p. 57.

ences, the four men maintained their controversy on the "abrogation and corruption" of the Scriptures, the Divinity of Christ, the Trinity, the mission of Mohammed, and the Koran. As both sides had probably expected, everybody wound up the debate with his convictions apparently unaltered. In this case, however, the real ending turned out to be happier than usual. For some ten years later two of the minor assistants on the Moslem side embraced Christianity. The more famous of these was Imad ad-Din. Baptized in 1866, he was later ordained to the priesthood in the Church of England. As a prolific author, a fearless preacher, and a notable Christian leader, he served the Church until his death in 1901. When he read a paper at the Parliament of Religions at Chicago in 1893, he was able to declare, "There was a time when the conversion of a Mohammedan to Christianity was looked on as a wonder. Now they have come and are coming in their thousands." At the end of his paper he added a list of more than a hundred converts who were then occupying influential positions in the State or in the Church in India.[15] In that achievement none had borne a larger share than he.

Before French left in 1859 for a long furlough in England, the C. M. S. had already been at work for some years in the Punjab, at the important cities of Amritsar, Peshawar,[16] and Multan. Though Robert Clark, Pfander, and their helpers enjoyed the warm encouragement of great civil administrators like John Lawrence and Robert Montgomery, they had to wait many years for any converts, and very few of these were Moslems. After his return in 1862, French and a fellow worker set out for the difficult frontier district of Derajat, west of the Indus on the borders of Baluchistan. Despite the need for a severe struggle with a new language, Pushtu, he was soon preaching in the bazaars of Dera Ismail Khan and among the tent villages of Afghans in the barren country round about. Everywhere hostility and apathy aggravated his hardships. Within less than a year, he was laid low with brain fever and ordered home, never, it was feared, to return. Yet after six years of parish work in England, he was back again at

15 Quoted in Robinson, *History of Christian Missions*, p. 470.
16 Since 1901, in the Northwest Frontier Province.

the front, eager to carry out new plans for a Training College
for native evangelists in northwestern India. Lahore, the capital
of the Punjab, was chosen as the center; and after twenty months
of organizing effort and many delays, the institution was opened
in November, 1870. The original four students had increased in
two years to twenty, of whom the majority were Moslems of the
Anglican Mission. How conservative was the curriculum may be
measured by the fact that the young men were obliged to study
not only Greek but also Hebrew for their biblical exegesis, while
their theological diet ranged from Chrysostom and Augustine to
Butler's *Analogy*. But though French could conceive of no theological education that did not correspond exactly with his own,
he took special pains to train his men in the practical work of
pastoral care and homiletics. They were encouraged to preach in
the bazaars and neighboring villages and to bring in enquirers.
French himself had been intensely active in this type of evangelism during the long months before the college opened, touring
over wide stretches of country around Peshawar and Rawalpindi
and as far north as the Kashmir border. Often he set himself to
deal directly with the mullahs and even preached in the mosques.
After his teaching began at Lahore, he joined in the public
preaching carried on by the students and shared their hardships.

The kind of greeting they sometimes encountered is illustrated
vividly by one occasion when French, Bateman, and others were
engaged in preaching at the Lohari gate of Lahore.

There was great excitement, and turnip-tops were flying freely, aimed
in the first place at French himself as the leader, but alighting with
impartiality on all his group of followers. French finding speech
impossible, declared that he would pray for them. "You pray! You
dog, you infidel!" they shouted, "You Christians have no *namaz*
[form of prayer]." Though French could have pronounced their
Moslem *namaz* as accurately as his scorners, he chose a better way.
He knelt down in the dust before them, and poured out his whole
heart to God in simple prayers, till by degrees the shouting fell to
silence, and all who listened were awed by his prophetic dignity.[17]

Except for a summer of arduous pioneering in Kashmir, French
remained at work in Lahore until his departure in 1874 for

[17] Birks, *op. cit.*, I, 258.

another stay of more than three years in England. It was at this time that the Anglican Society for the Propagation of the Gospel established the new diocese of Lahore, comprising the whole of the Punjab, Sind, and Kashmir, and French was appointed as its first bishop. He was consecrated in December, 1877, and early in the following year sailed for India, to take up the burden of his huge diocese. By this time the centers where work was mainly or wholly with Moslems had grown in number. Nearest to Lahore, in the central Punjab, were the stations at Amritsar and such lesser cities as Narowal and Batala. Far in the northwest at Peshawar, T. P. Hughes, scholar in Islamics, was the leader. Likewise close to the Afghan border were Bannu and Dera Ismail Khan. Farther south came the missions at Multan and Dera Ghazi Khan. And three or four hundred miles southward Karachi and Hyderabad were the outposts in Sind. Everywhere the prevailing activity of missionaries and Indian Christians was direct evangelism. But women's work was just beginning, with girls' schools and zenana missions; literary production was going forward through the energy of Imad ad-Din and others; and the founding of the Amritsar Medical Mission in 1882 marked an early stage in opening a new branch of the service of high promise for the future. In the difficult border regions, progress was wearisomely slow and conversions rare. Yet in Amritsar, during the thirty years before 1883, there had been baptized more than 250 converts from Islam.

It is because French was so notable an example of the earlier type of preacher and pathfinder and his energies so concentrated upon the Moslem that we have been justified in giving space to the details of his career. As an explorer he blazed trails in hard areas which others counted impossible and in that role he enjoyed a deeper satisfaction than at the post of an administrator. Even as bishop he found time in 1883 for an extended tour of Persia, where some of his adventures with the Moslem clergy resembled those of Martyn. When he resigned his office in 1887, he was free once more, at the age of sixty-two, to resume that pioneering for which his instinct was so strong. After long journeys through the Near East and North Africa in succeeding years, he reached the conviction that the future of missions to Moslems depended upon opening stations in Arabia. Viewing Muscat, on the coast of Oman, as the strategic point, he settled there early in 1891, and under every possible handicap began the work of evangelism. Within three weeks of his approaching death he was writing,

A sheikh of very wild description sat forty or fifty minutes with me this morning, and we read passages about our Lord's second coming. ...I have had the happiest morning of the week today, preaching in a large covered shed to a number of lepers.[18]

Soon after these last messages went home, he was stricken with fever and died on May 14, 1891. In a different sphere from Kipling's Explorer he too had heard

One everlasting Whisper day and night repeated—so:
"Something hidden. Go and find it. Go and look behind the Ranges—
"Something lost behind the Ranges. Lost and waiting for you. Go!"

French was not only mainly responsible for the founding of a college and for the opening of many frontier stations. He had also a share in initiating the Cambridge Mission to Delhi, which at intervals ever since has played a valuable part in the approach to the Indian Moslem. As early as 1854, the Society for the Propagation of the Gospel had started a mission at Delhi. It remained weak, however, until its affiliation with a new group which drew its strength from the University of Cambridge. There French and others had stirred some of the young clergy with the appeal that "the Universities were providentially fitted to train men who shall interpret the faith of the West to the East." First to respond, as the founder of this Cambridge Brotherhood, the Rev. Edward Bickersteth sailed for India with one companion in October, 1877. Within two years the Brotherhood had grown to the number of six, among whom were the Rev. Samuel S. Allnutt and the Rev. George A. Lefroy. Allnutt, a great teacher and scholar, founded in 1880 St. Stephen's College and St. Stephen's School and served as their principal for eighteen years. Until the end of the century the Moslem pupils were only a small percentage of the whole.

18 *Ibid.*, II, 386 f.

By 1920, however, there were a hundred in the college and twice that number in the school.

As an educator Allnutt is chiefly remembered; but it is as an evangelist to Moslems that Lefroy is in direct line of succession to Martyn and Pfander and French. While head of the Cambridge group from 1880 to 1899, he centered his energy and enthusiasm upon the mission to Islam. Lefroy learned Arabic in order to study the Koran and the theologians, and his command of Urdu was almost perfect. With this unusual equipment he threw himself into the bold enterprise of bazaar preaching and public disputation. So engaging were his vigorous friendliness and good humor and so keen his powers of attack and defense that he was soon enjoying the rare privilege of accepting invitations to carry on discussions in the mosques.

In a letter written in June, 1890, Lefroy relates,

I have been meeting some Mohammedans in one of their mosques in a much more intelligent and reasonable way than I ever did before, and really trying to get them to understand our creed. I must say they have been on the whole wonderfully courteous and willing to understand. . . . I had a close set-to of three hours last Friday morning with one of their leading teachers here. . . . It is exactly the kind of work which I most long for, but which only a short time since seemed so difficult, almost impossible to attain. It is, however, as you may imagine, terrible work arguing on the Trinity and such-like subjects in Hindustani. One has to tackle such questions with them, for they are just like the Greek Church of old and *must* deal with such matters.[19]

Seven months later he was writing of another encounter:

I got to the mosque as soon as I could, and instead of the twenty or thirty men I had been accustomed to meet previously, I found two hundred or three hundred all packed in, a table spread with books for discussion, and all on a grand scale. I felt I was in for it. We were at it for four hours, talking chiefly over internal discrepancies in the Gospel accounts. . . . After that I had two more meetings with the same disputant; one a very large one, over a thousand men packed quietly and listening for three hours. Then these ended, a proclamation appeared in print . . . a few days afterwards to announce the

[19] Montgomery, *Life and Letters of George Alfred Lefroy*, p. 69.

utter defeat in discussion of Rev. G. A. Lefroy, who had been unable
to say a word, and who was now invited to take refuge in Islam! [20]

Such an ending might well warrant the conclusion that the Moslem controversialists regarded the debates rather as a stimulating
game than as an opportunity for the pursuit of truth.

Far less peaceful than the hours in the mosques were those
spent in bazaar preaching.

We are encountering in our open street bazaar preaching a degree of
bigoted opposition such as I have never been through before.... It is
terribly trying on judgment and temper, especially in an atmosphere
of 105 or so!... In the bazaar we are having sore trouble. I accept it
all as a sign in various ways of progress as well as a means of disciplin-
ing, but it is not easy to rejoice in it.

Yet there were other moments more encouraging, of one of which
he wrote,

I am very happy this morning. We had last night the best preaching
I think I have ever had. It began at 6:30 poorly enough with constant
interruptions, but then I settled down to it . . . and God was with me
and I got well on to it, and we went on till eight o'clock, when I
finished in entire darkness, but with a considerable crowd all around
listening in perfect silence while I spoke of the Atonement as the
supreme manifestation of the love of God.[21]

Whatever may have been Lefroy's successes and failures as a
preacher and debater, none ever showed a greater zest than he
or a talent more marked. In view of his record, it is interesting
to learn from his address in 1906 at the Cairo Conference on
Missions to Moslems what he considered the qualifications for
this calling. First, he insisted, the evangelist must have a complete mastery of the Koran in Arabic and a thorough knowledge
of the commentaries, enriched by an acquaintance with the theological classics of Islam. But this training will be of little use
unless he displays in argument entire fairness and complete good
temper and patience. To these he must add a large-hearted sympathy that will prompt him to lead his opponent on from the
truth he already knows to Christ, *the* Truth. And never for an
instant must he lose hope. That missionary opinion had changed

[20] *Ibid.*, pp. 73 f.
[21] *Ibid.*, pp. 70, 72, 76.

in the fifty years since Pfander's prime is evident from these words of Lefroy on the value of controversy:

Most of the older controversial literature on the Christian side is ... very *hard* indeed, as though intended rather to confute the enemy than to win the disguised friend. Similarly much of our preaching seems to me rather as though we were hoping to convert men by throwing brick-bats at them, in the form of truth.[22]

Seven years before Lefroy took part in the Cairo Conference, he had been obliged to withdraw from active evangelism upon his promotion to be Bishop of Lahore. But his share in that meeting showed how close to his heart was the work among Moslems. So it remained during the last years of his life, when, as Bishop of Calcutta, he was Metropolitan of India. At the age of sixty-five he died in January, 1919.

We have thus far been concerned with the work of the English Church Missionary Society because that society was the first to emphasize the direct approach to Moslems and because such leaders as Pfander, French, and Lefroy offer the best examples of the type of evangelism familiar to a past generation. But another enterprise in the Punjab, begun still earlier, had been active all the while—the mission of the American Presbyterians.[23] It was as far back as 1836 that the Rev. John Newton founded the station at Ludhiana, which grew to be a strong center where the work ever since has been partly with Moslems. This Punjab Mission expanded during the next fifteen years to include stations at Fategarh, Jullundur, and Ambala, all cities with large Mohammedan elements in the population. It is as pioneers in education that the Presbyterian leaders have made their most notable contributions. At Ludhiana the first high school in northern India was established. With the arrival in 1848 of the Rev. Charles W. Forman, Lahore was occupied and the school begun which was later to become famous as Forman Christian College. Under the Rev. J. C. R. Ewing (Sir James Ewing), who served as president from 1888 to 1918, the college rose to the foremost place in education in northern India and its leader became the

[22] *Methods of Missionary Work among Moslems*, p. 225.
[23] The Presbyterian Church in the United States of America.

best known and the most trusted foreigner in the Punjab. By the year 1900 there were over 300 students and in 1937 over 1,000, one-fourth of whom were Moslems. Since all these students receive Christian religious training and many share in a well-planned program of Christian social service, the college is rightly counted a valuable factor in the process of reaching educated Mohammedans in this chief Moslem center of India. Indeed, the Punjab schools of this mission and the others have long been recognized as the most effective agency in Moslem evangelization. But a close second has been the continuous sale and distribution of the Scriptures, in which the same mission has always been active, as well as the production of Christian books and tracts especially written for the followers of Islam. Here, too, as in the many works of Dr. E. M. Wherry, the Presbyterians have made valuable additions to a type of literature which is still inadequate to the need.

A Punjab mission larger in numbers than the Presbyterian or the C. M. S. is that of the American United Presbyterians. But only a very small fraction of their staff is active in the predominantly Moslem district of Rawalpindi in the Punjab and at Kohat in the Northwest Frontier Province. At Gordon College, in Rawalpindi, there are many Moslem students, and the clientele of their hospital at Taxila is almost wholly Moslem. Evangelistic itineration and bazaar preaching supplement the extensive work of these two institutions.

Even in the Punjab the population is only a little more than 50 percent Mohammedan, and by far the greater part of missionary activity is concerned with Hindus and Sikhs. It is only when we move outward to its northern and western borders that we come to areas overwhelmingly Moslem, where a larger proportion of the meager Christian forces are necessarily in direct touch with Islam. As in other lands, like Arabia, where Islam is all-powerful and material civilization backward, it is here that medical service has proved the most effective method of approach and that the missionary physician has stood out as the most successful pioneer.

One example of such achievement is the career of the Neve

brothers in Kashmir. Kashmir, the northernmost tip of India, really belongs less to India itself than to Central Asia, bordered as it is on the north by Turkestan and on the east by Tibet. It is now a native state recognizing British supremacy; and though 90 percent of its population of 3,650,000 is Mohammedan, it is ruled by a Hindu Maharaja. In this province, as long ago as 1864, the Rev. Robert Clark, of the C. M. S., began regular work in the face of popular hostility and the determined opposition of the authorities. In the following year the C. M. S. Kashmir Medical Mission began, with the arrival at Srinagar of Dr. W. J. Elmslie, who, in spite of continued obstruction, was soon treating as many as 4,000 patients a year. It was not till after two decades, however, that the value of the mission began to be fully appreciated. Toward the close of that period Dr. Arthur Neve arrived, in 1882, and his brother Ernest, in 1886. Both had received the best of medical training at Edinburgh and each supplemented the other in the double enterprise of medicine and surgery in the hospital and extensive itineration for preaching and healing throughout the province and even beyond its borders. In 1919, after war service in France, Arthur Neve died, leaving to his brother the leadership of the hospital. When the news of his death reached Srinagar, it was an organized group of Mohammedans who passed this resolution: "In recognition of the innumerable favors which the Kashmiris in general, and Moslems in particular, enjoyed at his hands, this Association, on behalf of the Mussulmans of Kashmir, places on record the deep sorrow and extreme regret felt by the latter on the lamented and untimely demise of the late Dr. Arthur Neve." [24]

As to the methods of the hospital and the response of Moslems, Dr. Ernest Neve has written:

Medical mission work in Kashmir is to a great extent among Mohammedans. . . . Only those who know the Orient will understand that, with few exceptions, our readings and preachings are acceptable to all the patients, whether Mohammedan or Hindu. . . . Amongst those with whom we come in contact, the attitude toward Christianity varies greatly. Some are bitterly hostile. Others are a step farther on,

[24] Neve, *A Crusader in Kashmir*, pp. 64 f.

and listen with interest, smiling somewhat cynically at any unpalatable truth. Others are really anxious to hear, and ask us to preach to them. Those, however, who have the moral courage to come out and make an open profession of faith have to endure obliquy and the scoffs, jeers, and persecution of their fellow-countrymen for His sake. . . . In St. Luke's Church, in the Hospital waiting rooms, in the wards, and in the village not only have people gathered for medical relief . . . but witness has been regularly and steadily borne. In the year 1926 more than 3300 Gospels were sold to patients and their friends. If our methods are sound, and our lives at all adequately emphasize our teaching, there should be no room for doubt as to results. Already they are following. The confidence of the people has been won; the attitude of Hindus, Mohammedans, and Sikhs is most friendly; there is little or no *odium theologicum*. . . . There are abundant indications for those who have sympathy to feel compassion, and wisdom to perceive, that there is a remarkably widespread reverence in Kashmir for the name and work of Christ. . . . In spite of religious intolerance, and social and official opposition, the Spirit of Christ is moving in the land, and the future holds in store spiritual blessings to which hitherto Kashmir, with its unhappy history of tyranny and religious persecution, has been a stranger.[25]

Another intrepid physician, who gave eighteen years of strenuous service to the cause of winning Moslems, was Theodore L. Pennell. As a young Fellow of the Royal College of Surgeons who had won many honors and prizes, he offered himself to the C. M. S. for work in India. Late in 1892 he was stationed at Dera Ismail Khan, one of the centers in the Northwest Frontier Province at which French had earlier labored. In that province, which stretches for some 500 miles along the Afghan border, the population, composed of Pathans, Baluchis, Jats, and others, is more than 90 percent Mohammedan. Exploiting an amazing gift for languages, Pennell soon learned Urdu and Pushtu and began to preach in all the neighboring villages. In the following year he established the Medical Mission at Bannu, which was thenceforth to remain his headquarters and where within a few months he had to deal with more than 100 patients a day. Not content to serve only in the routine of hospital work, he started

[25] *Ibid.*, pp. 77, 79, 82, 88 f., 212. The annual average of new patients in 1934 was 23,000. In addition to the Mission Hospital at Srinagar, there is also a C. M. S. hospital for women at Anantang and a Church of England Zenana Mission Society Hospital for women at Ranawari, a suburb of Srinagar.

a boys' school, which in five years had risen to the status of a high school. As an enthusiastic athlete, he trained the boys to skill in sports and in later years often toured the cities of western India with his football teams to play match games. Some of his most valuable converts from Islam were former students who had worked and played with him at Bannu. But Pennell's favorite form of evangelistic adventure was to don Pathan dress and to go on tour, with two or three stalwart converts, to distant villages in the wilder parts of the country. Preaching in the bazaars was usually exciting and risky, for the Moslem mullahs were everywhere his bitter opponents, and at times he was even stoned. Yet by frequent visitations to the most unpromising centers, he often succeeded in winning the confidence of hostile tribes; and in his eyes the chance to face the Moslem directly with the Christian message was always worth the hazards. His militant zeal, however, never led him to violent polemic in his preaching. "To my mind," he once said, "much more good can be done with a bazaar audience by patient exposition of the spirituality of Christianity than by however brilliant a demonstration of the faults of Islam." [26]

Before his too-early death in 1911—the year he received the Kaisar-i-Hind gold medal for service to India—Pennell had spoken of his work at a meeting in Queen's Hall, London:

Afghanistan is a closed land . . . yet the influence of medical missions has penetrated through and through. I suppose there are few, if any, villages in East and South Afghanistan which have not sent their quota of patients to our Frontier hospitals. These patients have heard the Gospel preached in our out-patient departments; have, many of them, lain week after week in the wards, receiving the ministrations of the Christians, watching our lives and gauging the reality of our professions, and then they have gone back to their distant homes and retailed their experiences . . . while the old men and young warriors gathered around to listen to all they have seen and heard across the Frontier. Often a Testament or other book, carefully secreted from prying eyes, is smuggled back to their homes and studied in private, and passed on in secret to some friend, and thus the people have become familiarized with the Gospel story. . . . Medical missions are their own advocate, inasmuch as they have everywhere proved them-

[26] A. M. Pennell, *Pennell of the Afghan Frontier*, p. 187.

selves an immense success. Our very success is often the most embarrassing feature we have to deal with. . . . Last year in the Bannu hospital alone, we dealt with 34,000 individual cases . . . yet for this and the work at our three out-stations we have only four qualified medical men (two English and two Indian) and one qualified medical woman.[27]

In treating of an area as large as that of India, our method has inevitably had to be selective and, even within the limits of northern India and its borders, we have made no mention, for example, of such C. M. S. enterprises as Edwardes College at Peshawar, the high schools at Amritsar, the hospital at Quetta, and the little stations in the intensely difficult field of Sind. Outside of northern India, too, in the eastern province of Bengal, there are more than 25,000,000 Moslems and among the Christians are to be found about 16,000 who are either converts from Islam or their descendants. Yet it is in the north that Islam maintains its political and cultural seats of power and its strongest centers of resistance; and it is there that the most notable efforts have been made to win its followers.

It was in the heart of northern India and at the center of Shiah Islam that there was held in 1911 at Lucknow the second world conference of missionaries to Moslems. Like its predecessor at Cairo in 1906, the conference was initiated by Dr. Zwemer, of the Arabian Mission, who presided over its sessions from January 23 to January 28. One hundred and eighty delegates from eight different Moslem countries met to consider together such problems as "The Political Changes in the Moslem World," "Islam among Pagan Races," "Literature for Workers and Moslems," "Reform Movements in Islam," and "Work among Women." Even more clearly than the Cairo Conference, Lucknow emphasized the fact that Islam is a world problem and that missionaries throughout the world who face Islam need the help which can come only from a closer coördination of their knowledge, their experience, and their effort. As a result of carrying this conviction into practical action, there arose from the Lucknow Conference committees for aiding the production and distribution of Chris-

[27] *Ibid.*, pp. 398 f., 401.

tian literature for Moslems, the development of centers for training missionaries, and the founding of an invaluable quarterly which still flourishes—*The Moslem World.*

When we review the field of India as a whole, we find that accessions from Islam have been continuous for a century or more, coming nearly always singly and slowly, here and there. In the Punjab alone such converts now number several thousand, many of whom are outstanding leaders in the Church. Indeed, it was estimated more than thirty years ago that among the pastors and teachers of northern India were at least 200 former Mohammedans. The visible fruits of endeavor have thus been more encouraging than in the Near East or North Africa or even in Iran, though it must be remembered that the number of Moslems in India is greater than in all these countries put together.

It is when we consider this immense total of 78,000,000 Mohammedans that we reach the obvious conclusion that Indian Islam is a neglected field. Though the Moslems constitute 23 percent of the population, hardly more than 2 percent of the 5,000 Protestant missionaries are devoting their full time to the service of these Moslems, and still fewer are adequately equipped for such work. The chief reason, of course, is that since Moslems in most areas are not only a minority but a peculiarly exclusive and unresponsive minority, it has always been easy to turn from them to more readily exploited opportunities. And of such opportunities India has long had many to offer, with its mass movements, for many years past, among the depressed classes and the lower castes. It is only natural that the attention of most missions should have been chiefly absorbed in meeting the demands of those who have been eager to accept Christianity rather than in laboring to change the hearts of those who despise and reject it. But however plain the reasons may be, the more difficult cause has suffered in consequence. Few missionaries have been set apart for this special task; there is a deplorable lack of Indian evangelists capable of dealing with Moslems effectively; and there is extremely little Christian literature in any language used by Moslems except Urdu. Aside from such contacts as are furnished

by the Christian colleges, the class most completely neglected is
that of the educated Mohammedans, who are now more than ever
self-conscious and articulate.

For the last fifteen years, however, thanks in large measure to
the influence of the National Christian Council of India, the
needs and opportunities in the Moslem field have been brought
home with increasing urgency to the missionary forces. A greater
degree of concerted effort has been chiefly evident in the increased production of literature. Especially through the Christian
Literature Society of Madras and the Punjab Religious Book
Society millions of pages of books and tracts have been issued,
designed with a view to presenting Christianity to Moslem readers.
A further recent example of coöperation in the service of the
Indian Moslem is the Henry Martyn School of Islamics, an encouraging enterprise which offers abundant opportunities for
future developments of high value. Founded in 1930 at Lahore,
through the joint efforts of five British and American missions,
the school has set as its aims to provide a teaching center for the
study of Islamics, to prepare Christian literature for use with
Moslems, and to sponsor special studies by the staff of different
aspects of Indian Islam. Under the Rev. L. Bevan Jones as principal, the school proceeded rapidly to prove its usefulness in all
these directions. At Lahore it not only began the training of
missionaries, but succeeded at the same time in establishing cordial relations with Mohammedan leaders at that center. Its influence was soon extended by the practice of giving courses of
lectures and organizing study groups at such other cities as Lucknow, Calcutta, and Serampore, as well as at a number of hill
stations. After seven or eight years of work, the financial resources
of the school became so straitened that to save money it was
obliged to move from Lahore to Landour, Mussoorie, in the
United Provinces, where its more settled work is now carried on.
But its activities in itineration are still maintained. To enrich
its already effective contribution to the cause, the school now
needs not only larger funds to permit its return to Lahore, but
a closer integration with a more aggressive missionary program
for work with Moslems on the part of all the Churches.

XIV

The Netherlands Indies

THE NETHERLANDS Indies, more familiarly known as the Dutch East Indies, comprise the greater part of that wide stretch of islands which run from the Malay Peninsula on the west to British New Guinea on the east. They lie south of the Philippines and north of Australia. Extending for more than 3,000 miles from west to east, they cover an area of 735,000 square miles and include a population of nearly 61,000,-000, chiefly of the Malay race.[1] In these volcanic tropical islands, with their dense vegetation, their magnificent scenery, and their heavy rainfall, is to be found a rich variety of agricultural and mineral wealth—especially rice, rubber, sugar, tobacco, and coffee, together with petroleum and tin.

The main islands are Sumatra, Java, Celebes, Borneo, and New Guinea, half of which is under Dutch control. Sumatra, though fourteen times the size of Holland, contains the same number of inhabitants—about 8,000,000. Java, in less than a third of the area, supports a huge population of nearly 42,000,000, with the record density of 817 to the square mile. It is here that modern material civilization is most apparent, for the island contains some 3,400 miles of railway for trains and steam trams and 16,000 miles of roads. Dutch Borneo with 2,000,000 population and Celebes with 4,000,000 are far less developed, especially in their mountainous interiors. Most of their commercial activity depends upon the Chinese inhabitants, who number, throughout the whole Netherlands Indies, as many as 650,000. East of Celebes lie the Moluccas, a group composed of innumerable small islands and several large ones, such as Gilolo and Ceram; and south and southwestward lie the islands known as Amboina and Timor.

---

[1] Census of 1930, and so with other figures.

Following the Portuguese, who first appeared in the islands in 1511, the Dutch entered the East Indies at the end of the sixteenth century; and in 1602 their smaller trading companies were united by the establishment of the Dutch East India Company. Seventeen years later there was founded in Java the town of Batavia, the capital of the Indies, now a thriving city of more than 250,000 inhabitants. Within a generation, Portuguese rule had been wholly excluded, and until the middle of the eighteenth century the East India Company continued to increase in prosperity. After a long period of decline, during which the company was abolished, the government of the Netherlands took direct charge of the administration of the Indies. Extending their conquests gradually throughout the nineteenth century, the Dutch have long since obtained complete control of this vast archipelago, maintaining a government paternalistic in character and efficient in operation. It was not until the beginning of the present century that evidence of a nationalist awakening appeared. Contemporaneous with similar movements in India, there arose an increasing demand for Western education and for participation by the better classes in political activity. In response to these signs of new life, the government instituted in 1918 a semiparliamentary body called the Volksraad, whose membership for the past ten years has been half Indonesian. Since it now shares legislative powers with the Governor-General, it marks the first stage in the process of self-government. In Java there are already provincial councils, and local government is almost entirely exercised by native civil servants under Dutch regents.

During the same modern period the educational system has been extensively developed. There are now 17,000 public elementary village schools with two or three-year courses, and another 2,400 with five or six-year courses. A far smaller number of primary schools meet the needs of those who want instruction through the medium of the Dutch language, and a still smaller number carry the pupils through the secondary grades. In the field of higher education there are now an engineering college, a law college, a theological college, and a medical and dental college, besides various "gymnasia" and junior colleges.

The spread of Islam in the East Indies, which is still in active operation, has been largely the result of peaceful persuasion exerted by Moslem traders in the course of many centuries. No one knows just when the process began; but since Arab merchants were numerous at Canton as early as the eighth century, there is good reason to believe that some of them found their way southward to the Malay islands perhaps as long as 1,200 years ago. It is clear, at least, that until the arrival of the Portuguese at the beginning of the sixteenth century the Arabs had been for 500 years in full control of the trade with the East. And before the end of that period, Moslem missionaries from southern India were also to be found in the archipelago.

It is to the proselytizing efforts of these Arab and Indian merchants that the native Mohammedan population, which we find already in the earliest historical notices of Islam in these parts, owes its existence. ... In every instance, in the beginning, their work had to be carried on without any patronage or assistance from the rulers of the country, but solely by the force of persuasion, and in many cases in the face of severe opposition, especially on the part of the Spaniards.[2]

As early as the end of the thirteenth century, there was a Mohammedan kingdom in Sumatra; and during the next 200 years Islam, already established on the coasts, made rapid progress in the inland districts. Yet one large pagan group, the Bataks, long remained unconverted, and only in recent times has Islam made headway among that branch of them known as the Tobas.

In Sumatra the invading religion had to deal chiefly with uncivilized animists. But in Java its representatives encountered a civilization of a high order, already deeply rooted for many generations in the culture and faith of Hinduism and Buddhism. The advance of Islam was therefore slow and difficult, and its dominance has never succeeded in extinguishing the many traces of earlier ages. Though the first stages of Moslem influence appear at the close of the twelfth century, no great success was achieved for another 200 years. During the fifteenth century, however, the native followers of Mohammed had so increased in numbers and power that there ensued a civil war, which ended in 1478 with

[2] Arnold, *The Preaching of Islam*, pp. 365, 363.

the overthrow of one of the reigning dynasties and the emergence in eastern Java of a line of Moslem rulers. But in the west of Java the progress of Islam was much slower, and not until the middle of the sixteenth century did the native monarch give way to Mohammedan control. The conversion of central Java was a process even longer and less thoroughgoing. In course of time, however, more through gradual penetration than through political influence, the remainder of the natives conformed to the faith, so that today the whole population of the island, save for some 77,000 indigenous Christians, is nominally Moslem.

In the Molucca Islands, Islam may be traced as far back as the fifteenth century. Though its advance in that area was seriously retarded for a time by the Portuguese conquest, the majority of the people have long since become adherents. But in Borneo and Celebes, Islam has been very slow in making converts outside of the coastal regions and its forces are still occupied in winning the heathen population of the interior.

Sometimes indeed the sword has been drawn in support of the cause of religion, but preaching and persuasion rather than force and violence have been the main characteristics of this missionary movement. The marvelous success that has been achieved has been largely the work of traders, who won their way to the hearts of the natives by learning their language, adopting their manners and customs, and began quietly and gradually to spread the knowledge of their religion by first converting the native women they married and the persons associated with them in their business relations. Instead of holding themselves apart in proud isolation, they gradually melted into the mass of the population, employing all their superiority of intelligence and civilization for the work of conversion and making such skillful compromises in the doctrines and practices of their faith as were needed to recommend it to the people they wished to attract. . . . Beside the traders, there have been numbers of what may be called professional missionaries—theologians, preachers, jurisconsults, and pilgrims.[3]

Since Islam is still spreading rapidly in many parts of the Indies, it is possible to watch the process, to describe the methods employed, to note the motives of conversion, to estimate the effects

[3] *Ibid.,* p. 405.

of the religion upon the natives, and to draw conclusions valuable for the cause of Christian missions both there and elsewhere.[4]

The progress of Islam today is being furthered by the display of that power and prestige which characterize the Moslem trader, teacher, and official, a power and prestige at once political, social, and religious. Though the rulers of the islands are no longer Mohammedan and a Christian government maintains a position described as neutral, the high standing of Islam in the eyes of the natives has lost little by the change. In some respects, indeed, its cause has benefited through the replacement of Moslem by Dutch domination. For now it is Christianity which has to bear the disadvantage of being the religion of the foreign overlords, and Islam can offer itself as a protection against alien encroachment.

Neutral the state may be, in the sense that it does not deliberately exert its force to spread Islam and in the further sense that it suppresses any religious activities which appear politically dangerous. But the neutrality which the government observes is everywhere favorable to the reputation of the prevailing religion and helpful to the influence of its propaganda. The Malay tongue, for example, has been adopted by the Dutch as the official language for the whole archipelago. In Java, however, the indigenous languages are also used. Generally written in the Arabic character and spoken by very few who are not Mohammedans, Malay is regarded, next to Arabic, as the sacred language of all the Indies; and few natives learn it without adopting the faith with which it is identified. The higher classes have to acquire it if they are to have any dealings with the government, and the lower classes readily follow their example. Since the subordinate civil officials, moreover, are naturally recruited from Malay-speaking Moslems, these political agents, clerks, and interpreters carry their religion with them wherever they go. Even more advantageous to Islam has been the expansion of popular education. In most of the

4 Any reliable summary of this process, however brief, will owe much to the well-known work of Gottfried Simon—*Islam und Christentum im Kampf um die Eroberung der animistischen Heidenwelt* (trans. as *The Progress and Arrest of Islam in Sumatra*), as well as to the careful studies of H. Kraemer.

elementary government schools learning to read and write means studying Malay in the Arabic alphabet under the guidance of Mohammedan teachers. In these circumstances, it is not surprising that people still pagan are encouraged to believe that all wisdom is Mohammedan wisdom and that they can become truly civilized only through Islam. With the lower ranks of the civil service largely confined to Moslems, with education mediated through Moslems, and with the coastal trade chiefly in Moslem hands, the native heathen naturally count it to their advantage to accept Islam. That is the obvious path to progress, whether political, cultural, or economic.

Islam is not only associated with progress. It appears also as an agency of protection. In the midst of the revolution occasioned by the influx of European power, with all its disturbing changes, an uncivilized people feels helpless. It lacks the resources to resist disintegration. Like unorganized and unskilled labor, exploited by rich and ambitious capitalists, it is at the mercy of its rulers. It needs some rallying point, some weapon of defense that can command respect. The factory worker finds it by joining a powerful labor union. The East Indian pagan finds it by embracing Islam. For in his eyes Islam is clearly the religion of the brown man, as against the white man. More than that, it is the religion which the white man favors and respects, of which, indeed, he even seems to be afraid. Once a Moslem, the native can feel sure of preserving his nationality and maintaining his self-respect. He can share in that power and prestige of which the Moslem is so obviously proud. And he is all the more likely to take the step, because while he is still a heathen his Mohammedan neighbor regards him with disdain and yet when he has surrendered to Islam he is welcomed as a brother.

Existing conditions, then, offer every practical inducement for the heathen to become a Moslem. The non-religious attractions to conversion are varied and compelling. But it would be a mistake not to recognize how heavily they are reinforced by other motives definitely religious. Indeed, so close an observer as Gottfried Simon declares that in the East Indies the religious motive is fundamental. This does not imply, however, that such an impulse is any higher than those we call practical. Because of what religion already means to the native, there is rarely any longing for a purer faith, for inward peace, or for communion with God. In the common nature-religion of uncivilized peoples, the aim of the cult is to win material goods from powerful gods and spirits, and the cult is everywhere supplemented by magical rites designed to serve the same purpose. From the standpoint of the heathen animist, then, the Moslem shows every sign of enjoying prosperity and success. He must be in command of resources that make him irresistible. Undoubtedly his God is invincible. The Mohammedan, in turn, does all he can to confirm this conclusion. He even encourages the further belief of the despised pagan that adherents of Islam are endowed by Allah with secret wisdom and magical powers. The followers of the Prophet not only possess all earthly advantages. They likewise control all the mysterious forces of the unseen world. It is easy to see, therefore, why the natives of the Indies, responding to all these pressing incentives, should so long have been turning by the tens of thousands to Islam.

But what does their new religion do for them? Once they are converted, what sort of Moslems do they make? As in the case of the African Negro, no full answer can be given that is acceptable to all observers. Yet certain results seem beyond dispute. As might be expected, the convert is highly proud of his new status, for he has been taken into the brotherhood of a world religion. This pride in membership, admirable up to a certain point, easily degenerates into a conceited sense of superiority, expressing itself in contempt for his heathen neighbors and all their ways. Quite as commonly it is inflamed to a fanaticism which rouses in him a strong animus both anti-Christian and anti-European. But though the convert is proud of his religion, he knows very little about it. Even when the village teacher gathers about himself a group of young men, he is not only incompetent to give any secular instruction but has little to impart of Moslem learning. His pupils may hear the Koran read, but only in an alien tongue; and mechanical memory work from Malay catechisms offers an education more formal than real. As with Roman Catholicism in Latin America, the religious authorities have more to gain from popular ignorance than from popular enlightenment.

Yet the only kind of teaching which the newly won heathen is really anxious to receive, his masters are quite prepared to give—the kind of "wisdom" which consists in magical practices. With magic in general the pagan is already familiar, and the spirits with whom he has had intercourse still continue to be available. But now he can add to his equipment the spells and formulas, the talismans and amulets, which the Moslem expert is ready to provide. Mohammed figures as the mediator of the mystic powers of Allah, and the teachers are accepted as his representatives. These sheikhs are thus valued far less as teachers than as sorcerers, who take the place of the old magicians of the heathen past and are revered with a far more slavish devotion. In fact they are treated with almost divine honors, and after their death they become village saints to whose grave the people make pilgrimage. In other words, Islam in the East Indies is more concerned to exploit than to eradicate the superstitions of the pagans. By leaving their animism largely undisturbed and their ignorant fears still active, it makes easy the transition from the old to the new. No real change of heart is demanded.

Even a relaxed and degenerate Islam, however, must stand for certain laws. And it is just so far as these traditional requirements are made and met that Islam can claim any success worthy of its own standards. Among the laws commonly insisted upon are those concerned with food, especially the prohibition of eating swine's flesh. The duty of daily prayers, too, is constantly impressed upon the people, though it is regularly observed only by the stricter Mohammedans. With greater fidelity the religious tax is paid to the teachers, from whom no account is expected. The annual fast is almost universally kept, with surprising devotion. And as for the pilgrimage to Mecca, few Mohammedan lands send such a high percentage of believers to the sacred city.[5]

Islam is more successful in promoting obedience to these religious observances and external ceremonies than in achieving any

[5] E.g., 1914-15, 28,427; 1921-22, 28,878. Sometimes one-half the pilgrims in Mecca are from the Netherlands Indies.

moral transformation. The convert from paganism is still too much imbedded in his animistic environment to react against it with any new sense of sin. Mohammedan ethics justify him in continuing to raid and plunder the heathen tribesmen, for marauding can be encouraged as holy warfare. And the practice of divorce grows so extremely common that the morality of Moslem family life is often below that of the heathen.

In view of the evidence, these pictures of what Islam accomplishes among the masses of recently converted pagans are probably not too dark. It must be remembered, however, that these so-called "heathen-Mohammedans," drawn from many uncivilized tribes, are not the only Moslems in the Indies. Islam has been a power in the greater islands for five centuries and more, and among its adherents are millions whose civilization is still older. East Indian Mohammedanism, with perhaps 45,000,000 followers, is one of the major divisions of a world religion, in touch with movements in many other lands. As such, it has characteristics of its own and deserves to be judged at its best. And it can be seen at its best among the orthodox and educated in the middle classes of civilized society.

The outstanding characteristic of the Moslem Indies is the marked leaning toward the magical, occult, and mystical elements in Islam. This prevailing tendency is due partly to the natural inclination of the people, partly to their heritage of Hindu teaching and practice, and partly to the type of Islam which has been propagated. Each of the three influences, in fact, has served to reinforce the others. The most obvious method by which this mysticism has been implanted and nourished is the activity of the Darwish orders, whose members are growing in numbers throughout the islands. Usually belonging to these fraternities, nearly all the Moslem teachers of any repute try to give instruction in mysticism because only so can they retain their hold upon the people. A limited number of believers are capable of mystical discipline and experience of a more or less pure monistic type. But the higher mysticism, with its scholastic teaching, is relatively rare. Far more common, as in India and Egypt, are various simpler and coarser substitutes more easily appreciated by the average man. Among these is the practice of the *zikr*, stimulating group emotion with its recitations in unison and its hypnotic rhythmic exercises, often ending in intoxicated frenzy. Lower in the scale, as everywhere else in religious history, mysticism degenerates into sheer magic.

Another typical feature of Islam in the Indies is the widespread influence of the *hajjis*, those who have made the pilgrimage to Mecca. These, as we have seen, are exceptionally numerous, to be counted today by the hundreds of thousands. As traders and teachers they are everywhere to be found. Even more than elsewhere, their record as pilgrims heightens their prestige and affords them a position of leadership. Taking full advantage of their superior status, they not only derive personal benefit from their power but serve the valuable purpose of keeping a distant section of Islam in contact with what is going on in the rest of the Moslem world.

A further characteristic, more recently in evidence, is the rise of reforming movements. Here, of course, the Moslems of the East Indies are only sharing in a process familiar all over Asia— the effect upon ancient tradition of Western thought and modern education. Especially among people of the middle class in Java and the west coast of Sumatra, these influences have been at work for the last thirty years. Parallel with changes in the political sphere and often reinforcing them, new intellectual life has been manifest in religion. The clearest proof of this revival is the rapid growth of Moslem publications, for there are now more than a hundred newspapers and periodicals which are Islamic in their outlook or influence. Though a few are reactionary, the great majority are progressive.

A powerful movement of the modernistic type is the Mohammediyya, founded in Java in 1912 by a broad-minded *hajji*. It has since grown so rapidly that now every town of any size in Java or Sumatra has its local chapter and the organization has spread to Celebes and even to parts of Borneo. In sharp opposition to the conservative Islamiyya Association, the Mohammediyya rejects all tradition beyond the Koran and is ready to interpret even the Koran in the light of present-day knowledge. What the new movement really represents is a response, more or less conscious, to the successful methods of Christian missions, especially their educational and philanthropic enterprises. In this respect it offers a very close and interesting resemblance to the modern work of the Buddhist Shin sect in Japan. In both cases we notice the effort to prove that emancipated non-Christians can serve their people with an up-to-date energy equal to that of the Christians. The Mohammediyyas are active in propaganda and in the publication of literature, especially for the religious education of the young. Indeed, they are particularly concerned to develop a Youth Movement promoted by clubhouses, reading rooms, organized sports, and Boy Scout and Girl Guide troups. They are encouraging modern education by the founding of many secular schools. In developing social service they have established small hospitals and orphanages. Even the worship in the mosque has felt the effect of such changes as the introduction of hymn-singing and informal sermons, after the manner of Christians. To coördinate all these activities and to plan for others, there is held an annual conference known as the Mohammediyya Congress.

Of a wholly different sort is the Sarikat Islam which appeared, at the time of its organization in 1912, as a popular movement strongly nationalist. It voiced for a time the vague unrest and the political and economic hopes of an awakening people. As its influence gradually diminished with the rise of other political movements, it has become much more definitely Moslem in character and now appeals chiefly to those who are first Moslems and then nationalists.

Like most other Moslem lands, the Netherlands Indies have been included in the missionary plans of the Ahmadiyya Movement.[6] Of its two branches, the Lahore group has been at work in Java and Sumatra since 1924 and the Qadian group since 1929. Their representatives have proved, as usual, to be strongly controversial and anti-Christian in their attitude. Yet so far their efforts have met with little success, for Moslems of nearly all shades of opinion consider them heretics.

The vitality of East Indian Islam is evident not only from all

[6] See pp. 208 f.

these signs of its intellectual life in the more settled centers, but also from its unceasing missionary activity throughout the islands not yet wholly converted. In the island of Java and in those most nearly adjacent (like Lombok and Sumbawa), in the southwestern peninsula of Celebes, in the southern part of Gilolo, and in Central and South Sumatra, the population is already substantially Moslem, so that there is little further room for advance among pagans. But there are other parts of Malaysia where large numbers of the people are still heathen—the southern part of Northern Sumatra (the Batak country), the whole interior of Borneo and Central Celebes, the northern part of Gilolo, and such islands as Timor and Ceram, not to mention the wide territory of New Guinea. In these areas Moslem traders, teachers, and officials are at work, winning the same success by the same means that have extended the power of Islam for centuries past. Today, however, they encounter, on a scale never before so effective, the rival force of an expanding Christianity.

Christianity has had a continuous history in the East Indies for nearly four and half centuries. The religion entered the islands with the Portuguese traders and conquerors at the beginning of the sixteenth century, and its spread followed the line of Portuguese conquest. As in Latin America, the cross was planted wherever the ships of the invaders found entrance; and everywhere in large numbers the natives were compelled not only to yield to political domination but to accept the religion of their new masters. Chiefly by the use or the threat of force during two generations, the Roman Catholic communities about the year 1560 were widespread in the Moluccas, Solor, Timor, and Flores, and in smaller quantities in Celebes, Java, and Sumatra. At this time, indeed, they probably included as many as 200,000 Christians. As the power of Portugal waned from that time on, the Portuguese missions were abandoned, and a large proportion of their converts turned to Islam or relapsed into paganism. The Church was too wholly dependent upon foreign aid to survive; and its collapse was made all the more certain by the greed and cruelty and immorality of the European Catholics.

With the rise of the Dutch power at the end of the sixteenth century begins the story of Protestant advance. From that day to this, missionary evangelism has been chiefly among pagans, and most of the converts to Christianity have been converts from heathenism. During the same period, of course, the missionaries of Islam have been even more active and with far greater success. Only in recent times, as the Moslems have become more numerous and more accessible, has the Church begun to undertake their evangelization with adequate vigor and with fruitful results. But though our chosen subject is the Christian approach to the Moslem, we shall be justified in summarizing the progress of Christianity among pagans because every effort to win them is part of the larger endeavor to reach and serve Islam. The religious movements in these islands for 400 years may well be regarded as a race between Christianity and Islam to secure the allegiance of the heathen tribes. Narrowly viewed, from the standpoint of tactics, most of the missionary work of the Church has been simply the conversion of animists, like animists anywhere else. Broadly viewed, however, from the standpoint of strategy, the advance of Christianity in fields not yet claimed by its rival profoundly affects the relative position of the two great faiths and in a real sense constitutes a chapter in the Christian approach to Islam.

Unfortunately for the Christian Church, the efforts of missionaries were weakest in the earlier stages when the untouched heathen were greatest in number and Islam was far less widely and firmly established than it is now. As the Christian forces slowly increased in quantity and quality, the problem with which they had to deal was growing in complexity and difficulty, so that today a much stronger Church confronts a much harder task.

During the seventeenth and eighteenth centuries, religion in the Netherlands was under the control of the government, and in the Indies the functions of government had been conferred upon the East India Company. The company therefore regarded the Church as one branch of its activities. It employed clergymen of the Reformed Church to serve the interests of religion, much as it employed other agents to serve the interests of trade. Though the clergy were chiefly engaged in ministering to Europeans, they were often charged with missionary duties, and the power of the company was sometimes exerted to compel pagan natives to accept baptism. Missions, in other words, were looked upon as a government enterprise. As such, they could count upon strong local support, but on the other hand they made no appeal to the Christians in Holland. Moreover, it became increasingly difficult to obtain clergymen even of poor quality.

In 1795 Church and State in Holland were completely separated, and three years later the East India Company was abolished. By that time it had no more than seven ministers in its employ, and only the native preachers saved the missions from complete collapse. After an interval of seventeen years, the Netherlands, now transformed into a kingdom, assumed direct charge of the government of the Indies and retained there a control over the Church which had already been relinquished in the home country. In the course of the next thirty years, the Protestant Churches then in the islands were united as the Indian Church, which until 1927 remained the only Protestant body recognized by the government. All others occupied the status of "ethical associations." In contrast with the East India Company, the government maintained a policy of strict religious neutrality. It was usually willing to permit missions to the heathen, but for a long time opposed those to Moslems. It still requires that no missionary may serve anywhere without special permission from the Governor-General.

As a result of this evolution, missionary activity had to depend entirely on the initiative of private societies in the denominations. Such activity had already begun in 1797 with the formation of the Netherlands Missionary Society, the oldest and for long the only organization of its kind in Holland. Its first three missionaries went out to Java in 1814 and soon thereafter were appointed as clergymen of the Indian State Church. It was another twenty years before a second society sent its representatives to this field—the Basel Mission, from Germany. In 1861 the newly founded Netherlands Missionary Union began work among the Sundanese in western Java, and two years later the German Rhenish Missionary Society first entered the territory of the

Bataks of Sumatra and soon afterward the island of Nias, two fields that were later to prove immensely fruitful. During the next two or three decades, several other Dutch organizations had begun to send reinforcements, and since 1900 there have been added to the Continental societies missionaries of the Seventh Day Adventists and of the American Methodist Episcopal Church. Though there are now at least nineteen different societies active in the archipelago, there is but little duplication or overlapping. The work is distributed by territories, and the boundaries agreed upon are maintained in a spirit of coöperation. A sign of this readiness to work together is the Netherlands-Indian Mission Union, which holds a conference every two or three years for the discussion of common problems and which has appointed two permanent commissions.

The relations of all these societies with the government have become increasingly cordial and effective, and the range of action permitted them has grown continually wider. Until very recently there was a sharp distinction between the Indian Church and other bodies. The government appointed its ministers and bore the cost of its administration. Curiously enough, too, the government at the same time subsidized the Roman Catholic Church. This official aid, given to two Christian bodies by the neutral government of a population 97 percent non-Christian, was an anomaly against which the Volksraad made violent protest for many years. After long delay and many negotiations, an important change in the situation took place in 1935. Church and State were then separated, and though the government continues to contribute a large sum for ecclesiastical expenses, the Indian Church (Protestantsche Kerk) is at last completely free to live its own life. It is now constituted as a federation of regional indigenous Churches and a European Church, all united in a General Synod.

Coöperation with the government in the field of education has long been an advantage to the missionary cause. Until 1890 mission schools received no subsidy and had to encounter competition with government schools. Since that time they have enjoyed financial aid, subject to a law passed in 1915 that religious education must be optional with the parents of the pupils. In pagan districts like New Guinea, Central Celebes, and the central areas of Borneo, nearly all the schools are mission schools. The medical work of the Churches likewise benefits from government grants.[7] And encouragement has come not only from such direct assistance, but also from the greater freedom for missionary advance long since permitted by the state. Before 1880, for example, missionaries in Java were forbidden to live outside of the chief towns, where their work was chiefly confined to Chinese and Indo-Europeans. Since then they have been allowed to enter the interior. Today they are excluded from only a very few parts of the whole archipelago, such as Achin, in northern Sumatra, and Bantam, in West Java.

Coöperation between Church and State is made efficient by a unique institution established in 1906 and known as the Missions Consulate. In order that the government in all its relations with the missions might not have to deal with a score of different agencies, it requested the Churches to create a central authority to represent them. In response to this appeal the various societies united to choose this representative, who is accredited by the government as Missions Consul. He serves as an adviser to the state on mission matters and as an intermediary both among the missions themselves and between the workers in the field and the home societies.

A review of the present situation in the Netherlands Indies naturally begins with Java, for Java is the center of civilization and contains two-thirds of the whole population. Moreover, it is the area most solidly Moslem, so that nearly all the indigenous Christians are converts from Islam. For social and historical reasons, the island may be divided into West, Central, and East Java. The West is inhabited chiefly by the Sundanese, Central and East Java by the Javanese.[8]

---

[7] Because of the straitened condition of government finances since 1931, the drastic reduction of subsidies has greatly hampered the growth of schools and hospitals.

[8] Of the total population, 66 percent are Javanese, 22 percent Sundanese, 10.5 percent Madurese (in Madura and the neighboring mainland), and 1.5 percent Chinese and European.

In West Java there is little or no memory of the earlier Hindu civilization, and the people are more tenaciously attached to Islam than elsewhere. Work among them is more like that among Moslems in other lands, and its fruits are therefore relatively small. Yet they are small only in relation to the rest of Java, for in 1937, after some 80 years of effort by the Netherlands Missionary Union, there were about 5,000 baptized native Christians, who had been organized in 1934 as the Indigenous Church of West Java.

Central Java is the area in which there remains the strongest influence of the Hindu heritage, especially among the upper classes. It is still the cultural and political center of the island, where intellectual life is most active and where new movements of thought are most likely to flourish. Chiefly for these reasons it is far less thoroughly Islamized than the West. For nearly fifty years the chief society at work here has been the Mission of the Reformed Churches, a highly conservative Calvinistic body, with which the territory has been shared by the Salatiga Mission. During this time little effect has been produced upon the educated Moslems; but the approach to the lower classes has been so successful that by 1923 there were some 5,000 converts from Islam and 8 years later there was founded the autonomous Church of South Central Java, which then numbered more than 13,000 Christians and now counts as many as 16,000.

It is in East Java, where the allegiance of the people to Islam is the least strict, that Christianity has made the deepest impression. Here the Netherlands Missionary Society has been the chief force for several generations in the evangelization of Moslems. Even as early as 1911 there were 12,000 Christians, and that number had been almost doubled when, in 1931, there was established the Church of East Java, an independent body with a synod of its own in which there were only 3 Europeans out of 30 representatives. The Church now has more than 30,000 members, all converts from Islam.

In Java today the Christians still number only about 0.18 percent of the whole population. Not only are there millions of peasants who have never yet been brought into touch with the

Gospel, but little headway has been made in reaching the middle and upper classes, whose contacts with Christianity are chiefly through medical and educational work. Yet comparing results in Java with what has been accomplished in other Moslem lands, the success of the Church is unique in its extent and full of encouragement to all who labor elsewhere at the same task. The growth of the Christian movement has been impressively continuous for more than two generations. In 1873 there were 5,000 Christians, in 1906, 18,000. By 1915 the number had increased to 24,000, and by 1923 to 32,000. During the next eight or ten years the strength of the Christian bodies made possible not only a more active evangelism by the Javanese Christians but the formation of the three autonomous Churches. And today there are more than 50,000 indigenous Protestant Christians and 27,000 Roman Catholics.

In Sumatra four major societies are at work, partly with Moslems but chiefly with animistic tribes. Foremost among them is the Rhenish Mission in the Batak country, in northern Sumatra. The evangelization of these tribes is not only a remarkable feature of East Indian Christianity, it constitutes one of the most extraordinary achievements of the modern missionary enterprise.

The Bataks are a group of tribes which so long resisted the advance of Islam that when the Rhenish Mission entered their territory in 1863 most of them were still pagan. For the last seventy-five years there has been eager competition between the forces of the two great religions to win the allegiance of the people. The process has been hastened in recent times by the opening up of the country to the influences of government and of commerce, so that paganism has tended to disintegrate and the natives are turning either to Christianity or to Islam. The effect of Moslem energy is everywhere apparent. Propaganda is active, new mosques are being built, and village Koran schools are multiplying in number. Conversions to Islam have long been common and are still numerous. Yet Christian progress is both more rapid and more steady than Moslem. The Church is not only winning more heathen than Islam, it is also holding them more firmly; for though among the baptized there are many former Moslems, no Christians are deserting their religion. So successful had been the Rhenish Mission during its first half century of labor that in 1920, when Johannes Warneck was sent out to lead the Batak Mission, there were already 190,000 Christians. Since 1914 the society had been suffering from the effects of the war, but generous annual grants from the government of the Netherlands Indies enabled it to carry on its work. By 1930, when the number of Christians had risen to 325,000, there was organized the Batak Protestant Church, which has since become so entirely self-supporting that the Rhenish Mission now pays only the salaries of the European staff. The Church is likewise self-expanding. The Christians are not only active in evangelizing their neighbors. They exert an influence far beyond their own borders. As an ambitious and active people, the Bataks are emigrating to the larger towns of Sumatra and Java, bringing their religion with them. Even in ultra-Moslem Achin to the north, where the government forbids the entrance of missionaries, the Bataks are now penetrating; and wherever they go, they found their own churches. Thanks to the zeal of their genuine Christianity, their growth in numbers continues, sometimes at the rate of 25,000 a year. The process of increase is not by any means easy or unopposed. The Batak Christians not merely suffer from Moslem competition and persecution; they have even been subject to opposition and confusion at the hands of fellow Christians among the Roman Catholics and the Adventists. Schism, too, has marred the unity of the Church, for at the time of the recent split, seventy-five congregations set up for themselves. It is true, moreover, that hardly more than a third of the Batak people are Christians. Yet nowhere in the mission field are the prospects brighter. The Batak Church of today, with its 400,000 members, is a strong witness to the power of the Christian faith under the shadow of Islam.

Almost equally remarkable, on a smaller scale, has been the growth of Christianity in the little island of Nias, off the coast near the Batak country. Here, too, the Rhenish Mission began work in 1861. In the face of many difficulties and sometimes violent opposition, progress was painfully slow during the first 25 years, for in 1886 there were only 500 converts. But during the next 25 years the situation improved so rapidly that by 1911 the Christians had increased to 18,000. Five years later occurred an extraordinary revival movement, known as the "Great Repentance," which brought thousands to baptism and resulted in genuine moral renewal and increased missionary activity. No reaction to this upheaval appears to have taken place, for the growth of the Christian community has been continuous. In the year 1934 alone there were more than 6,000 baptisms, and twice that number of catechumens were under instruction. Today the Church of Nias, which held its first General Synod in 1936, includes 124,000 members, a total amounting to about two-thirds of the population of the island.

The Netherlands Indies include the southern two-thirds of the island of Borneo, an area larger than that of Spain. Its mountainous interior is thinly populated by various tribes, mostly pagan but partly Moslem, among which the Dyaks are the chief. Here the Rhenish Mission began in 1835 its long career of ninety years, at the close of which there were only 5,500 Christians. The mission was so severely straitened in its resources as a result of the war that in 1925 it transferred the field to the Basel Mission. Since then the expansion of the Christian community has been notably successful. By 1934 more than 9,000 had been added to its numbers, and the annual increase has since continued to be large. Though the opposition of Islam has been a serious obstacle, many Moslems are now counted among the converts. In 1936 the Dyak Church was organized, and in the following year the number of Protestant Christians in Borneo was reckoned as 30,000.

Celebes, with a much smaller area than Borneo, contains twice its population. Though there are now encouraging signs of Christian advance among the Toradjas in the center of the island, the greatest achievements have been in the northern peninsula, among the Minahassa tribes. Here the movement toward Christianity began about eighty years ago and has since proceeded at such a remarkable pace that the region is now almost wholly

Christian.[9] In 1934 there was established, as an independent unit within the Indian Church, the Minahassa Protestant Church, which included, four years later, nearly 250,000 members. The cultural progress of the people and their present high standards of education have aided the capacity of their Church for self-support. And since the Minahassans are now scattered all over the islands in various government and business positions, their spread becomes an important factor in the progress of Christianity.

In the eastward groups of islands known as the Moluccas and Amboina, Christianity goes back to Portuguese days, so that the Utrecht Missionary Union and the Indian Church, which have been active in the region in modern times, have had a Christian foundation on which to build. As a result of their heritage and of their own efforts, there has been developed a strong Christian community which was organized in 1938 as the Molucca Protestant Church (another independent unit in the Indian Church), with a present membership of about 200,000. Like the Minahassa Christians, the Amboinese have migrated in large numbers to other islands and are effective in spreading their faith in such pagan territory as New Guinea. In that easternmost section of the Indies, where the same missions are at work as in Amboina, there were already 7,000 Christians in 1920, a total which has since increased to more than 75,000. South of Amboina, in the Timor Archipelago, there is another new indigenous Church which includes about one-tenth of the population of the island.

When we turn from specific areas to view the East Indies as a whole, we find that in 1937 the number of native Protestant Christians was slightly over 1,500,000.[10] If we add to this the 450,000 Roman Catholics, the total amounts to more than 2,000,000 out of a population of 61,000,000, or somewhat over 3.25 percent of the whole. Though this percentage is undeniably small, it is higher than in any other field in Asia, despite the fact that at least four-fifths of the population are Moslem.

In the development of the Church thirteen societies of major

[9] The small islands of Sangi and Talaud, lying between northern Celebes and the Philippine Islands, are likewise almost wholly Christianized.

[10] In 1900 this total was 300,000 and in 1922 over 1,000,000. The rate of growth has thus been much faster than that of the population.

importance are now sharing, through the work of more than 500 missionaries, active not only in evangelism but also in the guidance of the educational enterprise, with its 33,000 pupils, and of the medical service, with its 111 hospitals and 200 dispensaries. But today, far more than ever before, the advance of Christianity is due in growing measure to the power of the indigenous Churches. Though they are still in need of considerable financial support from the home base, their capacity to propagate their faith has been abundantly proved.

If, in conclusion, we look toward the future, we find that one of the most obvious needs of the Church in the Indies is gradually to remedy what is now a grave defect—the lack of indigenous leadership. Very few leaders of strong personality and adequate training have arisen among the native Christians, even in such centers of civilization as Java. In this respect, indeed, the Church is less advanced than in Japan, China, or India, where the proportion of Christians is lower. One reason is the low standard of education. The effort to promote both popular education and higher education has come so recently, compared with other parts of the Orient, that its results are still meager.[11] The small share of the natives in public and political life is likewise of very recent date. Moreover, the centers of Christianity are largely in outlying districts, among untutored peoples. The missionaries, in consequence of all these facts, have been slow in transferring responsibility to indigenous Christians and have long kept them subordinated. Within the last five or six years, however, steps have been taken which may go far to improve the situation. As a minor but important factor, there has been established a Union Theological Training College first at Buitenzorg and now at Batavia. But vastly more effective as a stimulus than any school we may count the founding of the six autonomous Churches. Their new independence provides in itself a training ground and an incentive for the growth of leadership.

Another defect that calls for correction is the state of Christian literature. The Bible societies have long since made the whole

---

[11] The standard of literacy in the archipelago in 1930 was only 3.6 percent. But among the Bataks it was 12 percent and in Minahassa 45.7 percent.

Bible available in the chief languages of the Indies, and the steadily increasing sales of Scriptures may now be numbered by the hundreds of thousands. But most of the other literature in use is chiefly designed for Christians. The production and distribution of pamphlets and books written in Malay to meet the special difficulties of Moslems is still unsatisfactory in quantity and quality. And the lack of such necessary tools is only one sign of the fact that there is too little discrimination between the right mode of approach to the pagan and the right mode of approach to the Moslem. Not only the native evangelists but most of the missionaries fail to make use of the distinction and are inadequately equipped for dealing with the better trained elements in Islam.

The primary cause of these elements of weakness is the fact that Christian missions in the Indies have long been working chiefly among the peasant population. The favorable side of this situation is that the Christian community reproduces on a small scale the structure of society as a whole, with a broad base of the lower classes and a small apex of intellectuals. But the disadvantage of what has been termed the "excessive rural-mindedness" of the missions is the danger of neglecting the evangelization of those educated classes now so rapidly growing in numbers and the delay in developing the leaders who can undertake it with success. The need to reach these middle and upper classes among the ranks of Islam grows ever more pressing. For paganism is everywhere disappearing; Islam is still actively advancing; and the day is not far distant when the two faiths will confront each other as the only religions in the islands. Since Islam never proves in practice a preparation for Christianity, but rather the most baffling obstacle to its spread, the missionary task of the future promises to be more difficult than ever. Yet the achievements of the past give good ground for facing that future with undiminished hope.

XV
Negro Africa

NEGRO AFRICA is a loose term which we use, for want of a better, to cover the whole of Africa south of the northern tier of states formed by Morocco, Algeria, Tunisia, Libya, and Egypt. These latter countries are distinct from the rest of the continent, whether we think in terms of history, of culture, or of racial stock. Both in ancient and in modern times their most important relations have been with Europe, rather than with the rest of Africa. Moreover, they have been almost solidly Moslem from the earlier centuries of Islam. South of the Sahara, the immense variety of tribes, though they differ from one another, stand in contrast with North Africa as relatively uncivilized and destitute of any similar cultural background. They cover an area in which, for the most part, Islam has begun to flourish in comparatively recent times and in which it is still in course of active expansion. For all these reasons, they constitute a unit by themselves; and they present religious phe-nomena much more nearly analogous to those of the Netherlands Indies than to those of Algeria or Egypt. Negro Africa, like the Indies, is a region where Mohammedanism is spreading and where it competes with Christianity for the allegiance of hitherto pagan masses.

At the cost of dealing for a moment with a quantity of rather dry figures, we must first note the present extent of Islam throughout Negro Africa. According to a recent statistical survey by an Italian,[1] there are probably somewhat over 50,000,000 Moslems

---

[1] The work of Gasbarri, translated as "A Statistical Survey," in *The Moslem World* for July, 1937. Gasbarri's estimate follows fairly closely that of Professor Louis Massignon in the *Annuaire du Monde musulman* for 1925. (See Zwemer, *Across the World of Islam*, pp. 186 f.) It is on these two estimates, correct enough for our purposes, that the following statistics are chiefly based. Scientific accuracy is almost nowhere possible.

on the whole continent. Of these nearly half are to be found in those five countries of North Africa, from Morocco to Egypt, where the population averages 91 percent Moslem. The remaining 25,000,000 are distributed very unevenly over the remaining area, the strongest units, roughly speaking, being in the north, the weakest in the south.

Beginning in the northwest, we find four large French possessions with populations predominantly Moslem: Mauritania with 99 percent, Niger with 81 percent, Senegal with 75 percent, and French Guinea with 66 percent. In the other French territories in this area the proportions are smaller: the French Sudan 42 percent, the Ivory Coast 10 percent, and Dahomey only 8 percent. Like the French coastal provinces, the other colonies on the west coast include only a minority of Mohammedans—Portuguese Guinea 20 percent, Liberia 11 percent, and, under British control, Sierra Leone 30 percent and the Gold Coast 5 percent. As we move eastward to the British colony and protectorate of Nigeria, we find that though in the southern provinces Moslems constitute only about 13 percent of the inhabitants, in the northern they supply 68 percent. Still further eastward comes the French territory of Chad, 72 percent Moslem; the Anglo-Egyptian Sudan, 60 percent; Ethiopia, 37 percent, and the three Somalilands—Italian, British, and French—practically 100 percent. Lying south of the Sudan and Ethiopia are the British possessions of Kenya, Uganda, and Tanganyika, in which the proportion of Moslems is respectively 40, 20, and 10 percent, diminishing as we pass to the south. The island of Zanzibar, however, off the coast of Tanganyika, is solidly Mohammedan. South of Tanganyika, in Nyasaland, the Moslems form some 10 percent of the population. But in the vast remaining sections of Africa south of the equator Moslems are a negligible element, for only in the Union of South Africa is their proportion as high as 2 percent. From all these figures it is clear that Islam is strongest in the north and east, where the pressure of influence, either from North Africa or from Arabia, has been most continuous and powerful.

The extension of Islam in Negro Africa has been a growth of nearly a thousand years, for it was toward the end of the tenth century that Berber Moslems began to push southward from North Africa into the western Sudan. While this movement was still in progress, Islam first reached the Upper Nile and the East Coast. Further spread in the western Sudan went on during succeeding centuries, especially in the sixteenth, when Timbuctu became a powerful center of intellectual and religious life. Thenceforward, however, for another 300 years advance was relatively slight and sporadic. "It was only in the course of the nineteenth century that the great Negro Mussulman conquerors [between the Niger and the Nile] . . . served to bring to its culminating point the expansion of Islam in tropical Africa." [2]

To rehearse in historical detail the gradual extension of Islam is not within the proper scope of a brief study of the Christian approach to Moslems. More important from our point of view is to note the methods of that extension, to understand by what processes this flourishing growth has been achieved. The most obvious fact is that the spread of Islam, in contrast with the spread of Christianity, has been less often the product of direct effort or conscious propaganda than the inevitable by-product of other activities.

Among these other enterprises has been military conquest. Especially in the Sudan the conquerors of modern times have been Moslems, and some of their campaigns have been definitely of the type of *jihads,* or holy wars. The outstanding example of such expansion by force is the rise of the Fulani Empire a century and more ago. Toward the end of the eighteenth century, among the Fulah (or Fulbe) tribe of the western Sudan, there arose a powerful warrior-missionary, the Sheikh Othman Danfodio. When a pilgrim at Mecca he had been inspired by the reforming doctrines of the new puritanical sect of the Wahhabis. First he welded the scattered communities of his people into one powerful organization and then led them in revolt against their pagan ruler in the kingdom of Gober. His power increased with continued success until, one after another, he had subdued not only the pagan tribes over a wide area but also the Mohammedan Hausa states.

[2] M. Delafosse, "Islam in Africa," *International Review of Missions,* July, 1926, p. 534.

When he died at Sokoto, in 1816, the whole of Hausaland lay under his sway. His sons continued the work of conquest until the Fulani Empire at its height had grown to cover a large part of the western and central Sudan, including what is now Northern Nigeria. Not until the British administration took control of Nigeria in 1900 was the rule of the Fulahs brought to an end. Though the warfare conducted at intervals by this dominating tribe was sometimes prompted by religious motives, it was more often simply for conquest and quite as often it degenerated into mere slave-raiding. But whatever its purpose, it served to multiply conversions, for protection could be found by the heathen only through acceptance of Islam.

The slave trade has proved another line of approach to pagan Africans. The hunting of Negro slaves by Arabs from Muscat first introduced Islam to the natives of East Africa. The traffic, centering at Zanzibar and extending to Uganda and Nyasaland and beyond, was maintained with vigor until the rise of British rule. But though it offered a point of contact between pagans and Moslems, the slave trade had its defects as a method of propaganda. Since members of the brotherhood of Islam may not be enslaved, it was not to the interests of the raiders to encourage conversion; and since hunting slaves involved atrocities of every description, it left behind it a trail of bitterness and hatred. For these reasons the suppression of the traffic has really been favorable to the growth of Islam. Far more effective as a means of spreading the faith was the institution of slavery itself. "The constant replenishing of numbers with untold quantities of slaves, largely women, from whom grew up a stronger and always Moslem race, in the past loaded the dice heavily towards Islam. [But] slavery is now dying and will soon be dead." [3]

In Africa, however, as in the Netherlands Indies, peaceful methods have been far more productive of conversions than any form of violence. And no type of approach has proved more widely effective than the constant activity of traders. The Mohammedan merchant, in fact, has been the chief agency in pro-

[3] W. R. S. Miller, "Islam in Africa," *International Review of Missions* (July, 1926), p. 559.

moting his religion both in West and in East Africa. More advanced in culture than the peoples among whom he moves, he displays a self-confidence and an air of superiority which seldom fail to exert an influence. He impresses the natives not only as the bearer of valuable goods but as the representative of a higher religion, of which he is evidently proud. Though a trader by profession, he is none the less an unofficial missionary. In the course of his frequent visits to one village after another, he often succeeds by the mere pressure of example in winning to Islam first the chief and later the other members of the tribe. Or he may marry and settle for a while in one town, gradually converting its inhabitants to his faith. Such has been the story, constantly repeated, in area after area. The Mandingo, for instance, "have become the pioneers of Islam largely through obtaining an almost complete monopoly of the petty commerce of the Western Sudan. As merchants they traverse the entire territory from the Atlantic coast to northern Togo, Dahomey, and Nigeria, and even as far as the oases of the Sahara." [4] The Hausa people have played a similar role in the region farther east. Their language is the lingua franca of commerce for the western and central Sudan; their energy and aptitude for trade have carried them west to the Guinea coast and as far east as Cairo; and wherever they go they carry their faith with them.

Another agency of penetration, usually peaceful, has been supplied by the various Dervish Orders, which form so prominent a feature of the religious life of North Africa. During the nineteenth century, their active zeal proved a powerful factor in the advance of Islam, especially through the whole Sudan. One of the oldest and most widespread of these orders is the Qadiriyya, first introduced into western Africa in the fifteenth century.

Up to the middle of the nineteenth century most of the schools in the Sudan were founded and conducted by teachers trained under the auspices of the Qadiriyya, and their organization provided for a regular and continuous system of propaganda among the heathen tribes. The missionary work of this order has been entirely of a peaceful character, and has relied wholly upon personal example and

<hr/>

[4] Westermann, "Islam in the West and Central Sudan," *International Review of Missions* (Oct., 1912), p. 620.

precept and ... on the spread of education. ... The Tijaniyya, be-longing to an order founded in Algiers towards the end of the eighteenth century, have, since their establishment in the Sudan about the middle of the nineteenth century, pursued the same missionary methods as the Qadiriyya, and their numerous schools have con-tributed largely to the propagation of the faith; but, unlike the former, they have not refrained from appealing to the sword to assist in the furtherance of their scheme of conversion.[5]

Another society, with its center in the Libyan desert, is the Sanusiyya.

The success that has been achieved by the zealous and energetic emissaries of this association is enormous; convents of the order are to be found not only all over the north of Africa ... but throughout the Sudan, in Senegambia, and in Somaliland. ... Though primarily a movement of reform in the midst of Islam itself, the Sanusiyya sect is also actively proselytizing, and several African tribes that were previously pagan or merely nominally Moslem, have since the advent of the emissaries of this sect in their midst, become zealous adherents of the faith of the Prophet.[6]

The motives which impel the pagan to become a Moslem are numerous and urgent. An obvious ground of appeal is the fact that Islam presents itself as a black man's religion. Its representa-tives are usually either pure Negroes or mixed races like the Swahili or the Hausa. The immense gap in race and culture which sunders the European from the African is bridged for Islam by various intermediate stages, so that the Moslems whom the heathen sees and knows are felt to be essentially of his own kind. This sense of kinship is increased by the lack of race prejudice manifested by nearly every Mohammedan. Their social contacts with pagans are close, and they are quite ready to intermarry with them. Yet at the same time the African is always conscious of the superiority of the Moslem in religion, in education, and in standard of living; and the fact that the Moslem shares this sense of superiority makes it only the more convincing. In other words, the followers of Islam are different enough to attract, but not so different as to repel. And once the heathen has adopted the new faith, he is received at once on terms of equality into a

[5] Arnold, *The Preaching of Islam*, p. 329.   [6] *Ibid.*, pp. 334 f.

world-wide fraternity, in the power and prestige of which he will thenceforth have a part. That coveted prestige is heightened by the fact that for a long time past British and French colonial governments have shown marked favor toward their Moslem subjects. They have nearly always accorded them a respect and encouragement denied to pagans. By giving financial aid to Mohammedan schools and mosques, but still more by preferring Moslems as servants, civil employees, and soldiers, they offer added inducements to conversion. Though efficiency and convenience of administration may have been furthered by this policy, it has certainly promoted the spread of Islam.

The dominating motive for conversion, then, is the natural desire to rise in the world, to enjoy the social, political, and educational advantages which Islam can offer, and to win the self-respect and dignity that attach to membership in a predominant community. The acceptance of the new faith is thus more often than not a means to a secular end and not a religious end in itself. Yet the directly religious appeal of Islam is a force not to be overlooked. Aside from the social and economic superiority of the Moslem, which makes him an object of envy, he is plainly a man who has a superior God. He witnesses to the power of that God by his daily prayers and other devout observances. He evidently knows far more than the heathen about the uncertain spirit world. When on occasion he speaks of his beliefs, he tells of one omnipotent Deity and of the joys of a future paradise. His religion, moreover, like that of the Negro, is largely a matter of customary law and specific regulations, more readily understood than the Christian emphasis upon inner spiritual principles. But it is on a lower religious level, in which the pagan is more at home, that Islam presents the strongest attractions. If the Moslem teacher offered only a religion that was purer than native animism, his success would be less immediate. As the pagan views it, however, Islam is desirable not so much because it is higher in our sense as because it is more potent. The Moslem is in touch with powerful forces beyond the reach of the local medicine man. His charms and amulets and his efficacy as a miracle-worker excite unquestioning awe. To be able to draw upon these mysterious spiritual resources and to share in the benefits they produce is what any heathen, however unregenerate, would naturally desire.

The progress of Islam is made easy not only by the many advantages it offers but also by the low price for which they may be obtained. In contrast with Christianity, no abrupt break with the past is required. At least in Africa, the Mohammedan shows little repugnance to paganism and is prepared to allow many departures from orthodox Islam. The demands upon the convert, therefore, are far from exacting. Not merely is no inner change of heart expected, but even his outward habits and moral ideas need but few immediate alterations. Though open idolatry is of course discouraged, ancestor worship is usually permitted, and the confidence in magic is increased rather than diminished. Polygamy within limits may still be practiced, as well as concubinage without limits. The commands which call for renunciation or for discipline are simple and definite. Those which are chiefly emphasized are the prohibition of alcohol and the prescription of the prayers and the fast.

In view of the inducements to conversion and the ease with which the transition from paganism can be made, the wonder is not that Islam advances but that paganism has maintained for so long a time so many centers of resistance. In extensive regions, of course, the Negroes have not yet been subject to strong Mohammedan pressure. But in the lands where Islam is actively in evidence, and even where it is preponderant, there are many heathen tribes which still refuse to succumb. One limitation to its advance is the fact that Islam is characteristically a religion of nomads or of city dwellers. Its strength lies chiefly in the towns where its higher standards of civilization can be satisfied. It is the more backward agricultural peoples which find it hardest to change any of their ancient beliefs and practices. For these and other reasons it is fair to conclude "that the obstacles to the intensive development of Islam in Negro Africa are numerous and strong and that Islam shows no tendency to spread except in the towns, and that even there the importance of its progress depends to a large extent on the good-will of the colonial governments; finally, that among the rural communities which constitute the vast majority of the people its extension encounters a resistance which is by no means ready to give way." [7] As to where Islam is advancing today and at what rate of speed, the testimony of observers is not unanimous, and reliable facts are hard to obtain. It is safe to assert, however, that while progress has been retarded at a number of points and there are now few impressive movements making for increase, the number of Moslems in nearly every area where they are well established is steadily growing. To judge from experience in other lands and from the general laws of religious development, paganism in Africa is ultimately doomed, and the continent, so far as its people retain religion, will one day be divided between Islam and Christianity.

The Christian approach to Negro Moslems is affected not only by the extent of their religion and by its methods of growth but even more by its character. It is important, then, to ask the question, What effect has Mohammedanism upon the Negroes and what sort of Moslems do they make?

An answering judgment is not easy to express in any single form that will command general agreement. The standards and attitudes of observers are so far from uniform that their responses vary from harsh verdicts upon Islam at its worst to idealizations of Islam at its best. But even the soundest estimate has to take account of the fact that Negro Islam presents wide diversity in quality. Africans, that is, are Moslems in differing senses and in differing degrees. The range extends from fanatical orthodoxy in belief and practice to the thinnest of veneers, from a faith with centuries of tradition behind it to the knowledge of a few formulas and the possession of a few Koranic amulets among newly-won savages. At Timbuctu or Kano, for example, we find Mohammedans who can stand comparison in fidelity or in training with those in any land. Elsewhere, in some jungle tribe, it would be hard to distinguish Islam from paganism.

Despite this acknowledged variety, however, there are certain

[7] Delafosse, "Islam in Africa," *International Review of Missions* (July, 1926), p. 546.

generalizations which can be safely made. In the first place, it is true that the ambition of the new convert to improve his lot in life by a change in religion is seldom disappointed. On the whole, the acceptance of Islam by the Negro brings an advance in civilization and in material progress. It commonly raises his standard of living and helps him to develop a higher degree of social organization and to produce a more unified society over a wider area. Moreover, it makes for intellectual enlightenment. The coming of Islam means schools and the study of Arabic and the rudiments of Moslem law. Besides importing its own sacred language, Islam has used the Arabic alphabet to build up written languages, as in the Swahili, Hausa, and Fulani tongues. Whatever its limitations may be, this process of education has opened up to former heathen a whole range of new ideas and encourages in time a heightened self-respect and self-reliance. Morally, too, Islam has achievements to its credit. In addition to its curb upon the excesses of polygamy, it has put an end to cannibalism, human sacrifice, and female infanticide. It has greatly reduced the malign power of pagan sorcerers. To a remarkable extent it has even succeeded in stamping out the use of alcoholic drink. And at least in some measure it has led the Negro to appreciate the worth of the individual, who in heathenism is so wholly merged in the mass. Finally, it is obvious enough that just so far as the change from animism and polytheism to Islam has become genuine, it marks a tremendous forward step in religion. To pray regularly to one almighty God whose will is law and to confess His supremacy is to have risen to a new spiritual level. The contrast between the grotesque fetish house of past days and the village mosque with its daily summons to the faithful symbolizes a transformation not wholly external.

What Mohammedanism has failed to do for the Negro is no less apparent. Judged by its authoritative books and by its own best standards in other countries, the Islam which prevails in most of tribal Africa is of low quality. The education and civilization which it undoubtedly transmits may make for progress up to a certain point, but at that point there is a tendency to settle inertly without the vital energy for further growth. Aside from such important reforms as we have noted, tribal morality is but little altered. The position of women is worse than before, and slavery continues to be approved. Certain laws, it is true, are commendably observed; but any inward moral change is rarely achieved. Especially where Islam is not the faith of the majority nor of long standing, it accommodates itself so readily to ancient pagan beliefs and practices as to form an amalgam. The new religion is interpreted in such fashion as to cause the least possible break with the old. No more is given up than necessity requires, and what is accepted becomes colored by the background of the past. Animism and the use of magic are so prevalent in purely Moslem countries that they prove all the more adjustable to the Negro's version of Islam. Thus the Mohammedan teacher inevitably plays the role of a superior kind of tribal wizard, who differs from his predecessor less in kind than in degree of power. Such, for example, are the "marabouts" (to use the North African term), who are regarded with deep reverence not only as learned men equipped with their books and papers and rosaries, but as miracle workers who can offer printed pieces of the Koran as talismans and who encourage the trust in magic which they are ever ready to exploit. At the opposite end of the scale, then, to the best type of Sudanese Moslems, there are other varieties so superficial as to be hardly more than nominal.

When we turn from Islam to consider Christianity in Negro Africa, the fact most immediately evident is that native Moslems greatly outnumber native Christians. Though the Christians are somewhat easier to count than the Moslems, the figures for Ethiopia can only be roughly calculated and those for Roman Catholics in certain countries include whites as well as blacks. We shall not be far wrong, however, in stating that there are about 8,250,-000 Negro Christians, in addition to about 3,000,000 in Ethiopia.[8] The total of 11,250,000 Christians is thus less than half the number of Moslems in the same wide area. And the pagan population still constitutes a large majority of the whole. Another fact which emerges from a study of the religious map is that there are a few

[8] Statistics for both Protestants and Catholics are taken from *The Interpretative Statistical Survey of the World Mission of the Christian Church* (1938).

regions like Mauritania in the northwest and the Somalilands in the northeast where there are practically no Christians. On the other hand, there are several countries in the south, like Rhodesia, Angola, and Southwest Africa, where there are practically no Moslems. But in nearly all those main divisions of Negro Africa where Islam is strong there is a substantial number of Christians. They may be outnumbered by Moslems 100 to 1 as in French Guinea, or by even more as in the Anglo-Egyptian Sudan. In Nigeria, however, we find a proportion of about 14 to 1 and in Sierra Leone 10 to 1. More favorable is the situation in several other territories, as in Dahomey and Tanganyika, where the two bodies are not far from equal. In still another group of countries Christians are more numerous than Moslems, substantially so in Nyasaland and Uganda, and even more markedly elsewhere. In the Gold Coast, for example, there are about five Christians to one Moslem, in the Belgian Congo 26 to 1, and in the Union of South Africa more than 32 to 1.

In the Netherlands Indies, where there is similar competition between the two expanding religions, Christian missions, as we have seen, are actively at work along two lines—converting heathen tribes before they are won to Islam and converting Moslems themselves on an extensive scale. In Africa, too, there has long been fruitful effort to Christianize pagan peoples, as substantial native Churches can now testify. Some of these, like the Basuto, are beyond the present reach of Islam; others, like the Baganda, have been subject for several generations to constant Mohammedan pressure. But nowhere in Negro Africa has there yet been a direct approach to Mohammedans that can compare in strength or in success with that in the Indies. The Christian cause has advanced at many points by forestalling Islam, but at very few by actually winning Moslems.

It is true, of course, that wherever the work of Christian missions is carried on in Negro Africa, it affects to some degree the future advance of Islam. If we may express it in terms of inevitable competition, every gain for Christianity sets limits to the progress of the rival religion, because among Negroes Islam gains its converts from paganism and not from Christianity. In this indirect sense the growth of the Christian Church in Africa is part of the story of the Christian approach to Islam, for it is only through a native Church of growing power that Negro Moslems can ultimately be won. At the present time, then, it is chiefly this preventive and preparatory work that is in active operation, and only here and there or now and then are the Christian forces immediately concerned with Mohammedans. Partly for this reason and partly because the range of territory is so immense, we shall here cite only two examples of the kind of enterprise which now serves to check Islam and which affords unbounded future opportunity for that direct approach which as yet is too rarely attempted. Out of many possibilities we choose Nyasaland, a small country where Christians outnumber Moslems, and Nigeria, a large country where Moslems outnumber Christians.

Nyasaland, in the southeast section of Africa, covers only 40,000 square miles—a strip of territory over 500 miles long, varying in breadth from 50 to 100 miles. North of it lies Tanganyika, westward Northern Rhodesia, while Portuguese East Africa surrounds it both on the east and on the southwest. The great Lake Nyasa, which gives it its name, forms the larger part of its eastern boundary. Most of the country is mountainous, formed of lofty plateaus.

Despite the remoteness of this area, Portuguese adventurers penetrated in the seventeenth century to its southern portions, where at intervals they worked gold and silver mines. But it was not until David Livingstone discovered Lake Nyasa in 1859 that the modern development of the country began. His arrival came at a time of tribal migration, when two of the chief tribes now dominant were finding homes in new territory—the Ngoni from Zululand settling to the west of the lake and the Yao from the east establishing themselves along its southern borders. The warfare and slave-raiding which attended these movements had wrought such disturbance and suffering that the natives in large numbers welcomed the white men as supplying the only power which could protect them against oppression. From then on the advance of British influence was steady, in spite of the opposition of Arab slavers and their local allies. In 1891 there was proclaimed the Protectorate of British Central Africa, which in 1907 was given the name of Nyasaland. By 1937 the native population had reached a total of 1,620,000, an increase of more than 100 percent in one generation. These growing numbers find their support in what are now the chief industries—the raising of tobacco, tea, coffee, and cotton. And the advance of prosperity and of material civilization has been continuously promoted by the growth of communications through the telegraph, the railroads, and a network of 3,700 miles of roads. In this healthful and well-governed territory, Islam and Christianity have been progressing at the expense of paganism for the past eighty years.

The four chief tribes are the Ngoni, the Chewa, the Yao, and the Nyanja; and it is the Nyanja whose language is the lingua franca for most of the area. In the sixties of the last century, during Livingstone's time, Islam had no foothold among any of these peoples. A decade later, however, coast traders in slaves and ivory had begun to find their way into southeastern Nyasaland and to form centers of Moslem propaganda. It was not long before the new religion had won over many of the Yao tribe, though for some time it made little headway elsewhere. During the last thirty years most of the Yao, and an increasing number of the Nyanja, have become Moslems. It is largely among these two peoples, then, distributed around the southern shores of the lake and southward to Zomba, that Islam now flourishes. The total of Mohammedans was estimated in 1927 to be about 105,000.[9] A decade later the number had risen to 160,000, or 10 percent of the population.[10]

During the same period Christianity has been advancing over a wider area and at a more rapid pace. While Livingstone was in England in December, 1857, he presented to a great meeting in the Senate House in Cambridge a moving appeal to initiate a mission to Central Africa. "I go back to Africa," he declared, "to try to make an open path for commerce and Christianity. Do you carry on the work which I have begun. I leave it with you." Within a few months the call had been answered by Cambridge and Oxford, and within another two years by the Universities of Durham and Dublin. Through their combined action there had

---

[9] S. S. Murray, *Handbook of Nyasaland*, 1932, p. 388.
[10] Gasbarri, "A Statistical Survey," *Moslem World*, July, 1937.

been formed by 1860 what came to be known as the Universities'
Mission to Central Africa. The Rev. Charles S. Mackenzie, a
Cambridge graduate with missionary experience in Natal, was
chosen as its leader, and on January 1, 1861, was consecrated
bishop at Capetown and commissioned "to the tribes dwelling
in the neighborhood of Lake Nyasa and the River Shiré." Accompanied by three priests and three laymen, Bishop Mackenzie
joined Livingstone near the Zambesi; but not until July did they
succeed in establishing their first headquarters in the Shiré Highlands south of the lake. Their arrival coincided with a period of
slave-raiding and tribal warfare which kept the country in such
turmoil that any settled work was impossible. Within six months
the bishop died of fever, and a year later two others of the party.
Conditions, indeed, were so desperately unpromising that the
bishop who came out to succeed Mackenzie resolved to remove
the Mission to Zanzibar; and it was not until 1882 that its forces
succeeded in returning to the shores of Lake Nyasa. At the end
of the next decade Nyasaland became a separate bishopric; and
since then centers of work have been successively opened, chiefly
along the eastern borders of the lake and near its southern end.
The cathedral of the diocese and a college for training evangelists
are on the island of Likoma.

Before the Universities' Mission had resumed its work in this
area, the Free and United Presbyterian Churches of Scotland had
organized the Livingstonia Mission. Its first expedition set out
in 1875 under the leadership of E. D. Young, one of whose companions was Dr. Robert Laws, the future head of the Mission, who
was to render distinguished service for more than fifty years. They
brought with them the first steamer to be launched on Lake
Nyasa. Thanks to this means of communication and to conditions
somewhat less disturbed than a decade earlier, the new venture
met with no fatal reverses. After the founding of several smaller
stations at Bandawe and elsewhere, the Mission in 1894 established
its famous center of Livingstonia, far up in the northern part of
Nyasaland close to the western shore of the lake.

A third enterprise directly traceable to the influence of Livingstone was the Church of Scotland Mission, organized in 1876.

After a preliminary exploration, its first party, consisting of a doctor and five artisans, settled at Blantyre in the Shiré Highlands a hundred miles south of the lake. During the next twenty years its expanding forces opened further important stations in the same southern district at Zomba, Domasi, and Mlanje. In 1889 another Presbyterian body, the Mission of the Dutch Reformed Church of South Africa, entered the field, making Mkhoma its chief center and taking as its province a wide region inland from the southwest shore of the lake. These four bodies remain the leading missionary groups in Nyasaland, and their spheres of activity are so arranged as to cover the main divisions of the country and to avoid overlapping and competition. Next in point of numbers are the Zambesi Industrial Mission (1892), the American Seventh-Day Adventists (1902), and three still smaller organizations, all of which have their assigned portions in a total field now adequately occupied.

The present flourishing condition of the Church in Nyasaland may be attributed to the early adoption by nearly all the missions of two wholesome policies—the training and use of Africans as teachers and preachers and the extensive development of elementary and industrial education. The training of the native Christians begins with the catechumens, who are commonly expected to have some reading knowledge of the New Testament before they are baptized. Indeed, a direct acquaintance with the Scriptures is everywhere counted a fundamental necessity. The whole Bible has been translated into the Nyanja and Yao tongues, and three other peoples have the New Testament in their own languages. Those Christians whose devotion and ability fit them for evangelistic work are given more advanced instruction and sent out to preach in the villages of their own people. A further stage in the process has been the raising up of a native ministry. By the year 1925 there were 17 ordained Africans in all the Churches, and thirteen years later the number had risen to 58—a total larger than that of ordained missionaries. There is good ground, then, for the statement that "the young African Church in Nyasaland is a product of African Christianity itself." The two largest native Churches are the Church of Central Africa, Presbyterian,[11] and the Anglican diocese of Nyasaland, which together have over 100 organized congregations and nearly 900 lesser groups, for which services are regularly held. The size of the Christian community throughout the whole country and the expansive power of that community may be realized by noting that in 1925 there were 66,000 baptized Christians and in 1938, 174,000. If we add the Roman Catholic natives,[12] the total is 275,000—a figure which may be set against the 160,000 adherents of Islam, but which is less than 2 percent of a population still overwhelmingly pagan.

So effective has the work of education proved in promoting Christianity that it may well be said that the Church has grown out of the school. With the Scots characteristically in the lead, the emphasis upon missions as a teaching force has been so constant for two generations that today the greater part of the country is covered with a network of Christian schools. In the Protestant missions there are 1,600 elementary schools [13] with 120,000 pupils, and 6 high schools with 560 pupils, in which nearly all the teaching is done by some 2,000 natives. The educational policy of the missions conforms to the course laid down by the Government Education Code and qualifies the schools for the receipt of government grants-in-aid. That they deserve such recognition was affirmed by the Phelps-Stokes Commission in 1924, whose report stated that "no colony in Africa offers to its government such quantity and quality of educational work as that maintained in Nyasaland by the Mission Societies."

The foremost centers of higher education are the Overtoun Institution at Livingstonia and the Henry Henderson Institute at Blantyre. At these stations there are high schools, normal schools, and technical schools, with courses for teachers, evangelists, clerks, and hospital attendants. Apprentices are trained in agriculture, printing, carpentry, and building; and women in sewing and domestic craft. At both centers, too; there are well-

---

[11] Formed in 1926 by the union of the Churches connected with the three Presbyterian Missions—the two Scottish and the Dutch Reformed.

[12] The product of two missions established in 1901 and 1902.

[13] Including Roman Catholic and numerous government schools, the total is 4,000.

equipped hospitals.[14] The whole educational system, culminating in such institutions as these, exerts a powerful leavening influence upon the villages throughout wide reaches of the country. Christian ideals and standards are thus affecting the life of pagan society and preparing for the future growth of the Church.

In relation to Islam in Nyasaland, the main result of expanding Christianity has been to limit the spread of its rival. It has been clearly shown that wherever Christianity is the first religion to appear, Islam is unable to advance. The Christian school and the Christian church have proved definite barriers to Moslem progress. But there is evidence already that the growing Church is reaching Mohammedans directly. In this region they are far from fanatical and, knowing little of their own religion, they are easy to approach. Indeed, in many villages Christian schools have been opened at the invitation of Moslem headmen, and Moslem pupils sit beside pagan. Thus in spite of the lack of any organized effort aimed primarily at the followers of Islam, there is every year a small but steady influx of converts.

Nigeria lies in West Africa, at the extreme inner corner of the Gulf of Guinea, where the broad delta of the Niger stretches along the coast. It reaches into the interior as far north as French West Africa; on the west it is bounded by Dahomey, and on the east by the French Cameroons. The country, framed as it is around the Niger and its chief affluent, the Benue, may be divided into two well-marked regions, the wide valleys along the two great waterways, and the plateaus of the Northern Provinces. Nearly two-thirds of the land is covered with forest, and its total area of 343,000 square miles [15] is nearly three times the size of the British Isles.

This whole region, known officially as the Colony and Protectorate of Nigeria, has gradually reached its present organization by a series of stages. For centuries, of course, it was only the coastal area that was known to Europe. The Portuguese had been trading

---

[14] Throughout the country there are 23 other mission hospitals and 60 dispensaries.

[15] Exclusive of the mandated territory of British Cameroons, which is administered as part of Nigeria.

with the natives for some eighty years before the first English ship sailed into the little port of Benin in 1553. By the end of that century, Benin had become a regular center for European merchants. A hundred years later the slave traffic began to flourish, reaching ever more scandalous dimensions until in 1807 it was declared illegal for all British subjects. Thenceforth the trade in slaves remained in the hands of the Spanish and Portuguese, with Lagos as one of its main depots. Partly with the aim of ending this iniquity, a British force captured Lagos in 1851, and ten years afterward the territory surrounding it was ceded to Great Britain and became the nucleus of the future Nigeria. By 1886 it had attained the status of the Colony and Protectorate of Lagos. Meanwhile British pioneers had long since been exploring the interior by way of other routes than the Niger, until finally the course of the river was discovered. These successful expeditions led to the formation of several trading companies, which combined in the United African Company, rechartered in 1886 as the Royal Niger Company. It was not until 1900 that the crown took over the territories of the company and formed the two protectorates of Northern and Southern Nigeria. With these the government of Lagos was soon united; and finally, on January 1, 1914, the two divisions were amalgamated to form the Colony and Protectorate of Nigeria.

Under the first governor, Sir Frederick Lugard, the British soon won control of all the northern districts. The decadent Fulah empire in Sokoto and Kano collapsed with hardly a struggle, and the Mohammedan emirates on its southern and eastern borders were rapidly subdued.

In an amazingly short time the whole face of the country changed. ... The days of continual inter-tribal wars, slave-hunting raids, and autocratic tyranny passed away almost as though they had never been. ... Little by little, sometimes by force, often by a show of power that overawed resistance, the country was brought into the condition in which it is today.[16]

Under the governor, each of the 22 provinces has its British Resident, though in most of them indirect rule now prevails, with

16 Maxwell, *Nigeria*, pp. 51 f.

the administration in the hands of the paramount chiefs and their officials. More than 2,300 miles of railway and 12,000 miles of telegraph wire link the various parts of the country to one another. Trade has greatly developed in the past twenty years, for Nigeria has important products such as palm oil, palm kernels, cocoa, and groundnuts. The exports greatly exceed the imports in value, and the total of both now amounts to more than $250,000,000 a year.

The present population is slightly over 20,600,000, about 60 percent living in the Northern Provinces. The people are so far from homogeneous that nearly 250 tribes, large and small, may be counted. But the chief tribes—the Yoruba and Ibo in the south and the Hausa and Fulani in the north—include more than 12,-000,000 members. The great majority of the natives live in small towns and villages; and with some exceptions like the Fulani, who are pastoral nomads, their main occupation is agriculture. In terms of religion, Northern Nigeria is markedly different from Southern. In the Northern Provinces about two-thirds of the population are Mohammedan and about one-third still remain pagan, while the Christians constitute hardly more than a half of one percent of the whole.[17] In the Southern Provinces, however, the proportions are altered, for there the percentage of pagans is roughly 80, of Christians about 7, and of Moslems about 13.[18]

Christian missions began in Nigeria nearly a century ago. A number of Nigerian slaves, who had been set free in Sierra Leone and had there become Christians, made their way back to their own land in 1839. In answer to their appeal for teachers, the English Wesleyan Methodist Mission in the Gold Coast dispatched the Rev. T. B. Freeman to Badagri, near Lagos, where he arrived in 1842. At about the same time the Church Missionary Society sent the Rev. Henry Townsend to the same place. Both missionaries also visited Abeokuta—a larger town in this western edge of the Yoruba country—and found there a warm welcome. Eight years later the American Southern Baptists entered this field. And

[17] Census of 1931.

[18] The Census of 1931 for Southern Nigeria is quite unreliable as to religions, and no pretense to accuracy can be claimed for these figures. But the contrast with Northern Nigeria is plainly marked.

meanwhile, in 1846, the first representatives of the United Free Church of Scotland Mission reached the Calabar River, at the other end of the coast. Thus four of the eight leading societies now at work began their enterprise in the same period, and the history of their expansion thus covers almost a hundred years.

From our point of view, the story of Christian missions in Nigeria is marked by three successive stages of growing importance. For the first sixty years practically all the work was carried on among the heathen of Southern Nigeria. Since in that region Moslems were then relatively few and the response among pagans encouraging, the meager Christian forces were seldom in touch with Islam. But in winning adherents who might later have succumbed to Mohammedan pressure, they met with increasing success. For the next thirty years the occupation of Northern Nigeria went steadily forward. Yet attention was still concentrated on the heathen Negroes, chiefly because the government forbade the entrance of missions into those provinces in which Islam was completely dominant. Finally, during the last few years, a change of policy has opened up to several societies a number of centers in purely Moslem territory, so that today the direct approach to Mohammedans is at last in energetic progress.

As in the Netherlands Indies on a large scale and in Nyasaland on a smaller, the rapid advance of Christianity among pagans is a factor highly significant for the future relations of Christianity and Islam. The expansion of the Church in Nigeria, therefore, plays a part in the long process of winning the African Moslem; and a brief account of its achievements is relevant to our main theme.

The first two organizations to enter Nigeria, the C. M. S. and the Methodist Missionary Society, still remain in the lead; but it is the former which has since become responsible for the largest Church, whose members include more than half the Protestant Christians in the country. During the fifties, the C. M. S. enjoyed a period of steady growth in its small Yoruba Mission in the southwest corner of Nigeria, adding to its first two stations those at Lagos, Ibadan, and Oyo. In 1860 there were already 2,000 Christians. The succeeding decade, however, witnessed so much tribal warfare that it may be counted a period of disappointments and reverses. Yet the work at Lagos went on, and the Christians elsewhere remained faithful, despite the withdrawal of missionaries, so that by 1872 the number of converts had doubled and four of them had received ordination. Meanwhile, there was pioneering activity in another area. In 1857 Samuel Crowther, originally a slave boy but by that time a priest in the Anglican Church, was commissioned by the C. M. S. to open a Niger Mission staffed by Africans. His success in founding stations up the river at Onitsha and other points led to his consecration in 1864 as Bishop of the Niger Territories. For the next twenty-seven years, with his African clergy, he labored indefatigably under difficult conditions, extending the work along the river and establishing new centers in the Delta at Bonny and Brass. Besides the physical trials that went with ceaseless travel, he had not only to encounter with his people occasional persecution, but to combat the evil effects wrought by the white traders in his diocese. As a saintly character and a zealous pioneer his record was without blame; but before his death in 1891 there was disturbing evidence that he was incapable of firm administration. Indeed, the discipline among his clergy and their churches became so lax that there was marked deterioration everywhere, and a change of organization and of personnel was urgently demanded. A new period of strong leadership and higher standards began in 1893 with the arrival of Bishop Herbert Tugwell, who assigned two African assistant bishops to the reviving work in Lagos and the Yoruba Mission and devoted himself with ardor to the Niger Mission.

Before the bishop's retirement in 1920, there had been steady advance in the older mission; but it was along the Niger and in the Delta that the most notable growth was achieved. By the year 1919 it became necessary to set off this area as a second diocese, which has since had a bishop and a Negro suffragan of its own. It was a few years later that there began a mass movement toward Christianity among the pagans in the Isoko country west of the river, a process which lasted for nearly 10 years and brought 20,000 converts into the Church. Less spectacular but quite as impressive was the expansion of the great native church in the Delta, long known as the Delta Pastorate, which has grown from a little group in a mud-and-thatch hut at Bonny to an array of 80,000 Christians, all in self-supporting churches with African pastors. Not only in the Delta but throughout the two Anglican dioceses this development of self-support has long been a settled policy. Since there is relatively little poverty in the country, the Christians are always able to build their own churches and usually pay their own ministers, catechists, and teachers. Nearly all the pastoral care of the congregations is in the hands of Africans, and in the synods of both dioceses the Africans greatly outnumber the English. The rate of increase in this Anglican Church may be measured by the fact that between 1925 and 1938 the schools increased by almost 60 percent and the number of Christians more than doubled.

Only the need for brevity prevents us from following the course of other missions, smaller in comparison but with large achievements to their credit.[19] The English Methodists, for example, and the American Southern Baptists are very strong in Lagos and the Yoruba country. In Calabar, on the eastern edge of the coast, the Church of Scotland and the Qua Iboe Mission have important work; and in Northern Nigeria the Sudan United Mission and Sudan Interior Mission [20] have multiplied their endeavors in the pagan belt. In fact, except for the northern tier of Moslem provinces, most of the strategic points in the country are now adequately occupied. Among the fourteen societies represented in the field, there is a gratifying degree of coöperation, made more efficient during the past ten years by the formation in 1930 of a United Christian Council of Nigeria.

The present extent of Nigerian Christianity is revealed by the statistics of 1938, which record 580 missionaries (excluding wives), 200 African clergy, 3,400 organized churches, and 411,000 Protestant Christians, to which should be added some 200,000 Roman Catholics. The Christian Church is responsible for main-

19 Most of these societies are now active in Northern as well as in Southern Nigeria.

20 The Sudan Interior Mission has grown from 11 missionaries in 1911 to 190 in 1938.

taining nearly 90 percent of the schools in the country, which include, among the Protestant bodies, 2,500 elementary schools, but as yet only 15 middle schools and only one institution of college grade. In their contribution to medical service, however, the missions are relatively backward in terms of quantity, for only 19 missionaries are physicians and there are no more than 21 hospitals.

Such a Church, with its evident power of self-propagation, suggests immense possibilities for the future. Yet against the encouragement which its growth affords must be set not only the fact that even now there is only one Christian among every 32 inhabitants, but also the evidence of recent observers that in Southern Nigeria Islam is spreading faster than Christianity.

The direct work with Moslems, as we have noted, amounts to only a tiny fraction of the whole, but it is with that fraction that we are chiefly concerned. The enterprises now in operation are the outcome of patient and persistent endeavor through a period of forty years.

Though the C. M. S. before 1900 had penetrated farther north than the other missions, which were then largely confined to the Yoruba country and the Delta, its leader was eager to press onward to the more difficult Moslem areas. In January, 1900, accompanied by two clergymen and two laymen, one of whom was Dr. W. R. S. Miller, Bishop Tugwell led an expedition overland from Lagos to Kano. Arriving in April at that Moslem capital in the far north, the party interviewed the Emir of Kano, who sharply refused to allow them to remain. Returning southward to Zaria, in another emirate, they met with a similar rebuff; and their journey ended, in the beginning of 1901, almost at the borders of Southern Nigeria. This initial venture of faith bore little fruit for some time; but the easy conquest of this whole region by the British during the next two years wrought changes from which the Mission was later to benefit. Yet the openings still remained few, for the authorities were wary of stirring Mohammedan feeling, and the principles of indirect government obliged them to admit no form of missions unwelcome to the subordinate Moslem rulers. In 1905, however, Dr. W. R. S.

Miller succeeded in obtaining permission from the British and from the local emir to open work at Zaria, where in course of time he was joined by several other missionaries. Thus at last, after sixty years of Nigerian missions, a courageous group found a foothold in a Moslem stronghold in Hausaland. During the next sixteen years it was to remain the sole missionary base in that inhospitable area; for though the government granted freedom of access to all the pagans in the wide lower belt of Northern Nigeria and the work there increased steadily, further progress in the Mohammedan emirates was forbidden.

The enterprise at Zaria not only aroused no hostility but made encouraging headway. A hospital and dispensary were promptly opened; a boys' school was founded, and later, with the arrival of women workers, a girls' hostel. Dr. Miller added to his hospital labors the task of translating the Bible into Hausa, which was to require thirty years for completion. Nor were the members of the staff afraid of evangelism. "I was not supposed," Dr. Miller writes, "to itinerate and preach in the villages, but I managed perfectly openly and honestly to continue doing this all the [twenty-five] years I lived in Zaria." [21] As a result, there was gradually formed a little church of converts from Islam, many of whom were ready to testify to their faith among their own people. The next step in advance was the establishment in 1921, by government permission, of a book depot at Kano. The opening may seem small, but the city to which it gave entrance is of vast importance. Kano, in fact, may be called the metropolis of north central Africa, a market center for an immense region and a great focus of Moslem influence. Already in one of its suburbs there was a large church, under an African pastor, composed of immigrant Christians chiefly from pagan provinces. The new book station, however, was to be an agency for reaching Moslems; and in that endeavor it has results to show. Without arousing any sort of trouble for the authorities, the C. M. S. workers have formed a group of Christians, some of whom are former Moslems and all of whom have united in building a little church of their own.

21 W. R. S. Miller, *Reflections of a Pioneer,* pp. 93 f.

Within the last five years the policy of the government has become so much more flexible that applications for initiating missions in regions hitherto closed have been considered intelligently on their individual merits. In consequence, the C. M. S. has begun medical work at two points in the Katsina Emirate and at Chafé, in Sokoto, while the Sudan Interior Mission has opened centers in all four provinces along the northern boundary. Here we may hope to see in the coming decade the same fruits which have justified the earlier ventures at Zaria and Kano.

The full story of the present missionary effort to reach the Moslem would include other countries to which we have hardly referred, such as Liberia, French Equatorial Africa, the Anglo-Egyptian Sudan, and Kenya. Nyasaland and Nigeria, however, must serve as examples of the two lines of approach now pursued—the Christianizing of pagans in competition with Islam and the newer and more difficult enterprise of evangelizing Mohammedans themselves. Of the former endeavor the consequences are encouragingly evident on a large scale; but the fruit of the latter has only just begun to be gathered. It is only in terms of faith, and not of statistics, that we can look forward to the conversion of African Islam.

In viewing the prospect, however, certain factors are plain to the eye. Our earlier summary of the methods by which Islam progresses among Negroes has shown clearly enough why that religion advances more easily than Christianity. The sum of the reasons is that on the whole it works with the grain; it concedes much to the low human nature it finds and demands but little. And because its expansion depends to so small a degree upon organization, it is fair to say, as Canon Gairdner once put it, that "it adds cubits to its stature without taking thought." Christianity, in contrast, labors under the disadvantage of being the religion of the dominant white man. The European, moreover, is not only of a proud alien race but he has too often forgotten the need to develop among African Christians the power of self-support and self-propagation and to guide converted pagans toward the winning of their Moslem neighbors. The white missionary, too, is commonly ignorant of Islam, for there are few indeed in Negro Africa who possess the necessary qualifications to meet its followers. And perhaps hardest of all the handicaps is the fact, to which every worker in the field can testify, that Islam is distinctly not a stepping-stone to Christianity. Tribes once won to Islam are more than doubly hard to convert to Christianity.

Yet there are factors, even on the worldly level, favorable to Christianity. If Islam can bring to the native social advancement and a heightened self-respect, Christianity has proved that it can offer these advantages in even fuller measure. If Islam contributes to many followers a meager education and some degree of intellectual advancement, these benefits come far more abundantly with the spread of Christianity. As concrete evidence we need only cite the 27,000 Christian schools in Negro Africa and the spread of the Scriptures in more than 200 languages and dialects. Moreover, if Islam spreads more rapidly than Christianity, it is consequently the more superficial; and the lack of intolerance and fanaticism makes the average Negro Moslem all the easier to approach. On the other hand, Christianity, where it is successful, penetrates more deeply than Islam, and its adherents for that very reason are the more settled in their allegiance. Yet our confidence in the ultimate outcome is not fundamentally based on any favorable balance among such practical factors, but rather on the faith which remembers the promises of God and which finds in Christ alone the redemption for which Africa is waiting.

PART THREE

Problems and Policies

Foreword

A REVIEW of twelve centuries of background and a historical survey of modern missions to Moslems in eight typical countries afford us ample material for summarizing in conclusion some of the problems which attend the Christian approach to the Moslem and the policies which now guide it. Whether we think in terms of problems or of those attempts at solution which we may call policies, we find them to be of three different kinds—those which are common to all mission fields, those which are common to all Moslem mission fields, and those which are characteristic of particular Moslem areas.

Certain questions are of so general a nature that they arise wherever Christian missionaries are active—among Japanese university students, among the depressed classes in India, among Moslem sheikhs in Cairo, or among the pagan tribes of Southern Rhodesia. They are common to all partly because they relate to human nature in general. So far as men and women are alike everywhere, they present to the evangelist difficulties and opportunities which, if we express them only in broad terms, are much the same from country to country and from age to age. Yet it is only when stated abstractly that they seem everywhere the same: the moment they are dealt with concretely at any one point, no two situations are quite alike.

But there is another group of questions which are inevitably common to all mission lands because they are concerned with what the missionary brings with him, rather than with what he finds in his chosen field. Chief among these is the *purpose* of missions, which depends in each case on the missionary's convictions about the nature of Christianity and the nature of the Church. The ultimate goal which he sets himself is determined not by the various conditions which he encounters but by the beliefs in which he was reared and the matured faith which he has already made his own. In his view of the final objectives of missions, a High-Church conservative differs from an ultra-liberal Protestant not because their fields are different but because they themselves are different. Indeed, as often happens, their fields may be the same. The variation in their aims arises from contrasting interpretations of the task in hand; and these in turn are the outcome of opposing ideas as to the meaning of Christianity and the significance of the Church. As long as Christian missionaries represent diverse schools of thought, so long will their divergencies be reflected in any area to which they go. The problems and policies which result are everywhere familiar because they are not the product of local conditions. They simply reproduce certain standard types well known in Christian lands.

Wherever Christian leaders are engaged in the missionary enterprise, they have to decide sooner or later just what it is they are trying to do. Are they simply proclaiming the gospel, acting only as heralds? Or are they concerned also to organize churches, and, if so, what kind? Is the institution to be of central importance and baptism an essential factor? Or are these leaders to be content with manifesting the spirit of Jesus or with sharing religious values or with promoting general uplift? Shall they view the non-Christian religions as works of Satan or as incomplete revelations or as permanent alternatives to Christianity, requiring only modification through Christian influence? Are they to preach a Christ who alone is adequate to save or is His position only relative? Is their mission to be an anxious search party looking for the truth with the aid of local search parties, or is it to be a royal embassy bearing good tidings to all men? In our own day all of these attitudes toward the aim of missions find expression in one quarter or another. But it is not within the scope of this book to deal with missionary theology or missionary methods in general. For our purposes, the important point to note is that the answers to such questions are not to be supplied by reference to Islam or to conditions in Moslem countries. The questions arise everywhere and everywhere demand response. What response they shall receive will be determined by fundamental convictions about Christ and His Church.

The problems, then, which chiefly concern us here are those which are peculiar to Mohammedan lands. Some appear wherever Islam is to be found; others are characteristic only of certain areas. It is the difficulties encountered everywhere which are the hardest to deal with, for it is they which are most deeply rooted in stubborn facts. The two most important of these we may now consider—"The Presentation of the Message" and "The Care of the Convert."

XVI

The Presentation of the Message

AMONG the inevitable obstacles to the proclamation of the Christian message we may count as foremost the *claims* of Islam. For Islam, like Christianity, is rigorous and unyielding in its affirmations. Unlike the religions of India, it is neither accommodating nor amorphous. It has a rigid bony structure. It does not deal in shades of gray, but in blacks and whites. Mohammed is the last and the greatest of God's prophets. The Koran is the verbally infallible Word of God. Unbelievers are destined to an eternal hell. And the *denials* of Islam are as formidable as its assertions. Moreover, they are chiefly directed against Christianity. The Christian Scriptures have long since ceased to be reliable. The doctrine of the Trinity is false. Christ is not the Son of God. Christ did not die upon the cross nor rise again. To approach non-Christians with a message which is new and strange to them is often difficult enough. But to approach them with a message which expressly affirms what their own infallible dogmas expressly deny calls for the limit of hardihood. And as if these obstacles were not baffling enough, the missionary has also to reckon with the *misunderstandings* of Islam—those false interpretations of Christianity which are embedded in the revelation of Mohammed. Chief among these are the conception of Christ's sonship as a physical begetting by God and the idea of the Trinity as composed of the Father, Jesus, and the Virgin Mary. Whether we consider the claims or the denials or the misunderstandings of Islam, it is clear that in each case the Christian gospel has been judged and condemned in advance. It cannot count on a free field or a fair hearing, for the hearers are literally prejudiced. So far as they are orthodox Moslems, their minds are already made up. And their convictions are not merely private judgments, open to revision. They are solidly based on a revelation accepted as divine.

The difficulties of approach are further aggravated by the fact that orthodox Christianity is a religion of the same general type. Christianity, too, has a rigid bony structure and deals in blacks and whites. It relies upon a revelation regarded as unique and final. It has its own extreme claims and its own flat denials. The Bible is the Word of God and the norm for all doctrine. Christ is God himself incarnate, perfect God and perfect Man. In Him God was reconciling the world unto Himself. Through His life and death and resurrection, redemption is offered to all mankind. Exalted to God's right hand, He is ever active as a living Saviour. Only through Him can men win forgiveness and find salvation. Every man's destiny beyond the grave depends in some fashion on his relation to Christ. And implicit in these bold affirmations are the denials of Moslem claims. The Koran is *not* an infallible revelation. Mohammed is *not* the supreme apostle of God. Implicit also in the claims of Christianity are its *demands*. Christ being what He is, it is not enough that He should be honored and admired. He is not finally content to be accepted as a wise teacher or even as a major prophet. Because He is prepared to give everything, He has no hesitation in asking for everything. He calls for complete surrender, for unqualified discipleship, and exclusive devotion.

It is in the face of this complex of irreconcilable factors that missionaries to Moslems have to solve what is commonly their first and hardest problem—the presentation of the Christian message. As evangelists they have to decide what to say and how to say it. In proclaiming the gospel to alien minds there are of course two factors to be taken into account—what it means to the teacher and what it is likely to mean to the taught. The speaker's conviction and his past experience constitute, no doubt, the primary element; but another is supplied by the aptitude and the previous habits and beliefs of the hearers. The first factor is determined by the type of religious experience characteristic of the evangelist and by the current theology in which that experience is expressed. Since the Protestant missionary enterprise of the nineteenth century was chiefly the product of the Evangelical Movement, the language and substance of its preaching were naturally those of orthodox evangelical doctrine. In these earlier days the question of what to say and how to say it was not a problem, for the missionary message was largely standardized according to the evangelical model. When seeking to convert others, the missionary preached that form of Christian truth which had converted him. Nor was he greatly interested to adapt himself to what his hearers already knew and felt. Indeed, this second factor, for several generations, was usually neglected and frequently ignored. The whole process of development during the past century has thus been partly due to changing theology at home and partly to the increasing consideration of the other man's point of view, the growing concern for the capacities, the prejudices, and the peculiar needs of Moslem audiences.

What we have described as the evangelical model is of course familiar to any student of theology as "The Plan of Redemption" or "The Economy of Salvation." God created Adam in a state of innocence, but Adam sinned and fell. This Original Sin infected all his descendants, who therefore lay under the wrath of God. Only repentance and forgiveness could save them from everlasting punishment. To make this possible, God sent His only Son, Jesus Christ, who suffered on the cross the penalty due to human sin and thereby redeemed us through His blood. Vindicated and exalted through His Resurrection and Ascension, He now reigns as Lord and will one day return to earth as the Judge of all mankind at the General Resurrection. Meanwhile all men are steeped in sin and in dire need of pardon. This they can obtain by repentant acceptance of Christ as Saviour, through perfect faith in His redeeming power and in the promises of God. Those who so receive Him will be sanctified by His Holy Spirit and will receive the reward of heaven. Those who persist in rejecting Him will go to hell. In these terms we have outlined, all too roughly, the general scheme of doctrine, with no attempt to make it plausible and with no allowance for such variations as Predestination. To the main points of Original Sin, Vicarious Atonement on the Cross, and the Last Judgment we may add the further dogma of an infallible Bible, which records and ratifies the whole plan of salvation. Such, then, was the essence of the Gospel; and, as has been observed, "the unchanging nature of religious truth is often taken to justify an equally invariable method of announcing it."

Whatever may be the virtues and defects of this standard statement of the gospel, one fact is obvious. It is a mode of presenting the Christian message which gives the strongest emphasis to those dogmas which most readily antagonize the Moslem. It throws into high relief those very features which he is most likely to resent—especially the Deity of Christ, the atoning death on the Cross, and the infallible Bible. During the same period, moreover, when this form of proclamation was the recognized model, Islam was regarded as primarily the work of the devil, Mohammed as the "false prophet," and the Koran as a tissue of falsehood. A further characteristic of the age (not yet wholly outgrown) was to think of religions not as forms of experience with an inner vitality of their own, but as dogmatic systems confronting one another. Each one of these three factors—the character of the message, the attitude toward Islam, and the conception of religion—tended to reinforce the others. The historic consequence was that the approach to the Moslem became a head-on collision, a contest between two armies with banners. And the enterprise was commonly known for several generations as the great "Moslem Controversy."

Examples of this mode of preaching and writing we have already described in treating of India, the country where it was tried with the greatest enthusiasm and on the most extensive scale. Martyn and Pfander and French and Lefroy, though differing from each other in many respects, were all illustrations of evangelists who had confidence in the same type of approach; and together their lives span a century. Before the end of that century, however, there were factors at work which have since operated to change the prevailing attitude toward controversy as a missionary method.

Changes in the missionary message have been changes less in substance than in emphasis and in manner of presentation. They were made possible, and indeed inevitable, by the general development of Christian theology. To some degree, it is true, the actual content of Christian preaching suffered certain alterations depending, of course, on the training and home associations of the preacher. It was only natural that the same ideas which found a welcome in more liberal pulpits and writings in England and America should be reflected before long in mission lands, and that those dogmas which in certain circles at home were being abandoned should be gradually eliminated from the utterances of not a few teachers in the field. Among these doctrines were the expectation of a visible second coming of Christ as Judge; the verbal infallibility of the Bible; the Calvinistic theory of a substitutionary Atonement; and the orthodox belief in a hell of fire for unbelievers. If such changes in the substance of the message were apparent, still more marked and more widely accepted was the change in emphasis. This modification took the form not so much of substituting new doctrine for old as of minimizing, or at least simplifying, all doctrine. With it went the tendency, responsive to another note in current thought, to centralize attention on Christ Himself, on the character and life of the historical Jesus— to lay stress, in short, upon His persuasive personality and not simply upon His official function as Mediator. This aim of simplifying the message was greatly encouraged by the increasing realization that our theologies were essentially Western and that since Christianity was primarily a matter of life and experience, Christ should be presented in a form as little "encrusted" as possible. Many, therefore, who might not be prepared to alter their own cherished dogmas were unwilling to make them compulsory.

Parallel to this development and reinforcing it at certain points, have run other lines of change. One of these, of course, was the increasing concern for the environment and traditions, the existing beliefs and capacities of the Moslem, especially a fuller knowledge of his theology and of his mysticism at their best. Further encouragement to this attitude of appreciation was given by that growing study of pedagogy which has been remolding our educational system and which is always reminding us that the teacher must find and note aptitudes in the taught, must discover points of contact, and must lead from the known to the unknown. Quite as transforming in its effect has been a still more recent change which we may attribute in part to theology but chiefly to the psychology of religion—the tendency to view religion not simply as a system of beliefs but as essentially an inner experience. The missionary had usually looked on Islam as a set of doctrines to be compared with his own set. He saw it only externally and so viewed it merely as a hostile force. For some time past, however, he has grown more accustomed to consider what Islam means in the hearts of believers, what it does for them in terms of experience. And that shift of attitude tends to substitute sympathy and understanding for intellectual criticism and dogmatic combat.

By the beginning of the twentieth century, then, some of the most ardent missionaries to Moslems were ready to express grave doubts about the effectiveness of the controversial method. At the Cairo Conference in 1906, for example, D. M. Thornton, while acknowledging that the need to remove misunderstandings might lead to doctrinal discussion, urged his colleagues to avoid theological hairsplitting, to preach a simple gospel with moral and spiritual emphasis, and never to begin or provoke a controversy. And at this gathering there was general agreement that where polemic could not be avoided, it should always be conducted in the spirit of patience, fairness, and love. Writing a few years later from India, Dr. Weitbrecht notes that nearly all missionaries are opposed to the use of disputation; and at the Lucknow Conference in 1911 Dr. Bowman insisted that though a Moslem can sometimes be convinced by pure argument, he will become a merely intellectual Christian, whose devotional and spiritual life has been neglected. Such, too, was the view of Dr. Crawford of Syria, expressed in 1915, when he wrote "Convince [the Moslem] that you are more eager to have him feel the mastery of Jesus over the conscience than you are to establish any particular doctrine, and he begins to take hold of truth by the right handle." [1]

Each succeeding decade has produced an increasing volume of testimony to the same effect, not from half-hearted academic ob-

[1] In *Vital Forces of Christianity and Islam*, pp. 144 f.

servers but from stalwart evangelists in the field. Dr. Esselstyn, who died in the service of the cause in Iran, wrote in 1921,

Avoid argument, controversy, and disparaging references to Mohammed, the Koran, and Islam. If reference must be made to the things of Islam, speak of that which is good.... Never display heat or temper.... Preach sympathetically. Regard Moslems simply as lost sinners whom God loves and for whom Christ died, and preach accordingly.[2]

Typical of the experience of more than one missionary is the testimony of Dr. John Van Ess, of Basrah:

Twenty-five years ago I visualized myself as a knight of the Cross sallying forth to attack the citadel of Islam. I had bright and well-tried armor, sharp and shining weapons. It was to be a battle and a triumph. As the years went by ... the ideas of battle and conflict, of strife and victory and vindication, have receded. I have discarded the old conception of citadels and arenas and all the imagery so foreign to Himself, and have tried to learn from Him His own method and language, His thought and purpose, His ideas and ideals, and to measure success by what He approved.... I believe in the Atonement with all my heart, but I cannot teach it. Only Christ can do that, for only after an Arab has walked with Christ and seen His purity and his own need, can he feel the need of that Saviour. And so my message and my task have been: to get the Arab to walk with Christ, and to talk with Him, to love and trust Him.[3]

To show how nearly unanimous in this matter is opinion in the field today, we may cite the views of three other missionaries, each of whom speaks out of a rich experience. Dr. Bevan Jones, of Lahore, reminds us that persistence in arid controversy—a kind of long-range bombardment—generally embittered the Moslem, and even when it succeeded produced only intellectual converts who showed no evidences of Christ's redeeming love. "Can that method be right whereby we win the argument but lose the man, and that a man for whom Christ died?"[4] Dr. J. Christy Wilson, of Tabriz, is equally certain that

"The Great Moslem Controversy" has gone into the limbo of things that are past.... Today the one who would present Christ to the

[2] Esselstyn, "What to Preach to Moslems," *Moslem World,* Jan., 1922.
[3] Van Ess, "A Quarter Century in Arabia," *Moslem World,* April, 1929.
[4] L. B. Jones, *The People of the Mosque,* p. 298.

Moslem heart should be an expert at avoiding argument.... Intellectual disputation still remains a favorite indoor sport in the lands of the East.... The ordinary Mohammedan in almost any land would about as soon argue as eat.... Our task involves not only the winning of the intellectual consent to the truth of Christianity, but the far more difficult problem of winning the heart and will also for Christ.[5]

As a deep student of Islam and a Christian who is as far as possible from being a shallow liberal, Dr. Kraemer declares

that especially in the world of Islam to present Christianity as a set of doctrines is the most awkward way conceivable... Islam itself is creedal and doctrinal to the core. To present Christianity as a set of doctrines is to rouse the militantly intellectualist spirit of Islam... and to move entirely outside the religious sphere.... The missionary approach, in so far as it is dependent on its own initiative, must abjure all doctrinal approach and invite the Moslem to penetrate into the living world of Biblical realism.[6]

In place of a frontal attack launched on the intellectual level, the best of modern missionaries to Islam pursue a mode of approach which was seldom neglected by their predecessors but which was never quite trusted to bear full fruit—the method of intimate personal fellowship, of loving service, of sympathetic testimony, and of united prayer. Believing that the essence of conversion is direct experience of the saving power of Christ, they seek to lead the Moslem to that experience by helping him to sense his deepest needs, by appealing to what he has already known of God in his inner life, and by sharing with him what Christ has done for them. In counting upon Christ Himself, and not theories about Him, to exert a drawing power, they are aided by the fact that "the character of Christ does attract the Mohammedan, and is doing so more and more.... The most hopeful single note in the Islamic world today is the, to many, irresistible attraction of the Person of Jesus Christ." [7] To make the Moslem feel that attraction through deepening friendship, through a guided study of the New Testament, through leisurely conference, and through

---

[5] Wilson, "Presenting Christ to Moslems," *Moslem World*, Oct., 1935.
[6] Kraemer, *The Christian Message in a Non-Christian World*, pp. 356 f.
[7] Gairdner, in *Reports*, Jerusalem Meeting of the I. M. C., I, 209, 197.

that prayer together which confesses that God's Spirit alone can convert—this is the primary aim on which all else depends.

Such a procedure is based on the principle, which psychology and history alike confirm, that so far as possible experience ought to precede the acceptance of formulated doctrine. The way to learn of Christ's divinity is through contact with Christ Himself and not through previous submission to dogmatic assertions. By following this natural order, what might otherwise be an external collision becomes an internal evolution. Until Christ has had time to show His divine power He cannot be really recognized as divine. But once He has wrought in the inner life what only God can work, the moment has come when doctrine can properly meet a growing need and when the teacher can help to express the new experience in terms that will then seem to the convert as true and vital as they have to countless other generations of Christians. There is no question, then, of abandoning Christian doctrine in favor of a merely moral or emotional appeal. It is simply a matter of choosing the right time and employing the right means. For all evangelists who have the courage to seek the Moslem are agreed that sooner or later, by one means or another, he is entitled to all the truth we have. That truth may need restatement and such variation in form as may suit individual needs. It must not be set in an unvarying mold. But nothing can ultimately be adequate to the demands of those who have paid the price of forsaking Islam except the full faith of historic Christianity.

Despite a change of atmosphere and a development in method, there still remain, therefore, both the problem and the privilege of presenting Christian truths. There is first of all the difficulty of being understood. For one thing, the religious Arabic of Islam and the religious Arabic of Christianity have grown so far apart that the meanings of words, still more their connotations, now differ widely. Another obstacle is raised by those prepossessions of the Moslem mind which make Son and Trinity and Sin and Atonement convey one meaning to the hearer and another to the teacher. It is this need to be sensitive to the Moslem understanding both of words and of ideas that requires the most thorough scholarship and justifies the careful training in Islamics which is now supplied by the schools in Cairo and Jerusalem, and at Landour in India. And the knowledge of Moslem background ought to include a sympathetic understanding not only of theology but of the higher aspects of that widespread mysticism, which many believe offers the field in which Christians and Mohammedans can meet with the greatest hope of fruitful results.

Granted the equipment for guiding the Moslem who seeks to understand the truths of Christianity, the teacher naturally thinks of these truths as including both points of contact and points of contrast. If we use this classification, now so familiar in other fields, the doctrines held in common look impressive in their number and importance. What is strongest and best in Islam seems to find answering counterparts in our own religion: faith in one supreme God, a living God who dominates the whole of life; the fraternity of Islam, the brotherhood which binds together all believers; morality as the Law of God; Jesus as a sinless prophet; revelation through an inspired Book; the future Resurrection and Last Judgment, together with Heaven and Hell. If on all these vital points Moslem belief is to be accepted as equivalent to Christian, the elements of contrast might easily appear to be greatly outnumbered. But a closer scrutiny reveals the fact that within these seeming contacts there lurk the most vigorous contrasts. Not even here are the two religions really at one. We cannot pass over these doctrines as already agreed upon because in the very field which they cover Christianity has a wealth of contribution to make.

The monotheism of orthodox Islam centers in a God who has been described as "a loveless will-force" and who stands for autocratic and unlimited omnipotence. In the character of the Christian God supreme moral goodness is dominant. At the heart of His nature are holiness and love. He is a Father whose seeking and saving energy wins us to fellowship with Him. Moreover, the brotherhood of Islam, so admirably genuine within its limits, falls far short of the Christian ideal. "Islamic fraternity, that of 'a chosen people,' will be superseded in only one way ... by the demonstration of a brotherhood which goes deeper, reaches further, rises higher, and embraces more widely." [8] Again, while it

8 *Ibid.*, I, 204.

is true that for both religions the moral law is determined by the will of God, Islam is essentially legalistic after the manner of the Pharisees. The Gospel, on the contrary, proclaims an ethical freedom achieved by fellowship with Christ, "for he that loveth another hath fulfilled the law." And corresponding to this contrast in ideals is the difference in the two conceptions of sin—in the one case superficially conceived in legal terms, in the other interpreted deeply as alienation from the life of God. To choose but one more example, the two views of revelation are really at odds—the one mechanical, the other truly personal. "In Islam [revelation] is a set of immutable divine words that take the place of God's movable acts and His speaking and doing through the living man Jesus Christ. The foundation of Islam is not, The Word became flesh. It is, The Word became book." [9] "In the place of the pre-existent Word revealed in time as the Arabic Koran we offer the pre-existent Word revealed in time as the human Christ." [10] Herein lies the fundamental reason for not trying to match a verbally inspired Koran with a verbally inspired Bible. To do so is to descend to the Moslem's idea of divine revelation.[11]

But even if agreements were closer than they actually are, they would serve only as starting points. For "we must pass on from similarities to differences. The similarities . . . furnish contacts, but they do not furnish impacts. . . . A gospel is not only *good* but it is *news; and the new in it is the news.*" [12] And since an evangelist is by definition a bringer of good news, his mission is not fulfilled until he has shared with the Moslem whatever the Moslem is able to receive of "the unsearchable riches of Christ." When the right moment arrives in the process of conversion, he must "be ready always to give an answer to every man that asketh him a reason of the hope that is in him." Sooner or later the convert must be given the chance to know all that he is capable of understanding of such distinctively Christian teaching as the doctrines of the

[9] Kraemer, *op. cit.*, pp. 217 f.
[10] Browne, "The Christian Approach to Moslems," *East and West*, Oct., 1926.
[11] A searching treatment of this problem of contrasts underlying apparent agreements, appears in Arthur Jeffery's article, "The Presentation of Christianity to Moslems," *International Review of Missions*, April, 1924.
[12] Buck, *Christianity Tested*, pp. 112 f.

Incarnation, the Atonement, the Trinity, and the Kingdom of God. In that process of giving and receiving, the wise missionary will bear in mind that a man is not saved by doctrine through mental exertion but by grace through faith. He will remember that some of the purest Christians who ever lived could not stand an examination in theology. He will act on the principle that experience of Christ takes precedence (always in importance and usually in time) of theories about Christ. Even if standardized creeds should rightly remain his guiding norm, he will adapt himself flexibly to what the particular Moslem already knows and already seeks. He will be suspicious of any dogma which cannot be translated into moral terms that make a difference in the Christian life. While not withholding from the beginner anything "which a Christian ought to know and believe to his soul's health," his deepest concern will be that the Christian newly won shall be eager to serve and constant in prayer.[13]

[13] No attempt has here been made to discuss the question of converting agnostics who are only socially or politically Moslems. These are to be found in nearly all Mohammedan countries, especially in such Europeanized centers as Cairo. Though their background differs from that of unbelievers in Buddhist or Christian countries, the necessary mode of approach is quite distinct from that demanded for a convinced Moslem; and the problem is not essentially different from what confronts us in the endeavor to convert an agnostic in any other field.

XVII

The Care of the Convert

THE PROCESS of winning converts to Christianity and aiding them to develop an indigenous Church is difficult enough in any field. It is exceptionally hard in Moslem countries, harder than elsewhere to win them and harder to care for them after they are won. The peculiar obstacles which Moslems face before conversion account for the fact that there are so few converts; the peculiar obstacles which they face after conversion explain why so few are able to enjoy a normal church life. And the two sets of difficulties are closely interrelated.

The factors which keep the Moslem from becoming a Christian have been set forth at many points in earlier pages. In the last chapter we have noted the religious hindrances—the claims and the denials of Christianity and Islam and the severe demands involved in Christian allegiance. Such a review is enough to remind us how painful it is to move from one exclusive religion to another, when each one proclaims it is the only way of salvation. But there are many other barriers to a change of faith. There is the heritage of the past, which perpetuates in memory and tradition the centuries of hostility between Christendom and Islam, from the far-off days of bloody crusading to the recent days of European imperialism. There is the known record of all the vices and follies of modern Western civilization, and especially the spectacle of nations locked at frequent intervals in deadly struggle. In the Near East there is the living example of those Oriental Churches which display so little that can command admiration and whose members have so long been despised as spiritless or viewed with suspicion as disloyal to the state. Beyond these broader reasons for avoiding Christianity there are further deterrents more practical and personal. The law of apostasy, which condemns to death

the Moslem who forsakes his faith, may no longer be operative in
more than one or two countries; but at least it remains in the
background as a menacing reminder of what the apostate deserves.
And as substitutes there must still be encountered the pains and
penalties involved in commercial boycott, in loss of employment,
in disinheritance, and in vindictive social persecution, often ending in destitution and misery. To rehearse all these factors, religious, historical, legal, and social, is to understand why so few
Moslems become Christians. It is to understand also the forms of
pressure which sometimes cause the convert to relapse.[1]

Once a Moslem has surmounted all these barriers and becomes
an enquirer known to the missionary or the native evangelist, the
process of preparing him for baptism is similar in most respects
to the same process in any non-Christian land. Its details, that is,
are determined chiefly by the needs and capacities of the individual and by the convictions and traditions of the teacher or
pastor. What a Moslem should be required to know and believe
before he is baptized depends on what he is capable of understanding and on what his particular guide regards as indispensable.
We therefore observe in the mission field a great variety of practice. The minimum demands may be the acceptance of Christ as
Lord and Saviour, together with a knowledge of the Apostles'
Creed, the Lord's Prayer, and the Ten Commandments. But on
other occasions the catechumen may be obliged to confess his
faith in the Trinity and the Atonement, to learn various proofs
of these doctrines, to master the details of a church catechism,
and explicitly to disavow Mohammed as a true prophet. Fortunately, however, it is commonly agreed that personal faith is
far more important than the intellectual acceptance of dogmas and
that the evidences of a changed life are more significant than the
acquiring of credal information. Whatever tests of orthodoxy may
be applied, the emphasis is laid on the expression of faith in moral
conduct, on the readiness to witness to that faith, and on the need
to nurture the spiritual life by Bible study and prayer.

[1] Replies to a questionnaire prepared in 1933 under the auspices of the Near
East Christian Council and sent to missionaries in six Moslem countries revealed
important facts in regard to some 500 converts. Of these, 5 percent had been completely lost to sight and 15 percent had relapsed.

Since baptism should be recognized as the beginning of the Christian life and not its goal, the period of probation is seldom extended beyond one or two years. Whether the sacrament will then be administered privately or before whatever congregation may be available has usually depended on the degree of religious freedom which is locally enjoyed. Though there have been circumstances in which a public baptism would be only a solemn form of suicide, such extreme risks are seldom encountered today. There are but few places where secret baptism is necessary, and missionary policy is almost everywhere in favor of performing the rite in the presence of a Christian group.

Both before and after baptism, the position of the convert is nearly always one of hardship and sometimes one of danger. He has broken with his own community, and the penalties are usually prompt and painful. The reaction of his former associates is likely to be vigorous and unsparing. He is often thrown out of employment or subject to a trade boycott. Time and again he becomes financially dependent. And so the economic care of the convert has long since been a missionary problem—the problem of how to help him without hurting him. It is obvious, of course, that to refuse all aid of any kind is to deny every principle of Christian brotherhood. It is equally plain that indiscriminate giving would injure the sincere believers and attract large numbers of the insincere. But between these two extremes lie so many possible compromises that the practices of no two missions are quite alike, and the methods used are subject to wide variation. There is now general agreement, however, as to certain policies, and growing strictness and caution in applying them. It seems to be proved by experience that responsibility for the enquirer or convert should not be accepted until he has made every effort to shift for himself; but if his acceptance of Christianity has rendered him destitute, the church is bound in some way to provide for him. The most effective kind of help is to find him the employment for which he is best fitted, a solution often impossible in most Mohammedan lands. Or he may be given work for the church or mission or missionary—an alternative less desirable, since it tends to segregate him from his fellows and to increase his sense of dependence. If no sort of employment can be offered soon enough to be of value, the next best remedy is a financial loan. If it can be sufficiently large to enable the convert to make a new start in trade or handicraft, it will probably do him more good than harm. Of all forms of assistance, the least to be commended is a mere dole.

But the need to earn a living is not the only need of the new convert. Whether or not he suffers economic penalties, he is more than a mere economic man. When he cuts himself off from the brotherhood of Islam, he usually finds himself an isolated individual, with no social environment to compensate him for the fraternal solidarity which he has forsaken. An outcast from his former group, a member of a despised minority, debarred from the normal opportunities for marriage, he is more than likely to experience a disheartening loneliness and to feel that every man's hand is against him. In these circumstances it is all too probable that he will count the missionary who has guided him as his only friend and will attach himself solely to that one source of support and comfort.

In those non-Moslem mission lands where flourishing churches exist, the difficulty is not so acute, since in the first place the new Christian usually has less persecution to endure and in the second place he finds an organized group prepared to receive him. In most Mohammedan areas, however, there is either no real Christian community at all or else, as in Syria and Egypt, there are Christian bodies none too ready to welcome a newcomer; for, as we have noted in our survey of Near Eastern conditions, the native Christians of the older Churches and even many of the Protestant Church members feel no concern for winning Moslems. Unhappy experience through a long past has taught them to view Mohammedans with fear and distrust. Less excusable is their chilly and suspicious attitude toward the Moslem convert. In their eyes, more often than not, he is an unwanted outsider of dubious sincerity, whom they are most reluctant to receive into fellowship.

The only remedy for such a situation is the gradual Christianizing of the Church so that it will become what from the beginning it was meant to be—a warm-hearted family eager to receive and prepared to nurture every new member. But it is not likely to achieve that distinction unless it is filled with the missionary spirit. A Church which has not been interested enough to seek for converts will not be interested enough to nourish them. As one missionary in India has put it, "Only a Church that has a program leading to the winning of converts will ever develop an atmosphere warm enough to care for them." The ideal for which we should strive is that the local church, however it may be composed, should be active in the evangelistic process from the very start, so that in some degree the Mohammedan enquirer shall be associated with its fellowship at every stage. Instead of the missionary and his convert forming a semiforeign element apart from the local church, the native minister and his congregation ought to assume responsibility for evangelism, for grafting the newly baptized into their own body, and for his subsequent training and pastoral care. Only as a valued member of a Christian group can he find the social life that he sorely needs, with its opportunities for friendly intercourse and recreation. In view of the sacrifices he has made, he has the right to expect a genuine home in which he may be cheered by a sense of brotherhood at least as true and warm as that which he once knew. Above all, it is only in and through the Church that he can count upon growing in wisdom and grace and in the knowledge of Christ. To know that this ideal is being realized today in growing measure at little centers of Christian devotion in more than one Moslem land is to take hope for the future.[2]

It is of course the mutually exclusive character of the Islamic community and the Christian Church which creates for the convert this acute problem. As things stand, he has to be a member of one or a member of the other. He cannot have it both ways. And the situation is aggravated by the fact that even in areas under Christian government the Islamic fraternity is not simply a private religious association, so that a change would mean only a change of religion. Even where Islam cannot achieve its ideal as a Church-State, it is still an all-embracing social system. Still

---

[2] Iran offers especially encouraging examples of such churches, including a few in which all the members are former Moslems.

heavier are the consequences where Islam is wholly or partly in control of the state, as in Egypt or Syria. For a man to leave Islam means, therefore, to break all possible ties by which he has been bound and to tear himself loose from the whole fabric in which he has always been safely woven. In the Near East at any rate, by taking the critical step of accepting baptism he deserts a dominating community intensely proud and loyal, to share the fortunes of a weak but rival community, viewed with scorn by those who have held it in subjection for centuries. Thus the circumstances are quite different from those which confront a Chinese or Japanese who joins the Church. In terms of theology, baptism does not vary with varying climates; in terms of bitter experience, it *involves* far more in countries under the sway of Islam.

The latest attempt to review this familiar problem and to propose a solution has been the Inquiry on the Evangelization of Moslems, conducted in 1938 by the Near East Christian Council, which published its findings in November of that year.[3] As a result of extensive correspondence and prolonged conference, certain conclusions were reached which have since been the subject of much comment and criticism. One section of the *Report* treats of the presentation of the message and sets forth principles which we have already considered. The other section, more radical in its proposals, deals with the very obstacle with which we are now concerned—the fact that "in the thought of the Moslem a change of religion is primarily a change of group-connection and group-loyalty." "The greatest handicap against which the Christian missionary has to strive is the power of Moslem solidarity." "There are thousands of men and women who believe in Christ and are trying to follow Him, but they cannot bring themselves to face the break with their own community." "Even where the deterrent is fear or unwillingness to take the consequences, it is still true that this bond of Brotherhood is one of the strongest bulwarks of Islam; and so long as the Christian missionary undertaking appears to be a frontal attack against this great and (to the Moslem) precious fellowship, so long that powerful instrument will effectively oppose the progress of the Gospel."

[3] *Report*, published at the American Mission Building, Beirut, Lebanon, 1938.

ically within Islam. And on this subject the following resolution was adopted:

This Conference of Christian workers amongst Moslems wish to place on record that while we recognize with gratitude the wide interest in our Lord Jesus Christ evident throughout the Moslem world today, and that many real believers in Christ may never reach the point of identifying themselves with the Christian fellowship, yet we maintain that it is our aim and purpose as Christian missionaries to encourage and teach all to realize the vital necessity of open witness to Christ within the fellowship of the Christian Church. At the same time realizing our failure in the past we urge the Church in each country to seek to develop the evangelistic spirit, and to eliminate those unworthy elements in itself which repel or are a stumbling block to the new convert, and that we should endeavor to make it a real fellowship where race, nation and class are lost in a new life in Christ.[4]

And this recommendation was subsequently approved by The Moslem Lands Group at the Tambaram Meeting. These conclusions may thus be accepted as the matured convictions of a representative body. They undoubtedly reflect the views of a majority of missionaries to Islam.

All are agreed that unbaptized followers of Jesus exist in considerable numbers, a few of whom are ready to testify to their belief. All are likewise agreed in rejoicing at this fact and in recognizing that this degree of discipleship is vastly better than no discipleship at all, and that it constitutes a hopeful stage in Christian growth. The critical point at issue is whether that stage of discipleship should be gradually accepted as final. Should it be encouraged and applauded as a permanent status, or simply regarded as good enough so far as it goes but incomplete in view of the ultimate purpose of the Church's mission? In short, is it a solution or it is an evasion?

Here is one of those general problems, referred to in a previous paragraph, which must be dealt with in the light of our fundamental beliefs as to the goal of missions and the nature of the Church. That is why devoted missionaries of equal experience in the same field differ in their replies. For it is not simply a

---

[4] *The World Mission of the Church* (Findings of the International Missionary Council, Tambaram), p. 141.

matter of technique or method; it is really a matter of theology, to be determined by our deepest convictions. Bearing this in mind, there is good reason to believe that most of the men and women who are giving their lives to the cause of missions among Moslems are deeply sympathetic with the pain and distress which must attend the passage from Islam to Christianity. Knowing their own failures as disciples under conditions far less severe, they are not prepared to judge the secret believer. Rather they are ready to welcome any sign in him of an awakening response to the power of the living Christ. Nor would they willingly force the pace of his Christian growth. But such sympathy and understanding are consistent with the firmest resolution not to sanction as complete any form of Christian discipleship which falls short of a surrender to Christ without qualification. The believer will have to decide what price he is willing to pay, but he may need to be reminded that the less he gives the less he will receive; and enlistment under the protection of a saving clause is not the unreserved enlistment which Christ demands and which He rewards with His unlimited gifts. And in one sense at least it remains forever true that outside the Church there is no salvation. To be grafted into the Body of Christ is to draw upon resources divine and human, in sacrament and fellowship, without which the Christian can never grow to full stature.

Conclusion

WHOEVER has taken the pains to study the history of the Christian approach to the Moslem for the past thirteen centuries and to review the efforts of the Church today in the world of Islam will be acutely aware of the baffling obstacles that beset the enterprise. Whatever else the observer may feel as he surveys the task, he is certain to be conscious of the obvious difficulties. It is true, of course, that these are so far from uniform as to vary greatly in different areas. At one end of the scale are those few regions where Christian activity is completely excluded, like central Asia and Afghanistan. Nearest to them in order come those countries where opportunity is greater but results are still meager, as in Arabia, Turkey, Syria, Egypt, and North Africa. More encouraging are other fields, such as Iran and India, where opposition is less rigid and where converts can be numbered by hundreds and even thousands. At the other end of the scale we find the Netherlands Indies, where the path of advance is perhaps most nearly open and where there are large indigenous Churches formed of converts who were once Moslems. Generally speaking, it is in the areas first won to Islam among Arabic-speaking peoples of Semitic stock that the strongest centers of resistance are to be found. The further we move outward toward races whose traditions are less fixed and in whose environment other elements are more largely mingled, the readier is the response. Just what are the many obstacles which confront the Christian evangelist in greater or less degree we have more than once recited. Some are inherent in the essential nature of his mission; others are the regrettable product of the movements of secular history or the wages of the corporate sins of Christendom. But however they may vary in intensity and whatever may be their causes, the immense difficulties are clear to every observer and painfully present to every laborer.

One outcome of these obvious difficulties has been the almost uniform reluctance of the Christian Church to engage in the enterprise of winning Islam. No missionary opportunity of comparable importance has been so widely and continuously neglected. To cite only the Protestant record of the last century and a half, everywhere we find that direct work with Mohammedans has been the adventure of only a courageous few, a tiny minority of the 27,000 Protestant missionaries now active in the non-Christian world. A still more disturbing result of the hardships that are known to attend the quest for the Moslem is the conviction of many in Christian lands that missions to Mohammedans are either impossible or undesirable. To assert that such missions are difficult is to accept a plain truth. But to affirm that they are therefore impossible is to fly in the face of all the facts; and to insist that they are not needed is to repudiate the faith of historic Christianity and to deny the claims of Christ.

So far from being impossible, the genuine conversion of Moslems to Christianity is in progress today in every country where Islam is known and Christian missionaries are to be found. Indeed, considering how few pioneers are dedicated to this enterprise and trained for its prosecution and how heavy are the handicaps under which they labor, the results are greater than might have been expected. They indicate at least what fuller success we might count upon if the Church were ever to set itself seriously and devoutly to the task. Yet even if the fruits of effort were far more discouraging than they are, it would still remain true that whatever ought to be done can be done and that nothing is impossible to the God whose purposes we serve.

For the divine call to win Islam to the faith of Christ is inescapable. From its insistent urgency there can be no refuge. No reasons can be advanced for its denial that do not equally apply to Christian missions everywhere else. If Christ is needed anywhere, He is needed everywhere. If He is all in all to those whom He has found and redeemed in America, in Europe, in China, and in India, He is eager to mean no less to those in Islam who as yet know only His name. For the commission of the Church of Christ is not to spread monotheism and to persuade men to honor Jesus as a mere prophet. If that were so, we might well view Islam as no proper field of endeavor. The Church is charged with a mission to share with all men the unsearchable riches of Christ, and to know the love of Christ which passeth knowledge, that they may be filled with all the fullness of God. It is a call to make Him known by word and deed to those whom He seeks through us and who still await the coming of His Light.

The command of Christ which summons us to be His fellow workers in seeking to win for Him the community of Islam is a call to the whole Church. The task is too arduous and immense to be left to the valiant efforts of little half-neglected groups, representing but a fraction of the mighty Christian forces potentially available. Two hundred and fifty million Moslems offer a field for service which cannot be adequately exploited except by strong and well-trained missions, supported by every major Christian communion. Until the response from the older and younger Churches is commensurate with the need, no one can know what vast changes God might bring to pass. For in this field, as in others, it is true that "he which soweth sparingly shall reap also sparingly; and he which soweth bountifully, shall reap also bountifully." Faith is a daring experiment, but it ends in the richest experience. And that experience begins to ripen not when we are skeptically waiting but when we are trustfully acting.

But whether the enterprise of reaching and winning Islam is to be carried on by a rapidly growing number of faithful volunteers, or whether for generations to come it is to be hampered and delayed by its present limitations, the cause demands the united efforts of every variety of Christian missionary. Provided only that the ultimate aim is to make Christ known and to play a part, through His power, in advancing His Kingdom, there is room for every sort and kind of worker and for every type of service.

One of the most hopeful and impressive movements of modern times is the movement toward organic Church unity, represented by the great Conferences at Lausanne and Edinburgh. The fundamental principle which has guided all who have shared in this cause is the firm conviction that we must seek not for uniformity but for "a synthesis of differences." Uniformity not merely requires the use of force; it sacrifices all the riches of our existing diversity. Equally fatal is the remedy of reducing that diversity to a weak common denominator, for an impoverished Christianity is even worse than a disunited Church. The only process which can both strengthen and unite the separated branches of the visible Church is the healthful process of building together into one united Body all that is sound and positive in every group, all the varied contributions which each has to make. Every one of them has some marked defect which needs to be supplemented or overcome; every one of them has some treasure of its own, for the neglect of which the rest are the poorer. Living apart, they lead narrow lives, too often satisfied with their own limitations; but once incorporated into a living organism, all that is best in each enriches the expanded life of the whole.

The same principle applies to that far smaller group of Christians who have dedicated their lives to the service of the Moslem. Today they fortunately represent a very wide diversity in origin, in training, in attitude, and in method. Some are extreme conservatives (whom "Liberals" would call "Fundamentalists") devoted wholly to a type of evangelism familiar for a century past. Other missionaries accept much that modern thought and scholarship have contributed to the study of the Bible and theology and are ready to experiment with new types of evangelism. Still others are physicians, some of whom welcome every chance for preaching the Gospel, while others are content to let their faith shine through their deeds. Others yet again are training mothers how to take care of babies, or teaching mathematics to Mohammedan boys, or translating new books of devotion into some alien tongue. And with all this variety of vocation goes an equal variety in the interpretation of what is vital in Christianity and of what constitutes the aim of Christian missions. On a wide arc reaching from one extreme to another, their beliefs and purposes might be plotted. At one end we might put the strictest Calvinists, who are emphasizing the supreme importance of salvation through the blood of Christ and the pressing need for such evangelism as will achieve a growing series of individual conversions and open professions. At the other end we might put the educators, who are meeting the insistent demand for Western secular culture and who aim to transmit it in a Christian atmosphere of high ideals and unselfish service to the community. They think in terms not of baptisms and church organization, but of gradual leavening and permeation which will prepare the way for richer results in the future. And between these extremes may be noted almost every possible variety of intermediate types.

Given a diversity in attitude and method of so broad a range, there is a natural temptation for the workers to view each other with some degree of suspicion and to deplore the fact that there is not a greater approach to uniformity. Those who are nearest to one another in this imaginary arc may find it easy to be fraternal in thought and action. But the further apart are their ideals and practices, the harder it grows to welcome their fellow workers as allies. Thus it comes to pass that one little group on the right wing may condemn what it takes to be the vague secularism and the diluted Christianity of some other group on the left wing. The latter, in return, may enjoy an ill-concealed sense of superiority to a rival body which it regards as hopelessly antiquated and narrow-minded.

If it were necessary that all missionaries to Islam should be as closely as possible identical in their beliefs and methods, we should then face the difficult task of deciding which type was the right one. But happily there is no such necessity, for it is not a question of right and wrong. It is not a matter of "either or" but of "both and." If we take a broad view from the standpoint of past history and of future development, we acknowledge a crying need for all sorts of missionaries and all varieties of service. There are so many different kinds of things to be done that it takes all kinds to do them. Each variety of worker and each type of method are reaching some class of Moslem which the others cannot reach and achieving in that class results which the others could not achieve. If it is true, for example, that a liberal university will produce fruits beyond the powers of a determined little evangelical group, it is equally true that a determined little evangelical group will produce fruits beyond the powers of a liberal university. The translator can reach thousands who may never enter a hospital; the physician can touch thousands who may never read a tract. Moreover, this same diversity not only widens the range of action in the field; it also widens the range of appeal among the home Churches. There are thousands who will give to support a great interdenominational college, with broadly stated aims, who would not pay a cent to support the evangelism of a conservative sect; and the reverse is just as emphatically true.

Since these things are so, practical common sense and true Christian charity alike demand that we welcome such diversity and make it our aim to promote that healthful unity which means "a synthesis of differences." It is not enough that one type of missionary should merely tolerate another and regard divergences as unfortunately inevitable in an imperfect world. Rather he should rejoice in the fact that the weakness of one is the strength of another and the limitations of one are redeemed by the virtues of another. He should understand with such sympathy the purposes and ideals of his brothers in the cause that he can state them fairly and appreciate how helpfully they supplement his own. By such weaving together of varied strands of endeavor, the fabric of the whole will be strengthened and enriched.

Every man hath his proper gift of God, one after this manner, and another after that. . . . Now there are diversities of gifts, but the same Spirit. And there are differences of administrations, but the same Lord. And there are diversities of operations, but it is the same God which worketh all in all.

APPENDIXES

I. NORTH AFRICA *(Exclusive of Egypt)*

LIBYA, under Italian government since 1911, has a small population of only 888,000, 87 percent of which is Mohammedan. In spite of a few previous attempts, there has been no Protestant mission there for several years.

Algeria, Tunis, and Morocco are sufficiently alike to form a group by themselves. Algeria, a French possession, has neither complete autonomy nor is it entirely assimilated to France, for its status is a compromise between self-government and annexation as a part of France proper. It contains a population of 6,250,000 natives, practically all Moslems, and nearly 1,000,000 Europeans, mostly French. Tunis, a French Protectorate since 1883, includes a population of 2,400,000 Moslems and 213,000 Europeans. Aside from the very small area under international administration in the Tangier Zone, Morocco comprises the 13,000 square miles which constitute the Spanish Protectorate and the 200,000 square miles included in the French Protectorate. The total population is 7,100,000, of which 6,650,000 are Moslems. Thus in all three countries there are as many as 15,300,000 Mohammedans.

The chief racial stocks in the three territories are Arab and Berber. Though there are few pure-blooded Arabs, Arab blood, culture, and traditions predominate. The Berbers are the inhabitants of pre-Islamic times, tribes of mixed racial descent, of which the most notable groups are the Riffs in Morocco and the Kabyles in Algeria. Some Berbers have kept their racial dialects, but the majority speak Arabic. In addition to the city dwellers, there are some nomadic Bedawi, but throughout the country most of the Arabs and Berbers are agriculturists. Islam is of the Sunni type. Its most characteristic feature is the prevalence of Sufiism and the powerful influence upon the masses of the various Dervish orders and their leaders.

The long period of French government and French influence in Algeria and Tunis has resulted in the rapid advance of European civilization and culture. The development of communications, for example, has provided over 3,000 miles of railways in Algeria and 1,300 in Tunis, besides an elaborate network of roads of all grades. Progress in education, too, has been consistent. Except for elementary primary schools, Europeans and natives in Algeria attend the same schools. The higher schools, or Lycées, in the larger towns prepare for the University at Algiers, with its 2,300 students. French is spoken by an increasing number and is on its way to becoming the literary language of the masses. In Algeria and Tunis there is thus a very strong French influence among the educated classes, which is not incompatible with close relations between these classes and similar groups in other Moslem lands, especially Egypt. Educated Moslems, as in Egypt, are of two types—those who have received an orthodox Mohammedan training and those whose training has been French. Among the latter (again as in Egypt), there is a growing indifference to religion. In Morocco, however, the whole process of Europeanization is of course far less advanced, for until 1910 there were hardly any traces of Western civilization. But, for a generation past, economic and educational progress has been rapid, and the same changes, felt earlier in the other states, are already evident.

In these three countries the missionary situation resembles in certain respects that of Egypt, with its powerful Moslem majority and its half-European civilization. There are two important differences, however. Algeria, Tunis, and Morocco are definitely under the rule of Western Powers, and in none of these states is there any ancient Christian minority such as is everywhere found in the Near East. Christianity is represented primarily by the Roman Catholic Church and its large French membership. This negative feature constitutes one of the most severe handicaps under which Protestant missions labor, for there are no indigenous Christian communities into which Moslem converts can be fitted, no homes for their nurture. The convert finds himself isolated, cut off from his heritage, his society, and his employment, with no Christian group solidarity to enjoy in compensation.

In Algeria and Tunis, the oldest Protestant missions and the largest in number of workers are the British North Africa Mission (1881) and that of the Brethren (1883), which together include more than half the missionaries in these countries. Next in numbers and in years of service is the Algiers Mission Band, founded by Lilias Trotter in 1888. The chief American contribution has been made since 1908 by the Methodist Episcopal Church Mission, which now confines its work to Algeria. With its 350 baptized Christians, most of whom are of non-Moslem origin, and with its four native clergy, the Methodist Mission supplies the nearest approach to an indigenous Protestant Church. The Seventh Day Adventists, after fourteen years of work, have more than 200 communicant members of similar mixed origin. Both the Adventists and the North Africa Mission are also active in Morocco, together with three other missions, of which the two most important are the Southern Morocco Mission (1888) and the Church of England Bible Churchmen's Missionary Society. At Casablanca, in Morocco, is the headquarters of the Anglican Diocese of North Africa.

With the government providing educational and medical service on a large scale, particularly in Algeria and Tunis, there is little scope for missionary activity in these spheres. In fact, there are no more than a score of small mission schools in this entire area, and but seven dispensaries. The Tulloch Memorial Hospital at Tangier is the only missionary hospital between Egypt and the Atlantic. A few hostels and orphanages complete the tale of institutions. Missionary work, in other words, is largely confined to evangelism, personal and public, and the sale and distribution of Christian literature, for all of which there is freedom. In addition to the Arabic version, the Bible has now been translated into Kabyle and portions into other Berber dialects. Converts from Islam are few and scattered, the majority being Kabyles. Several conferences of converts have been held in the past two or three years, at the last of which there were not far short of one hundred present.

II. THE BALKANS

In Rumania, Bulgaria, Yugoslavia, and Albania there are about 3,381,000 Moslems. In Rumania, with its population of 20,000,000, there are only 260,000 Mohammedans, mostly Turkish-speaking and of Turkish origin. But in the other countries Islam is both relatively and absolutely much stronger. In Bulgaria, out of the 6,100,000 inhabitants 821,000 are Moslems, three-quarters of whom are Turks. In Yugoslavia, where the population is 15,700,000, as many as 1,600,000 are Moslems, nearly all Slavic. Among the 1,000,000 inhabitants of Albania 70 percent are Mohammedans.

The Bulgarian (Protestant) Church, mainly the result of the American Board Mission founded in 1871, attained full self-government and self-support in 1936. In the following year the Church formed by the Methodist Episcopal Mission was united with it. This Bulgarian Church, however, has no organized work for Moslems; and contacts between Moslems and the few Congregational and Methodist missionaries are only rare and occasional. What little has been attempted in the direct approach to Mohammedans has been chiefly by the Deutscher Hülfsbund für Christliches Liebeswerk im Orient. During the first ten or fifteen years of this century, an Armenian (Abraham Amirkhanjanz) and a Turk (Johannes Aweteranian) worked under this society on behalf of Moslems with great devotion and very little success. The Hülfsbund, however, has since maintained, on a small scale, the effort to reach Moslems. In view of the fact that this constitutes most of the meager record for Bulgaria and that practically nothing is being done for Islam in the other countries, it is evident that Protestant Missions have not yet seriously undertaken the conversion of Moslems in the Balkans.

III. PALESTINE

Palestine, though far better known to the West than most Moslem countries, is but a very small fragment of the world of Islam, for it contains only about one three-hundredth of the total number of Mohammedans. Controlled by the British since 1918, the country is now administered under a Mandate which came into force in 1923. The population in 1939 was 1,467,000, of which 849,000 were Moslems, 424,000 Jews, and 114,000 Christians, including Orthodox, Roman Catholics, Armenians, Jacobites, Copts, Anglicans, and Protestants. Except for most of the Jews, the language of the country is Arabic. The Moslems, who are of Arabic stock, are the most backward section of the community.

Thanks to British rule, to Hebrew energy, and to the activities of Christian missions, the three chief elements of the population are well supplied with educational facilities. There are over 1,400 schools in this small country. In the 402 schools maintained by the government, the great majority of the pupils are Mohammedan, and the Moslems have in addition 184 private schools. The 622 Jewish schools provide entirely for the training of Jewish children, while the 193 Christian schools care for most of the Christian children, with a substantial Moslem minority in the few which are of secondary grade. The only university is the Hebrew University of Jerusalem. On condition that schools maintain a certain standard of efficiency, they receive small grants-in-aid from the government, and there is no attempt on the part of the state to interfere with Christian schools. Medical service is likewise amply supplied by government, Jewish, and Christian agencies, so that in Palestine there is said to be one hospital bed to every 420 inhabitants.

Until the British regime began, Christian mission work, as in Turkey and Syria, was largely concerned with Oriental Christians. For the last twenty years, however, the emphasis upon the direct approach to Moslems has steadily grown, and increasing advantage has been taken of complete religious freedom. What was reported in 1927 is still true: "Evangelistic work with Moslems meets with far less hostility than at any other period, especially in country districts; but with greater readiness to hear goes a reluctance to accept Christianity, and converts are few." Every form of missionary method is actively employed—evangelism, both public and personal, the sale and distribution of the Scriptures and other Christian literature, schools of primary and secondary grade (of which 41 are Protestant with 4,800 pupils), medical work in the hospitals (7) and dispensaries (10), and such social service as that rendered by the Y.M.C.A. and Y.W.C.A.

In the small area of Palestine there are 24 different Protestant organizations at work. The missions of foremost importance are those under the Church of England Diocese of Jerusalem—the Church Missionary Society (1851) and the Jerusalem and the East Mission (1887)—which supply one-third of the Protestant missionaries and with which are connected 70 percent of the 4,400 Protestant Christians. The vast majority of this total, of course, have been drawn from various Oriental Churches, chiefly the Orthodox. Six Continental Societies are also represented, and six American, including the Christian and Missionary Alliance, the Seventh Day Adventists, and the Friends. Through the United Missionary Council of Syria and Palestine and the Near East Christian Council, a large number of these too numerous missions are ready to practice a degree of coöperation much greater than formerly. Several societies, moreover, led by the C. M. S., contribute to the support of the Newman School of Missions at Jerusalem (opened in 1928), a center like the School of Oriental Studies in Cairo and the Henry Martyn School in India.

IV. RUSSIA AND CENTRAL ASIA; AFGHANISTAN

The number of Moslems under the government of the Union of Soviet Socialist Republics may be roughly estimated as about 20,-000,000, of which the largest groups are to be found in Kazan (in European Russia) and in the areas formerly known as the Caucasus and Russian Turkestan. The policy of the Soviet government excludes all missionary work from these areas. Here, then, is the largest Moslem population (under any one government) which remains completely untouched.

Sinkiang, the great Chinese province lying north of Tibet and west of Mongolia, includes Chinese Turkestan, Kulja, and Kashgaria. In this huge area there are only 4,360,000 people, the majority Mohammedan. The chief Christian venture in Sinkiang has been the Swedish Mission in Kashgar, begun in 1891. Growing Soviet influence and revolts against Chinese rule among the Moslem inhabitants resulted in the expulsion of the Mission in 1937. The following year the three members of the China Inland Mission, who had been working at Urumtsi in the north, were forced by the Soviet authorities to leave the country. There is thus no Christian missionary activity at present in Sinkiang.

Afghanistan, with its all-Mohammedan population of 10,000,000, is the only country under Moslem rule which absolutely prohibits every form of Christian missions. Afghans can be reached only by the missions in eastern Iran and in the Northwest Frontier Province of India.

V. IRAQ

Iraq (Mesopotamia), freed from the Turks during the World War, was assigned by Mandate to Great Britain. In 1927 Britain recognized Iraq as an independent state, and with its admission to the League of Nations in 1932 the Mandate was terminated. Of the population of about 3,560,000, over 90 percent are Moslems, slightly less than half Sunnis and slightly more than half Shiites. Christians of ancient Oriental Churches (Assyrians, Chaldeans, and Jacobites), together with 91,000 Jews, constitute the remainder of the population. The language of the country is Arabic. During the last eighteen years the government has made rapid strides toward meeting the growing popular demand for education. The state primary schools have now about 93,000 pupils, and the intermediate schools, 11,400. Most of the smaller number of private schools receive state grants. There are colleges of medicine, law, and teacher training. The state supports at least seventeen hospitals and a larger number of public dispensaries.

Islam is of course the religion of the state. The old system of millets, or religious communities, still prevails, each being guaranteed the free exercise of its own religion. The religious and philanthropic activities of Christian missions are expressly permitted by law. Since 1924 every subject has had the right to register a change of religion, even though it be from Islam to Christianity; and there have been a very few instances of the latter. Though there is thus legal freedom for missionary work, enquirers and converts have an uneasy sense of lack of security.

Previous to the World War, the English Church Missionary Society had stations at Baghdad and Mosul, where the work was chiefly medical. Before the end of the war, however, the mission was permanently closed. In 1924 there was organized the United Mission in Mesopotamia, the three constituent bodies being the Reformed Church in America (Dutch), the Reformed Church in the United States (German), and the Presbyterian Church in the United States of America. The primary aim of the new venture is the evangelization of Moslems. Five stations at strategic points are now occupied by twelve missionaries—Baghdad (population 300,000), Mosul, Hillah, Kirkuk, and

Dohuk. Though there are two schools at Baghdad with not a few Moslem pupils, the chief activities of the Mission are evangelistic, including not only preaching and personal work but the distribution of literature and the use at several centers of reading rooms and book-shops. There are three still smaller missions, two English and one American. As the survey in the *International Review of Missions,* January, 1939, expressed it, "Missionary work is small in extent and somewhat difficult to carry on." [1]

VI. CHINA

The number of Moslems in China is variously estimated. A probable total is about 9,000,000, out of a population of some 425,000,000. They are to be found in nearly every province, but are especially numerous in the north and west. Kansu, in the extreme northwest, is their strongest center.

"They are in large part, although by no means entirely, of foreign descent, and with some exceptions they attempt little or no direct missionary work. While not always easily distinguished in appearance from the non-Moslems, they have been and are a rather distinct and self-contained portion of the population. They have changed only slightly if at all, the institutions and thought of China, but they have themselves been strongly influenced by their environment and in many respects have conformed to the life of the country." [2]

"In religious practices Moslems largely preserve their separation from those of the Chinese about them and maintain those common to their fellow-believers in other lands. Usually they do not use pork and tend to abstain from opium and . . . from alcoholic drinks. They repeat the creed, fast during the month of Ramadan, give alms to their own poor, and some few of them make the pilgrimage to Mecca. They . . . maintain their own worship in Arabic (although occasionally in Chinese) in mosques. . . . Usually they are not at all fanatical. As a rule only their religious leaders and teachers pray five times a day. Generally, too, it is only these who understand Arabic." [3]

In the year 1912, at Peking, there was founded an Association for the Progress of Islam, the beginning of a forward movement of a more or less modernist type which in various forms has since resulted in the production of much literature, the establishment of better Moslem schools, the organization of Young Men's Moslem Associations,

[1] The strong schools in Basrah (near the Persian Gulf) under the Arabian Mission of the Reformed Church have been noted in the chapter on Arabia.

[2] Latourette, *History of Christian Missions in China,* p. 17.

[3] Latourette, *The Chinese,* II, 171 f.

and so forth. The vast majority, of course, have remained little affected.

Christian work with Moslems before 1917 was negligible in amount, for not until that year was there any concerted effort on behalf of Islam. As a result of an extended visit of Dr. Zwemer, a Committee on Moslem Work was then formed, which remained under the auspices of the National Christian Council until 1926. In 1926 the Society of Friends of the Moslems of China was organized. Thanks to the leaders of these groups, a beginning has been made in the production of Christian literature for Moslems, including a diglot version of St. Matthew and St. John in Arabic and Chinese. In the past twenty years the very few small books and tracts available have increased in quantity to a total of about thirty-five books and as many tracts. A *Primer on Islam* has been issued by the Christian Literature Society, to inform the Christian Church of China about the Moslem population within its borders. There still prevails, however, a general neglect of the great opportunities that await a more concentrated effort to approach the Chinese Moslem. There are extremely few missionaries equipped and commissioned for this special task. The China Inland Mission, which probably has the best record, includes only four or five such men. As a result of almost exclusive attention to non-Moslems, there are probably no more than a hundred Christian converts from Islam, mostly in central and eastern China. One of them, however, is an Anglican bishop in eastern Szechuan.

VII. BRITISH MALAYA

British Malaya comprises the Straits Settlements (of which Singapore is the chief), the Federated Malay States, and the Unfederated Malay States. The total population of about 5,400,000 includes not only 2,224,000 Chinese, but over 2,250,000 Malay Moslems. As among kindred peoples in the Dutch East Indies, Islamic beliefs are mixed with others of earlier days, when animism and later Hinduism prevailed. Shamanism and the use of magic are common. Yet also, as in the Indies, the advance of modern civilization has resulted in a revival of Islam, with the organization of schools and of religious societies as one of its features. In the Straits Settlements and the Federated States, primary vernacular education is compulsory and about 90 percent of the children are in school.

Since Chinese and Indians form so large a part of the population and are so much easier to approach than the Malays, nearly all missionary work has been concerned with these races. For fifty-five years the Mission of the American Methodists has been active in Malaya, but only to a very small degree in the service of Mohammedans. For many years, however, the literary work of W. G. Shellabear made valuable contributions to the cause, with the production of a Malay grammar and dictionary, the translation and revision of the Bible, as well as of hymns and tracts, and the publication of a religious journal in Malay. The only other large mission is that of the English Society for the Propagation of the Gospel.

The missionary forces are now in contact with Malays by means of Christian schools and hostels and through the distribution of literature. But direct evangelistic work among them is meager and spasmodic, and not a single missionary is giving his whole time to it. For the most part, the Moslem population is untouched, and there are scarcely any converts from Islam.

VIII. PHILIPPINE ISLANDS

The great archipelago to which the United States fell heir after the Spanish War of 1898 is composed of 466 islands of more than a square mile in size and supports a population of about 16,000,000, chiefly of the Malay race. Over 90 percent of the people are Christians, descendants of the Filipinos converted during the Spanish occupation. Since 1898 the various Protestant missions have been responsible for building up Protestant Churches with a baptized membership of 250,000, the great majority of whom were formerly nominal Roman Catholics. The remainder of the population is pagan or Mohammedan. The Moslems, known as Moros, are mostly concentrated in the southern islands of Mindanao and the Sulu Archipelago and number about 500,000.

Few of the missions have ever devoted themselves to the conversion of pagans and still fewer to the winning of Moslems. The 2 small missions which have achieved marked success in the approach to Islam are those of the Episcopal Church and of the American Board. The Brent Hospital at Zamboanga, in Mindanao, has been maintained by the Episcopal Mission for thirty-six years, with a total staff of about 30 members. This hospital now treats 800 in-patients per year and some 10,000 dispensary patients, most of them Mohammedan. In the same town this mission conducts a settlement house and a school for Moro girls. In the district around Lake Lanao, in Mindanao, Dr. Frank C. Laubach, of the American Board, has developed since 1929 a remarkable enterprise for the benefit of the Moros of that region. He has carried out a literacy campaign, using an original technique, which has resulted in teaching more than 60 percent of the inhabitants to read. Under his leadership, too, the Mission has been active in the improvement of agriculture, in the establishment of a press and library, in community betterment, and in carrying out a medical program through the operation of a dispensary and the promotion of health education. Through the expanding influence of these two missions, the attitude of Moslem Moros toward Christianity and Christians has been largely transformed over wide areas.

IX. MADAGASCAR

This great island off the southeast coast of Africa, a French possession since 1896, covers 241,000 square miles and sustains a population of 3,800,000. Including the adjacent Comoro Islands, the number of Moslems is probably about 700,000. Apart from this minority, Christian missions in Madagascar have been increasingly successful. The *Statistical Survey* of 1938 reports nearly 300 Protestant missionaries, 960 ordained natives, 300 schools, and 212,500 baptized Christians. The Roman Catholics claim over 500,000 members. Yet the missions are so distributed as to neglect the areas and tribes predominantly Moslem; a large number of the missionaries are unaware of the extent of Islam in the island; and except by accident practically no effort is being made to reach the Malagasy Moslem. Here is a field, like British Malaya, which is well occupied, but in which the Christian forces have confined their attention to non-Christians far more accessible than the Mohammedans.

Bibliography

Books on Islam as a religion are not included in this list. Readers desiring elementary volumes on this subject are referred to: L. Bevan Jones, The People of the Mosque, London and New York, 1932; H. Lammens, Islam, London and New York, 1929; C. S. Hurgronje, Mohammedanism, rev. ed. New York, 1937.

In each group books are listed first and then articles. In references to articles: M.W. = *The Moslem World;* I.R.M. = *The International Review of Missions.*

Part One

Twelve Centuries of Background

Adeney, W. F., The Greek and Eastern Churches. New York, 1908.

Altaner, B., Die Dominikanermissionen des 13 Jahrhunderts. "Breslauer Studien zur historischen Theologie," Vol. III, 1924.

Arnold, Sir Thomas, The Preaching of Islam. 2d ed., London, 1913.

Attwater, D., The Catholic Eastern Churches. Milwaukee, 1935.

—— The Dissident Eastern Churches. Milwaukee [1937].

Bechler, T., Die Herrnhuter in Ägypten. Herrnhut, 1936.

Becker, C. H., Islamstudien. Leipzig, 1924.

Browne, L. E., The Eclipse of Christianity in Asia. Cambridge, 1933.

Burkitt, F. C., Early Eastern Christianity. London, 1904.

Cambridge History of India, Vol. IV, The Mughul Period. New York, 1937.

Chew, S. C., The Crescent and the Rose. London, 1937.

Chronicles of the Crusades. "Bohn's Library," 1848.

Diehl, Charles, History of the Byzantine Empire, trans. by G. B. Ives. Princeton, 1925.

Dozy, R., Spanish Islam, trans. by F. G. Stokes. London, 1913.

Emhardt, W. C. and G. M. Lamsa, The Oldest Christian People [Nestorians]. New York, 1926.

Fortescue, A., The Lesser Eastern Churches. London, 1913.

Fritsch, E. Islam und Christentum im Mittelalter. Breslau, 1930.

Graf, G. (ed.), Die arabischen Schriften des Theodor Abû Qurra. Paderborn, 1910.

Grousset, R., Histoire des Croisades et du royaume franc de Jérusalem. Paris, 3 vols. 1934.

Guerreiro, F., Jahangir and the Jesuits, trans. by C. H. Payne. London, 1930.

Güterbock, C., Der Islam im Lichte der byzantinischen Polemik. Berlin, 1912.

Haines, C. R., Christianity and Islam in Spain, A.D. 756-1031. London, 1889.

Janin, R., The Separated Eastern Churches, trans. by P. Boylan. London, 1933.

Jarric, Pierre du, Akbar and the Jesuits, trans. by C. H. Payne. London, 1926.

Keller, A., Der Geisteskampf des Christentums gegen den Islam bis zur Zeit der Kreuzzüge. Leipzig, 1896.

Kindi, al-, Apology for Christianity, trans. by Sir William Muir. London, 1882.

Lane-Poole, S., The Moors in Spain. 7th ed., London, 1897.

Latourette, K. S., The First Five Centuries. New York, 1937.

Lea, H. C., History of the Inquisition of the Middle Ages. 3 vols. New York, 1887.

—— History of the Inquisition of Spain. 4 vols., New York, 1906-7.

—— The Moriscos of Spain. Philadelphia, 1901.

Lemmens, L., Die Heidenmissionen des Spätmittelalters. "Franziskanische Studien," Vol. V, Münster-i-W., 1919.

Lupton, J. H., St. John of Damascus. London, 1882.

Maclagan, Sir Edward, The Jesuits and the Great Mogul. London, 1932.

Merriman, R. B., The Rise of the Spanish Empire in the Old World and the New. New York, 4 vols. 1918-34.

Mesnage, J., Le Christianisme en Afrique. Paris, 1915.

Munro, D. C., The Kingdom of the Crusaders. New York, 1935.

Peers, E. A., Ramon Lull. London, 1929.

Prutz, H., Kulturgeschichte der Kreuzzüge. Berlin, 1883.

Schmidlin, J., Catholic Mission History, trans. by M. Braun. Techny, Illinois, 1933.

Smith, Margaret, Studies in Early Mysticism in the Near and Middle East. London, 1931.

Stevenson, W. B., The Crusaders in the East. Cambridge, 1907.

Stewart, John, Nestorian Missionary Enterprise. Edinburgh, 1928.

Tabari, Ali, The Book of Religion and Empire, ed. and trans. by A. Mingana. Manchester, 1922.

Tritton, A. S., The Caliphs and Their Non-Muslim Subjects. Oxford, 1930.

Vine, A. R., The Nestorian Churches. London, 1937.
Zwemer, S. M., Raymund Lull. New York, 1902.

Altaner, B., "Sprachstudien...im Dienste der Mission des 13 und 14 Jahrhunderts," *Zeitschrift für Missionswissenschaft,* XXI (1931), 113-36.
Barge, H., "Der Dominikanermönch Ricoldus und seine Missionsreise nach dem Orient," *Allgemeine Missions-Zeitschrift,* XLIII (1916), 27-40.
—— "Luthers Stellung zum Islam und seine Übersetzung der Confutatio des Ricoldus," *Allgemeine Missions-Zeitschrift,* XLIII (1916), 79-82, 108-21.
Bishop, E. F. F., "An Eighteenth Century Literary Missionary to Moslems [Callenberg], M.W., Oct., 1933, pp. 397-403.
Boyd, E. I. M., "Ricoldus," M.W., Jan., 1918, pp. 45-51.
Darbishire, R. S., "The Moslem Antagonist" [Crusading Period], M.W., July, 1938, pp. 258-71.
Grabmann, M., "Die Missionsidee bei den Dominikanertheologen des 13 Jahrhunderts," *Zeitschrift für Missionswissenschaft,* I (1911), 137-46.
Groeteken, A., "Zur mittelalterlichen Missionsgeschichte der Franziskaner," *Zeitschrift für Missionswissenschaft,* I (1911), 52-70.
Guillaume, A., "Theodore Abu Qurra as Apologist," M.W., Jan. 1925, pp. 42-51.
Hamilton, J. T., "Moravians in Moslem Lands during the Eighteenth Century," M.W., Jan., 1920, pp. 82-86.
Hutton, J. E., "Moravian Missions in Moslem Lands," M.W., April, 1924, pp. 125-30.
Mandonnet, P., "Fra Ricoldo de Monte-Cruce," *Revue biblique,* 1893, pp. 182-202.
—— "Pierre le Vénérable," *Revue thomiste,* I (1893), 328-42.
Munro, D. C., "The Western Attitude toward Islam during the Period of the Crusades," *Speculum,* VI, 3, 329-43.
Schanzlin, G. L., "Religious Background of the Indian Moghuls," M.W., April, 1933, pp. 179-86.
Simon, G., "Luther's Attitude toward Islam," M.W., July, 1931, pp. 257-62.
Slosser, G. J., "Early North African Christianity," M.W., April, 1933, pp. 137-42.
Soucek, J., "V. B. de Budov," M.W., Oct., 1927, pp. 401-4.

Part Two

The Modern Age

GENERAL WORKS

Anderson, R., History of the Missions of the A.B.C.F.M. to the Oriental Churches. 2 vols., Boston, 1872.

Barton, J. L., The Christian Approach to Islam. Boston, 1918.

Brown, A. J., One Hundred Years [Presbyterian Missions]. 2d ed., New York, 1936.

Cash, W. W., Christendom and Islam. New York, 1937.

—— The Expansion of Islam. London, 1928.

—— The Moslem World in Revolution. London, 1925.

Centenary Conference on Missions, Reports. London, 1888.

Christian Literature in Moslem Lands, Prepared by a Joint Committee. New York, 1923.

Committee on the War and the Religious Outlook, The Missionary Outlook in the Light of the War. New York, 1920.

Conferences of Christian Workers among Moslems, 1924. New York, 1924.

Continuation Committee Conferences in Asia, 1912-1913. New York, 1913.

Dodd, E. M., and R. W. Dodd, Mecca and Beyond. Boston, 1937.

Ecumenical Missionary Conference, 1900, Addresses and Papers. New York, 1900.

Foreign Missions Convention at Washington, 1925, Addresses. New York, 1925.

Gairdner, W. H. T., The Rebuke of Islam. London, 1920.

Herrick, G. F., Christian and Mohammedan. New York, 1912.

Hutton, J. E., History of Moravian Missions. London, 1923.

Jerusalem Conference of Christian Workers among Moslems, 1924. London, 1925.

Jerusalem Meeting of the I. M. C. 1928, Reports. 8 vols. New York, 1928.

Kraemer, H., The Christian Message in a Non-Christian World. New York, 1938.

Levonian, L., Moslem Mentality. Boston [1928].

Lucknow, 1911, Papers Read at Conference at Lucknow, January, 1911. London, 1911.

Madras Series, Papers Based upon the Meeting of the I. M. C. at Tambaram, Madras. 7 vols. New York, 1939.

Mathews, Basil, Young Islam on Trek. New York [1926].

Mohammedan World of Today, Papers Read at the First Conference on Behalf of the Mohammedan World, held at Cairo, April, 1906. New York, 1906.

Moslems, Methods of Missionary Work among, Papers Read at the First Missionary Conference on Behalf of the Mohammedan World, held at Cairo, April, 1906. New York, 1906.

Mott, J. R. (ed.), The Moslem World of To-day. New York, 1925.

Parker, J. I., Interpretative Statistical Survey of the World Mission of the Christian Church. New York, 1938.

Rice, W. A., Crusaders of the Twentieth Century. London, 1911.

Robinson, C. H., History of Christian Missions. New York, 1915.

Sailer, T. H. P., The Moslem Faces the Future. New York [1926].

Shedd, W. A., Islam and the Oriental Churches. Philadelphia, 1904.

Statesman's Year Book.

Stock, E., History of the Church Missionary Society. London, 1899-1916.

Strong, W. E., Story of the American Board. Boston, 1910.

Titus, M. T., The Young Moslem Looks at Life. New York, 1937.

Vital Forces of Christianity and Islam, by Eight Authors. London, 1915.

Watson, C. R., What Is This Moslem World? New York, 1937.

Wherry, E. M., S. M. Zwemer, and C. G. Mylrea, (edd.), Islam and Missions: the Lucknow Conference. New York, 1911.

Woodsmall, R. E., Moslem Women Enter a New World. New York, 1936.

World Missionary Atlas and Statistics. New York, 1925.

World Missionary Conference, 1910 (Edinburgh), Reports. 9 vols. New York, 1910.

World Mission of the Church, Findings of the International Missionary Council, Tambaram, Madras. New York, 1939.

World Statistics of Christian Missions. New York, 1916.

Zwemer, S. M., Across the World of Islam. New York [1929].

—— The Law of Apostasy in Islam. London [1924].

—— The Moslem World. New York, 1908.

"La Conquête du monde musulman, Missions évangéliques anglo-saxonnes et germaniques," *Revue du monde musulman,* Nov., 1911.

Gasbarri, C., "A Statistical Survey of Islam," M.W., July, 1937, pp. 273-93.

International Review of Missions, Surveys, annual and decennial, 1913-40.

Jeffery, A., "Three Cairo Modernists," I.R.M., Oct., 1932, pp. 498-515.

Mohammedan World Number, *Missionary Review of the World,* Oct., 1937.

Morrison, S. A., "Modern Types of Moslem Thought," M.W., Oct., 1925, pp. 374-84.

—— "New Tendencies in Islamic Religious Thought," I.R.M., April, 1927, pp. 199-216.

TURKEY, SYRIA, AND PALESTINE

See Part Two, "General Works."

Allen, H. E., The Turkish Transformation. Chicago, 1935.

Barton, J. L., Daybreak in Turkey. Boston, 1908.

—— Story of Near East Relief. New York, 1931.

Bliss, Daniel, Reminiscences. New York, 1920.

Davis, H. C. M. (ed), Some Aspects of Religious Liberty . . . in the Near East. New York, 1938.

Davis, W. S., Short History of the Near East. New York, 1922.

Greene, J. K., Leavening the Levant. New York, 1916.

Hamlin, C., Among the Turks. New York, 1877.

Hocking, W. E., The Spirit of World Politics. New York, 1932.

Jenkins, H. D., An Educational Ambassador to the Near East (Mary M. Patrick). New York, 1925.

Jessup, H. H., Fifty-Three Years in Syria. 2 vols. New York, 1910.

Kohn, H., Nationalism and Imperialism in the Hither East. London, 1932.

Patrick, M. M., A Bosporus Adventure. Stanford University, California, 1934.

Richter, J., History of Protestant Missions in the Near East. New York, 1910.

Ross, F. A., C. L. Fry and E. Sibley, The Near East and American Philanthropy. New York, 1929.

Scherer, G. H., Mediterranean Missions, 1808-1870. Beirut, n.d.

Stein, L., Syria. New York, 1926.

Washburn, G., Fifty Years in Constantinople. Boston, 1909.

Allen, H. E., "The Outlook for Islam in Turkey," M.W., April, 1934, pp. 115-25.

Anderson, S., "The Future of Missions in Turkey," M.W., Oct., 1923, pp. 367-78.

Anonymous, "Turkish Women as Pioneers," I.R.M., Oct., 1928, pp. 645-54.

Barton, J. L., "Missionary Problems in Turkey," I.R.M., Oct., 1927, pp. 481-94.

—— "The Near East Relief," I.R.M., Oct., 1929, pp. 495-502.

Bishop, E. F. F., "Problems of the Holy Land," Church Overseas, July, 1930, pp. 243-56.

Browne, L. E., "Religion in Turkey, Today and Tomorrow," M.W., Jan., 1929, pp. 14-24.

Carleton, A., "Aleppo as a Moslem Centre," M.W., April, 1937, pp. 132-34.

—— "Church and State in the Near East," M.W., July, 1938, pp. 279-84.

Coate, W. A., "The Function of the Secondary Schools in Palestine," I.R.M., April, 1936, pp. 184-94.

Freidinger, W. A., "American Mission Press" [at Beirut], M.W., April, 1923, pp. 163-66.

Levonian, L., "Islam and the Evangelical Churches in the Near East," I.R.M., July, 1935, pp. 392-96.

Morrison, S. A., "Religious Liberty in Turkey," I.R.M., Oct., 1935, pp. 441-59.

—— "Social Work in the Near East," I.R.M., July, 1933, pp. 400-414.

"Newman School of Missions at Jerusalem," M.W., July, 1932, pp. 301-2.

Nielsen, A. J., "Damascus as a Mission Centre," M.W., April, 1923, pp. 160-62.

—— "Islam in Palestine," M.W., Oct., 1935, pp. 354-58.

Riggs, E. W., "The American Board and the Turks," M.W., Jan., 1924, pp. 1-4.

—— "The Missionary Outlook in Turkey," M.W., April, 1923, pp. 127-32.

Riggs, H. H., "The Missionary Situation in Turkey," I.R.M., April, 1938, pp. 195-200.

Vrooman, L., "Issues in Missionary Education in the Near East," I.R.M., Jan., 1933, pp. 50-62.

—— "The Place of Missions in the New Turkey," I.R.M., July, 1929, pp. 401-9.

Warburton, M. C., "Christian Education in the Near East," I.R.M., July, 1938, pp. 453-62.

EGYPT

See Part Two, "General Works," and books on the Near East under "Turkey, Syria, and Palestine."

Alexander, J. R., A Sketch of the Story of the Evangelical Church in Egypt. n.p., 1930.

Educational Conference at Assiut, 1937, Papers. Egypt Inter-Mission Council, n.p., 1937.

Gairdner, W. H. T., D. M. Thornton. London, 1908.

Harris, E., New Learning in Old Egypt. New York, 1932.

Hogg, R. L., A Master Builder on the Nile. New York, 1914.

Morrison, S. A., The Way of Partnership: Egypt and Palestine. London, 1936.

Padwick, C. E., Temple Gairdner of Cairo. London, 1929.

Watson, A., The American Mission in Egypt, 1854-1896. Pittsburgh, 1898.

Watson, C. R., In the Valley of the Nile. New York, 1908.

Bateman, J. E., "Medical Evangelism in Cairo," M.W., Oct., 1925, pp. 370-73.

"Egypt and Religious Liberty," I.R.M., Oct., 1933, pp. 530-48.

Elder, E. E., "The Evangelical Church in Egypt," I.R.M., Oct., 1937, pp. 514-25.

Fairman, W. T., "Nationalism and Evangelism in Egypt," M.W., July, 1923, pp. 231-35.

Gairdner, W. H. T., "El-Azhar Collegiate Mosque and the Mohammedan Propaganda," East and West, July, 1911, pp. 256-73.

—— "The Study of Islamics at Cairo," M.W., Oct., 1922, pp. 390-93.

Gwynne, L. H., "An Effort towards Unity in Egypt," East and West, Jan., 1924, pp. 1-6.

—— "Towards a Better Understanding between East and West," East and West, Oct., 1925, pp. 364-69.

Ibrahim, G. E., "Work among the Blind in Egypt," M.W., July, 1932, pp. 276-82.

Lasbrey, F. O., "Evangelistic Work in the Old Cairo Hospital," M.W., July, 1924, pp. 279-85.

Manley, G. T., "Policy of the Christian Church in Egypt," Church Missionary Review, June, 1922, pp. 143-54.

Menzies, J. R., "The Nile Mission Press," M.W., April, 1936, pp. 161-69.

Morrison, S. A., "The Church in Egypt," Church Missionary Review, June, 1927, pp. 134-46.

—— "El Azhar Today and Tomorrow," M.W., April, 1926, pp. 131-37.

—— "A New Approach to the Moslem Student," M.W., Oct., 1922, pp. 373-85.

—— "The Theory and Practice of Evangelism with Special Reference to Egypt," I.R.M., Oct., 1930, pp. 550-62.

Philips, D. G., "The Awakening of Egypt's Womanhood," M.W., Oct., 1928, pp. 402-8.

—— "The Feminist Movement in Egypt," M.W., July, 1926, pp. 277-85.

"Religious Freedom in Egypt," M.W., Oct., 1930, pp. 344-51.

"Religious Liberty in the Near East—Egypt," East and West Review, Jan., 1938, pp. 62-64.

Sailer, T. H. P., "Problems of Education in Egypt," I.R.M., July, 1912, pp. 498-510.

Sergius, Q., "Why Copts Become Moslems," M.W., Oct., 1936, pp. 372-79.

"Student Problem in Egypt, The," *Church Missionary Review,* Dec., 1922, pp. 277-84.

Thornton, D., "Eastern and Western Education in Cairo," *East and West,* July, 1906, pp. 278-85.

Ward, A., "The Egyptian (Coptic) Church," *East and West,* Oct., 1908, pp. 429-36.

IRAN

See Part Two, "General Works."

Cash, W. W., Persia, Old and New. London, 1929.

Century of Mission Work in Persia. Board of Foreign Missions, Presbyterian Church in the U.S.A., n.p., 1936.

Filmer, H., The Pageant of Persia. Indianapolis, 1936.

Hoare, J. N., Something New in Iran. London, 1937.

Richards, J. R., The Open Road in Persia. London, 1933.

Richter, J., History of Protestant Missions in the Near East. New York, 1910.

Shedd, Mary L., The Measure of a Man, the Life of William Ambrose Shedd. New York, 1922.

Speer, R. E., The Hakim Sahib; the Foreign Doctor, J. P. Cochran of Persia. New York, 1911.

Sykes, Sir Percy, History of Persia. 3d ed., London, 1930.

Wilson, Sir Arnold T., Persia. London, 1932.

Wilson, S. G., Persian Life and Customs. New York, 1900.

Wishard, J. G., Twenty Years in Persia. New York, 1908.

Boyce, A. S., "Government Education for Girls in Persia," M.W., July, 1920, pp. 290-92.

Cash, W. W., "The Anglican Church in Persia," M.W., Jan., 1930, pp. 45-49.

—— "Church Building in Persia," *Church Overseas,* Oct., 1928, pp. 330-36.

Donaldson, D. M., "Intellectual Awakening in Modern Iran," I.R.M., April, 1936, pp. 172-83.

—— "Modern Persian Law," M.W., Oct., 1934, pp. 341-49.

Fisher, C. B., "Mission Schools in Persia," M.W., July, 1930, pp. 251-56.

Fleming, M. R., "The Open Door in Persia," M.W., Oct., 1920, pp. 364-66.

Frame, J. D., "An Interchurch Conference in Persia," M.W., Jan., 1926, pp. 19-24.
—— "The Persian Shias," I.R.M., April, 1927, pp. 216-25.
"Hamadan Conference, The," M.W., Jan., 1913, pp. 106-8.
Hawkes, J. W., "Fifty Years of Mission Work in Persia," M.W., July, 1923, pp. 236-41.
Hoffman, R. E., "Changing Medical Work in Persia," I.R.M., July, 1933, pp. 361-66.
Irwin, J. M., "Evangelism in Iran Today," M.W., Jan., 1936, pp. 16-24.
Jordan, S. M., "Constructive Revolutions in Iran," M.W., Oct., 1935, pp. 347-53.
Linton, J. H., "Evangelism in Persia," I.R.M., Jan., 1931, pp. 84-91.
—— "Towards a United National Church of Persia," *Church Overseas,* April, 1930, pp. 152-65.
Miller, W. M., "Early Efforts among Mohammedans in Persia," M.W., Oct., 1933, pp. 333-47.
Moorhatch, A., "A New Day in Persia," M.W., Oct., 1924, pp. 392-96.
Potter, J. L., "Religious Liberty in Persia," M.W., Jan., 1913, pp. 41-46.
Rice, W. A., "Bahaism from the Christian Standpoint," *East and West,* Jan., 1913, pp. 22-43.
Richards, J. R., "Bahaism in Persia Today," M.W., Oct., 1931, pp. 344-51.
Schuler, H. C., "Methods of Evangelism in Persia," M.W., Jan., 1921, pp. 48-52.
Shedd, W. A., "Among Moslems and Christians in Western Persia," I.R.M., Jan., 1917, pp. 99-112.
—— "The Religious Outlook in Persia," *East and West,* July, 1909, pp. 257-66.
Stileman, C. H., "Progress and Development in Persia," *East and West,* April, 1915, pp. 121-40.
Stocking, A. W., "Education and Evangelization in Persia," M.W., Oct., 1913, pp. 391-400.
Thompson, W. J., "The Awakening of Persia," *Church Missionary Review,* March, 1920, pp. 36-44.
Wilson, J. C., "The All-Persia Church Conference," M.W., April, 1928, pp. 159-66.
Wysham, W. N., "The New Persian Church," M.W., April, 1932, pp. 116-20.
Young, H. B., "Contrasts in Iran," M.W., Oct., 1936, pp. 380-84.
Zwemer, S. M., "Persia Faces the Future," *Church Missionary Review,* March, 1927, pp. 42-50.

ARABIA

See Part Two, "General Works."

Harrison, P. W., The Arab at Home. New York, 1924.

Mason, A. de W. and F. S. Barny, History of the Arabian Mission. New York, 1926.

Sinker, R., Memorials of the Hon. Ian Keith-Falconer. Cambridge, 1888.

Storm, Harold W., Whither Arabia; a Survey. London, 1940.

Zwemer, S. M., Arabia, the Cradle of Islam. New York, 1902.

Zwemer, S. M., and J. Cantine, The Golden Milestone. New York, 1938.

Beatty, J., "Desert Doctor," *American Magazine*, Oct., 1938.

Dame, L. P., "Four Months in Nejd," M.W., Oct., 1924, pp. 353-62.

—— "From Bahrain to Taif," M.W., April, 1933, pp. 164-78.

—— "Objectives in Arabia," M.W., April, 1930, pp. 179-84.

Harrison, P. W., "The Arab Mind and the Gospel," M.W., July, 1922, pp. 225-29.

—— "The Gospel and the Bedouin," M.W., Oct., 1914, pp. 368-70.

MacCallum, E. P., "The Arab Nationalist Movement," M.W., Oct., 1935, pp. 359-74.

Mylrea, C. S. G., "Arabia—a Retrospect, 1912-22," *Church Missionary Review*, Dec., 1922, pp. 269-76.

—— "Kuweit, Arabia," M.W., April, 1917, pp. 118-26.

Storm, W. H., "Hadramaut—Its Challenge," *World Dominion*, Jan., 1937, pp. 53-57.

Van Ess, J., "Educating the Arab," M.W., Oct., 1931, pp. 379-86.

—— "A Quarter Century in Arabia," M.W., April, 1929, pp. 196-99.

Van Peursem, G. D., "Methods of Evangelism in Arabia," M.W., July, 1921, pp. 267-71.

INDIA

See Part Two, "General Works."

Birks, H., Life and Correspondence of Thomas Valpy French. 2 vols. London, 1895.

Clark, R., The Punjab and Sindh, Missions of the C.M.S. (1852-84). London, 1885.

Garlick, P. L., The Way of Partnership: With the C.M.S.. in India. London, 1938.

Henderson, L. F., The Cambridge Mission to Delhi. London, 1931.

Jones, L. B., The People of the Mosque. London, 1932.

McLeish, A., The Frontier Peoples of India, a Missionary Survey. London, 1931.

Martin, C. H., Allnutt of Delhi. London, 1922.

Montgomery, H. H., Life and Letters of George Alfred Lefroy. New York, 1920.

Muir, Sir William, The Mohammedan Controversy. Edinburgh, 1897.

Neve, E. F., A Crusader in Kashmir [Arthur Neve]. London, 1928.

Padwick, C. E., Henry Martyn. London, 1922.

Pennell, A. M., Pennell of the Afghan Frontier. London, 1914.

Pennell, T. L., Among the Wild Tribes of the Afghan Frontier. London, 1909.

Pfander, C. J., The Mizanu'l Haqq: The Balance of Truth, ed. by W. St. C. Tisdall. London, 1911.

Sargent, John, Memoir of the Rev. Henry Martyn. London, 1819.

Smith, George, Henry Martyn. New York [1891].

Speer, R. E., Sir James Ewing. New York, 1928.

Titus, M. T., Indian Islam. London, 1930.

Wherry, E. M., Islam and Christianity in India and the Far East. New York, 1907.

Bjerrum, H., "The Tamil Moslems of South India," M.W., April, 1920, pp. 172-75.

Chowdhury, D. A., "The Bengal Church and the Convert," M.W., Oct., 1939, pp. 342-50.

—— "Evangelism in Bengal," M.W., Oct., 1931, pp. 368-78.

Jones, L. B., "The Educated Moslems in Bengal," M.W., July 1916, pp. 228-35.

Kraemer, H., "Islam in India Today," M.W., April, 1931, pp. 151-76.

Neve, E. F., "The C.M.S. Kashmir Medical Mission," Church Overseas, Oct., 1934, pp. 307-19.

Sweetman, J. W., "Islam in India," M.W., Oct., 1937, pp. 348-61.

—— "Modernity in Indian Islam," East and West Review, April, 1937, pp. 138-42.

Takle, J., "Islam in Bengal," M.W., Jan., 1914, pp. 3-19.

Walter, H. A., "Islam in Kashmir," M.W., Oct., 1914, pp. 340-52.

Warren, W. P., "Islam in Southern India," M.W., Oct., 1931, pp. 352-67.

Zwemer, S. M., "Islam in India," M.W., April, 1925, pp. 109-14.

THE NETHERLANDS INDIES

See Part Two, "General Works."

Rauws, J., et al., The Netherlands Indies. London, 1935.

Richter, J., Die evangelische Mission in niederlandisch Indien. Gütersloh, 1931.

Simon, G., Islam und Christentum im Kampf um die Eroberung der animistischen Heidenwelt. Berlin, 1910. Translated as The Progress and Arrest of Islam in Sumatra. London, [1912].

Adriani, N., "Spiritual Currents among the Javanese," I.R.M., Jan., 1917, pp. 113-25.

Archer, R. L., "Muhammadan Mysticism in Sumatra," M.W., July, 1938, pp. 231-38.

Browne, L. E., "Missionary Work among the Muslims of the East Indies," *Church Overseas,* July, 1934, pp. 195-206.

Delius, E., "The Spirit of Islam in Sumatra," M.W., April, 1935, pp. 145-55.

Gunning, J. W., "Government, Islam, and Missions in the Dutch East Indies," I.R.M., April, 1917, pp. 209-20.

—— "Missions among the Moslems of Java," M.W., Jan., 1915, pp. 63-75.

Kraemer, H., "Spiritual Currents in Java," I.R.M., Jan., 1924, pp. 101-8.

—— "A Survey of the Netherlands Indies," M.W., Jan., 1937, pp. 44-55.

Meulen, J. F. W. van der, "Education in the Dutch East Indies," M.W., Oct., 1929, pp. 374-82.

Rauws, J., "Islam and Christianity in Malaysia," M.W., July, 1911, pp. 241-47.

Simon, G., "The Religious and Civilizing Influence of Islam upon the Backward Races," M.W., Oct., 1912, pp. 387-404.

Vandenbosch, A., "Christianity and Government in Netherlands India," M.W., April, 1932, pp. 134-45.

Van Kekem, E. G., "The East Java Mission," M.W., Jan., 1940, pp. 20-35.

Van Randwijck, S. C., "The Need for a More Highly Trained Pastorship in the Netherlands Indies," I.R.M., Oct., 1936, pp. 453-60.

NEGRO AFRICA

See Part Two, "General Works."

Blyden, E. W., Christianity, Islam, and the Negro Race. London, 1887.

Cash, W. W., The Changing Sudan. London, 1930.

Cooksey, J. J., and A. McLeish, Religion and Civilization in West Africa. London, 1931.

[Mackay, A. M.] Mackay of Uganda, by His Sister. New York, 1890.

Maxwell, J. L., Nigeria ... Christian Progress. London [1927].

Miller, W. R. S., Reflections of a Pioneer [Nigeria]. London, 1936.

—— Yesterday and Tomorrow in Northern Nigeria. London, 1938.

Philp, H. R. A., A New Day in Kenya. London, 1936.

Roome, W. J. W., Can Africa Be Won? London, 1927.

—— A Great Emancipation: A Missionary Survey of Nyasaland. London, 1927.

Walker, F. D., The Romance of the Black River [C.M.S. Nigeria Mission]. London, 1930.

Watson, C. R., The Sorrow and Hope of the Egyptian Sudan. Philadelphia, 1913.

Allen, Roland, "Islam and Christianity in the Sudan," I.R.M., Oct., 1920, pp. 531-43.

Delafosse, M., "Islam in Africa," I.R.M., July, 1926, pp. 533-68.

Farrant, H. G., "Northern Nigerian Opportunity," M.W., Oct., 1937, pp. 337-47.

Gairdner, W. H. T., "Islam in Africa," I.R.M., Jan., 1924, pp. 3-25.

Hampson, A. R., "Moslems in Capetown," M.W., July, 1934, pp. 271-77.

Hartmann, M., "Islam and Culture in Africa," M.W., Oct., 1911, pp. 373-80.

Hetherwick, A., "Islam and Christianity in Nyasaland," M.W., April, 1927, pp. 184-86.

Hofmeyer, A. L., "Islam in Nyasaland," M.W., Jan., 1912, pp. 3-8.

Lasbrey, B., "Problems of a Church in Tropical Africa [The Niger Diocese, Nigeria]," *East and West Review,* Oct., 1938, pp. 312-19.

Lighton, G., "The Numerical Strength of Islam in the Sudan," M.W., July, 1936, pp. 253-73.

Locke, A. H., "A New Day in Northern Nigeria," M.W., Jan., 1938, pp. 54-60.

Macintyre, J. L., "Islam in Northern Nigeria," M.W., April, 1912, pp. 144-51.

Meinhof, K., "A Plea for Missionary Work among the Moslems of Central Africa," M.W., April, 1911, pp. 155-63.

Miller, W. R. S., "Islam in Africa," I.R.M., July, 1926, pp. 533-68.

Peel, W. G., "Islam Not a Stepping-Stone toward Christianity," M.W., Oct., 1911, pp. 365-72.

Plessis, J. du, "Government and Islam in Africa," M.W., Jan., 1921, pp. 1-23.

Roome, W. J. W., "The Border Marches of Islam," M.W., July, 1920, pp. 220-40.

—— "Islam in Equatorial and Southern Africa," M.W., July, 1914, pp. 273-90.

—— "Islam in the Western and Eastern Sudan," M.W., April, 1914, pp. 120-36.

—— "Islam on the Congo," M.W., July, 1916, pp. 282-90.

Walker, F. D., "Islam and Christianity in West Africa," M.W., April, 1929, pp. 129-33.

Westermann, D., "Islam in the Eastern Sudan," I.R.M., July, 1913, 454-85.

—— "Islam in the West and Central Sudan," I.R.M., Oct., 1912, pp. 618-53.

Zwemer, S. M., "Islam at Capetown," M.W., Oct., 1925, pp. 327-33.

—— "Islam in Africa," M.W., July, 1925, pp. 217-22.

—— "Islam in Africa," I.R.M., July, 1926, pp. 533-68.

—— "Islam in Madagascar," M.W., April, 1940, pp. 151-67.

—— "A Survey of Islam in South Africa," I.R.M., Oct., 1925, pp. 73-91.

Part Three

Problems and Policies

See Part Two, "General Works."

Mott, J. R. (ed.), Evangelism for the World Today. New York, 1938.

Near East Christian Council Inquiry on the Evangelization of Moslems, Report. Beirut, Lebanon, 1938.

Tisdall, W. St. C., Muhammadan Objections to Christianity. 2d rev. ed., London, 1911.

Watson, C. R. (chairman), The Presentation of Christianity to Moslems, Report of a Committee. New York, 1917.

Allen, C. H., "Conditions for Baptism," M.W., Jan., 1931, pp. 59-68.

Bomford, T., "The Right Angle of Approach," M.W., July, 1911, pp. 283-88.

Browne, L. E., "The Christian Approach to Moslems," East and West, Oct., 1926, pp. 316-20.

—— "Islam," East and West Review, Oct., 1935, pp. 301-11.

Chowdhury, D. A., "A Christian Approach to Muslims," I.R.M., April, 1934, pp. 223-33.

Christensen, J., "The Theological Approach," M.W., July, 1939, pp. 229-39.

Elder, J., "The Care of the Convert," I.R.M., April, 1936, pp. 153-71.

—— "A Cross Section of the Moslem Mind," M.W., Oct., 1930, pp. 352-58.

Esselstyn, L. E., "What to Preach to Moslems," M.W., Jan., 1922, pp. 66-70.

Fairman, W. T., "The Approach to Moslems," M.W., July, 1926, pp. 272-76.

Ford, G. F., "On the Support of Converts," M.W., July, 1914, pp. 251-54.

Gairdner, W. H. T., "The Christian Church as a Home for Converts from Islam," M.W., July, 1924, pp. 235-46.

Heinrich, J. C., "'Shell-shocked' Converts," M.W., July, 1928, pp. 246-49.

Jeffery, A., "The Presentation of Christianity to Moslems," I.R.M., April, 1924, pp. 174-89.

Linton, J. H., "The Cost of Victory to a Moslem Convert," M.W., April, 1925, pp. 156-63.

Macdonald, D. B., "Whither Islam?" M.W., Jan., 1933, pp. 1-5.

Merrill, J. E., "The Christian Approach to Moslems," I.R.M., Oct., 1922, pp. 551-60.

Morrison, S. A., "The Indigenous Churches and Muslim Evangelism," I.R.M., July, 1936, pp. 306-20.

—— "Missions to Muslims," I.R.M., Oct., 1938, pp. 601-15.

News and Notes; Monthly Paper of the Missionaries to Moslems League, Medak, Nizam's Dominions, India.

"Oriental Churches and Islam, The," M.W., Jan., 1925, pp. 38-41.

Stanton, H. U. W., "Christ and Controversy," M.W., April, 1922, pp. 115-21.

"Temptations of Moslem Converts, The," M.W., Oct., 1933, pp. 348-55.

Wilson, J. C., "Love Must Win Persian Converts," M.W., Jan., 1926, pp. 25-36.

—— "Presenting Christ to Moslems," M.W., Oct., 1935, pp. 336-46.

Appendices

NORTH AFRICA

See Part Two, "General Works."

Cooksey, J. J., The Land of the Vanished Church. London [1928].

Blackmore, J. T. C., "The Educational Work of the French Government in Algeria," I.R.M., April, 1930, pp. 266-76.

Cooksey, J. J., "Islam in North Africa," M.W., Oct., 1934, pp. 350-55.

Haldane, J., "Morocco Today," M.W., Jan., 1930, pp. 63-69.

—— "New Forces in Old Morocco," M.W., April, 1932, pp. 146-52.

"Missions in Morocco," M.W., July, 1912, pp. 258-62.

Padwick, C. E., "Lilias Trotter of Algiers," I.R.M., Jan., 1932, pp. 119-28.

Roome, W. J. W., "Islam in North Africa," M.W., Jan., 1915, pp. 38-57.

Smith, H. B., "A Philosophy of Missions for North Africa," M.W., Jan., 1939, pp. 13-30.
Zwemer, S. M., "North Africa as a Mission Field," I.R.M., Oct., 1923, pp. 556-66.

THE BALKANS

See Part Two, "General Works."
Bousquet, G. H., "Islam in the Balkans," M.W., Jan., 1937, pp. 65-71.
Erickson, C. T., "Albania, the Key to the Moslem World," M.W., April, 1914, pp. 115-19.
"Islam in Albania," M.W., July, 1938, pp. 313-14.
"Islam in Jugoslavia," M.W., July, 1938, pp. 309-10.
Sanders, I. T., "The Moslem Minority of Bulgaria," M.W., Oct., 1934, pp. 356-57.
"Two Pioneer Missionaries in Bulgaria," M.W., Oct., 1927, pp. 375-82.
Zwemer, S. M., "The Moslems in South-eastern Europe," I.R.M., Oct., 1927, pp. 495-510.

RUSSIA AND CENTRAL ASIA

See Part Two, "General Works."
Cable, M., et al., The Challenge of Central Asia. London, 1929.
Kunitz, J., Dawn over Samarkand: The Rebirth of Central Asia. New York, 1935.
Bobrovnikoff, S., "Moslems in Russia," M.W., Jan., 1911, pp. 5-31.
Cable, A. M., "Central Asia as a Mission Field," I.R.M., April, 1929, pp. 179-87.
Catrice, P., "Islam in Central Asia," M.W., July, 1934, pp. 246-56.
Grimwood, E. E., "The Problem of Central Asia," M.W., Jan., 1938, pp. 22-27.
Högberg, L. E., "Missions in Chinese Turkestan," M.W., April, 1911, pp. 131-35.
Massignon, L., "Islam in the U.S.S.R.," M.W., Oct., 1927, pp. 359-369.
Mayer, J. de, "Islam and National Responsibility, I. Russia," M.W., April, 1914, pp. 137-44.
—— "Turkestan, a Neglected Mission Field," M.W., Jan. and April, 1922, pp. 35-52, 142-60.
Raquette, G., "Eastern Turkestan as a Mission Field," I.R.M., April, 1925, pp. 252-59.
—— "An Ordeal in Central Asia," M.W., July, 1939, pp. 271-74.

IRAQ

Foster, H. A., The Making of Modern Iraq. Norman, Okla., 1935.
Main, E., Iraq: From Mandate to Independence. New York, 1935.

Badeau, J. S.., "Mosul," M.W., Jan., 1930, pp. 16-19.
Morrison, S. A., "Religious Liberty in Iraq," M.W., April, 1935, pp. 115-28.
Van Ess, J., "The Mesopotamia Mandate," M.W., Jan., 1924, pp. 54-57.

CHINA

See Part Two, "General Works."
Andrew, G. F., The Crescent in Northwest China. London, 1922.
Broomhall, M., Islam in China. London, 1910.
China Mission Year Book, Shanghai, 1916, 1918, 1919.
Christian Occupation of China, The (pp. 353-58). Shanghai, 1922.
Latourette, K. S., The Chinese. 2 vols. New York, 1934.
—— History of Christian Missions in China. New York, 1929.
Taylor, Mrs. Howard, The Call of China's Great Northwest. London, 1924.

Botham, M. E., "Chinese Islam," M.W., July, 1924, pp. 261-68.
—— "Islam in Kansu," M.W., Oct., 1920, pp. 377-90.
—— "Methods of Evangelism among Chinese Moslems," M.W., April, 1921, pp. 169-78.
—— "Modern Movements among Chinese Mohammedans," M.W., July, 1923, pp. 291-99.
Harris, G. K., "Literature for Chinese Moslems," M.W., April, 1927, pp. 190-93.
—— "The Moslem Mind and the Gospel in China," M.W., Oct., 1929, pp. 403-6.
—— "The Moslems of China Today," M.W., Oct., 1935, pp. 399-403.
—— "Spiritual Results among Moslems in China," M.W., April, 1933, pp. 156-63.
Hayward, H. D., "The Kansu Moslems," M.W., Jan., 1934, pp. 68-80.
Mason, Isaac, "Christian Literature for Chinese Moslems," M.W., April, 1920, pp. 164-67.
—— "The Future of Islam in China," M.W., Jan., 1940, pp. 76-84.
"Missionary Conferences on the Moslem Problem in China," M.W., Jan., 1918, pp. 97-98.
Pickens, C. L., "The Challenge of Chinese Moslems," Chinese Recorder, July, 1937, pp. 414-17.

—— "The Christian Church and Chinese Islam," M.W., Jan., 1939, pp. 63-72.

"Resolutions on Work among Moslems (Conference of July, 1933)," *Chinese Recorder,* Oct., 1933, pp. 633-36.

Zwemer, S. M., "The Fourth Religion of China," M.W., Jan., 1934, pp. 1-12.

—— "Islam in China," M.W., Jan., 1918, pp. 1-3.

BRITISH MALAYA

Browne, L. E., Christianity and the Malays. London, 1936.

Means, N. T., Malaysia Mosaic, a Story of Fifty Years of Methodism. New York, 1936.

Cherry, W. T., "British Malaya as a Mission Field," M.W., Jan., 1923, pp. 30-38.

"M.D.," "Mohammedanism in Malaya," *East and West,* July, 1913, pp. 241-53.

Shellabear, W. G., "Christian Literature for Malaysia," M.W., Oct., 1919, pp. 379-84.

Wheeler, L. R., "Islam in Malaya," I.R.M., April, 1928, pp. 342-53.

THE PHILIPPINE ISLANDS

Laubach, F., "Christianity and Islam in Lanao," M.W., Jan., 1935, pp. 45-49.

—— "A Literacy Campaign among the Moros," M.W., Jan., 1933, pp. 38-45.

—— "My Experience with Moslems," *Missionary Review of the World,* Oct., 1937, pp. 485-89.

MacLaren, Mrs. J. D., "Brent Hospital," *Spirit of Missions* (Episcopal), Sept., 1938, pp. 365-66.

"Missionary and the Moro," *Missionary Herald* (A.B.C.F.M.), Oct., 1937, pp. 437-41.

Pickens, C. L., "With the Moros of the Philippines," M.W., Jan., 1940, pp. 36-40.

Young, A., "Winning Moros to Christ," *Spirit of Missions* (Episcopal), Feb., 1938, pp. 64-68.

Index

a new birth, and total surrender to our Lord. There are some who believe that some spiritual equivalent of baptism, free from the false significance which has grown up in the thought of the Moslem, can and must be devised.

That these proposals meet with favor in the eyes of not a few missionaries is evident enough from the findings of the Inquiry. But the *Report* itself includes many adverse criticisms from other evangelists. Several of these are worth recording as typical of many others. "A flank attack is good, but not if we have to abandon our frontal position to make it. We should not let our desire to get around the obstacles be first in our minds; Christ should be first always." "A Moslem who had become a Christian—a devoted follower of Jesus Christ and living a new life in Christ—would find it quite impossible to retain true living connection with the Moslem social-political group ... because he would, if true to his Master and Lord, be forced to pass judgment and criticize the ideas of life in this social-political group, having discovered that they are quite incompatible with his Christian faith." "Religion has to do with life, family life, political life, responsibilities for theories and practice of social living; and I find it difficult to picture anything but a maimed and halting religious experience if there is not complete association in these family and community affairs with the environment which has its source in Christ." "We hardly believe it possible for any man or woman to be able *to go on* living a Christian life—having the Christian's communion with God—if he or she deliberately chooses not to come out as a Christian." "The price of salvation is the same as it was in Christ's time. The church will be founded by those who are willing to pay the cost of open profession."

These comments are, of course, only examples of individual opinion. A more formal and impressive verdict upon the proposals of the Inquiry was passed by the Conference of Missionaries to Moslems, held at Delhi in December, 1938. On that occasion sixty delegates from eight Moslem countries gathered for two days of consultation before the Tambaram (Madras) Meeting. Among other topics, they discussed at length the suggestion for developing groups of followers of Jesus who shall remain socially and polit-

Proceeding to answer the question, "What methods or lines of approach offer hope of better success?" the *Report* offers first the unimpeachable reply that "the way to overcome these hindrances is more devotion, more effort, more prayer, and above all, more love." But supplementing this answer are further suggestions, which take the line that "we must try to find a way *around* these obstacles so that we shall not be in a position of attacking Islam frontally and at its strongest points." Among the concrete proposals to this end, the most notable is phrased as follows:

It is the conviction of a large number of workers among Moslems that the ultimate hope of bringing Christ to the Moslems is to be attained by the development of groups of followers of Jesus who are active in making Him known to others while remaining loyally a part of the social and political groups to which they belong in Islam. The ideal is that there should thus come into being a church whose only head is Christ, and which does not carry the stigma of being an alien institution drawing men away from their natural political and social connections. . . . To such followers of Jesus the term "secret believer" has been applied, sometimes with a degree of deprecation. To clarify our attitude toward such believers it might be stated that we lovingly encourage secret believers to go forward in the Christian life without publicly professing themselves as Christians in the sense of separation from the fellowship of their own people. But the purpose of such a course is to make possible a more effective witness to the power of Christ in their own lives, among their own people. Experience has shown that unless such effective witness develops into a *group* of such believers, a solitary believer seldom survives. The essential function of the church can never be ignored. The aspiration here expressed is that the church of Christ might take root within the social-political body called Islam, and not as an alien body encroaching from without. If such a line of effort is to be followed, certain very practical questions must be met. The first is that the name Christian, in the Near East, has almost exclusively a racial and social group-connotation, and does not suggest either a new way of life or a spiritual rebirth within. If a group of believers is to grow up as indigenous and not alien, they cannot take on themselves that particular name. Some other terminology must be developed. Similarly, baptism is almost universally recognized as the sign of the definite transfer to a new group-connection, and is thus the inevitable signal for casting out the convert from the fellowship of his own people. It does not mean to the Moslem, as it does to the Christian, repentance,

CATHOLIC THEOLOGICAL UNION

3 0311 00166 6879

BP 172 .A32 1942
Addison, James Thayer,
 1887-1953.
The Christian approach to
 the Moslem

DEMCO